THE
EMERGENCE
OF THE CHURCH

CONTEXT, GROWTH,
LEADERSHIP & WORSHIP

ARTHUR G.
PATZIA

InterVarsity Press
Downers Grove, Illinois

InterVarsity Press
P.O. Box 1400, Downers Grove, IL 60515-1426
World Wide Web: www.ivpress.com
E-mail: mail@ivpress.com

InterVarsity Press® is the book-publishing division of InterVarsity Christian Fellowship/USA®, a student movement active on campus at hundreds of universities, colleges and schools of nursing in the United States of America, and a member movement of the International Fellowship of Evangelical Students. For information about local and regional activities, write Public Relations Dept., InterVarsity Christian Fellowship/USA, 6400 Schroeder Rd., P.O. Box 7895, Madison, WI 53707-7895, or visit the IVCF website at <www.ivcf.org>.

Cover photograph: Scala/Art Resources

ISBN 0-8308-2650-5

Printed in the United States of America ∞

Library of Congress Cataloging-in-Publication Data

Patzia, Arthur G.
   The emergence of the church : context, growth, leadership & worship / Arthur G. Patzia.
      p. cm.
   Includes bibliographical references and index.
   ISBN 0-8308-2650-5 (paper : alk. paper)
      1. Church history—Primitive and early church, ca 30-600. I. Title.
BR165.P35 2001
270.1—dc21

                                                                          2001039359

24 23 22 21 20 19 18 17 16 15 14 13 12 11 10 9 8 7 6 5 4 3 2 1

20 19 18 17 16 15 14 13 12 11 10 09 08 07 06 05 04 03 02 01

*Dedicated to my wife, Dorothy,
and our family*

CONTENTS

MAPS & FIGURES

Preface

The use of the term *emergence* for this study of the early church is deliberate because I believe that it best captures the dynamic nature of the early Christian communities described in the New Testament. There are, as the footnotes and bibliography indicate, many fine studies on the birth, origin, history, nature and theology of the first-century church. However, most of these works do not trace the *development* of the church in the first century. Many analyze the church according to different authors of the New Testament, such as the church in Matthew, John or Paul; others focus on the church in certain geographical areas, such as the church in Jerusalem, Antioch, Ephesus, Rome and so forth.

My goal, on the other hand, is to focus on the emergence of the church from the time of Jesus to the end of the first century. At certain points we will examine nonbiblical and early Christian literature that may be helpful in understanding the early church or that gives us a perspective on where the church was heading after the first century. But most of our discussion will center on the documents of the New Testament.

A number of people find the concept of emergence troubling, believing that it subjects the church to the vicissitudes of history and human personalities rather than to the direct guidance of God. Many, therefore, argue for a "divine blueprint" or "transcendent reality" of the church to which all individual churches of the first century conformed. However, this "'big bang' theory of church origins," as N. T. Wright notes, is a myth that has been exposed by many credible New Testament scholars who have correctly discerned that there is considerable diversity among the churches in the first century. In these circles it is more common—and appropriate—to speak of pluriformity rather than uniformity. For those who wish to "get back to the New Testament church," who feel that the first church is somehow better, more pure, and the like, I propose that there was no normative church in the first century.

All this is not to say that the emergence of the church was haphazard, that it was solely a sociological phenomenon, or that there were no controlling norms. The early church believed that it was the community of Jesus whom God raised from the dead, the true Israel of God. It was also convinced that every believer received God's gift of the Holy Spirit and that the Spirit not only created them as a community but guided them throughout their development. But the end result in all of this was not a discernible uniformity. Churches with a Jewish background, such as in Jerusalem and Antioch, differed considerably from certain churches in the Greco-Roman world, such as those in Ephesus, Corinth and Rome.

Sometimes scholars use the term "early Catholicism" to capture the ideas of emergence. Basically, it means that the church began as a rather free and loosely organized community and then developed by the end of the first century into a more structured organization with certain standardized patterns of leadership and worship as well as a normative theology. We shall examine this hypothesis more thoroughly during the course of our study to see whether it is a helpful and legitimate way to understand the churches that we find in the New Testament.

The subtitle indicates that the book is divided into several discernible sections. Part one deals with the geographical, religious and cultural background to the New Testament and the impact this background had on the early church. I begin by concentrating on Palestine and its surrounding areas because this was the territory that Jesus and his disciples covered during their ministry. A brief explanation of Jewish sects and parties and the characteristics of Palestinian Judaism helps us to appreciate the struggles that Jesus and the succeeding church had within this context.

The following discussion of the Greco-Roman world exposes some of the issues that Christianity faced as it expanded beyond Palestine "to the ends of the earth" (Acts 1:8). Most of this discussion applies directly to Paul's missionary activity and helps to explain the problems he and others faced in evangelizing Gentiles and establishing churches in cities and regions dominated by Greco-Roman culture, religion and politics. I hope that readers will appreciate this section not only as foundational to the book but also as a useful commentary on issues that arose in the course of the church's expansion.

The essence of part two is the relationship between Jesus and the church. What were Jesus' aims? Did he succeed? Did he intend to found the church? Here we introduce the "Third Quest" for the historical Jesus that is in vogue in Jesus research today. This quest, as interpreted by many capable scholars, shows that Jesus' mission was to renew or reform Israel and not to begin a new religious community separate from Judaism.

Since Pentecost is often designated as the founding or birth of the church, I examine Easter, Pentecost and intervening events from Luke's perspective, because he is the first Christian theologian to write a history of the church. This provides a transition to part three, which details the emergence of churches beginning from Jerusalem and spreading throughout the Roman Empire. This development also leads to exploring the concept of diversity in more detail and examining reasons for the separation of Christianity from Judaism as well as Gentile Christianity from Jewish Christianity.

In part four I investigate the concepts of church leadership, ministry and order. Here the theory of early Catholicism comes under close scrutiny in the attempt to understand how the church understood its ministry and how different individuals or groups of individuals functioned in the church. In the process, I find some confirmation that leadership in the church moved from charismatically endowed individuals to certain specific and well-defined offices.

Part five's discussion of worship probably illustrates the concept of emergence more than any other section. Here the church is seen seeking self-understanding, seeking its own identity as the people of God vis-à-vis their former way of life in Judaism or paganism. After addressing the concept of house churches, I describe certain basic elements from the New Testament that identify believers as Christians and that form part of most worshiping communities. In the end, I argue that there is enough evidence to talk about the components of worship but not enough to hazard a reconstruction of an early worship service that would be normative for all churches in the first century.

Deep appreciation and gratitude is extended to a large number of individuals who made the writing and publishing of this book possible: first, to the many scholars whose writings have enriched my understanding of the early church; second, to students at Fuller Theological Seminary who enrolled in my classes on "The Emergence of the Church" over the last fifteen years; third, to Fuller Theological Seminary for sabbatical time from my teaching responsibilities; fourth, to the staff at Fuller Seminary Northern California, especially Dr. Curt Longacre and Shelly Ahn, who assumed additional administrative responsibilities that enabled me to free up more time for research; fifth, to Dr. Cecil White, librarian, and Sister Patricia Wittman, library technician, at St. Patrick's Seminary library for valuable assistance in locating reference materials and granting special research privileges; sixth, to readers and critics of earlier drafts of my manuscript, Curt Longacre, Dr. Anthony Petrotta, Judy Joy, Dan Olson, and Joo Ean Ong; and seventh, to my wife, Dorothy, who endured more lonely hours of separation than she deserved while I isolated myself in the study with books and computer.

Last, but not least, I thank Dr. Dan Reid, academic and reference book editor for InterVarsity Press, who accepted my proposal for this manuscript, believed that it was an important study for the church today and affirmed that I had the ability and perseverance to complete the project. Thanks, Dan, for your confidence, guidance, suggestions and support.

Arthur G. Patzia
Menlo Park, California

Abbreviations

1 Clem.	*1 Clement*
1QS	*Rule of the Community* (or *Manual of Discipline*) from Qumran Cave 1
AB	Anchor Bible
ABD	*Anchor Bible Dictionary.* Edited by David Noel Freedman. 6 vols. New York: Doubleday, 1992.
AJT	*Anglican Journal of Theology*
Ant.	Josephus *Jewish Antiquities*
Apol.	Tertullian *Apologeticus (Apology)*
Apol. 1	Justin Martyr *Apology 1*
Apos. Trad.	Hippolytus *Apostolic Tradition*
BA	*Biblical Archaeologist*
BAFCS	The Book of Acts in Its First-Century Setting
Bapt.	Tertullian *De baptismo (Baptism)*
BBR	*Bulletin for Biblical Research*
BDAG	Bauer, W. F., F. W. Danker, W. F. Arndt, and F. W. Gingrich. *Greek-English Lexicon of the New Testament and Other Early Christian Literature.* 3rd edition. Chicago: University of Chicago Press, 2000.
BJRL	*Bulletin of the John Rylands University Library of Manchester*
CBQ	*Catholic Biblical Quarterly*
Cels.	Origen *Contra Celsum (Against Celsus)*
De Bapt.	Tertullian *De Baptismo (On Baptism)*
Did.	*Didache*
DJG	*Dictionary of Jesus and the Gospels.* Edited by Joel B. Green, Scot McKnight and I. Howard Marshall. Downers Grove, Ill.: InterVarsity Press, 1992.
DLNTD	*Dictionary of the Later New Testament and Its Developments.* Edited by Ralph P. Martin and Peter H. Davids. Downers Grove, Ill.: InterVarsity Press, 1997.
DNTB	*Dictionary of the New Testament Background.* Edited by Craig A. Evans and Stanley E. Porter. Downers Grove, Ill.: InterVarsity Press, 2000.
DPL	*Dictionary of Paul and His Letters.* Edited by Ralph P. Martin and Gerald F. Hawthorne. Downers Grove, Ill.: InterVarsity Press, 1994.
Ep.	Pliny the Younger *Epistulae (Epistles)*
ExpT	*Expository Times*
EvQ	*Evangelical Quarterly*
Geog.	Strabo *Geography*
GNS	Good News Studies
Haer.	Irenaeus *Adversus haereses (Against Heresies)*
Hist. Eccl.	Eusebius *Historia ecclesiastica (Ecclesiastical History)*
HTR	*Harvard Theological Review*

HTS	Harvard Theological Studies
IDB	*The Interpreter's Dictionary of the Bible.* Edited by G. A. Buttrick. 4 vols. Nashville: Abingdon, 1962.
Ign. *Eph.*	Ignatius *To the Ephesians*
Ign. *Magn.*	Ignatius *To the Magnesians*
Ign. *Phld.*	Ignatius *To the Philadelphians*
Ign. *Pol.*	Ignatius *To Polycarp*
Ign. *Rom.*	Ignatius *To the Romans*
Ign. *Smyrn.*	Ignatius *To the Smyrnaeans*
Ign. *Trall.*	Ignatius *To the Trallians*
Int	*Interpretation*
ISBE	*International Standard Bible Encyclopedia.* Edited by Geoffrey Bromiley. 4 vols. Grand Rapids, Mich.: Eerdmans, 1979-1989.
J.W.	Josephus *Jewish War*
JBL	*Journal of Biblical Literature*
JETS	*Journal of the Evangelical Theological Society*
JRH	*Journal of Religious History*
JSNTSup	Journal for the Study of the New Testament Supplement Series
JSOT	*Journal for the Study of the Old Testament*
JTS	*Journal of Theological Studies*
LCC	Library of Christian Classics
Life	Josephus *Life of Flavius Josephus*
Neot	*Neotestamentica*
NIBCNT	New International Biblical Commentary on the New Testament
NICNT	New International Commentary on the New Testament
NIGTC	New International Greek Testament Commentary
NIDNTT	*New International Dictionary of New Testament Theology.* Edited by Colin Brown. 4 vols. Grand Rapids, Mich.: Eerdmans, 1986.
NovTSup	Supplements to Novum Testamentum
NTS	New Testament Studies
Odys.	Homer *Odyssey*
Omn. Prob. Lib.	Philo *Quod Omnis Probus Liber Sit (Every Good Man Is Free)*
Refut.	Hippolytus *Refutation of All Heresies, or Philosophoumena*
SBLDS	Society of Biblical Literature Dissertation Series
SBLMS	Society of Biblical Literature Monograph Series
SBT	Studies in Biblical Theology
SJSJ	Supplements to the Journal for the Study of Judaism
SJT	*Scottish Journal of Theology*
SNTSMS	Society for New Testament Studies Monograph Series
Spec. Leg.	Philo *De Specialibus Legibus (On the Special Laws)*
TDNT	*Theological Dictionary of the New Testament.* Edited by G. Kittel and G. Friedrich. Translated by G. W. Bromiley. 10 vols. Grand Rapids, Mich.: Eerdmans, 1964-1976.
TS	*Theological Studies*
TynBul	*Tyndale Bulletin*
VC	*Vigiliae Christianae*
WBC	Word Biblical Commentary
ZTK	*Zeitschrift für Theologie und Kirche*

1

THE GEOGRAPHICAL, RELIGIOUS & CULTURAL BACKGROUND TO THE EARLY CHURCH

Before discussing the emergence of the early church, one must explore the world into which the church came. As mentioned in the preface, the idea and structure of the church was not a "once-and-for-all" event. Rather, the church emerged over a period of time from within the historical womb of Judaism in a concrete historical setting with specific geographical, ethnic, political, social and cultural realities. All of these factors influenced early Christianity and helped shape the church in the first century A.D.

A major portion of this section deals with the land of Palestine and the nature of Palestinian Judaism as embodied in its religious groups (sects or parties) and institutions (temple and synagogue). By highlighting certain historical events prior to the first century A.D., I hope to answer some of the questions often asked by people who begin studying the New Testament: How did we get here? What happened in Palestine during the period between the Old and New Testaments, those four hundred long years of silence from the prophecy of Malachi to the arrival of Jesus the Messiah?

Information such as this is important for understanding the ministry of Jesus as well as the emergence of the early church in Jerusalem and surrounding regions. But it is not sufficient. Thus, I also move beyond Palestine to discuss the Greco-Roman world, because this is where the expansion of the early church took place. In many respects, this world is quite different from the one in Palestine, one in which the church encounters new political and religious challenges.

Even a brief knowledge of this culture will help one to understand how the church attempted to communicate its message of God's love through Christ and maintain its witness "in the midst of a crooked and perverse generation" (Phil 2:15). However, not everything about this world was evil. The rapid growth of the church, for example, was facilitated by the prevalence of a common Hellenistic culture, the Greek language, peaceful conditions throughout the empire *(pax romana)*, improvements in land and sea transportation and the social structure of the household. For many reasons, it was a good time for God to begin this phase of salvation history, because many conditions were in place that enabled the gospel to be proclaimed freely and the church to succeed.

1.1. Geographical Background[1]

1.1.1. Palestine. Palestine (also referred to as the Promised Land, the land of the Philistines, the land of Canaan, the land of Israel and the Holy Land) is the name generally used to designate the territory from the western coast of the Mediterranean Sea and across the Jordan River to the east. Because of its strategic location in the Near East between the Mediterranean Sea and the desert, Palestine was a corridor between the ancient civilizations of Egypt and Mesopotamia and often became the object of invading empires. One invasion occurred in 722 B.C., when the Assyrians defeated the northern kingdom of Israel, carried away thousands of Israelites and resettled them in various parts of

---

[1]For background reading, see Paul Barnett, *Jesus and the Rise of Early Christianity: A History of New Testament Times* (Downers Grove, Ill.: InterVarsity Press, 1999); Albert A. Bell Jr., *Exploring the New Testament World* (Nashville: Thomas Nelson, 1998); Shaye J. D. Cohen, *From the Maccabees to the Mishnah* (Philadelphia: Westminster Press, 1989); Everett Ferguson, *Backgrounds of Early Christianity,* 2d ed. (Grand Rapids, Mich.: Eerdmans, 1993); K. C. Hanson and Douglas E. Oakman, *Palestine in the Time of Jesus* (Minneapolis: Augsburg Fortress, 1998); John H. Hayes and Sara R. Mandell, *The Jewish People in Classical Antiquity* (Louisville: Westminster John Knox, 1998); James M. Jeffers, *The Greco-Roman World of the New Testament* (Downers Grove, Ill.: InterVarsity Press, 1999); Helmut Koester, *History, Culture, and Religion of the Hellenistic Age,* vol. 1 (Philadelphia: Fortress, 1982); William S. LaSor, "Palestine," *ISBE* 3:632-49; A. R. C. Leaney, *The Jewish and Christian World 200 B.C.-A.D. 200* (Cambridge: Cambridge University Press, 1984); Eduard Lohse, *The New Testament Environment* (Nashville: Abingdon, 1976); James D. Newsome, *Greeks, Romans, Jews* (Philadelphia: Trinity Press International, 1992); Calvin J. Roetzel, *The World That Shaped the New Testament* (Atlanta: John Knox, 1985); D. S. Russell, *The Jews from Alexander to Herod* (Oxford: Oxford University Press, 1967); N. T. Wright, *The New Testament and the People of God* (Minneapolis: Fortress, 1992), pp. 147-214. Additional sources are mentioned in Raymond E. Brown's *An Introduction to the New Testament* (New York: Doubleday, 1997), pp. 55-96.

the Assyrian Empire (2 Kings 17). Another invasion took place at the hands of the Babylonians. Under the leadership of Nebuchadnezzar, they invaded Palestine, destroyed the temple in 587 B.C. and took many Jewish people (mainly from the upper classes) into captivity (2 Kings 24—25; Jer 39—41). There are strong suggestions that the scribal schools and the synagogue originated during this Babylonian captivity of the Jews (see 1.2.1.3).

The Persian defeat of the Babylonian Empire had a profoundly positive effect on Palestine, for Cyrus, the founder of the Medo-Persian Empire, permitted the exiled Jews to return to their homeland. While Palestine remained under Persian rule (c. 532-332 B.C.), Zerubbabel returned in 537 B.C. to rebuild the temple (completed c. 516 B.C.), Ezra reestablished worship and the cultic system in Jerusalem (c. 458 B.C.), and Nehemiah returned to repair the wall and gates of the city (see the books of Ezra, Nehemiah, Haggai).

The Hellenistic invasion of Palestine began with the military and cultural expansion of Alexander the Great (332-323 B.C.). After his death his territories were divided among his generals, the *diadochi* ("Successors"). In time, a series of atrocities against the Jewish people by several foreign dynasties ruling Palestine between 323 and 163 B.C. led to a major Jewish revolt under the leadership of Judas Maccabeus ("the Hammer") and other Jewish patriots. The Jews were especially incensed when Antiochus IV Epiphanes erected a statue of Zeus on the temple altar, an event that became known as "the abomination of desolation" (1 Macc 1:54).

Under Maccabean rule (165-63 B.C.), certain Jewish leaders of the Hasmonean dynasty were able to gain political and military control of their land, restore many of their religious customs and institutions and even expand territorially.[2] The Jewish festival of Hanukkah, also known as "the Festival of Lights," celebrates the cleansing of the temple and the relighting of the candelabras.[3] Most Maccabean leaders who ruled Palestine during this period brought peace, stability, prosperity and religious freedom to the Jewish people. Some, however, were corrupt and cruel. Alexander Janneus, for example (103-76 B.C.), governed with abominable cruelty (Josephus *Ant.* 13.13.5 §372; 13.14.2 §380). His

---

[2]This is a dynasty of Jewish high priests and kings who ruled 142-63 B.C. The name may come from the great-grandfather (Hasamonaios) of Mattathias, a priest in the village of Modein who essentially began the Maccabean revolt (1 Macc 2:1-41; *Ant.* 12.6.1 §265; 16.7.1 §187; 20.8.11 §189; 20.10.3 §238; 20.10.5 §247). See Tessa Rajak, "Hasmonean Dynasty, *ABD* 3:67-76; Harold. W. Hoehner, "Hasmoneans," *ISBE* 2:621-27l; Joseph Sievers, "Hasmoneans," *DNTB*, pp. 438-42.

[3]Much of this brief history of the Maccabees is recorded in 1 and 2 Maccabees and the writings of Josephus, a Jewish historian and apologist who lived around A.D. 37-100 (*Ant.* 12.7.7 §§323-26).

policies polarized the political and religious leaders of the Jews. Some historians believe that those "zealous for the law" (*ḥasîdîm*) were eventually identified as the Pharisees, a group who desired to purify worship and interpret the Torah correctly. Those who were unable to cope with the secularization of their religion and the atrocities of the high priests may have fled to the desert and become Essenes or founders of the Qumran community (see 1.2.1.6).

Rome ruled most of the Western world by 146 B.C. Under the military leadership of Pompey, the Roman army marched into Jerusalem, captured the city in 63 B.C. and subsequently profaned the temple by entering into the inner sanctuary (Josephus *J.W.* 1.7.6 §§152-54; cf. *Ant.* 14.4.4 §§70-73).[4] Thus began the Roman domination of various parts of Palestine and the series of rulers mentioned in the New Testament referred to as kings, governors, tetrarchs, ethnarchs and procurators.

The ignominy of Roman rule raised all kinds of theological questions for the Jews. First, they resented the foreign occupation of *their land,* a territory given to them by God as his covenant people, which was, along with the temple and Torah, a sacred symbol and pillar of their faith.[5] Second, they believed in a theocracy but wondered whether God had abandoned them again. Various solutions to these concerns emerged within different religious groups, including accommodation (Pharisees), passive resistance (Essenes) and active revolt (revolutionary movements).[6]

Beginning around A.D. 66, rebellions and revolutions by certain Zealots provoked Rome to commission the general Titus to destroy the city of Jerusalem and its temple. The loss of the temple in A.D. 70 was a major blow to the Jewish faith. Still, although they were unable to offer sacrifices, the Jews continued to observe the sabbath, practice circumcision, read and study the law, and so forth. Tensions between the Jews and Rome increased, however, when Hadrian became emperor in A.D. 117. In A.D. 135 Rome decisively crushed another rebellion, this one led by Bar Kokhba ("Son of the Star"). Jerusalem again was destroyed and then rebuilt as a military camp called Aelia Capitolina. (Aelia was the Hadrian family name, and Capitolina referred to the Roman sky-god Jupiter.)

---

[4]See Lester L. Grabbe, "Jewish History: Roman Period," *DNTB,* pp. 576-80; Brian M. Rapske, "Roman Governors of Palestine," *DNTB,* pp. 978-84.

[5]See James D. G. Dunn's discussion of the fourfold foundation of Second Temple Judaism (monotheism, land, Torah and temple) in his *The Partings of the Ways* (Philadelphia: Trinity Press International, 1991), pp. 18-36; see also Dale C. Allison Jr., "Land in Early Christianity," *DLNTD,* pp. 642-44; Lawrence H. Schiffman, "Israel, Land of," *DNTB,* pp. 554-58; N. T. Wright, *New Testament and the People of God,* pp. 226-27.

[6]See Steven D. Fraade, "Palestinian Judaism," *ABD* 3:1060; David Rhoades, "Zealots," *ABD* 6:1043-54.

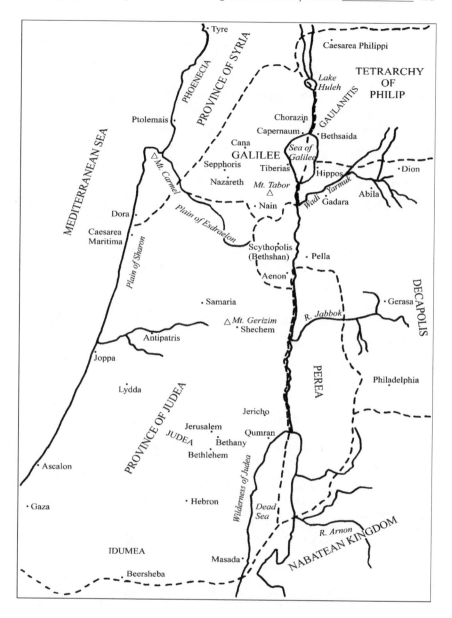

Map 1. Palestine in New Testament times

At the time of Jesus, Palestine was divided into several provinces or territories: Judea, Galilee, Syria, the tetrarch of Philip, Decapolis, Perea and the Nabatean Kingdom (see map 1). It is estimated that the total population of Palestine in the first century was between 1.5 and 2 million people, with about 500,000 to 600,000 Jews living in Judea.[7]

1.1.2. Judea. In some New Testament writings, the significance of Judea centers on Bethlehem in Judea as the place of Christ's birth predicted by the prophet Micah (Mic 5:2) and as the location of John the Baptist's first public ministry (Mt 3:1-6; Lk 3:1-6).[8] All four Gospels indicate that Jesus' temptation and much of his subsequent public ministry were in Judea, where many people were eager to hear his message (Mt 4:25; Mk 3:8; Lk 4:44; 5:17; 6:17; 23:5; Jn 7:3; 11:7). John, however, gives the impression that Jesus experienced considerable opposition in Judea from the Jewish authorities, especially the Pharisees (Jn 7:1). And when the Evangelists recorded sayings about the siege and destruction of Jerusalem, they warned that "those in Judea must flee to the mountains" (Mt 24:16; Mk 13:14; Lk 21:21).

Although some of Jesus' public ministry took him to different parts of Judea, one gets the impression from the Gospels that he spent most of his Judean ministry in Jerusalem, the leading city of the time because of its cultural and religious significance. Its population was probably between 60,000 and 120,000.[9]

1.1.3. Galilee. This small Roman province during the time of Jesus was mainly Jewish, although most of its inhabitants spoke both Aramaic and Greek.[10] There must have been something unusual about the Galilean dialect,

---

[7]Bruce M. Metzger, *The New Testament: Its Background, Growth, and Content,* 2nd ed. (Nashville: Abingdon, 1983), p. 39; see *J.W.* 3.3.5 §§51-58; Lohse, *New Testament Environment,* p. 120; Rodney Stark, *The Rise of Christianity* (Princeton, N.J.: Princeton University Press, 1966), pp. 57-58. Further suggestions and sources are listed in R. Brown, *Introduction to the New Testament,* pp. 561-62, with estimates of forty to fifty thousand Jews in Rome in the first century A.D. See also Paul R. Trebilco, "Jewish Communities in Asia Minor," *DNTB,* pp. 562-69.

[8]See further, Chris J. Seeman, "Judea," *DNTB,* pp. 616-24.

[9]Metzger, *New Testament,* p. 39. This figure is a substantial revision of Joachim Jeremias (*Jerusalem in the Time of Jesus* [London: SCM Press, 1969], p. 27), whose estimate of 25,000 prevailed for years. Recent studies disagreeing with Jeremias include David A. Fiensy, "The Composition of the Jerusalem Church," in *The Book of Acts in Its Palestinian Setting,* ed. Richard Bauckham, BAFCS 4 (Grand Rapids, Mich.: Eerdmans, 1995), pp. 237-65 (see p. 214 and n. 3 for additional references). For additional estimates, especially on feast days, see also E. P. Sanders, *Judaism: Practice and Belief 63 B.C.E-66 C.E.* (Philadelphia: Trinity Press International, 1992), pp. 125-27. On Jerusalem, see Peter W. L. Walker, ed., *Jerusalem: Past and Present in the Purpose of God* (Cambridge: Tyndale Press, 1992).

[10]Rainer Riesner estimates a population between 200,000 and 300,000 ("Galilee," *DJG,* p. 252). See also Sean Freyne, *Galilee from Alexander the Great to Hadrian 323 B.C.E. to 135 C.E.: A Study of Second Temple Judaism* (Edinburgh: T & T Clark, 1998); William S. LaSor, "Galilee," *ISBE* 2:386-91; Sherman E. Johnson, *Jesus and His Towns* (Wilmington, Del.:

because Peter is betrayed by his "accent" (*lalia,* Mt 26:73) when he denies Jesus, and the audience at Pentecost recognizes Galilean as a native language (Acts 2:7). After Rome destroyed Jerusalem in A.D. 70, the Galilean city of Tiberias, near the Sea of Galilee, became an important center of rabbinic learning where the Mishnah (c. A.D. 200) and the Palestinian Talmud (c. A.D. 400) were completed.

Galilee also held a strategic place in the life and ministry of Jesus. Mary and Joseph made their home in the city of Nazareth, where the angel Gabriel appeared to Mary and prophesied the birth of Jesus (Lk 1:26-38). Jesus spent the greater part of his life as a carpenter's son in this town (Mt 2:23; 13:54; Mk 1:9; Lk 4:16) and did not leave until he began his public ministry when he was approximately thirty years old (Lk 3:23). Apparently Jesus was well received as a local citizen (Mk 6:3; Lk 2:42; 4:16) and was recognized by many as Jesus *from* or *of* Nazareth (Mt 21:11; 26:71; Mk 1:24; 10:47; 14:67; 16:6; Lk 4:34; 18:37; 24:19; Jn 1:45; 18:5, 7; 19:19; Acts 2:22; 3:6; 4:10; 6:14; 10:38; 22:8).

A change of attitude occurred when Jesus began preaching in other areas (Cana, Capernaum, Nain, Tiberias, Magdala) and the synagogues of Galilee (cf. Lk 4:15-30). At this point many of his own townspeople rejected him because his words and deeds challenged the current interpretations of Scripture (Mk 6:1-6; Lk 4:28-30). Nathaniel's contemptuous question, "Can anything good come out of Nazareth?" (Jn 1:46), and the doubting attitudes of others (Jn 7:41-42) probably reflect the inability of individuals to see greatness in the familiar. But neither did the Jews expect the Messiah to come from Galilee (Jn 7:41, 52).

All the Gospels narrate some events of Jesus' Galilean ministry. Many of the miracles, including the first one in Cana (Jn 2:11), were performed in Galilee. In addition, a significant number of parables reflect the type of agricultural and pastoral setting common to this land. But eventually Jesus, disappointed by the lack of response to his message of repentance, pronounced judgment on the Galileans (Mt 11:21-24; Lk 10:12-15) and withdrew with his most loyal followers to the Greek centers outside of Galilee, such as the hills of Tyre (Mk 7:24), the Decapolis (Mk 7:31) and Gaulanitis (Mk 8:27).

Matthew and Mark make Jesus' Galilean ministry the focal point of their Gospels. For Mark, Galilee epitomizes the success of Jesus' ministry over the opposition and the rejection he experienced in Jerusalem. Mark also predicted this province as the location where the Lord would return after his resurrection to be reunited with his disciples (Mk 14:28; 16:7). Matthew develops this Galilean motif further and places the risen Lord's commission to the eleven dis-

---

Michael Glazier, 1989); James F. Strange, "Galilee," *DNTB,* pp. 391-98. On the significance of Galilee for scholars associated with the "Third Quest" for the historical Jesus, see part two.

ciples on a mountain in Galilee, not Jerusalem, as one might expect from Acts 1:8 (Mt 28:16-20; see 2.5.1. below on "Galilean Christianity").[11]

1.1.4. Samaria. Samaria (named for its capital city) is situated geographically between Judea and Galilee.[12] The New Testament references to personal and religious animosity between the Jews and Samaritans (Jn 4:9, 27), to Samaria as a territory that Jesus and the disciples avoided passing through if possible (Lk 17:11; Jn 4:4) and to the Samaritan rivalry to Jewish worship (Jn 4:20-26) are best understood by certain historical tensions that go back to the seventh century B.C. when Assyria captured northern Israel (2 Kings 17:6, 24; Ezra 4:1-4; 10:18-44; Neh 2:11—6:14).

Not everything in the Gospels about the Samaritans is negative. The Samaritan woman's report about her encounter with Jesus at Jacob's well (Jn 4:1-42) led "many Samaritans" to believe in Jesus (Jn 4:39) and even to invite him to stay longer in their territory. John records that those who heard truly believed in Jesus as "the Savior of the world" (Jn 4:42). This stands in stark contrast to the Samaritan village that refused hospitality to Jesus and his disciples (Lk 9:51-55). Later, Samaria became the focal point of Philip's evangelistic activity (Acts 8:4-25).

1.1.5. Decapolis. The region of Decapolis (from the Greek *deka,* "ten," and *polis,* "city") was a federation of ten Greek cities adjacent to Galilee and Samaria east of the river (see map 1).[13] Its origins go back to the Hellenizing policies of Alexander the Great and his successors, who established settlements and Greek culture in the territories that they conquered. The few references in the Gospels indicate that Jesus healed a demon-possessed man from "the country of the Gerasenes" (variant, Gergesenes, Mk 5:1-20), that he taught in the Decapolis (Mk 5:20; 7:31) and that some of his followers also came from there. Matthew, for example, records that "great crowds followed him from Galilee, the Decapolis, Jerusalem, Judea, and from beyond the Jordan" (Mt 4:25).

1.1.6. Perea. Perea (Greek, "beyond") signifies the Transjordan, the land

---

[11]On Galilee, see L. E. Elliott-Binns, *Galilean Christianity,* SBT 16 (Chicago: Allenson, 1956); Richard A. Horsley, *Galilee: History, Politics, People* (Valley Forge, Penn.: Trinity Press International, 1995); Ben Witherington III, "Galilee and the Galilean," in *The Jesus Quest* (Downers Grove, Ill.: InterVarsity Press, 1994), pp. 14-41.

[12]See further Robert T. Anderson, "Samaritans," *ISBE* 4:303-8; William S. LaSor, "Samaria, Country of," *ISBE* 4:298-303; H. G. M. Williamson and Craig A. Evans, "Samaritans," *DNTB,* pp. 1056-61; Andrianus van Selms, "Samaria," *ISBE* 4:295-98.

[13]Pliny, a first-century historian, identifies the original cities as Damascus, Dion, Gadara, Gerasa (or Galasa), Hippos (or Hippo), Canatha (or Kanatha), Pella, Philadelphia (present-day Amman, the capital of Jordan), Raphana (or Rephana) and Scythopolis. See Roy E. Ciampa, "Decapolis," *DNTB,* pp. 266-68; Victor P. Hamilton, "Decapolis," *ISBE* 1:906-8.

"beyond the Jordan" *(peran tou Iordanou).*[14] John the Baptist began his public preaching and baptizing "in Bethany across the Jordan" (Jn 1:28; cf. 10:40-41) and may even have baptized Jesus there (implied in Jn 1:29-34, though the baptism is placed "at the Jordan" in the Synoptic Gospels). Apparently, John's activity created enough interest among the Jewish leaders in Jerusalem for them to send a delegation of priests and Levites to check out his credentials and message (Jn 1:19-42; 3:26). Jesus also found refuge in this region when the Jews in Judea were harassing him (Jn 10:39-42).

From this brief historical review one can appreciate the following realities:

1. Divergent nationalities, cultures and religions invaded Palestine over the years.

2. A variety of attitudes developed within Judaism in reaction to the religious, political and cultural events of the time.

3. The Hellenistic culture had a profound effect upon the entire Mediterranean world, including the Hellenization of the Jews.

4. In spite of foreign influences and oppression, most Jews continued to revere their traditions, develop their theology and remain faithful to the Torah.

5. Jewish religious sects, such as the Sadducees, Pharisees, scribes and Essenes, emerged in response to certain historical, political and religious influences.

6. The Roman Empire was an inescapable political reality during the time of Jesus and the early church.

1.2. Cultural and Religious Background

1.2.1. Palestinian Judaism. As a religion, Judaism went through many stages of development from its initial conviction as God's chosen nation with the call of Abraham and the Mosaic covenant to the types of Judaisms current in the first century.[15] We have already discussed briefly how some religious leaders

---

[14]The place name Perea (Greek *Peraia*) occurs only as a textual variant in Lk 6:17.

[15]Today, it is more correct to speak of "types of Judaisms" or "multiple" and "varied" Judaisms rather than "Judaism," because scholars have shown that the idea of a normative Judaism in the first century is inaccurate. For further discussion, see Albert I. Baumgarten, *The Flourishing of Jewish Sects in the Maccabean Era: An Interpretation,* SJSJ 55 (Leiden: E. J. Brill, 1997); Bruce D. Chilton, "Judaism," *DJG,* pp. 398-405; Chilton, "Judaism and the New Testament," *DNTB,* pp. 603-16; Steven D. Fraade, "Palestinian Judaism," *ABD* 3:1054-61; Steve Mason, "Chief Priests, Sadducees, Pharisees and Sanhedrin in Acts," in Bauckham, ed., *Palestinian Setting,* pp. 115-77; Mason, "Theologies and Sects, Jewish," *DNTB,* pp. 1221-30; Anthony J. Saldarini, *Pharisee, Scribes, and Sadducees in Palestinian Society* (Grand Rapids, Mich.: Eerdmans, 2001); Günter Stemberger, *Jewish Contemporaries of Jesus: Pharisees, Sadducees, Essenes* (Minneapolis: Augsburg Fortress, 1995); James C. VanderKam, *An Introduction to Early Judaism* (Grand Rapids, Mich.: Eerdmans, 2000).

attempted to bring the nation back to its core through the restoration of temple worship and covenant faithfulness to God. We also noted some serious diversions and challenges to Judaism under Hasmonean and Roman rule. Many of these political and religious challenges continued and even intensified into the first century A.D. and affected both Jesus and the early church.[16]

In the following pages we will trace the emergence of several significant responses to the crises that Judaism faced during this period of history. In essence, each group had an interest in the restoration of Israel and the survival of the nation as God's covenant people. But we will also see that the responses varied with each group and that each one had a different vision of how to attain its goals.

1.2.1.1. Pharisees. The Pharisees are the Jewish religious group most frequently mentioned in the New Testament as opposing Jesus and the early church. Although the precise circumstances surrounding their origin are unknown, it is generally accepted that the Pharisees are descendants of the Hasidim, a group of pious Jews who emerged during the time of the Maccabees. The name comes from the Hebrew *pᵉrûšîm* ("separatist") or *parûšhîm* ("specifiers")—that is, people whose life was governed by certain rules and regulations.[17]

In addition to the New Testament, the Pharisees' history and beliefs are recorded in Josephus's writings and rabbinic literature.[18] Josephus personally examined several religious groups and became a Pharisee, a "sect," he clarifies for his Roman readers, "having points of resemblance to that which the Greeks call the Stoic school" (*Life* 1-2 §§10-12). Saul was also a Pharisee prior to becoming a Christian (Phil 3:4-6).

---

[16]The period from Ezra to the fall of Jerusalem in A.D. 70 is often referred to as Second Temple Judaisms. Note N. T. Wright: "Though we may rightly speak of the 'Judaism' of this period, it is often easier linguistically to refer to the singular 'Judaism' as a generic entity to which they all belong. The period is regularly known as 'second-temple Judaism,' indicating the time roughly from the fourth century BC to the second century AD (even thought the second Temple itself had been destroyed in AD 70), or occasionally 'middle Judaism,' indicating the time between 'early Judaism' (the pre-exilic period) and the 'later Judaism' of the rabbis and beyond" (*New Testament and the People of God*, p. 147 n.1).

[17]Stephen Westerholm, "Pharisees," *DJG*, p. 610; Paul L. Redditt, "Hasideans," *ABD* 3:66.

[18]*Ant.* 18.1.3 §§12-15; *J.W.* 2.8.2-14 §§62-66; for references and evaluation of the rabbinic literature, see Jacob Neusner, *The Rabbinic Traditions About the Pharisees Before 70* (Leiden: E. J. Brill, 1970); Westerholm, "Pharisees," p. 610; Günter Stemberger, *Jewish Contemporaries of Jesus*. Since it is difficult to get an accurate picture of the Pharisees from these sources, it is not surprising that a number of scholars disagree with each other. See James D. G. Dunn, *Jesus, Paul and the Law* (Louisville: Westminster John Knox, 1990); Steve Mason, "Pharisees," *DNTB*, pp. 782-87; E. P. Sanders, *Jesus and Judaism* (Philadelphia: Fortress, 1985); Sanders, *Judaism*, pp. 380-451; Anthony J. Saldarini, "Pharisees," *ABD* 5:289-303.

The Pharisees pursued primarily religious interests but also became involved politically when it furthered their religious agenda.[19] More specifically, the Pharisees were a religious group concerned with applying the traditions of ritual purity to the context of everyday life.[20] Although ritual purity, especially table fellowship and avoidance of "sinners," may have been their central concern, several sources also discuss issues relating to picking grain on the sabbath (Mt 12:1-5 par. Mk 2:22-28; Lk 6:1-5), healing on the sabbath (Mt 12:10 par. Mk 3:2; Lk 6:7; cf. 13:14; 14:3; Jn 5:10; 9:16), fasting (Mt 6:16-18; Mk 2:18-20), tithing (Mt 23:23 par. Lk 11:42) and additional denunciations mentioned in Matthew 23. According to Pharisaic standards, most ordinary Jews residing in towns and villages surrounding Jerusalem—the "people of the land" ('am hā'āres)—were too slack in observing these rules. One can detect the Pharisees' disdain when John writes: "But this crowd [ochlos], which does not know the law—they are accursed" (Jn 7:49).[21]

Most of the controversies with Jesus emerged out of the body of oral traditions that developed within this group, material commonly referred to as the traditions or customs of the fathers, elders or Moses (see Mt 15:2; Mk 7:3, 5; Acts 6:14; 15:1; 21:21; 22:3; 26:3; 28:17; Gal 1:14; Josephus *Ant.* 13.10.6 §297). The Pharisees' mastery of these oral traditions made them one of the most successful and popular movements within pluralized Judaism.

Scholarly debates continue around the nature of first-century Pharisaism, the different representations of them in the Gospels and their role in shaping Palestinian Judaism. Still, the New Testament clearly indicates that the confrontation that Jesus experienced continued in the early church as well, for the Pharisees were actively antagonistic toward the mission of the early church, not only in the persecution by Saul the Pharisee (Acts 8:1-3; Gal 1:13-14; Phil 3:5-6), but later as opponents of Paul's gospel and mission to the Gentiles (Acts 15:5; 23:6).

Josephus identifies the Pharisees as one of three sects *(hairesis)* or philosophical schools within Judaism (Pharisees, Sadducees, Essenes; see Acts 15:5; 26:5) who lived a rather peaceable and virtuous life in the community. They believed strongly in fate as well as the immortality of the soul, eternal rewards for the

---

[19]Anthony J. Saldarini refers to them as a "religio-political interest group" in *Pharisees, Scribes and Sadducees in Palestinian Society* (Wilmington, Del.: Michael Glazier, 1988), p. 94.

[20]See Jacob Neusner, *From Politics to Piety: The Emergence of Pharisaic Judaism* (Englewood Cliffs, N.J.: Prentice Hall, 1973), esp. pp. 143-54.

[21]For a similar attitude, see Rabbi Akiba's comment in *b. Pesaḥim* 49b. E. P. Sanders discredits older (but still popular) views that these were sinners excluded from salvation and synagogue worship (*Jesus and Judaism,* pp. 174-211).

righteous and eternal punishment for the wicked (Josephus *J.W.* 2.8.14 §§162-66; *Ant.* 13.5.9 §172; 18.1.3 §§12-15). The New Testament focuses more on what they opposed than on what they believed. The most significant reference comes from Luke's description of Paul's trial before the Sanhedrin, a council that included Pharisees and Sadducees: "The Sadducees say that there is no resurrection, or angel, or spirit; but the Pharisees acknowledge all three" (Acts 23:8).

After the fall of Jerusalem, the Pharisaic movement went through a period of declining influence as a popular party within Judaism. Debates continue among scholars as to whether the Pharisaic tradition is reflected in rabbinic Judaism. "As far as we can tell," writes Westerholm, "Pharisaism was a phenomenon of the pre-70 period. To depict the post-70 situation as the triumph of the Pharisees is over-simplistic and misleading. It was not until years later that the rabbis established effective leadership of the people; when they did so, they did not appear as Pharisees."[22]

1.2.1.2. Sadducees. The commonly accepted view is that the name for this group comes from the personal name Zadok, a priest during the reign of David (2 Sam 15:24) and Solomon (1 Kings 1:34-35), who essentially became the father of the Jerusalem priesthood. The Sadducees' rise to power, influence in Jewish society and religious beliefs are chronicled in Josephus, the New Testament and rabbinic literature and are discussed widely by scholars dealing with the intertestamental period. From these sources we learn that they came from the priestly aristocratic class, generally supported Hellenism and were interested in politics and religion.[23]

The Sadducees are mentioned fourteen times in the New Testament, but the references do not differentiate their role from other religious leaders. In some cases they are paired with the Pharisees in their opposition to Jesus (Mt 3:7; 16:1, 6, 11-12) and leaders of the early church (see Acts 4:1-2; 23:6; note Acts 5:17, where they are called a "sect" *[hairesis]*). In other places they are singled out, such as when they debate the resurrection of the dead with Jesus (Mt 22:23, 34; Mk 12:18; Lk 20:27). Since they regarded only the written Pentateuch as legally binding and rejected the legal authority of the oral law (the "tradition of the elders"), they also came into conflict with the Pharisees. As members of the Sanhedrin, the Sadducees were involved in the trial and crucifixion of Jesus (Mt 26:59; Mk 14:55, 60-64), in opposition to leaders of the early church (Acts 4:1-3; 5:17-41), in the trial and martyrdom of Stephen (Acts

---

[22]Westerholm, "Pharisees," p. 611.
[23]Gary G. Porton, "Sadducees," *DNTB*, pp. 1050-52; E. P. Sanders, "Aristocrats and Sadducees," in *Judaism*, pp. 317-40.

6—7) and in the arrest of Paul (Acts 22—24).[24]

Both Josephus (*Ant.* 18.1.4 §16; *J.W.* 2.8.14 §§162-66) and the New Testament claim that the Sadducees denied the resurrection of the dead, the immortality of the soul, rewards and punishment after death and the existence of angels and spirits (see Acts 23:8 and the references above). They also believed in free will, that is, that humanity is solely responsible for its own destiny. After the destruction of the temple (their center of power) in A.D. 70 and the emergence of rabbinic Judaism, they no longer played a significant role in Judaism.

1.2.1.3. Scribes. In the first-century world, essentially anyone who could read and write was considered a scribe. This ability set people apart from the general public and led to significant roles in politics, local government, commerce and religion. While some scribes came from the "priestly aristocracy," many were ordinary priests or individuals from all segments of society. Their scribal activity usually was a supplement to their regular vocation or trade—not unlike the apostle Paul, a "leather worker." Consequently, one needs to visualize a significant number of priests circulating throughout the towns and villages of Palestine. As such, they represented a larger class of people than a few opponents of Jesus and the early church that we meet in the New Testament.[25]

In New Testament times, scribes *(grammateus)* performed a number of different functions within Judaism. Beyond ordinary scribal activity, they were "teachers" (*didaskaloi,* Lk 2:46), "teachers of the law" (*nomodidaskaloi,* Lk 5:17; Acts 5:34) and "lawyers" (*nomikoi,* Lk 7:30). In these and other cases they are depicted as the custodians and interpreters of the Jewish Scriptures.

The identity of the scribes is unclear in the New Testament. They may be a separate group of Jewish religious leaders who came from the priestly or Sadducean aristocracy (Mt 7:29 par. Mk 1:22). In the New Testament they are mentioned twenty-one times in relation to the chief priests and eighteen times with

---

[24]Graham H. Twelftree, "Sanhedrin," *DJG,* pp. 728-32; Twelftree, "Sanhedrin," *DNTB,* pp. 1061-65.

[25]Most scholars date the origin of the scribal school during the exilic period, when studying, collecting, editing, copying and guarding the Scriptures took on new significance. Ezra, for example, is called "a scribe skilled in the law of Moses" (Ezra 7:6). The tradition is that from him there developed an unbroken line of scribes of the Great Synagogue. Mishnah ʾ*Abot* (1:1) states: "Moses received Torah from Sinai and delivered it to Joshua, and Joshua to the Elders, and the Elders to the Prophets, and the Prophets delivered it to the Men of the Great Synagogue. These said three things; Be deliberate in judging, and raise up many disciples, and make a hedge for the Torah" (R. Travers Herford, *The Ethics of the Talmud: Sayings of the Fathers* [New York: Schocken, 1962], p. 19). See further, Donald A. Hagner, "Scribes," *ISBE* 4:359-61; Graham H. Twelftree, "Scribes," *DJG,* p. 733; Twelftree, "Scribes," *DNTB,* pp. 1086-89; Anthony J. Saldarini, "Scribes," *ABD* 5:1012-16.

the Pharisees. However, reference to "the scribes of the Pharisees" (Mk 2:16; Acts 23:9; see also Acts 5:34 on the Pharisee Gamaliel, a "teacher of the law") indicates membership within that group.[26] Whatever their identity and alliance, they are depicted as major opponents of Jesus, repeatedly questioning his message, lifestyle, interpretation of the law and right to speak on behalf of God. In a number of cases Matthew and Luke appear to tone down or qualify scribal opposition to Jesus.

The book of Acts records several encounters of the early church with the scribes and other religious leaders. Their opposition is now directed toward Peter and John and the boldness with which they proclaim the gospel—particularly the resurrection of Jesus (Acts 4:1-22). Later, members of "the synagogue of the Freedmen" (see 3.1) succeed in stirring up the populace "as well as the elders and scribes" against Stephen (Acts 6:8-15). In this light, it is quite possible that scribes were part of the crowd that supported Saul in the persecution of the Jerusalem church (Acts 8:1-3).

Little is known about individual members of the Great Synagogue before the fall of Jerusalem in A.D. 70. Hillel and Shammai, both contemporaries of Jesus, were important rabbinical teachers who attracted many disciples and formed "schools." As far as we know they had no direct contact with Jesus or members of the early church. Gamaliel, however, a great scribe and rabbi renowned for his teaching (including Saul, Acts 22:3), demonstrated moderation and wise counsel in order to avoid a serious conflict between Jewish authorities, Peter and the apostles (Acts 5:17-42).[27]

1.2.1.4. Priests. Since Israel was to be "a priestly kingdom and a holy nation" (Ex 19:4-6), it is not surprising that much of the Bible devotes itself to discussion about the nature and function of this office. Priests were individuals who represented the people before God through the cultic rituals in the temple, particularly performing sacrifices on their behalf.[28] Only the high priest, however, could perform the sin offering on the Day of Atonement and enter into the holy of holies.

There appear to have been three classes of priests functioning in Palestine during the first century A.D. As in the Old Testament, the New Testament mentions that the high priest was appointed to offer "gifts and sacrifices" (see Heb

---

[26]A textual variant on Mk 2:16 has "scribes *and* the Pharisees."

[27]On rabbinic Judaism, see Bruce D. Chilton, "Rabbinic Traditions and Writings," *DJG,* pp. 651-60.

[28]For a list of other functions, see L. D. Hurst and Joel Green, "Priest, Priesthood," *DJG,* p. 634; Wayne O. McCready, "Priests and Levites," *ISBE* 3:965-70; and Bruce Chilton and Craig A. Evans, *Jesus in Context: Temple Purity and Restoration* (Leiden: E. J. Brill, 1997). E. P. Sanders offers a lengthy discussion on the priesthood in *Judaism,* pp. 45-189.

8:3) as "God's high priest" (Acts 23:4) and "leader" of the people (Acts 23:5). He also served as the head (president) of the Sanhedrin, the highest ruling council of the Jews (Mt 26:3; Acts 4:1-6). Annas and his son-in-law Caiaphas, although appointed high priests at different times, collaborated during the events of Jesus' trial and crucifixion (Mt 26:3, 57; Lk 3:2; Jn 11:49; 18:13-14, 24, 28) and the confrontation with Peter and John (Acts 4:6). Ananias was the high priest before whom Paul appeared when he was arrested in Jerusalem (Acts 23:2) and who spoke against Paul before the Roman governor Felix in Caesarea (Acts 24:1).

A second classification is the "chief priests" *(archiereus)*, who appear to have a higher rank and administrative authority than other priests. For example, they conspired with Judas concerning the betrayal of Jesus before his arrest (Mt 27:6; Lk 22:4-5; see also Acts 9:14; 26:10). In addition to their association with the high priest and the Sanhedrin, they also aligned themselves with other religious groups, such as the elders, scribes and Pharisees in their opposition to Jesus (see Mt 2:4; 16:21; 20:18; 26:59; Mk 8:31; 10:33; 14:43; Lk 9:22; 19:47; 23:10; Jn 7:32; 11:47; 18:3; Acts 4:23; 5:24; 25:2).[29]

Although we are not informed about the ordinary or rank-and-file priests during the first century, it is safe to assume that they were part of the religious establishment that continued to function in some capacity as long as the temple was standing. Zechariah, who with his wife Elizabeth was blessed with the birth of their son John the Baptist, appears to be such a priest (Lk 1:5-80). Perhaps the great number of the priests who "became obedient to the faith" were from this rank (Acts 6:7).[30]

The epistle to the Hebrews makes the most significant theological references to the priesthood in the New Testament. Here Jesus is presented as the supreme and eternal high priest who, through his death, has abolished the need for any earthly priesthood. The author of 1 Peter invites all believers to consider themselves "a holy priesthood" (1 Pet 2:5).

1.2.1.5. Herodians. Not much is known about the Herodians apart from three brief references in the New Testament (Mt 22:16; Mk 3:6; 12:13). In these verses they align themselves with the Pharisees in order to conspire against Jesus because he healed a man with a withered hand on the sabbath (Mk 3:6) and in order to question Jesus' position regarding paying taxes to Caesar (Mk

---

[29]These verses are just a sample of the sixty-four times "chief priests" are mentioned in the New Testament.

[30]David A. Fiensy estimates that there may have been as many as two thousand ordinary temple priests in Jerusalem ("The Composition of the Jerusalem Church," in Bauckham, ed., *Palestinian Setting,* p. 228. See also Steve Mason, "Chief Priests, Sadducees, Pharisees and Sanhedrin," esp. pp. 142-47.

12:13 par. Mt 22:16). In this last episode they believed they could "trap" Jesus or at least put him on the horns of a dilemma: if Jesus said no to Caesar, he would be accused of treason against Rome, while affirming the payment of taxes could lead to questions about his theocracy.

This group probably originated from tangled political and religious relationships between Rome and the Hasmoneans, though it is impossible to reconstruct these relationships with confidence. As difficult as it is to imagine Pharisees entering into an alliance with supporters of Herod, religion and politics sometimes make strange bedfellows. One possibility is that the Herodians were some kind of royalist group, with a separate identity, that developed a special relationship to Herod. Bruce Chilton suggests that they were a "Pharisaic group" who enjoyed some support from the royal family, especially on their teaching of purity.[31] A more convincing solution places them within the Sadducean circle, because in principle the Pharisees were "anti-Hasmonean, anti-Herodian and anti-Roman."[32] Either way, they were a group to whom the Pharisees appealed in their opposition to Jesus and his message.

There are no further references to this group in the New Testament, even though the early church in Palestine was under Herodian rule. Herod Agrippa I's persecution of the church, killing of James and arrest of Peter (Acts 12:1-5) were political moves on his part to gain favor with the Jews. The "Jews" who were pleased by this action probably were a small minority within Judaism who found the message and spread of Christianity threatening.

1.2.1.6. Essenes. Although the Essenes are not mentioned by name in the New Testament, they do represent a movement within Judaism that sought to form an alternative community of the "true" Israel. The _precise_ origin of the movement is debated, but scholars agree that it began during Hasmonean rule when a number of Jewish pietists _(ḥasîdîm)_ protested the illegitimacy of the ruling high priesthood and when certain rulers inflicted severe atrocities on the Jewish people and their faith.

The Essenes were not a monolithic sect. Some members believed that total separation from society was necessary and thus established a monastic-like community at Qumran in the Judean desert. The Dead Sea Scrolls (DSS), written by this group over a period of years, describe in detail their beliefs and practices. Basically they were an eschatological movement who believed they were called to prepare the way of the Lord _in the wilderness_ (their interpretation of Is 40:3-11). Entrance into the community was regulated by strict rules, including

---

[31]Bruce Chilton, "Judaism," _DJG,_ p. 402; Harold W. Hoehner, "Herodians," _ISBE_ 2:679-81; Hoehner, "Herodian Dynasty," _DNTB,_ pp. 485-94, esp. 493-94.
[32]Hoehner, "Herodian Dynasty," p. 325.

celibacy, communal ownership of property, a one-year period of probation, intensive study of the Torah, an initiatory baptism, ritual purifications, prayers, and so forth.[33]

Other Essenes did not become part of the Qumran community and chose to live within society. They married, possessed private property and engaged in normal social and political contacts. When political tensions with Rome eased under Herod's rule, they may have carried out intensive missionary activities that resulted in the founding of additional Essene communities in Judean towns and villages. The "gate of the Essenes" (Josephus *J.W.* 5.4.2 §145) indicates that they continued to enter the city and perhaps participate in temple ritual as well.

It is difficult to assess whether the Essenes had much impact on Jewish society or early Christianity, since there is no trace of their type of Judaism after A.D. 70. John the Baptist has (though not convincingly) been identified as an Essene. His physical demeanor and messianic message (see Mt 3:1-14; Mk 1:2-4; Lk 3:1-20) suggest a monastic lifestyle. However, his interpretation of Isaiah 40:3 was different. Instead of "in the wilderness prepare the way of the Lord" (Qumran), he saw his mission as a public one: "*A voice cries out in the wilderness,* 'Prepare the way of the Lord.' "

There is no clear or convincing evidence that Jesus had any direct contact with the Essenes, although some contemporary scholars have attempted to identify him with their Teacher of Righteousness because both were messianic figures. Similar religious concepts and vocabulary in the Qumran literature and the Fourth Gospel (e.g., darkness, light, truth and falsehood) are probably due to the commonality of these ideas rather than to direct influence.[34]

1.2.1.7. Revolutionary Movements. Although I have referred to some of the

---

[33]Primary source material includes Philo *Hypothetica* 11.1-18 and *Omn. Prob. Lib.* 75-76; Josephus *J.W.* 2.8.2-13 §§119-61; *Ant.* 18.1.5 §§18-22; Hippolytus (a third-century bishop), *Refut.* 9.4. For translations of the DSS, see G. Vermes, *The Dead Sea Scrolls in English*, rev. ed. (Sheffield: Sheffield University Press, 1988); Florentino García Martínez, *The Dead Sea Scrolls Translated* (Leiden: E. J. Brill, 1994); Michael Wise, Martin Abegg Jr. and Edward Cook, *The Dead Sea Scrolls: A New Translation* (San Francisco: HarperCollins, 1996). Selected studies with helpful bibliographies include Todd S. Beall, "Essenes," *DNTB*, pp. 342-48); George W. Buchanan, "Essenes," *ISBE* 2:147-55; John J. Collins, "Dead Sea Scrolls," *ABD* 2:85-101; Collins, "Essenes," *ABD* 2:619-26; William S. LaSor, "Dead Sea Scrolls," *ISBE* 1:883-97; James C. VanderKam, *The Dead Sea Scrolls Today* (Grand Rapids, Mich.: Eerdmans, 1994); and Michael O. Wise, "Dead Sea Scrolls: General Introduction," *DNTB*, pp. 252-66. E. P. Sanders provides an excellent discussion on the origins, history, practices and beliefs of the Essenes and the Dead Sea Sect in *Judaism*, pp. 341-79.

[34]For suggestions on possible connections between Jesus and the Essenes in Jerusalem, see Rainer Riesner, "Jesus, the Primitive Community, and the Essene Quarter of Jerusalem," in *Jesus and the Dead Sea Scrolls*, ed. James Charlesworth (New York: Doubleday, 1992), esp. pp. 215-17.

political, social and religious turmoil in Palestine between the second century
B.C. and the first century A.D., it is necessary to identify the Jewish revolutionary
movements that were current during the time of Jesus and the early church
more precisely. Scholars applying a social-scientific methodology to the New
Testament era have enriched our knowledge of such movements significantly in
recent years.[35] Warren J. Heard provides such a perspective when he writes:

> Revolutionary movements were a Jewish response to the injustice of Israel's
> oppressors, particularly the Roman Empire. The first century was one of the most
> violent epochs of Jewish history, with the cauldron of unrest reaching its apex in
> the destruction of Jerusalem. . . . This in turn was punctuated by the mass suicide
> of Jewish rebel forces at Masada in A.D. 74. Sixty years later the smoldering embers
> from this war were fanned into flame by the Jewish leader Simon ben Kosiba, who
> led the second revolt against the Romans in A.D. 132-135.[36]

Josephus identifies two major Jewish "messianic" revolts that attempted to
overthrow Roman domination of Palestine. The first (c. A.D. 66) was led by
Menahem, son of Judas the Galilean, who started an insurrection against Herod
(Josephus *J.W.* 2.8 §§433-34). The second, under the leadership of Simon bar
Giora (c. A.D. 68), lasted two years before it was crushed by the Roman army
(*J.W.* 2.22.2 §§652-54; 4.9.3-8 §§503-44). A final messianic movement,
recorded by the Roman historian Dio Cassius (*Roman History* 59.13.3), was led
by Simon bar Kokhba ("Son of the Star") from A.D. 132-135. The defeat of this

---

[35]For further reading and helpful bibliographies, see Ernst Bammel and C. F. D. Moule, eds.
Jesus and the Politics of His Day (Cambridge: Cambridge University Press, 1984); Stephen C.
Barton, "Social-Scientific Approaches to Paul," *DPL*, pp. 892-900; Barton, "Social Setting of
Early Non-Pauline Christianity," *DLNTD*, pp. 1102-11; John H. Elliott, *Social-Scientific Criticism and the New Testament* (Minneapolis: Augsburg Fortress, 1993); John Gager, *Kingdom
and Community: The Social World of Early Christianity* (Englewood Cliffs, N.J.: Prentice Hall,
1975); Susan R. Garrett, "Sociology (Early Christian)," *ABD* 6:89-99; William R. Herzog II,
"Sociological Approaches to the Gospels," *DJG*, pp. 760-66; Bengt Holmberg, *Sociology and
the New Testament* (Minneapolis: Augsburg Fortress, 1990); Richard A. Horsley, *Jesus and
the Spiral of Violence: Popular Jewish Resistance in Roman Palestine* (San Francisco: Harper
& Row, 1987); Horsley, *Sociology and the Jesus Movement* (New York: Crossroad, 1989);
Richard A. Horsley and J. Hanson, *Bandits, Prophets and Messiahs: Popular Movements at
the Time of Jesus* (Minneapolis: Winston, 1985); Howard C. Kee, *Christian Origins in Sociological Perspective* (Philadelphia: Westminster Press, 1980); Bruce Malina, *The New Testament World: Insights from Cultural Anthropology* (Atlanta: John Knox Press, 1981); Wayne A.
Meeks, *The First Urban Christians* (New Haven, Conn.: Yale University Press, 1983); John E.
Stambaugh and David L. Balch, *The New Testament in Its Social Environment* (Philadelphia:
Westminster Press, 1988); Gerd Theissen, *Sociology of Early Palestinian Christianity* (Philadelphia: Fortress, 1978); Derek Tidball, *The Social Context of the New Testament* (Grand
Rapids, Mich.: Zondervan, 1984).
[36]Warren J. Heard in Heard and Craig A. Evans, "Revolutionary Movements, Jewish," *DNTB*, p.
936.

movement under the emperor Hadrian virtually ended all revolutionary attempts against the Romans.[37]

In addition to these messianic revolts, which attempted to reestablish a theocracy in Palestine, there were many other movements with different agendas. *Social bandits,* as identified by Horsley and Hanson, were peasants seeking agrarian reforms against severe economic injustice and taxation.[38] Members of *prophetic movements* were not messianic pretenders but individuals who believed and taught that God was about to defeat their enemies, transform society and usher in a new era of peace, justice and prosperity. Josephus describes some of them as "deceivers and impostors, under the pretense of divine inspiration fostering revolutionary changes, they persuaded the multitude to act like madmen, and led them out into the desert under the belief that God would give them tokens of deliverance" (*J.W.* 2.13.4 §259).

Many revolutionary movements were active in the first century. It is a mistake, however, to classify all of them as Zealots, even though they were *zealous* in their political and religious goals. The Zealots as an identifiable group "were not formed until the winter of A.D. 67-68."[39] Nor is the Fourth Philosophy mentioned by Josephus (*Ant.* 18.1.6 §§23-25) to be equated with all these groups.[40] Not all groups were armed rebels or guerrilla warriors; some were passive resisters who believed they could accomplish their goals by obedience to the Torah, righteous suffering and martyrdom.

This information helps us understand some of Rome's fear of Jesus as a possible revolutionary prophet, the references to Theudas and Judas the Galilean (Acts 5:36-39) and mistaken identification of Paul as "the Egyptian who recently stirred up a revolt and led the four thousand assassins out into the wilderness" (Acts 21:38; cf. Josephus *J.W.* 2.13 §§261-63; *Ant.* 20.8.6 §§169-72). Luke's use of "assassins" (*tōn sikariōn*) may refer to another group, the *sicarii* or "dagger men" (from the Latin *sica,* a curved dagger).[41]

1.2.1.8. The Temple. There were three temples over the course of Israel's history: Solomon's, the postexilic temple rebuilt by Zerubbabel in 516 B.C., and Herod's, which was destroyed in A.D. 70. The temple was always regarded as the "house of Yahweh" *(bêt yhwh)* or "house of God" *(bêt ʾelōim)* set in Jerusalem, the city of Zion. In addition to its religious or cultic role, it also served as a

---

[37]See Horsley and Hanson, *Bandits,* pp. 127-31; Benjamin Issac, "Banditry," *ABD* 1:575-80.
[38]Warren J. Heard provides a brief synopsis in "Revolutionary Movements," *DJG,* pp. 688-89.
[39]Ibid., p. 696.
[40]See further Horsley and Hanson, *Bandits,* esp. pp. 190-243; Terence D. Donaldson, "Zealot," *ISBE* 4:1175-79.
[41]Josephus *J.W.* 1.13.3 §§254-56; Horsley and Hanson, *Bandits,* pp. 200-16; Cohen, *From the Maccabees to the Mishnah,* pp. 164-66.

major symbol of Jewish national pride and unity. Symbolically, Jerusalem (Zion) was the cosmic mountain and the temple "the cosmic center of the universe . . . the place where heaven and earth converge and thus from where God's control over the universe is effected."[42]

During the first century the temple was a busy place of cultic, religious and social activity. The Jewish people, including those in the Diaspora, believed that God had ordained the temple with its priesthood, sacrifices and festivals, and they supported it with their worship and the payment of the temple tax. For the most part, Jesus is presented as honoring the temple, and a considerable part of his public ministry was spent in Jerusalem openly teaching (Mt 21:23; Mk 12:35; 14:49; Lk 19:47; 20:1; 21:37-38; 22:53; Jn 7:14, 28; 8:2, 20; 18:20) and healing (Mt 21:14; Jn 5:14) within the temple area.

Conflict and suspicion between Jesus and the religious authorities arose when some of his teaching mentioned the destruction of the temple (Mt 26:61; 27:40; Mk 14:58; 15:29; Jn 2:19; cf. Acts 6:14). This conflict came to a head when Jesus cleansed the temple because he was disgusted with the money changers (Mt 21:12-13; Mk 11:15-17; Lk 19:45-46; Jn 2:14-17). Scholars continue to debate whether this was merely a dramatic apocalyptic act or whether it was interpreted as a revolutionary one by the temple authorities. E. P. Sanders has argued quite passionately—and correctly—that "the threat of destruction and the gesture [cleansing] against the temple" was the main reason leading to Jesus' arrest and crucifixion.[43]

The temple continued to play a significant part in the life of the early church. Because most of the Jewish Christians saw themselves as the "true" rather than the "new" Israel, there was no need to break their relationships with existing patterns of worship (see 3.10.2). Thus Peter and John honored their prayer schedule (Acts 3:1) and preached and taught the gospel in the temple area (Acts 5:20-21, 42). Luke indicates that "all who believed . . . spent much time together in the temple" (Acts 2:44-46). Even Paul, according to Luke, remained faithful to ritual purification (Acts 21:26) and prayer (Acts 22:17) and argued vehemently that he did not desecrate the temple in any way (Acts 25:8). The situation is different with Stephen, because his speech about the temporary nature

---

[42]Carol Meyers, "Temple, Jerusalem," _ABD_ 6:359; see also N. T. Wright, _New Testament and the People of God,_ pp. 224-26. E. P. Sanders does a thorough job of describing the day-to-day operation of the temple, the function of the priests, and so forth in _Judaism,_ pp. 47-145, as does N. T. Wright in _Jesus and the Victory of God_ (Minneapolis: Fortress, 1996), pp. 406-28. See also Bruce Chilton, Philip W. Comfort and Michael O. Wise, "Temple, Jewish," _DNTB,_ pp. 1167-83.

[43]Sanders, _Jesus and Judaism,_ p. 302. See William R. Herzog II, "Temple Cleansing," _DJG,_ pp. 817-21.

of the law and the temple was interpreted as blasphemy by the Hellenistic Jews and ultimately led to his martyrdom (Acts 7).

The destruction of the temple in A.D. 70 was not a theological problem for the early church. Not only had Jesus predicted its demise as God's judgment on Israel (Mt 26:61; 27:40; Mk 15:29), but by that time believers had formed their own identity apart from Judaism (see 3.10.2). It was different for the Jews, however. The rabbinic response was to shift the focus from the Temple to the Torah, so that Judaism gradually became a religion of scribes rather than priests. Eventually their oral traditions were codified into the Mishnah and the Talmud.[44]

1.2.1.9. The Synagogue. The synagogue was the second major institution within Judaism. The word *synagōgē* is used to describe a "gathering" or "assembly" of people as well as to designate a "place" or "building" where people met. While there is unanimity among scholars about the first meaning, a current debate centers around the second. That is, at what period of time did *synagōgē* refer to a special building or meeting place, *a* or *the* gathering place for the Jews?

Howard Clark Kee and other scholars agree that, although *synagogue* designates a gathering of individuals in private homes and public buildings, there is no evidence to speak of synagogues as architecturally distinguishable structures in Palestine prior to A.D. 200.[45] A similar view is expressed by Eric Meyers, who concludes that in Palestine, "it was about a hundred years after the destruction of the Temple that the synagogue *as a building* began to emerge as a central feature of Jewish communal life."[46] Rainer Riesner, on the other hand, represents the traditional and probably majority opinion when he writes that "the synagogue was widespread by the 1st century AD, both in the Diaspora and in the land of Israel."[47]

---

[44]For issues on temple theology after A.D. 70, see Chilton, Comfort and Wise, "Temple, Jewish," pp. 1167-83; C. Meyers, "Temple, Jerusalem," 6:367-68; Philip W. Comfort, "Temple," *DPL*, pp. 923-25; Glenn N. Davies, "Tabernacle, Sanctuary," *DLNTD*, pp. 1154-56.

[45]Howard Clark Kee, "The Transformation of the Synagogue After 70 C.E.: Its Import for Early Christianity," *NTS* 36 (1990): 9.

[46]Eric Meyers, "Synagogue," *ABD* 6:255.

[47]Rainer Riesner, "Synagogues in Jerusalem," in Bauckham, ed., *Palestinian Setting*, p. 180. He provides an excellent bibliography on the subject in n. 2. A useful summary of different scholarly views on the synagogue is found in Richard S. Ascough, *What Are They Saying About the Formation of Pauline Churches?* (New York: Paulist, 1998), pp. 11-28. For further discussion of the issues, see Brad B. Blue, "The Influence of Jewish Worship on Luke's Presentation of the Early Church," in *Witness to the Gospel*, ed. I. Howard Marshall and David Peterson (Grand Rapids, Mich.: Eerdmans, 1995), pp. 473-97; Bruce Chilton, "Synagogue," *DLNTD*, pp.1141-46; Donald B. Binder, *Into the Temple Courts: The Place of Synagogues in the Second Temple Period* (Atlanta: Society of Biblical Literature, 1999); Bruce Chilton and Edwin Yamauchi, "Synagogues," *DNTB*, pp. 1145-53; Fredrick C. Grant, "The Ancient Synagogue," in *Ancient Judaism and the New Testament* (London: Oliver & Boyd, 1960), pp. 39-

Kee's position makes the picture of the synagogue in the Gospels and Luke-Acts rather anachronistic. That is, later patterns of synagogal worship are projected back into the time of the New Testament. No doubt some early assemblies were located in rooms of houses designated as places of prayer (*proseuchē*), but it is difficult to imagine that there were no specific *structures* designated for such gatherings in the first century. Jesus is depicted as teaching and performing miracles of healing in synagogues throughout Galilee (Mt 4:23; 9:35; Lk 4:15), in cities such as Nazareth (Mt 13:54; Mk 6:2; Lk 4:16) and Capernaum (Mk 1:21; Lk 7:5; Jn 6:59) and in Judea (Lk 4:44; cf. Jn 18:20). The centurion in Capernaum is loved by the Jews because he built a synagogue for them (Lk 7:5).[48]

Separate buildings also appear to exist in the Diaspora, where Acts describes Paul's visits to synagogues in such places as Pisidian Antioch (Acts 13:14), Iconium (Acts 14:1), Thessalonica (Acts 17:1), Berea (Acts 17:10), Athens (Acts 17:17), Corinth (Acts 18:4; note Acts 18:7: Titius Justus, whose house was "next door to the synagogue") and Ephesus (Acts 18:19; 19:8). While some passages could refer to a gathering of Jews anywhere, others suggest a separate structure. Edwin Yamauchi reminds us that to question Luke's account "is to underestimate the fragmentary nature of the archeological evidence and to disregard not only the testimony of the New Testament but also of Josephus . . . and Philo."[49]

Shaye Cohen defines the synagogue as "a tripartite institution: a prayer-house, a study hall or school, and a meeting-house."[50] From this description, it is not difficult to believe that the synagogue served as a model for the early Christian house churches and their worship liturgy. In the New Testament, synagogues are described as assemblies where people met for worship by reading Scripture, praying and receiving instruction (Lk 4:16-30; Acts 13:15; 14:1; 15:21; 17:2-3). It also was the place where justice was administered (Mk 13:9; Jn 9:22; 12:42; 16:2; Acts 22:19; 2 Cor 11:24). The personnel in charge of the synagogues are identified as either heads (*archisynagōgos*, Mk 5:22) or leaders (*archōn*, Mt 9:23; Lk 8:41). Their primary responsibility was to keep people faithful to the Torah. Another person functioned as a custodian who took care of the scrolls. When Jesus, for example, finished reading from the scroll, he rolled

57; Rachel Hachlili, "Synagogue," *ABD* 6:255; William S. LaSor and Tamara C. Eskenazi, "Synagogue," *ISBE* 4:676-84; Lee I. Levine, *The Ancient Synagogue: The First Thousand Years* (New Haven, Conn.: Yale University Press, 2000); Irina Levinskaya, "The Meaning of *Proseuchē*," in *The Book of Acts in Its Diaspora Setting*, BAFCS 5 (Grand Rapids, Mich.: Eerdmans, 1996), pp. 213-25; Wolfgang Schrage, "συναγωγή κτλ," *TDNT* 7:798-852.
[48]See Riesner's conclusions in "Synagogues in Jerusalem," p. 209.
[49]Edwin Yamauchi, "Synagogue," *DJG*, p. 784.
[50]Cohen, *From the Maccabees to the Mishnah*, p. 111.

it up and "gave it back to the attendant" (*hypērete,* Lk 4:20).

At the beginning of the Christian movement, Jewish Christians probably continued their relationship with the synagogue, as they did with the temple, even though they also observed specifically Christian customs (see Acts 2:39-42). As time went on, however, tensions between church and synagogue increased. This was true of Paul when he preached and interpreted the Scriptures in the Diaspora synagogues, for in most cases he was met with derision, hostility, expulsion and persecution (Acts 13:50-51; 14:2-6, 19-20; 17:5-9, 13-14; 18:6, 12-17). In addition, the warning that Jesus gave to his disciples about hostility and punishment in the synagogues (Mt 10:17; 23:34; Lk 21:12) was fulfilled toward the end of the first century in the Johannine community, where Jewish Christians (those who believed in Jesus as the Messiah) were threatened with expulsion from the synagogues (Jn 9:22; 12:42; 16:2). This hostility intensified and led to the inclusion of a curse (the Birkat ha-Minim; literally, "blessing of the heretics") against such "apostates" in the Eighteen Benedictions *(Shemoneh Esre)* that were recited in the synagogue service: "As for the apostates, let there be no hope, and in judgment cause the kingdom of arrogance soon to be destroyed. *Blessed art thou, O Lord, who humblest the proud.*"[51]

1.2.2. Hellenistic Judaism. *Hellenism* is a historiographical technical term designating the period of history ranging from Alexander the Great (356-323 B.C.) to Roman imperial rule (c. 30 B.C.)[52] For our purposes, we shall refer to Hellenism as a *process* during which Greek language and culture (art, literature, religion, science, philosophy, etc.) were spread throughout the ancient Near Eastern world.

In Palestine, most Hellenization took place during the rule of Alexander the Great and his successors. Although Hellenism may have been more pervasive in areas surrounding Judea and Samaria (such as Galilee, the Decapolis and cities in the Transjordan), it affected *all* of Palestinian Judaism, with the possible exception of the Qumran community. The research of Martin Hengel and others has shown that the artificial distinction between the Hellenism of Jews in the

---

[51]Translation from Frederick C. Grant, *Ancient Judaism and the New Testament* (London: Oliver & Boyd, 1960), p. 47. For further discussion, evaluation, interpretation, questions about dating and even later revisions of this curse, see R. Brown, *Introduction to the New Testament,* p. 82; Dunn, *Partings of the Ways,* p. 320, nn. 44-46; Craig A. Evans, "Christianity and Judaism: Partings of the Ways," *DLNTD,* pp. 159-170; William Horbury, "The Benediction of the Minim and Early Jewish-Christian Controversy," *JTS* 33 (1982): 19-61; N. T. Wright, *Jesus and the Victory of God,* p. 374 n. 9.

[52]See Hans-Dieter Betz, "Hellenism," *ABD* 3:127; Leon Morris, "Hellenism," *ISBE* 2:679-81; Greg R. Stanton, "Hellenism," *DNTB,* pp. 464-73; Walter T. Wilson, "Hellenistic Judaism," *DNTB,* pp. 477-82.

Diaspora and an "uncontaminated" Judaism of Palestine is invalid.[53] Widespread use of the Greek language, names, architecture, and the like all confirm that, by the Roman period, Palestinian Jews were significantly Hellenized in many areas of thought and life. In some cases the dispersion (Diaspora) of the Jews was forced upon them by conquering empires, but for most Jews the Diaspora was a voluntary choice determined by such factors as adventure and commercial opportunities.

The highest concentration of Jews outside of Palestine was in Egypt, especially in the city of Alexandria. Settlement there began as early as the sixth century B.C. and, according to the Hellenistic Jewish philosopher Philo (c. 15 B.C.-A.D. 50), may have totaled as many as one million (*Against Flaccus* 43). Alexandria was significant for the production of the Septuagint (LXX), the Greek translation of the Hebrew Bible. This translation eventually became the Old Testament version used by Paul and other Greek-speaking Christians. The writings of Philo, and eventually a form of Egyptian Christianity, also originated in Alexandria. Other regions with a significant Jewish population included North Africa, Italy (particularly Rome), Asia Minor, Greece and Syria (primarily the cities of Antioch and Damascus).[54]

The dispersion of the Jews from Palestine to various geographical regions beyond the borders of Palestine and surrounding Greek territories precipitated two reactions. First, it exposed the Jews to a variety of foreign cultures that made the assimilation of certain aspects of Hellenization inevitable. However, Jews retained certain key beliefs and practices, such as separation from Gentiles in table fellowship, excluding Gentiles from temple worship and avoiding intermarriage with Gentiles.[55] Though scholars today recognize the variety of Judaisms current in the first-century world, they talk about the four pillars of Second Temple Judaism that served as a unifying core for Palestinian and Diaspora Jews (see p. 22 n. 5). These convictions also were a "witness" to the Gentiles and in many ways prepared the pagan world for the advent of Christianity. Luke mentions some who became Jewish proselytes and others, sometimes referred to as "God-fearers," who were attracted to Judaism (Acts 6:5; 10:2; 13:42-48; 14:1-2).

---

[53]See esp. Martin Hengel, *Judaism and Hellenism,* 2 vols. (Philadelphia: Fortress, 1974); Hengel, *The "Hellenization" of Judea in the First Century After Christ* (Philadelphia: Trinity Press International, 1989); Hengel, *Jews, Greeks, and Barbarians* (Philadelphia: Fortress, 1980).

[54]Andrew Overman and William S. Green, *ABD* 3:1048-50; William R. Stegner, "Diaspora," *DPL,* pp. 211-13; Paul R. Trebilco and Craig A. Evans, "Diaspora Judaism," *DNTB,* pp. 281-96.

[55]For details, see Scot McKnight, "Gentiles," *DJG,* p. 259, and his monograph *A Light Among the Gentiles: Jewish Missionary Activity in the Second Temple Period* (Minneapolis: Fortress, 1991).

Although Diaspora Jews were separated from Jerusalem and the temple, they supported it by paying a temple tax (a half-shekel per year) and making pilgrimages whenever possible. Joachim Jeremias has estimated that over 100,000 pilgrims attended the Passover in Jesus' day.[56] Thus, it is not surprising to find nonresident Jews, along with those living in Jerusalem, celebrating the Feast of Pentecost (Acts 2:5).[57] Moreover, the "synagogue of the Freedmen" *(Libertinōn)* in Jerusalem included Hellenistic Jews from Cyrene, Alexandria, Cilicia and Asia (Acts 6:9). It is possible that these were descendants of Jews taken to Rome by Pompey around 60 B.C. who settled in Jerusalem after they were given their freedom. Stephen, who was persecuted by members of this synagogue, may have belonged to it before he became a Christian.

The apostle Paul is a classic example of a Hellenistic Jew. Tarsus, the city of his birth (Acts 9:11; 22:3), was Hellenized during the Seleucid period and competed with Athens and Alexandria as an educational center (see Acts 21:39: "a citizen of an important city"), having both philosophical schools and schools of rhetoric. It is not difficult to believe that Paul studied the Greek language, philosophy, rhetoric, oratory, and the like in such a setting. However, all this did not diminish Paul's appreciation for his Jewish heritage, training and traditions (see Phil 3:4-6). Current studies on Paul seek to recover and understand his Jewishness rather than to explain him solely as a Hellenized Jew of the Diaspora.[58]

1.2.3. Gentiles. In Scripture, non-Jewish people, those who do not belong to the nation (Hebrew, *gôy*) of Israel, generally are referred to as Gentiles, a translation of the Greek *ethnos* (pl. *ethnē*), that is, those who have a non-Jewish "ethnic" identity.[59] In a few cases the New Testament uses such synonyms as *Greeks* (*Hellēnas;* Jn 7:35; Acts 14:1; 18:4; Rom 1:14; 1 Cor 1:24), *pagans* (1 Cor 5:1; 10:20; 12:2), *uncircumcised* (Acts 11:3; Rom 2:26-27; 3:30; 4:9; Gal 2:7; Col 3:11) and *unbelievers* (Lk 12:46; 1 Cor 6:6; 10:27; 2 Cor 4:4) to mean the same thing.

---

[56]Jeremias, *Jerusalem in the Time of Jesus,* pp. 77-83 (but see above for additional figures). E. P. Sanders discusses the unreliability of calculating numbers at that time but still comments: "It seems to me not unreasonable to suppose that some hundreds of thousands celebrated Passover at Jerusalem" (*Judaism,* p. 127).

[57]For the catalog of places, see Bruce M. Metzger, "Ancient Astrological Geography and Acts 2:9-11," in *Apostolic History and the Gospel: Essays Presented to F. F. Bruce,* ed. W. Ward Gasque and Ralph P. Martin (Grand Rapids, Mich.: Eerdmans, 1970), pp. 123-33.

[58]So Craig C. Hill, "Hellenists, Hellenistic and Hellenistic-Jewish Christianity," *DLNTD,* pp. 462-69; William R. Stegner, "Jew, Paul the," *DPL,* pp. 503-11. For additional sources on the influence of Hellenistic Judaism on Christian thought, see Peder Borgen, *Early Christianity and Hellenistic Judaism* (Edinburgh: T & T Clark, 1966); Peder Borgen and Søren Giversen, eds., *The New Testament and Hellenistic Judaism* (Peabody, Mass.: Hendrickson, 1998).

[59]Douglas R. de Lacey, "Gentiles," *DPL,* p. 335.

There are a few references where the context suggests that *Gentiles* refers to the Romans, as in the case of the arrest and trial of Jesus (Mt 20:19; Mk 10:33, 42; Lk 18:32; 21:24) and of Paul (Acts 21:11; note a distinction in Acts 4:27: "both Herod and Pontius Pilate, with the Gentiles and the peoples of Israel, gathered together against . . . Jesus"). Barbarians (Rom 1:14; cf. Acts 28:2, 4, where NRSV translates as "natives") were an alien race or people thought to be less cultured than the Greeks.

Scholars disagree on the nature of Jewish attitudes towards the Gentiles. The older school of thought, which supported the idea of total resistance to Hellenism, promoted the idea that all Gentiles were "sinners" because they were ritually unclean. Such total separation, however, was not possible and may even have differed among Jewish groups within Judaism. The Old Testament places certain requirements on resident aliens (Gentiles living among Jews; see Lev 17—19): for example, respect for the Noachide commandments, which included such things as prohibitions against idolatry, murder, incest and eating certain foods.[60] This background helps us to understand the decision of the Jerusalem Council, which endorsed Paul's mission to the Gentiles but modified the Noachide commands by requesting that Gentile believers abstain "from things polluted by idols and from fornication and from whatever has been strangled and from blood" (Acts 15:20).

Although Jesus acknowledged Gentiles as sinners in the sense that they were exclusive in their friendships (Mt 5:47), pursued earthly goods (Mt 6:32) and misunderstood the true nature of prayer (Mt 6:7), he associated with and ministered to them and refused to take vengeance on them according to Jewish expectations.[61] Thus the Gentile mission of the early church emerged with the conviction that both Gentiles and Jews were sinners needing salvation.

1.2.4. The Greco-Roman World. This section will briefly discuss the cultural and religious forces that the church faced in the Greco-Roman world as it expanded from Jerusalem to Rome. The Hellenistic age is characterized by a combination of primitive, Near Eastern, Greek, Roman and Jewish ideas and practices. This phenomenon—often referred to as syncretism—occurs whenever two cultures come into contact and assimilate each other's ideas and practices.[62]

The inclusivism of the Greeks and Romans enabled them to transplant and assimilate foreign deities into their religious system quite easily. Thus many dei-

---

[60]See the helpful summary in ibid., p. 336.
[61]See examples and references in McKnight, "Gentiles," pp. 259-61. On current scholarship regarding sinners, see Michael J. Wilkins, "Sinner," *DJG,* pp. 757-60.
[62]Clinton E. Arnold, "Syncretism," *DLNTD,* pp. 1146-47.

ties in the Greek pantheon had Egyptian and Near Eastern roots. The Romans likewise adopted and renamed many of their gods from the Greeks.[63] This is illustrated rather vividly in the New Testament when Paul arrives in Ephesus and confronts the cult of the fertility goddess Artemis (Greek) or Diana (Roman). Acts 19:21-41 shows the significance of Ephesus as the "temple keeper" *(neōkoron)* of the goddess (Acts 19:35), the passion of the Ephesians for their religion and the threat that the gospel posed to it. This passage also reveals the civic nature of this local cult, which involved local magistrates, provincial authorities and the commercial enterprise of manufacturing and selling statues of the goddess.[64]

One can assume that the idolatry described in Athens (Acts 17:16-34) included a vast array of gods and goddesses from antiquity (Acts 17:16: "the city was full of idols"). The point here is not so much the identification or assimilation of gods but the inclusiveness of the Athenians with their altar to "an unknown god" (Acts 17:23). Although no inscription has been discovered with this *exact* phraseology, there are ancient literary sources that record the existence of altars to "all the gods." Paul uses this occasion not to proclaim a new god but rather to proclaim this "unknown god" as the only God, the creator and "Lord of heaven and earth" (Acts 17:24).

One interesting aspect of Greek religion was the view that their gods and goddesses were anthropomorphic in nature, that is, having the form and character of humans (from the Greek, *anthrōpos* [human] and *morphē* [form]). Paul and Barnabas encountered this phenomenon in the city of Lystra in Lycaonia (a district in central Asia Minor) on their first missionary journey (Acts 14:1-7). Their preaching and their healing of someone crippled from birth amazed the crowd and persuaded them to exclaim, "The gods have come down to us in human form" (*hoi theoi homoiōthentes anthrōpois katebēsan pros hēmas,* Acts 14:11). They identified Barnabas with Zeus, the head of the Greek pantheon, and Paul with Hermes, the messenger or chief speaker of Zeus (Acts 14:12).

The scenario that developed gives us a brief glimpse into some other aspects

---

[63]Jack Finegan provides a list of twelve chief deities in the Roman pantheon and their Greek equivalents in *Myth and Mystery* (Grand Rapids, Mich.: Baker, 1989), p. 192. See also Bell, "Greco-Roman Religion," in *Exploring the New Testament World,* pp. 123-60; J. R. C. Cousland, "Temples, Greco-Roman," *DNTB,* pp. 1186-88; Everett Ferguson, *Backgrounds of Early Christianity,* 2nd ed. (Grand Rapids, Mich.: Eerdmans, 1993), p. 143; Larry Hurtado, *At the Origins of Christian Worship* (Grand Rapids, Mich.: Eerdmans, 2000), pp. 7-38; Hans-Joseph Klauck, *The Religious Context of Early Christianity: A Guide to Graeco-Roman Religions* (Edinburgh: T & T Clark, 2000).

[64]On Artemis, see Paul Treblico, "Asia," in *The Book of Acts in Its Graeco-Roman Setting,* ed. David W. J. Gill and Conrad Gempf, BAFCS 2 (Grand Rapids, Mich.: Eerdmans, 1994), pp. 316-57.

of civic religion as it was practiced in this locale. Paul and Barnabas, who certainly did not want to be honored with a sacrificial procession and offering at the temple of Zeus for their mistaken identity as gods, responded by drawing attention to their humanity. This clash with polytheism gave them an occasion to witness to the one living and creator God (Acts 14:15-17).

The early church faced a similar challenge with the development of the imperial cult of the Romans. The external forms of this cult included "the dedication of altars and temples, erection of statues to the person in the appearance of a deity, commemorative inscriptions, sacrifices in the ruler's honor, instituting new festivals or renaming old ones and ascribing divine titles."[65] Attributing divinity to certain emperors created tremendous tension for the church because its theological exclusivism was grounded in monotheism and the belief that Jesus was the only true "Lord" (kyrios) and "Savior" (sōtēr).

In most cases the divinization of an emperor took place after his death. Julius Caesar, for example, was declared to be a god (Divus Julius) by a vote of the Roman senate. Honorific terms such as augustus ("worthy of reverence"), divus ("divine"), divi filius ("son of god") and dominus ("master, lord") were included in the titles of many emperors.

Many scholars assume that the most serious conflict between Christianity and Rome arose during the time of Domitian (A.D. 81-96), who may have demanded divine recognition and participation in emperor worship from all citizens.[66] While faithful Christians could not acknowledge Caesar as Lord (kyrios), they nevertheless were instructed to honor the state and its leaders (Rom 13:1-7; 1 Tim 2:1-2; 1 Pet 2:13-17). To quote Jack Finegan: "while they willingly prayed for the emperor . . . [they] were not willing to pray to the emperor."[67] Failure to comply led to a reign of terror and a series of religious persecutions of the church.[68]

It seems likely that this is the context in which the book of Revelation was written, since it opposes the imperial claims of Rome more than any other book in the New Testament. Embedded in all of its apocalyptic imagery, symbolism,

---

[65]Everett Ferguson, "Religions, Greco-Roman," *DLNTD*, p. 1008. See also Samuel Angus and A. M. Renwick, "Roman Empire and Christianity," *ISBE* 4:207-21; David E. Aune, "Religion, Greco-Roman," *DNTB*, pp. 917-26; Susan G. Cole, "Festivals, Greco-Roman," *ABD* 2:793-94; Donald L. Jones, "Roman, Imperial Cult," *ABD* 5:806-9; Howard F. Vos, "Religions of the Biblical World: Greco-Roman," *ISBE* 4:107-17; Brook W. R. Pearson, "Polytheism, Greco-Roman," *DNTB*, pp. 815-18; H. F. Vos, "Rome," *ISBE* 4:228-36.

[66]Leonard L. Thompson has seriously challenged this assumption in *The Book of Revelation: Apocalypse and Empire* (Oxford: Oxford University Press, 1990).

[67]Finegan, *Myth and Mystery*, p. 214.

[68]For details, see Ethelbert Stauffer, *Christ and the Caesars* (Philadelphia: Westminster Press, 1955), esp. ch. 11, "Domitian and John," pp. 147-91.

numerology, and the like is the strong message of hope and assurance for the church that Christ has already won the final battle by defeating the powers of darkness. Thus Ethelbert Stauffer notes: "The Book of Revelation began with an imperial acclamation: *Ipsi gloria et imperium:* To him be the glory and the dominion. It ends with an imperial advent cry: *Veni, Domine:* Come, Lord Jesus."[69] A similar theme was echoed much earlier in the Christ-hymn of the early church: "so that at the name of Jesus every knee should bend, in heaven and on earth and under the earth, and every tongue should confess that Jesus Christ is Lord, to the glory of God the Father" (Phil 2:10-14).

The early church had to face not only these major and official characteristics of Greek and Roman religion but also other beliefs and practices that conflicted with its faith. The root of many problems was the ancient and universal idea of spiritual forces or demons inhabiting the universe and humanity. This belief is present in both biblical and extrabiblical literature, where it is often discussed and developed within the context of idolatry, healing, exorcism, magic, Satan and the devil.[70]

The leaders of the early church had encounters with the demonic not unlike those that Jesus faced during his ministry. Although the reality of the spirit world was not denied, the church's approach to dealing with the demonic was changed in light of Jesus' resurrection and victory over the powers of evil and darkness. Thus Peter and John invoked the name of Jesus in the healing of the crippled man (Acts 3:6; see 5:16; 8:7). When Paul and Silas encountered the slave girl in Philippi "who had a spirit of divination" they exorcised the spirit in "the name of Jesus Christ" (Acts 16:16-18). Paul must also have exorcised the evil spirits in Ephesus in the name of Jesus, because when some "itinerant Jewish exorcists" (the sons of Sceva) attempted to use "the name of the Lord Jesus," their incantations failed to produce the desired results (Acts 19:11-16). The implication is that Paul was successful as an exorcist because he was a follower of Jesus and could invoke his name legitimately.

This account also illuminates certain first-century beliefs regarding healing

---

[69]Ibid., p. 191. For additional information, see David E. Aune, "Emperors, Roman," *DPL,* pp. 233-35; David A. deSilva, "Ruler Cult," *DNTB,* pp. 1026-30; Mark Reasoner, "Emperor, Emperor Cult," *DLNTD,* pp. 321-26; and Reasoner, "Persecution," *DLNTD,* pp. 907-14. A series of helpful essays is found in Richard A. Horsley, ed., *Paul and Empire* (Harrisburg, Penn.: Trinity Press International, 1997).

[70]Clinton E. Arnold, "Satan, Devil," *DLNTD,* pp. 1077-82; Daniel P. Fuller, "Satan," *ISBE* 4:340-44; Sydney H. T. Page, *Powers of Evil* (Grand Rapids. Mich.: Baker, 1995); Terence Paige, "Demons and Exorcism," *DPL,* pp. 209-11; David G. Reese, "Demons," *ABD* 2:138-42; Peter Schafer and Hans G. Kippenbert, eds., *Envisioning Magic* (Leiden: E. J. Brill, 1997); Graham H. Twelftree, "Demon, Devil, Satan," *DJG,* pp. 163-172. For a more complete treatment of the topic, see Twelftree's *Jesus the Exorcist* (Tübingen: Mohr, 1993).

and magic. The Ephesians believed that divine powers could be transmitted through personal possessions and so brought their "handkerchiefs or aprons" for Paul to touch (Acts 19:11). Others were involved in practicing magic (Acts 19:18-20). The reluctance of "believers" to abandon this practice and discard their books illustrates how difficult it was for new believers to relinquish their former way of life.[71] Paul also encountered a Jewish magician and false prophet named Bar-Jesus, or Elymas, on the island of Cyprus (Acts 13:4-12). The apostle's denunciation of Elymas's deception, accompanied by Elymas's temporary blindness and the conversion of the proconsul, Sergius Paulus, vindicated the power of God over the forces of evil.

Another conflict between Christianity and magic is narrated in Acts 8:9-24. When Philip began to evangelize in Samaria, he healed the sick, exorcised demons and through the proclamation of the gospel saw people come to faith and baptism and receive the Holy Spirit. Within the crowd was a former magician named Simon (commonly referred to as Simon Magus, from the Greek *magos,* a sorcerer, magician). Simon had established quite a reputation and following in Samaria, performing such extraordinary deeds of magic that he was given the title "The Great Power" ("This man is the power of God that is called Great," Acts 8:10).

Later postapostolic writings depict Simon as the father of the Gnostic heresies, especially the sect of the Simonians. His desire to purchase the gift of the Holy Spirit was rebuked by Peter, who along with John had come from Jerusalem to lay hands on the Samaritan believers so that they would receive the Holy Spirit. Peter's rebuke is recorded in Acts 8:20: "May your silver perish with you, because you thought you could obtain God's gift with money!"

Other New Testament documents also warn believers about demonic powers. James notes that even though demons believe and shudder in the fact that "God is one" (Jas 2:19), the so-called wisdom they claim is not heavenly "but is earthly, unspiritual, devilish" (*daimoniōdēs,* Jas 3:15). The letters to Timothy warn believers not to renounce their faith "by paying attention to deceitful spirits and teachings of demons" (1 Tim 4:1) and remind them that "wicked people and imposters" (*goētes*) will flourish and deceive them (2 Tim 3:13). Idolatry and sorcery (Greek *pharmakeia,* from which we get the word *pharmacy*) are mentioned together in Galatians 5:20. An equally strong warning occurs in the Apocalypse with reference to the continuing work of demonic spirits (Rev 16:14), and there are warnings against worshiping demons and idols (Rev 2:20).

_____

[71]The existence of such books is well-attested by extant magical papyri. For a sample, see C. K. Barrett, *The New Testament Background: Selected Documents,* rev. ed. (San Francisco: Harper, 1987), pp. 31-38.

In the author's mind, fallen Babylon (Rome) has become the dwelling place of demons (Rev 14:8).

Pagan belief in idols emerged in Corinth over the issue of eating meat that pagan devotees had offered to their gods (see esp. 1 Cor 8:4-13 and 10:14-22, where Paul contrasts Christian faith and practice with pagan idolatry and sacrifices). Many of the pagan feasts included sacrificial offerings of meat to the gods, with some of the meat eaten within the temple area and the rest sold in local meat markets, where it was bought by the public, including converts to Christianity. The fact that some believers would buy and eat such meat created a controversy within the Corinthian congregations. According to Paul, partaking in pagan meals is akin to idolatry (1 Cor 10:21): "You cannot drink the cup of the Lord and the cup of demons. You cannot partake of the table of the Lord and the table of demons."[72]

The New Testament also refers to a host of other spiritual beings that are presented as demonic powers because of their power over individuals. In an argument not unlike the one on idolatry in 1 Corinthians, Paul reminds the Galatians that *before* they became believers (when they "did not know God") they were enslaved "to beings that by nature *[tois physei]* are not gods" (Gal 4:8). He wonders why they would return to the enslaving powers of "the weak and beggarly elemental spirits" *(stoicheia)* after experiencing freedom in Christ (Gal 4:9-11).

The fact that Christians in Galatia would abandon the truth of the gospel and return to their old belief system is indicative of the pervasive control and power of these *stoicheia* (see Gal 1:6: "I am astonished that you are so quickly deserting the one who called you in the grace of Christ and are turning to a different gospel"). Although the meaning of this term is "essential components of the universe," such as earth, air, water and fire,[73] in some contexts (Heb 5:12; 2 Pet 3:10, 12), it signifies some form of spiritual powers in Galatians 4:3, 9. This appears to be the case in Colossians 2:8, 20 as well, where "elemental spirits of the world" *(stoicheia tou kosmou)* are discussed within the context of the Colossian heresy.

One problem in the church in Colossae was that believers were unable to break free from their syncretistic religious background even though they had placed their faith in the Christ who defeated all spiritual powers (Col 2:15). Thus Paul had to remind them to live in the assurance of Christ's superiority

---

[72]On these chapters, see Gordon D. Fee, *The First Epistle to the Corinthians,* NICNT (Grand Rapids, Mich.: Eerdmans, 1987), pp. 357-490; see also Brad B. Blue, "Food Offered to Idols and Jewish Food Laws," *DPL,* pp. 306-10; Dennis E. Smith, "Meal Customs (Greco-Roman)," *ABD* 4:650-53; Smith, "Meal Customs (Greco-Roman Sacred Meals)," *ABD* 4:653-55.

[73]Daniel G. Reid, "Elements/Elemental Spirits of the World," *DPL,* pp. 229-33.

(Col 1:15-20; 2:9-10) and not to return to their former deceitful philosophy and human traditions (Col 2:8, 18). Since they had "died to the elemental spirits of the universe," they could not continue to live as though they were still in subjection to them (Col 2:20).

Although the nature of the Colossian heresy is complex, the ancient belief in astrology was part of the problem and may account for the references to subjection, submission and slavery.[74] Daniel G. Reid notes the relationship between cosmic deities and demonic powers in literary sources and concludes that "it is not difficult to imagine a belief system, particularly at Colossae, in which Jewish and Hellenistic ideas would have been intermingled and celestial powers associated with angels, who were revered as controlling the fate of humans."[75]

The governing belief of astrology was universal solidarity, the correspondence between the movement of the gods above and events and individuals below.[76] Once people felt that they were subject to certain stellar or astral divinities, they looked for ways either to live harmoniously within the system or to free themselves when fate and determinism took over. There seems to be little doubt that some aspects of magic, sorcery, divination, and the like that we see in the New Testament were attempts to liberate individuals from such a fate. This could be the case with the elemental spirits in Galatians and Colossians as well.

In addition to the "elemental spirits of the world" (stoicheia tou kosmou), the New Testament also refers to thrones (thronoi), dominions (kyriotētes), rulers (archai), powers (exousiai and dynameis), cosmic powers (kosmokratoras) and spiritual forces of evil (pneumatika tēs ponērias; see Rom 8:38; 1 Cor 15:24; Eph 1:21; 6:12; Col 1:16; 2:10, 15; 1 Pet 3:22).[77] While it is possible that stoicheia tou kosmou is an inclusive term for all these concepts, they probably signify different realities of the spiritual world. The key thought in the gospel is that Christ has defeated these powers and reigns over them as the resurrected and exalted Lord.

The existence of these spiritual beings may indicate an early form of Gnosticism. "Magic and astrology," according to Arnold, "ultimately fed into the grand amalgam of teachings commonly called Gnosticism. Individual Gnostic teachers incorporated magical incantations, rituals of power, and astrological

---

[74]For a current treatment of the heresy, see Clinton E. Arnold, _The Colossian Syncretism: The Interface Between Christianity and Folk Belief at Colossae_ (Tübingen: Mohr-Siebeck, 1995).

[75]Reid, "Elements," p. 232. See further, Francesca Rochberg-Halton, "Astrology in the Ancient Near East," _ABD_ 1:504-7.

[76]Franz Cumont, _Astrology and Religion Among the Greeks and Romans_ (New York: Dover, 1912).

[77]Daniel G. Reid, "Principalities and Powers," _DPL_, pp. 746-52.

beliefs and symbols into their various systems of thought."[78] Amid all the diverse opinions on the origin, definition and influence of Gnosticism on the early church, several things are clear: (1) it was a religious and philosophical movement; (2) it was not monolithic;[79] (3) it emerged during the first and second centuries A.D. and became more systematized in subsequent centuries; and (4) a *gnōsis* (knowledge) of some type was a threat to many churches mentioned in the New Testament.[80] This heresy had serious ramifications for Christian theology in areas such as creation, anthropology, salvation and ethics.

Another religious phenomenon of the Greco-Roman world worth mentioning is the existence of various mystery religions. Although of ancient origin, the mystery religions flourished as private and public cults by initiating converts with secret rituals (hence "mystery" religions).[81]

Because there are no specific references to the mystery religions in the biblical texts, readers of the New Testament generally are unaware of their popularity or of the threat that they posed to Christianity. Most of our information about them comes from the postapostolic age, so one should be cautious about the influence of the mysteries on first-century Christianity. Nevertheless, we need to acknowledge their universal appeal to the populace through personal initiation, purification through baptism, communion with the deity through sacred meals, salvation through regeneration and a belief in immortality. Mithraism, one of the mystery religions, was adopted by the Roman army and spread rapidly throughout the empire. Franz Cumont invites us to consider Joseph Ernest Renan's opinion that if Christianity had not succeeded, "the world would have become Mithraic."[82]

Why, then, did Christianity succeed and the mystery religions fail? No doubt Samuel Angus was correct about his assessment of syncretistic religions: "A liv-

---

[78]Clinton E. Arnold, "Magic and Astrology," *DLNTD*, p. 704. He also draws attention to astral imagery in the Apocalypse and the apostolic fathers (p. 704).

[79]Arnold writes: "Gnosticism represented the grandest form of syncretism in combining aspects of Judaism, Platonism, Greco-Roman and Egyptian religions (including mystery cults), magic, astrology and Persian thought into various systems of redemption" ("Syncretism," *DLNTD*, p. 1150).

[80]The literature on the subject is voluminous. See helpful discussion and sources mentioned in Kurt Rudolph, "Gnosticism," *ABD* 2:1033-40; *Gnosis* (San Francisco: Harper, 1983); David M. Scholer, "Gnosis, Gnosticism," *DLNTD*, pp. 400-412; Edwin Yamauchi, "Gnosis, Gnosticism," *DPL*, pp. 350-54; "Gnosticism," *DNTB*, pp. 414-18. For a brief sample of some texts see Barrett, *The New Testament Background*, pp. 120-34.

[81]David E. Aune, "Religions, Greco-Roman," *DPL*, p. 792. See Ferguson, *Backgrounds*, pp. 235-82; Marvin W. Meyer, "Mystery Religions," *ABD* 4:941-45; Marvin W. Meyer, ed., *The Ancient Mysteries: A Sourcebook* (San Francisco: Harper, 1987); Joscelyn Godwin, *Mystery Religions in the Ancient World* (San Francisco: Harper, 1981).

[82]Franz Cumont, *Oriental Religions in Roman Paganism* (New York: Dover, 1956), p. 160.

ing religion must not conform to but transform, the spirit of the age."[83] The apostle Paul understood this truth at the personal level when he exhorted the believers in Rome: "Do not be conformed to this world, but be transformed by the renewing of your minds" (Rom 12:2).

One cannot leave this brief discussion of the Greco-Roman world without mentioning some of the philosophical systems that the early church encountered. Paul's debate with some Stoic and Epicurean philosophers in Athens is the only specific reference to philosophical schools (Acts 17:18; the "philosophy" in Col 2:8 refers to a syncretistic blend of ideas). Although Paul held some ideas in common with these philosophies, he differed with them in many respects. Students of Paul have noticed this and have compared Paul and other authors of the New Testament with Platonism, Epicureanism, Stoicism, Cynicism and Neo-Pythagoreanism.[84] On this issue, Terence Paige observes that while Paul "may have used philosophical vocabulary for his apologetic or didactic purposes, he was not constrained by the content or method of the philosophies in vogue" nor compelled "to reconcile his message with philosophy."[85] True wisdom, for Paul, is found in the gospel (1 Cor 1:21; 2:6-16; cf. Eph 1:15-18), not in the "wisdom" or "rulers" of this age (1 Cor 2:6).

Although there were many obstacles to the early church in the first century, one must not overlook some of the positive elements of the Roman Empire that facilitated the spread of the gospel. The political conquests of the Roman army and the establishment of provincial rulers enabled Rome to consolidate its vast empire. This led to an unprecedented long period of peace _(pax romana)_ during which trade, commerce and travel flourished. The book of Acts, which documents many of Paul's travels on land and sea, is a good indication of how conditions in the empire enabled the church to extend its mission.[86]

---

[83]Samuel Angus, _The Mystery Religions and Christianity_ (London: J. Murray, 1928), p. 253.

[84]See Terence Paige, "Philosophy," _DPL_, pp. 716-18; Ferguson, _Backgrounds,_ pp. 299-371. See also ch. 6, "Greco-Roman Philosophy," in Bell, _Exploring the New Testament World,_ pp. 161-84; and Raymond Brown's helpful analysis and bibliography in _Introduction to the New Testament,_ pp. 74-96.

[85]Paige, "Philosophy," p. 718. See Trols Engberg Pedersen, _Paul and the Stoics_ (Louisville: Westminster John Knox, 2000); Thomas Schmeller, "Stoics, Stoicism," _ABD_ 6:210-14; and Johan C. Thom, "Stoicism," _DNTB,_ pp. 1139-42. A similar conclusion is appropriate for those who have interpreted 2 Peter as an "assimilation of Epicurean rationalism" or the Johannine letters in terms of "Platonic dualism" (see Arnold, "Syncretism," p. 1149).

[86]See James E. Bowley, "Pax Romana," _DNTB,_ pp. 771-75; F. F. Bruce, "Travel and Communication (NT World)," _ABD_ 6:648-53; David A. Dorsey, "Travel; Transportation," _ISBE_ 4:891-97; David F. Graf, Benjamin Issac and Israel Roll, "Roads and Highways (Roman Roads)," _ABD_ 5:782-87; Brian M. Rapske, "Roman Empire, Christians and The," _DLNTD,_ pp. 1059-1063; Rapske, "Travel and Trade," _DNTB,_ pp. 1245-50; E. R. Thiele, "Roads; Highways," _ISBE_ 4:199-203.

Rome's attitude toward Christianity was generally favorable until the reigns of Nero (A.D. 54-68) and Domitian (A.D. 81-96). Initially the Roman authorities regarded the confession of Jesus as the Messiah a Jewish matter and did not prevent the Jews from administering justice in their own way when tensions arose between Jews and Christians (cf. Acts 5:18, 40; 7:58—8:1; 9:2, 23-24; 13:50; 18:12-17; 24:2-9). Thus the first persecution of the church was by Jews and not the Romans, except when the Roman authorities objected to certain provocations in Ephesus (Acts16:20-21), attempted to prevent a riot in Jerusalem (Acts 21:27-36) or deliberately acted in complicity with the Jews (Acts 12:2-4; 14:5). Once Paul appealed to his Roman citizenship (Acts 22:22-29), the Roman judicial system took over.[87]

1.3. Summary

The discussion above noted many significant elements of the political, social, cultural and religious environments of early Christianity. Believers interacted with this environment, spoke Greek, and used a Greek Bible (LXX). Familiar words and concepts were used, although in some cases with new meaning. Christian theology was developed and communicated in letters to churches and individuals by utilizing the oral and literary forms of the day.[88] Apart from their fellowship in the church, much of the early believers' vocational and domestic life went on as it had before they became Christians.

The decision to become a believer and identify with a local church, however, called for a radically new orientation to life that created some significant tensions.[89] For example, converts to Christianity were to live *in* the world yet not be *of* the world, to live in the spirit while still living physically in the flesh. They were to associate with their neighbors and bear witness to the gospel yet be separate from them. They continued to live in a corrupt and evil world and experienced trials, afflictions and death but were told that Christ had defeated the powers of evil and that in Christ they could experience a victorious life. They were told that their future was guaranteed but that they would have to wait for the final eschaton to realize it. They were subject to earthly authorities and asked to pray

---

[87]On the persecution of the church, see Ernst Bammel, "Jewish Activity Against Christians in Palestine According to Acts," in Bauckham, ed., *Palestinian Setting*, pp. 357-64; Geoffrey W. Bromiley, "Persecute; Persecution," *ISBE* 3:771-74; D. S. Potter, "Persecution of the Early Church," *ABD* 5:231-35; Reasoner, "Persecution," pp. 907-14.

[88]Arthur G. Patzia, *The Making of the New Testament* (Downers Grove, Ill.: InterVarsity Press, 1995), pp. 69-72.

[89]Larry Hurtado appropriately refers to Christian initiation as a "*replacement cultus*" because believers were expected to renounce their former religious life and its rituals and to make an exclusive commitment to Christ (*Origins of Christian Worship*, p. 4). For detailed discussions of such issues, see David A. deSilva, *Honor, Patronage, Kinship and Purity: Unlocking New Testament Culture* (Downers Grove, Ill.: InterVarsity Press, 2000).

for them while not compromising their confession of the lordship of Christ.

These are just a few examples of the theological ideas that these young believers from the Greco-Roman world had to process. The next challenge was to live out their faith within "the household of faith," the Christian church. If their pagan environment was an outside challenge to their faith, life within the church constituted another. A notable part of the New Testament illustrates how difficult this task was for early church leaders and writers.

2

JESUS &
THE CHURCH

Who was Jesus? How did he understand himself? What were his aims? How did he see his mission? These are just a few of the questions that have troubled biblical scholars over the years and have been the subject of innumerable books, articles and films on Jesus. Our concern is not to pursue these questions or to analyze the materials that have already been written.[1] Rather, we will examine a more specific question: Did Jesus intend to found the church?

When the French Catholic scholar Alfred Loisy studied the life of Jesus with respect to this question, he wrote: "Jesus foretold the kingdom, and it was the church that came."[2] The implication of this statement is that since the kingdom did not come during Jesus' lifetime, the early believers created the church instead. Now, some ninety-five years after Loisy, we do not appear to be any closer to resolving questions about Jesus and the church, even though many creative solutions have been proposed. It is no wonder, then, that the author of a recent and ambitious study of Jesus states:

---

[1]For a thorough though dated collection of secondary sources, see Craig Evans, *Life of Jesus Research: Annotated Bibliography* (Leiden: E. J. Brill, 1989). For current studies, consult the bibliographies in other works on Jesus suggested throughout this book.

[2]Alfred Loisy, *The Gospel and the Church* (New York: Prometheus, 1988), p. 145. The first translation of Loisy's book was made by Christopher Home and published by Charles Scribner's Sons in 1904. Loisy's conclusion makes good sense when one considers that the word "kingdom" *(basileia)* occurs 126 times in the Gospels, whereas "church" *(ekklēsia)* appears only three times (Mt 16:18; 18:17 [2x]).

Did Jesus intend to found a "church"? The question is hopeless. Of course he didn't; of course he did. The way the oft-repeated question puts it is impossibly anachronistic: it makes Jesus sound like a pioneer evangelist of the nineteenth century, throwing previous denominations to the winds and building his own tin tabernacle. Worse, it implies, almost with a sneer, that Jesus could hardly have envisaged the church as we know it today, or even as it has been for most of the last two thousand years; and that therefore the church stands condemned, untrue to the founder's intentions. What then did Jesus intend to do?[3]

2.1. The Search for Jesus

The history of New Testament scholarship shows that there have been many attempts to determine what can be known about the historical Jesus or to discern his intentions. Most modern studies are categorized as "quests" for Jesus, which together span a period of approximately two hundred years.[4] For the most part, these quests were not helpful in recovering the historical Jesus or in understanding his mission. Joachim Jeremias, a critic of such movements, sums up the results rather negatively:

> The rationalists pictured Jesus as a preacher of morality, the idealists as the ideal Man; the aesthetes extolled him as the master of words and the socialists as the friend of the poor and as the social reformer, while the innumerable pseudo-scholars made of him a fictional character. Jesus was modernized. These lives of Jesus are mere products of wishful thinking. The final outcome was that every epoch and every theology found in the personality of Jesus the reflection of its own ideals, and every author the reflection of his own views.[5]

A new approach, known as the Third Quest, was introduced into contemporary scholarship by N. T. Wright in the early 1980s, and it includes a significant number of biblical scholars.[6] This search is guided by two significant principles:

---

[3]N. T. Wright, *Jesus and the Victory of God* (Minneapolis: Fortress, 1996), p. 275.

[4]It is common to speak of the Old Quest (1778-1900), the No Quest (1900-1940) and the New Quest (1940-1980). For useful discussion of these quests, see Colin Brown, "Historical Jesus, Quest of," *DJG*, pp. 326-41; Joachim Jeremias, *The Problem of the Historical Jesus* (Philadelphia: Fortress, 1964); James Robinson, *A New Quest of the Historical Jesus* (London: SCM Press, 1959); Albert Schweitzer, *The Quest of the Historical Jesus* (New York: Macmillan, 1961).

[5]Jeremias, *Problem of the Historical Jesus*, pp. 5-6.

[6]The term appears in Stephen Neill and Tom Wright, *The Interpretation of the New Testament, 1861-1986*, 2nd ed. (Oxford: Oxford University Press, 1988); N. T. Wright, "Quest for the Historical Jesus," *ABD* 3:796-802; N. T. Wright, *Jesus and the Victory of God*. Wright's essay, "Jesus and the Quest," in *The Truth About Jesus*, ed. Donald Armstrong (Grand Rapids, Mich.: Eerdmans, 1998), pp. 4-25, is an abbreviated version of his thoughts in *Jesus and the Victory of God*. Wright selects twenty authors whose publications he feels are particularly important to the Third Quest. These include Otto Betz, Marcus Borg, G. F. Brandon, G. B. Caird, James

(1) a serious attempt to understand Jesus within the context of first-century Jewish and Hellenistic culture; and (2) a focus on the *facts* rather than the *sayings* of Jesus.

Based on the first principle, scholars work unapologetically as historians, claiming that we can know a great deal about Jesus as a Palestinian Jew by closely studying the Gospels and by fully utilizing Josephus, the Dead Sea Scrolls and, in some cases, rabbinic literature. With regard to the second principle, E. P. Sanders is one among many who is convinced that scholars must abandon the form-critical analysis of the Gospels, not only because scholars will never agree on the authenticity of Jesus' sayings (the Jesus Seminar notwithstanding), but also because that type of exegesis has "led many a New Testament scholar into a quagmire from which he has never emerged."[7] Historical facts, on the other hand, have a better chance of giving meaning or significance to the person and mission of Jesus. N. T. Wright has a similar commitment to history as he seeks to answer the following questions about Jesus: (1) How does Jesus fit into Judaism? (2) What were Jesus' aims? (3) Why did Jesus die? (4) How and why did the early church begin? (5) Why are the Gospels what they are?[8]

The rediscovery of Jesus the Jew has produced some interesting portraits. James D. G. Dunn, Martin Hengel, Geza Vermes and Irving Zeitlin see Jesus as a "charismatic" Jew. Others, such as David Flusser, Max Wilcox, Harvey Falk, E. P. Sanders and Ben F. Meyer, view him as a moderate reformer of Judaism,

---

A. Charlesworth, Bruce Chilton, Martin de Jonge, Seyne Freyne, A. E. Harvey, Martin Hengel, Richard Horsley, Gerhard Lohfink, John P. Meier, Ben F. Meyer, Douglas E. Oakman, J. K. Riches, E. P. Sanders, Gerd Theissen, G. Vermes and Ben Witherington III (*Jesus and the Victory of God,* p. 84). Although he acknowledges that other scholars could be added to this category, he places Burton Mack, John D. Crossan, and other participants in the Jesus Seminar and the Q Project in a separate category, a "revived New Quest because their presuppositions and methodology remain quite Bultmannian" (ibid, p. 84, nn. 6, 8). See also Marcus J. Borg and N. T. Wright, *The Meaning of Jesus: Two Visions* (San Francisco: Harper, 1998); and Mark A. Powell, *Jesus as a Figure in History* (Louisville: Westminster John Knox, 1998). In this discussion, no attempt will be made to list the publications of these authors unless they are quoted. Readers are encouraged to see the bibliographies in N. T. Wright's *Jesus and the Victory of God* and Ben Witherington's *The Jesus Quest: The Third Search for the Jew of Nazareth* (Downers Grove, Ill.: InterVarsity Press, 1995). For additional information, see W. Barnes Tatum, *In Quest of Jesus,* rev. ed. (Nashville: Abingdon, 1999); Walter F. Taylor Jr., "New Quests for the Historical Jesus," *Trinity Seminary Review* 15.2 (993): 69-83; James H. Charlesworth and Walter P. Weaver, eds., *Jesus Two Thousand Years Later* (Harrisburg, Penn.: Morehouse, 2000); Gerd Theissen and Annette Merz, *The Historical Jesus* (Minneapolis: Fortress, 1998); Walter P. Weaver, *The Historical Jesus in the Twentieth Century, 1900-1950* (Harrisburg, Penn.: Trinity Press International, 1999).

[7]E. P. Sanders, *Jesus and Judaism,* p. 131.

[8]N. T. Wright, *Jesus and the Victory of God,* pp. 91-112.

especially on issues of table fellowship, sabbath-keeping and purity laws. George F. Brandon stands quite alone in branding Jesus as a political Zealot. Martin Hengel, Richard Horsley and even Marcus Borg temper this view by branding Jesus more as a *social* than a *political* reformer. Those who have explored the concept of Messiah include James Charlesworth, Peter Stuhlmacher, James D. G. Dunn, M. de Jonge, Markus Bockmuehl and Ben Witherington III.

Recent archaeological activity in Galilee, especially the Roman capital of Sepphoris, has produced a new appreciation of the Galilean urban culture to which Jesus was exposed (Richard Batey, Sean Freyne, Richard Horsley). This development, including sociological (Gerd Theissen) and anthropological (Bruce Malina, J. Dominic Crossan) insights, has enlarged our vision of Jesus, even though some of the portraits seem rather bizarre. For example, Jesus is portrayed as the "Cynic Philosopher" (Mack), the "Cynic Peasant" (Crossan), the "Wandering Charismatic" (Theissen), the "Radical Reformer" (Borg, Horsley), the "Holy Man" (Vermes) and the "Millenarian Prophet (Allison).

As with any undertaking, decisions need to be based on the evidence that seems most reasonable and convincing. Although some of the portraits of Jesus alluded to are intriguing and provocative, they do not describe the *person* or fit the *purpose* of Jesus that one finds in the Gospels. In my view, the best solutions to understanding Jesus are the current proposals made by such scholars as Ben F. Meyer, E. P. Sanders and N. T. Wright.[9]

2.2. Jesus and the Restoration of Israel

Although there are some differences among scholars belonging to the Third Quest, they agree that Jesus had a *definite agenda* in mind during his public ministry *that focused on the restoration of Israel*. His words (proclamation of the kingdom, parables, etc.) and actions (healing miracles, table fellowship with sinners, etc.) indicate his conviction that the old Israel was to be cleansed and reconstituted in view of the nearness of God's kingdom. Ben Meyer summarizes Jesus' aims rather succinctly:

---

[9]N. T. Wright takes the concept of restoration further than either Meyer or Sanders by speaking of a "reconstituted" Israel around Jesus and the Twelve (*Jesus and the Victory of God*, p. 300). Note Witherington's critique of this concept in *Jesus Quest*, pp. 225-32. One could add R. David Kaylor to this list as well. In *Jesus the Prophet: His Vision of the Kingdom on Earth* (Louisville: Westminster John Knox, 1994), Kaylor sees Jesus calling for the renewal of Israel by returning to their covenant traditions. But with his focus on Jesus as a political or social reformer, Kaylor has more affinity with Freyne, Horsley and, to some extent, Crossan. An older, although valuable, work is R. Newton Flew, *Jesus and His Church: A Study of the Idea of the Ecclesia in the New Testament* (London: Epworth, 1938). Many of Flew's ideas are echoed and elaborated by Sanders in *Jesus and Judaism* (Philadelphia: Fortress, 1985).

The reign of God was the focal point. Proclamation and teaching centered on it; cures and exorcisms were signs of it. But what has neither been clearly seen nor probed for its consequences is that the reign of God as imminent meant the imminent restoration of Israel, and the reign of God as already overtaking Israel in Jesus' words and acts meant that Israel was already in process of being restored. His teaching was Torah appropriate to restored Israel and requisite to perfect restoration. His wonder-working signified the restoration of Israel and effected it by restoring the afflicted to their heritage as children of Abraham. The appeal to "the sinners" likewise belonged to this context. Offering forgiveness and eliciting conversion, it was designed to restore the outcasts to Israel. This is confirmed by Jesus' repeated efforts to reconcile the righteous to this move toward socio-religious integration.[10]

E. P. Sanders sees Jesus as a prophet within the tradition of "Jewish restoration eschatology."[11] Throughout his book, Sanders repeats and supports the following points, which together form the heart of his thesis:

Most of the things which we know about Jesus with virtually complete certainty fit him rather neatly into the category of a prophet of Jewish restoration. (1) He began his career as a follower of John the Baptist, who called on all Israel to repent in preparation for the coming judgment. (2) His call of twelve disciples points to the hope for the restoration of the twelve tribes. (3) His expectation that the temple would be destroyed and rebuilt corresponds to a known, if not universal, expectation about the restoration of Israel. (4) After his death and resurrection the disciples worked within a framework of Jewish restoration expectation. Thus our list of facts, including the behaviour of the early Christians, points towards an "orthodox" eschatological movement whose peculiar characteristic is that it continued, flourished, and even followed out

---

[10]Ben Meyer, *The Aims of Jesus* (London: SCM Press, 1979), p. 221. See also Meyer, *The Church in Three Tenses* (Garden City, N.Y.: Doubleday, 1971), pp. 31-53. One could mention a host of scholars who see Jesus acting with a definite plan. See N. T. Wright, *Who Was Jesus?* (Grand Rapids, Mich.: Eerdmans, 1992), pp. 100-103; Ben Witherington III, *The Christology of Jesus* (Minneapolis: Fortress, 1990), esp. pp. 140-43, 215, 268; Ralph P. Martin, *The Family and the Fellowship* (Grand Rapids, Mich.: Eerdmans, 1979). For a brief review of scholars such as C. F. D. Moule, C. H. Dodd and Joachim Jeremias, see Sanders, *Jesus and Judaism*, pp. 40-44. Some, however, see it differently. Sanders (*Jesus and Judaism*, p. 20) reacts to a statement by Henry J. Cadbury, who wrote, "What I wish to propose is that Jesus had no definite, unified, conscious purpose, that an absence of such a program is *a priori* likely and that it suits well the historical evidence" (*The Peril of Modernizing Jesus* [New York: Macmillan, 1937], p. 141). Likewise, C. K. Barrett claimed that Jesus did not envision a period of continuing history beyond his suffering "in which a Church organized in this world may find a place, but an apocalyptic act of vindication" (*Jesus and the Gospel Tradition* [London: SPCK, 1967]), p. 87).

[11]Sanders, *Jesus and Judaism*, p. 335.

the natural momentum of a realized Jewish eschatological movement by admitting Gentiles.[12]

N. T. Wright's thesis is quite similar to that of Meyer and Sanders because he sees Jesus within the prophetic tradition of individuals such as Elijah, Jeremiah and John the Baptist, calling the nation to repent and follow Jesus. "Jesus," claims Wright, "believed himself called to work as a prophet, announcing the word of Israel's god to his wayward people, and grouping around himself a company who, according to all the partial precedents and parallels, would be regarded as the true people of YHWH."[13]

Wright, however, develops his thesis of restoration around the theme of *exile,* arguing that as long as the nation was suffering and under Roman rule (the present evil age), it remained in exile. Jesus' call to repent, to receive forgiveness, to obey, to follow, and the like was his way of calling the nation to return from exile, to renew the covenant and receive the forgiveness of sins. Here was the king through whose work "YHWH was at last restoring his people."[14]

Whereas Meyer and Sanders see this restoration of Israel at the end of the age, Wright interprets Jesus' mission as one directed to the renovation of the present world order, the current space-time universe. This entailed "the end of the period when the Gentiles were lording it over the people of the true god, and the inauguration of the time when this god would take his power and reign and, in the process, restore the fortunes of his suffering people."[15]

The idea of a reformed, renewed or restored Israel does not imply that Jesus intended to set up a countermovement within Judaism. Indeed, Jesus proclaimed the kingdom of God to all Israel and lived within its national and religious culture. He did not attempt to form a community outside the people of God. The Jesus Movement, if we could call it that, was not intended as a "*surrogate* or *replacement* for Israel."[16] Jesus sought to establish the *true* Israel, not a *new* Israel. N. T. Wright suggests that Jesus would have answered the question "Who are we?" as follows: "we are Israel, the chosen people of the creator god. More specifically, we are the real, the true, Israel, in the process of being

---

[12]Ibid., p. 222. See also Sanders's "Jesus and the Kingdom: The Restoration of Israel and the New People of God," in *Jesus, the Gospels, and the Church: Essays in Honor of William R. Farmer,* ed. E. P. Sanders (Macon, Ga.: Mercer University Press, 1987), pp. 225-39.

[13]N. T. Wright, *Jesus and the Victory of God,* p. 196.

[14]Ibid., p. 272.

[15]Ibid., p. 95. For critiques of Wright's book and his exile thesis, see Robert H. Gundry, "Reconstructing Jesus," *Christianity Today,* April 27, 1998, pp. 76-79; and James D. G. Dunn's review of *Jesus and the Victory of God* by N. T. Wright, *JTS* 49 (1998): 727-34.

[16]Gerhard Lohfink, *Jesus and Community* (Philadelphia: Fortress, 1984), p. 34.

redeemed at last by this god, over against the spurious claimants who are either in power or mounting alternative programmes."[17]

This concept of a *true* Israel is supported by the existence of the Christian community after Easter, which saw itself *in continuity with Israel* and not as a new or separate movement or sect *(hairesis)*. C. F. D. Moule notes that the New Testament "nowhere countenances the term 'New Israel' " although there certainly was a sense in which "*God's* Israel, *true* Israel was so radically different from what counted as Israel in the contemporary world, that there is an undeniable sense in which it is 'new'."[18] Later we will discuss how this *newness* eventually created certain tensions within the community and ultimately led to a split between Judaism and those who confessed Jesus as Messiah and Lord.

2.3. Kingdom or Church?

Scholars who doubt that Jesus intended to found a church generally do so based on their understanding of eschatology. Jesus, they argue, was an apocalyptic visionary whose teaching on the kingdom of God anticipated the imminent end of the world. Hermann Samuel Reimarus (1694-1768) was one of the first Gospel interpreters to argue that Jesus was a Jewish political messiah or reformer who was possessed with the idea of delivering the Jews from their foreign oppressors and setting up an earthly kingdom. Unfortunately, this did not happen because Jesus suffered an ignominious death at the hands of the Romans. Jesus' cry from the cross, "My God, my God, why have you forsaken me?" (Mt 27:46; Mk 15:34) shows that he was deluded and that his mission failed. The misguided and disillusioned disciples then invented the mythical story of the resurrection, which eventually led to the creation of "the Christ of faith" in place of the "Jesus of history." With these ideas Reimarus laid the foundation for the quest of the historical Jesus, a search that continues to engage scholars to this present day.

Although Albert Schweitzer (1875-1965) did not see Jesus as a Jewish Zealot, he nevertheless embraced Reimarus's idea that Jesus expected the world to end during his lifetime. Schweitzer made the words of Matthew 10:23 ("truly I tell you, you will not have gone through all the towns of Israel before the Son of Man comes") pivotal to his understanding of Jesus' eschatology.[19] But something was not right with the script. The kingdom did not come as expected, so, according to Schweitzer, Jesus went to Jerusalem to purify the temple and has-

---

[17]N. T. Wright, *Jesus and the Victory of God,* p. 443; see also p. 278.

[18]C. F. D. Moule, *The Birth of the New Testament,* rev. ed. (San Francisco: Harper, 1982), p. 54.

[19]Schweitzer's views often are attributed to the ideas of Johannes Weiss, who argued for a complete eschatological interpretation of Jesus ("consistent eschatology"). Rudolf Bultmann held a similar view of eschatology but interpreted it in existential categories.

ten his death in a heroic attempt to force God's hand to establish the kingdom. Jesus thus died as a disappointed and mistaken eschatologist.

In such an interpretation of history, it is easy to understand that Jesus would not have envisioned a continuing community of believers. The calling and training of the twelve disciples simply enabled Jesus to summon people more quickly to repentance in view of the impending judgment. They were not in it for the long haul. Nor did Jesus' moral teaching have any abiding significance; at best, it was intended as an interim ethic. The concept of a thoroughgoing eschatology precluded the need for the church.

Since the pendulum of critical scholarship tends to swing radically from one extreme to the other, it did not take long for a different interpretation of Jesus' eschatology to emerge. Here C. H. Dodd normally is credited with replacing "futuristic eschatology" with "realized eschatology," meaning that the kingdom of God is *fully* present or realized in the life and teaching of Jesus. The key to Dodd's understanding includes several New Testament passages:

☐ "The time is fulfilled, and the kingdom of God is at hand [*ēngiken*]; repent, and believe in the gospel" (Mk 1:15 RSV; cf. Mt 4:17).

☐ "But if it is by the Spirit of God that I cast out demons, then the kingdom of God has come [*ephthasen*] upon you" (Mt 12:28 RSV; cf. Lk 11:20).

☐ "For, in fact, the kingdom of God is among [within] you" (*entos hymōn estin,* Lk 17:21).

This means that God is now asserting his sovereignty and rule over those who have accepted his message of the kingdom. Jesus' aim, according to Dodd, "was to constitute a community worthy of the name of a people of God, a divine commonwealth, through individual response to God coming in his kingdom."[20] The Twelve were recruited to confront humanity with this reality and to form the nucleus of what would become the church.

Reaction to Dodd's extreme view of Jesus' eschatology elicited a number of mediating positions more amenable to all of the Gospel material and that a larger number of scholars could embrace. Here we are indebted to such individuals as Dale C. Allison, George R. Beasley-Murray, Reginald H. Fuller, Archibald M. Hunter, Werner G. Kümmel and George E. Ladd, who coined such phrases as "inaugurated eschatology," "an eschatology in the process of realization," the "already-and-the-not-yet" or "promise and fulfillment."[21] Basi-

---

[20]C. H. Dodd, *The Founder of Christianity* (New York: Macmillan, 1970), p. 90.

[21]For a valuable discussion and bibliography for these and other authors, see C. Caragounis, "Kingdom of God/Heaven," *DJG*, pp. 417-30. On the christological meaning of kingdom sayings, see Martin de Jonge, *Early Christology and Jesus' Own View of His Mission* (Grand Rapids, Mich.: Eerdmans, 1998), pp. 34-43.

cally this means that although the kingdom is present in the ministry of Jesus its full consummation will not take place until the end of history.

The primary meaning of Hebrew/Aramaic *malkût* and Greek *basileia* is "reign," "sovereignty" or "kingly rule of God." This is basic to Jewish ideas about the very nature of God, namely, that he *is now and eternally the sovereign Lord.* But even as the prophets of the Old Testament affirmed this truth, they looked beyond the present to the future, to the "Day of the Lord" when God would conclusively and triumphantly intervene in the course of history and finally and absolutely establish his rule.[22] This concept, which reappears in New Testament eschatology in the categories of "this age" and "the age to come," means that although God's rule is already active in the person and works of Jesus, the perfection of God's reign will not be established until the consummation of this age, when God will abolish all evil and rule forever.

In this view of the kingdom, emphasis is given to the kingly rule or sovereignty of God upon those who accept his will. To pray "Your kingdom come. Your will be done" (Mt 6:10) is a request for God to establish his will as perfectly on earth as it is in heaven. As a divine act the kingdom is God's gift to humanity: "It is your Father's good pleasure to give you the kingdom" (Lk 12:32). It is to be received with the innocence of a child: "Let the little children come to me, and do not stop them; for it is to such as these that the kingdom of heaven [God] belongs" (Mt 19:14 par. Mk 10:14; Lk 18:16).

Since the kingdom of God is defined as the rule or reign of God, it is natural to ask how and where such a rule takes place. Must there not be a sphere, realm or domain over which God's rule is exercised? A rule cannot operate in a void. In other words, should there not be a geographical territory or at least a community of people that one could identify as the kingdom of God? Surely the Jewish nation, at least, thought that God was their king, ruling over his people and the land that they possessed. Could not Israel be equated with the kingdom of God?

Failure to distinguish clearly between rule and realm has led to some confusing and inaccurate conclusions about the kingdom of God. A liberal Protestant view proposed by Adolf Harnack internalized this concept in the human heart. The kingdom comes *to* and God rules *over* the hearts and souls of individuals. The kingdom, therefore, is some moral disposition within humanity.

Another approach, sometimes identified with the Social Gospel Movement, emphasized humanity's contribution to the kingdom. However, the kingdom is God's act of breaking into history through the person of Jesus to redeem sinful

---

[22]There are many Old Testament eschatological passages, but note especially Amos 5:18-20; Zeph 1:14-18; Isa 2:2-4; 11:6-9; Mic 4:1-14.

humanity, so it can never be defined exclusively as some renewed earthly and social utopia built by human efforts. Jesus did not call his followers to build, advance or promote the kingdom. Here A. M. Hunter wisely reminds us that the gospel "is not man's deed but God's seed. It is not *men* creating a new and nobler Christian society on the basis of the Sermon on the Mount."[23]

An older view, traced back to Augustine (354-430) and common among some theologians today, equates the kingdom of God on earth with the church. However, although the relationship between the two is difficult to differentiate at times, they must be viewed separately. The disciples of Jesus are not members of the kingdom *per se*. George Ladd argues this point rather persuasively and concludes:

> while there is an inseparable relationship between the Kingdom and the church, they are not to be identified. The Kingdom takes its point of departure from God, the church from human beings. The Kingdom is God's reign and the realm in which the blessings of his reign are experienced; the church is the fellowship of those who have experienced God's reign and entered into the enjoyment of its blessings. The Kingdom creates the church, works through the church, and is proclaimed in the world by the church. There can be no Kingdom without a church— those who have acknowledged God's rule—and there can be no church without God's Kingdom; but they remain two distinguishable concepts: the rule of God and the fellowship of men.[24]

From this observation one could say that Jesus did not deliberately or consciously set out to found the church; rather, the church was a logical corollary to Jesus' preaching of the kingdom. Here again Ladd is helpful:

> Jesus looked upon his disciples as the nucleus of Israel who accepted his proclamation of the Kingdom of God and who, therefore, formed the true people of God, the spiritual Israel. He indicated his purpose to bring into being his *ekklēsia* who would recognize his messiahship and be the people of the Kingdom and at the same time the instrument of the Kingdom in the world. However, Jesus and his disciples did not form a separate synagogue, nor start a separate movement, nor in spite of constant conflict with the Jewish leaders break with either the temple or synagogue in any outward way. His disciples formed an open fellowship within

---

[23]A. M. Hunter, *The Words and Works of Jesus,* rev. ed. (London: SCM Press, 1973), p. 91 (emphasis added). Eduard Schweizer adds: "He [Jesus] never speaks of building or advancing the kingdom; men can only receive it, inherit it, obtain it by entreaty, enter into it, for *God* will give it to them to possess" (*Church Order in the New Testament,* trans. Frank Clarke, SBT 32 [London: SCM Press, 1961], p. 20).

[24]George E. Ladd, *A Theology of the New Testament,* rev. ed. (Grand Rapids, Mich.: Eerdmans, 1993), p. 117. See also "The Kingdom, Israel, and the Church," ch. 8 in Ladd's *The Gospel of the Kingdom* (Grand Rapids, Mich.: Eerdmans, 1971), pp. 107-22.

Israel whose only external distinguishing mark was their discipleship to Jesus.[25]

Although the kingdom is not the church, it appears that Jesus envisioned the formation of a visible religious community (Hebrew, *qāhāl; LXX, ekklēsia*) committed to his mission to restore the people of Israel.

2.4. The Jesus Movement

On the basis of the preceding discussion, a number of important conclusions can be made about Jesus and his followers before his death and resurrection.

2.4.1. Jesus' Ministry. Jesus traveled throughout the country, villages and cities (see 1.1 above) seeking to gather the eschatological people of God by proclaiming the kingdom of God, healing, performing miracles and calling people to repentance and obedience. Although the Gospels were not written specifically as biographies in the modern sense of the term, they do provide a reliable historical picture of Jesus' activities.

2.4.2. Jesus' Role. It is more accurate to describe Jesus as a Jewish teacher (rabbi) within Israel's prophetic tradition than as a social or political reformer (Zealot), a Cynic philosopher or a charismatic holy man.

2.4.3. Responses to Jesus. Jesus' teaching appealed to a variety of people. Some were attracted to him because of his miracles and spectacular deeds (Lk 23:8; Jn 2:23; 4:48), which, in a number of cases, led to some form of belief in him (Jn 2:23; 4:48; 6:2). Others must have hoped that he was a political messiah who would deliver Israel from Roman oppression and establish God's rule on earth. This fact probably accounts for the many warnings against "false messiahs" who were leading Israel astray (Mt 24:5, 23-24; Mk 13:21-22). The messianic expectations at the time still left the disciples and populace wondering about Jesus. At the trial and crucifixion, for example, there was the feeling that *if* Jesus truly was the Messiah, he would be able to save himself (Mk 15:32; Lk 23:35) or at least squelch his interrogators' taunting (Mt 26:63, 68; 27:17, 22; Mk 14:61; Lk 23:2). Did any of them see Jesus as God's Messiah calling the nation back into its covenantal relationship?

Prior to the resurrection, it is doubtful that any of Jesus' followers, including the Twelve, *fully* understood the nature of his mission to restore Israel. Peter's confession, "You are the Messiah, the Son of the living God" (Mt 16:16; cf. Mk 8:29), and the epiphany of the disciples on the Emmaus road (Lk 24:31: "Then their eyes were opened, and they recognized him"), acknowledge the person but not the mission. The request by James and John to sit at Jesus' right and left hand (Mk 10:37) indicates that their messianic expectations were quite different

---

[25]Ladd, *Theology of the New Testament,* pp. 379-80. See also discussion below.

from Jesus' understanding of his fate (Mk 10:38-40). Even when the ascended Lord appeared to the disciples gathered in Jerusalem and instructed them about "the kingdom of God," there were national expectations in their response: "Lord, is this the time when you will restore the kingdom to Israel?" (Acts 1:6).

Nothing is said in the Gospels about the future of those who initially followed Jesus. Apart from the Twelve who "left all" and joined his itinerant ministry, the larger circle of disciples—that is, believers, adherents—would have remained within the context of their work and homes, probably attempting to live according to the new moral teaching they had heard as they waited for the kingdom of God. Here Gerd Theissen's distinction between a group of "wandering charismatics" who literally followed Jesus and local "sympathizers" who accepted his teaching but remained in their communities has some merit.[26] N. T. Wright talks about "cells of followers . . . scattered about Palestine . . . small groups of people loyal to himself, who would get together to encourage one another, and would act as members of a family, sharing some sort of common life and, in particular, exercising mutual forgiveness."[27]

There is, however, no evidence that Jesus actually intended to establish such groups committed to his cause, although some may have formed naturally on their own. Neither did Jesus leave any instructions as to how his followers should organize themselves in the future. Wright's claim that Matthew 18:19-20 reflects such groups with loyalty to Jesus ("Again, truly I tell you, if two of you agree on earth about anything you ask, it will be done for you by my Father in heaven. For where two or three are gathered in my name, I am there among them") more than likely fits into a post-Easter situation and the structure of the church as it developed in the Matthean community.

2.4.4. The Twelve. Apart from this larger number of disciples, including the "seventy" mentioned in Luke 10:1-16,[28] Jesus selected and trained twelve individuals who symbolically represented the twelve tribes of Israel, thus confirming his intention to restore or "reconstitute" (N. T. Wright) all Israel (Mt 10:5-6).

---

[26]See Gerd Theissen, _Sociology of Early Palestinian Christianity_ (Philadelphia: Fortress, 1978), pp. 10-16.

[27]N. T. Wright, _Jesus and the Victory of God,_ p. 297.

[28]There is no way of knowing how serious the people who followed Jesus were or how committed they were to his teaching. At the time of Jesus' death, Lk 23:49 mentions the presence of "all his acquaintances _[gnōstoi],_ including the women who had followed him from Galilee." After the resurrection there were "other women" besides Mary Magdalene, Joanna and Mary the mother of James (Lk 24:10). On the road to Emmaus there was Cleopas plus a companion (Lk 24:13, 18). In Acts 1:23, two names (Joseph called Barsabbas [or Justus] and Matthias) are recommended to replace Judas among the Twelve. There were 120 in the upper room (Acts 1:15) and, according to Paul, 500 to whom the risen Christ appeared (1 Cor 15:6).

The historicity of their call (Mt 4:18-22; Mk 1:16-20; Lk 5:1-11; 6:12-16; Acts 1:2), their commission (Mt 10:1-15; Mk 6:7-13; Lk 9:1-6) and the eschatological claim that they will "sit on twelve thrones, judging the twelve tribes of Israel" (Mt 19:28) surely goes back to Jesus himself and is well-attested in early Christian tradition (1 Cor 15:5).[29] Gerhard Lohfink notes that the Twelve were "created" or "instituted" (from the Greek *poiein*) and may represent different factions within Judaism of the day who were chosen from different regions in order to signify that Jesus was seeking to draw together *all* Israel.[30]

Even though Jesus' mission was directed exclusively to Israel (Mt 7:6; 15:24, 26; Mk 7:27), there are indications that he envisioned a future inclusion of Gentiles as well (see, e.g., Mt 8:11-13; 22:1-10; Lk 13:28-29; 14:16-24). E. P. Sanders states it best by noting "that Jesus started a movement which *came to see the Gentile mission as a logical extension of itself.*"[31]

2.4.5. The Last Supper. Before his arrest, trial and execution, Jesus shared the Last Supper, a Passover-type meal, with his disciples in an "upper room" in Jerusalem (Mt 26:17-30; Mk 14:12-25; Lk 22:7-23), which established a new covenant and anticipated the messianic banquet at the end of the age (see 5.8).

2.4.6. Opposition to Jesus. Some of Jesus' words and deeds created opposition with the religious establishment and ultimately led to his death at the hands of the Romans. Sanders is probably correct that the action of cleansing the temple and certain sayings about the destruction of the temple precipitated Jesus' death more than any other events, including his confrontations with the Pharisees on matters of laws on the sabbath, hand-washing, food, eating and associating with sinners, the charge of blasphemy, and the triumphal entry into Jerusalem.[32]

2.4.7. Summary. If it is valid to claim that Jesus' main mission was the restoration of Israel, what about our opening question concerning whether or not he intended to found the church? Was N. T. Wright correct to say, "of course he didn't; of course he did"? If, for the moment, we define *church (ekklēsia)* as a gathering of the people of God, a community of believers in whom the reign of God is actualized, the answer is *affirmative.*[33] Of course Jesus came to gather

---

[29]Sanders, *Jesus and Judaism,* 98-106.

[30]Lohfink, *Jesus and Community,* p. 11.

[31]Sanders, *Jesus and Judaism,* p. 220.

[32]Ibid., pp. 61-76, 294-318. This was noted much earlier by Flew, *Jesus and His Church,* pp. 39-42.

[33]For more discussion on *ekklēsia* and related terms, see below. In the Gospels, *ekklēsia* appears only in Mt 16:18 and 18:17. Note I. Howard Marshall, "New Wine in Old Wineskins: The Biblical Use of the Word '*Ekklēsia,*'" *ExpT* 84 (1972-73): 359-64; Marshall, "Church," *DJG,* 122-25.

such a community.[34] But this is only true if we conceive of such a movement *within* and not separate from the Judaism of Jesus' day. This explains why, with the exception of the content of his message and the ministry of the Twelve, he provided no new directions for corporate religious life. Jesus expected his followers to worship within the parameters of the temple and synagogue and to honor Israel's religious leaders. The disciples did not feel compelled to form some special religious group within the Jewish nation, as, for example, was the case with Qumran.

However, if we think of *church* sociologically or in terms of a physical structure with elaborate architecture, a complex constitution, an ordained hierarchy of officials to govern the community, intricate liturgical forms, and the like, the answer would be negative. This is not what Jesus had in mind in the formation of his *ekklēsia*. But this does not necessarily mean that he would condemn such structures either. Architectural, ecclesiastical and liturgical simplicity are not virtues in themselves. The history of the emerging church shows that such developments were natural, necessary and helpful. The challenge facing the early church (as it is today) was not to mistake structure and form for substance. In various ways the church found it necessary to remind believers of Jesus' words, that the essence of their faith is to love God and their neighbors (Lk 10:27) and to worship God "in spirit and truth" (Jn 4:24).

On a concluding note, Gerhard Lohfink offers sound advice on the origin of the church in the preface to *Jesus and Community:*

> Critical theology has long asked emphatically if the historical Jesus really founded a church. Yet it has become increasingly clear that this question is posed in the wrong way. It is not much of an exaggeration to say that Jesus could not have founded a church since there had long been one—God's people, Israel. Jesus directed his efforts to Israel. He sought to gather it in view of the coming reign of God and to make it into the true people of God. What we now call church is nothing other than the community of those ready to live in the people of God, gathered by Jesus and sanctified by his death. From this perspective, it is foolish to look to the historical Jesus for a formal act of founding the church. But it is very meaningful to ask how Jesus gathered Israel and how he envisioned the community of the true Israel, because right here we reach the

---

[34]According to Kevin Giles, "Jesus did call into being the Christian community, the church theologically defined. Then and now he forgives the sins of those who repent and believe and makes them members of his family. He calls them a flock, is present with them as their shepherd, sends them into the world on mission, sustains them with spiritual food, and provides them with leaders. If these things constitute the church then Jesus is most certainly the founder of the church" (*What on Earth Is the Church?* [Downers Grove, Ill.: InterVarsity Press, 1995], p. 45).

ultimately decisive question of *what the church should be like today.*[35]

Lohfink then proceeds to write two hundred pages on "what the church should be like today," especially in the area of "community" (*Gemeinde*). Our task, however, is to move in another direction and examine the type of community that emerged after the resurrection as described in Acts and the New Testament epistles. Only then can one decide whether the church—both New Testament and contemporary—is a distortion or a natural development in continuity with Jesus' original vision. Perhaps there is some truth in Loisy's statement that Jesus came proclaiming the kingdom but we got the church instead! Those who responded to Jesus' message of the kingdom and who lived according to his teaching formed the type of community—an *ekklēsia*—that God intended Israel to be.

2.5. Jesus: From Easter to Pentecost

On the basis of the preceding discussion, one can conclude that Jesus intended to restore Israel by gathering together an eschatological community *(ekklēsia)* in anticipation of the coming kingdom of God. This community thought of itself as the true Israel and initially had no intention of forming its own identity with different religious observances. There is, so to speak, nothing that one would identify as a *church* at this point. On the other hand, the community that Jesus initially gathered clearly formed the basis of the church that emerged after Easter and Pentecost. These two events transformed this community into what came to be called the church *(ekklēsia)* of God.

2.5.1. Easter. The trial, crucifixion and burial of Jesus left his disciples and followers sad, bewildered, orphaned and hopeless. Cleopas's sad response to the "stranger" on the Emmaus road, his hope that Jesus would have been the one who would redeem Israel (Lk 24:17-24), probably expressed the mood of all who witnessed Jesus' death and had placed their hope in him. Although Jesus had spoken both directly and metaphorically about his resurrection (Mt 12:40; 26:61; 27:40, 63; Mk 8:31; 9:31; 10:34; 14:58; 15:29; Jn 2:19-20), even those who prepared his body for burial did not understand the significance of these sayings. Mary Magdalene's discovery of the empty tomb suggested theft to her, not resurrection of the body (Jn 20:2; note Jn 20:9: "for as yet they did not understand the scripture, that he must rise from the dead").[36]

---

[35]Lohfink, *Jesus and Community,* p. xi.

[36]Note Martin de Jonge's interpretation: "In their attempts to grasp the meaning of Jesus' death, his followers were led by their conviction that Jesus had indeed been sent by God at a crucial moment in history and that God had vindicated him. He had died on the cross, but he was no criminal or revolutionary, much less a pious man or a prophet who, in the eyes of his executioners, had deluded his followers and himself" (*Early Christology,* p. 13).

The confirmation to the disciples that Jesus of Nazareth was the resurrected Lord took place through a number of postresurrection appearances, which included those at the tomb and other locations (see the resurrection accounts in Mt 28:1-10; Mk 16:1-8; Lk 24:1-12; Jn 20:1-18), as well as several postresurrection meals where Jesus' identity was confirmed (Lk 24:30-43; Jn 21:13-14; cf. Acts 1:3; 10:37-41).[37]

In many ways one could say that *the church began at Easter.* Now, for the first time, the disciples finally realized that the reign of God had been present and active in the life and teaching of Jesus. Those who experienced this assurance assembled together with new conviction and enthusiasm. Their certainty of the "living Christ" was a decisive confirmation of all that Jesus imparted to them during his earthly ministry.[38] For the moment at least, their confession of Jesus as the Messiah *(Christos)* did not create any tensions within Judaism nor even foreshadow the possibility that this group would later emerge as a separate entity within Judaism.

The nature of the Christian community before the ascension of Jesus is difficult to reconstruct, because the biblical narratives do not deal with it in any complete or systematic way. Many followers of Jesus undoubtedly stayed within the vicinity of Jerusalem and formed a group of believers there. Matthew (28:16-17) and Mark (14:28; 16:12, 14) focus on the resurrection appearances in Galilee, events that may account for the formation of some type of Galilean Christianity.[39] Luke, on the other hand, locates the event in Jerusalem (Lk 24:36-53; Acts 1:3-14). There is no geographical clue where the appearance to "more than five hundred brothers and sisters" (1 Cor 15:6) took place, although many scholars suspect that it was Galilee.[40] What existed prior to Pentecost, and probably even after, were two communities of believers convinced of the resurrection and confessing Jesus as Messiah: one in Galilee and the other centered in Jerusalem in the vicinity of the temple.

---

[37]For further discussion on the significance of these meals, see the discussion on the Lord's Supper in 5.8.

[38]This point is presented with considerable conviction by Adolf Schlatter in *Die Geschichte der Ersten Christenheit* (Gütersloh: C. Bertelsmann, 1926); Eng. trans., *The Church in the New Testament Period,* trans. Paul P. Levertoff (London: SPCK, 1955). He writes that there is no uncertainty how the church came into being: "The Church gives it clearly and unambiguously by pointing to what happened on Easter Day" (p. 3). This certainly is true when one notes how often the fact and significance of the resurrection is mentioned in early Christian preaching and theology.

[39]This possibility has been explored by L. E. Elliott-Binns, *Galilean Christianity,* SBT 16 (Chicago: Allenson, 1956); and Ernst Lohmeyer, *Galiläa und Jerusalem* (Göttingen: Vandenhoeck & Ruprecht, 1936).

[40]F. F. Bruce, *The Book of the Acts,* rev. ed., NICNT (Grand Rapids, Mich.: Eerdmans, 1992), p. 43.

The ascension (Lk 24:50-51; Acts 1:9) marks the end of the "forty-day" period of postresurrection appearances of the Lord. According to Luke's theology, this "completes his [Jesus'] earthly ministry and, together with the outpouring of the Holy Spirit, inaugurates 'the last days'."[41] After this event, the disciples returned to Jerusalem from the Mount of Olives, worshiped and blessed God in the temple (Lk 24:52-53), fellowshiped and prayed together in the upper room (Acts 1:12-15) and awaited the promised Holy Spirit (Lk 24:49; Acts 1:8).

2.5.2. Pentecost. It is difficult to construct an accurate chronology of the events between Jesus' resurrection and Pentecost because the information in the biblical text is selective rather than complete. Luke mentions the disciples' *public* expressions of joy and blessing in the temple after they had witnessed the ascension of Jesus at Bethany (Lk 24:52-53), but in Acts the believers (numbering c. 120 persons) return to Jerusalem from the Mount of Olives, meet *privately* in an upstairs room for prayer (Acts 1:13-14) and wait for the fulfillment of Jesus' promise to send the Holy Spirit (Acts 1:8).

Pentecost (from the Greek *pentēkostē*, "fiftieth"), also called the Feast of Weeks, is the second of three obligatory festivals for the Jews (the other two are Passover and Tabernacles [or Booths]). Initially an agricultural festival in thanksgiving for the firstfruits, it was celebrated seven weeks after the cutting of the first barley and cereal grains (Ex 23:16; 34:22; Lev 23:15-21; Num 28:26-31; Deut 16:9-12; 2 Chron 8:13). Calculations place it on the fiftieth day from the first Sunday after Passover. At a later date in Judaism, probably after the destruction of the temple in A.D. 70, it commemorated the giving of the law to Moses on Mount Sinai (Ex 19:1: "On the third new moon after the Israelites had gone out of the land of Egypt, on that very day, they came into the wilderness of Sinai"). On the Christian calendar it commemorates God's gift of the Holy Spirit to the church (Acts 2:1-13).

In addition to Luke's comments about the ascension, the only other significant recorded event is the election of Matthias to replace Judas (Acts 1:26). The fact that it seems necessary to bring the number of disciples back up to twelve confirms the conviction that this group represents the twelve tribes of Israel, the entire nation that Jesus was seeking to reconstitute. Matthias, who qualifies for the position of apostle because he was a follower of Jesus as well as an "eyewitness" to the resurrection (Acts 1:21-22), was selected by lot over the other candidate, "Joseph called Barsabbas, who was also known as Justus." Since there

---

[41]Kevin Giles, "Ascension," *DJG*, p. 50. Most scholars agree that the *forty* are not literal days but symbolic, denoting an indefinite period of time. However, on the Christian calendar, Ascension Day is celebrated on the fortieth day after Easter.

are no other references to Matthias in the New Testament, we do not know if he played any significant role in church leadership. One gathers from Luke that his appointment had more significance for prophetic fulfillment (Acts 1:20) and numerical value (the Twelve) than for practical reasons.[42]

2.5.3. Luke and the Birth of the Church. Although Easter led to the formation of a community of believers in Jerusalem and Galilee confessing Jesus as the resurrected Lord and Messiah, his followers still had not received the promised Holy Spirit, which would enable them to begin their *public* ministry: "But you will receive power *[dynamis]* when the Holy Spirit has come upon you; and you will be my witnesses *[martyres]* in Jerusalem, in all Judea and Samaria, and to the ends of the earth" (Acts 1:8). Through this miraculous and creative act of God, the disciples received confirmation and power for their mission.

Luke's account of Pentecost in Acts includes the descent of the Spirit with both audible and visible manifestations (Acts 2:1-4), the crowd's amazement (Acts 2:5-13), Peter's proclamation of the gospel (2:14-36) and the call to repentance (Acts 2:37-42). Here Luke's goal is to develop the theme of fulfillment that began with the story of Jesus in his Gospel ("an orderly account of the events that have been fulfilled *[plērophoreō]* among us" Lk 1:1) and to extend that to the birth and history of the church.[43] Pentecost fulfilled the prophecy of Joel (see Acts 2:16-22) as well as the promises of the Holy Spirit made by Jesus (see Mt 10:20; Lk 12:12; 24:49; Jn 14:16-31). The "roll call of nations" present in Jerusalem represented Jews from the Diaspora who came to celebrate Pentecost.[44] Luke's reference to "visitors from Rome, both Jews and proselytes" (Acts 2:10) is particularly noteworthy because it may help explain the origin of the church in Rome (see 3.7.8).

---

[42]Thus David Seccombe, "The New People of God," in *Witness to the Gospel,* ed. I. Howard Marshall and David Peterson (Grand Rapids, Mich.: Eerdmans, 1998), p. 351: "Peter cites only scriptural necessity as the reason for replacing Judas, but this begs the question what the necessity related to. In the light of Jesus' promise to the apostles that they would 'sit on thrones judging the twelve tribes of Israel' (Luke 22:30), and their question to him at the ascension about the restoration of Israel (Acts 1:6-8) it is hard to imagine that Luke did not intend his readers to see it in connection with Israel's restoration and the twelve-fold foundation of its community (see Rev. 21:14)."

[43]See the commentary and extensive bibliographies in Ben Witherington III, *The Acts of the Apostles* (Grand Rapids, Mich.: Eerdmans, 1998); Marshall and Peterson, eds. *Witness to the Gospel;* C. K. Barrett, *Acts* (Edinburgh: T & T Clark, 1994), 1:106-26.

[44]Most commentaries on Acts provide helpful discussions on this list. For additional reading, see Bruce Metzger, "Ancient Astrological Geography and Acts 2:9-11," in *Apostolic History and the Gospel,* ed. W. Ward Gasque and Ralph P. Martin (Grand Rapids, Mich.: Eerdmans, 1970), pp. 123-33; James M. Scott, "Luke's Geographical Horizon," in *The Book of Acts in Its Graeco-Roman Setting,* ed. David W. J. Gill and Conrad Gempf, BAFCS 2 (Grand Rapids, Mich.: Eerdmans, 1994), pp. 483-544. C. K. Barrett sums up the difficulties this passage creates when he laments: "The list of names, including both countries and races, presents severe problems and has never been satisfactorily explained" (*Acts,* 1:121).

It is important to remember that Pentecost is God's "gift" of the Holy Spirit to the church and needs to be distinguished from the "gifts" of the Spirit *to believers* (Rom 12:6-8; 1 Cor 12:8-10, 28-30; Eph 4:7-11) as well as the "fruit of the Spirit" expected *of believers* (Gal 5:22-24). The manifestation of glossolalia (from the Greek, *glōssa,* commonly referred to as "speaking in tongues") in Luke is presented as *speaking in known foreign languages.* This differs from other New Testament passages, where it is some kind of *unknown* and unintelligible language that needs to be interpreted (see 1 Cor 13:1; 14:2, 9).

It is difficult to explain some of Luke's phrases regarding the miracle of languages. Is this a miracle of *speaking?* That is, were the disciples able to speak in all the languages of the hearers? This appears to be the meaning of Acts 2:4: the disciples "began to speak in *other* languages *[heterais glōssais]* as the Spirit gave them ability." Or, is this a miracle of *hearing?* In other words, the "Spirit-filled" disciples spoke in their own language (presumably Hebrew, Aramaic, Greek and a Galilean dialect), which the visitors recognized as their own native language or dialect (Acts 2:8: "And how is it that we hear, each of us, in our own native language?" *[hekastos tē idia dialektō]*). F. F. Bruce concludes:

> The disciples, suddenly delivered from the peculiarities of their Galilaean speech, praised God and rehearsed his mighty works in such a way that each hearer recognized with surprise his own language or dialect. No such surprise is expressed when Peter addresses the multitude (vv. 14-36), though it may be inferred that in this address he continued to speak without those Galilaean peculiarities that might otherwise have hindered people from other parts from understanding him.[45]

Another option is to take the "other languages" *(heterais glōssais)* as an unknown tongue, some type of "spirit language," which implies a miracle of speaking *and* hearing.

No amount of exegetical or psychological research will satisfactorily explain this event. The most one can say with reasonable certainty is that a miracle of language took place. The presence of all these nations in Jerusalem is Luke's way of informing his readers that representatives of the entire Jewish world witnessed the fulfillment of God's promise to send the Spirit and heard the gospel as presented by Peter (Acts 2:14-36). Peter placed considerable emphasis on the fact that his fellow Israelites (Acts 2:22, 29; the "entire house of Israel," 2:36) knew with absolute certainty that God had made the crucified and resurrected Jesus of Nazareth both Lord *(kyrios)* and Messiah *(Christos).* For the disciples, the coming of the Spirit was a creative act of God that confirmed their mission and was the means by which the living Christ became available and

---

[45]Bruce, *Acts,* p. 115.

active for all humanity. From now on they were enabled and commissioned to act on behalf of the risen Lord to proclaim the gospel to the entire world (Acts 1:8).

So, is this where the church *really* began? Should we take Peter's proclamation of the gospel (Acts 2:14-36) and the subsequent formation of a repentant and baptized community (Acts 2:37-42) as the "First Christian Church of Jerusalem"? If, as argued earlier, Easter marked the formation of a community *(ekklēsia)* that recognized Jesus as the exalted Lord, is Pentecost simply another affirmation of that realization? In Luke's theology, it appears to be much more. Catholic theologian Rudolf Schnackenburg captures the essence of Pentecost in relationship to the founding and self-awareness of the primitive church when he writes:

> It [the church] cannot be understood without its foundation and endowment which took place "from on high" by God's eschatological action. Every attempt to understand it purely from the point of view of religious sociology for example, as the formation of a group within Judaism, as a sect with an apocalyptic bent which then developed in the Hellenistic world into an independent yet syncretistic religious society, breaks down because of the witness it bears to itself. . . . The consciousness of having received the Holy Spirit from the exalted Lord and Messiah, as the first fruits and pledge of redemption (see Rom 8:23; 2 Cor 1:22; Eph 1:13f.; Tit 3:6f.), distinguishes its character from the whole of Judaism, including the Qumran community, to say nothing of paganism and its cults.[46]

All this is not to say that, by attributing the founding of the church to a divine act of God, we ignore all the historical and sociological insights from scholars over the years. Individuals such as John Gager, Howard C. Kee, Bruce J. Malina, Wayne Meeks, Gerd Theissen, Robin Scroggs, and the like have provided many valuable perspectives on the social factors at work in the first century that affected early Christianity.[47] Neither were Luke, Paul, Peter, James, John and other church leaders oblivious to such dynamics. Nevertheless, the underlying conviction in the New Testament is that the church is God's church, his creation, and that the community of believers is his flock (see 5.10 and concluding remarks).

What we have at this early stage of church history, therefore, is the nation of

---

[46]Rudolf Schnackenburg, *The Church in the New Testament* (Freiburg: Herder, 1965), pp. 16-17.

[47]See references cited earlier. Another valuable source utilizing the social sciences is Rodney Stark, *The Rise of Christianity* (Princeton, N.J.: Princeton University Press, 1996). As a sociologist with an interest in history, Stark is concerned with the growth of the church, not its origin.

Israel identified by its belief in YHWH, committed to the Torah and observance of the cultic system associated with the temple in Jerusalem. But within that large group there is a small minority of Jewish men and women who see themselves as the *true* Israel. They realize that God is at work in the person of Jesus and thus readily confess him as their Messiah. They also know that God has given the Holy Spirit to authenticate and empower their mission to restore Israel (note Peter's Pentecost sermon, where the prophetic fulfillment also includes the "universal restoration" [*apokatastasis,* Acts 3:21] of the nation). On this basis it seems appropriate to refer to these believers as "the church."

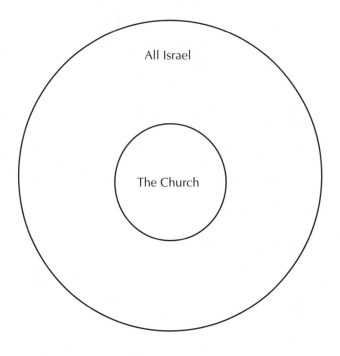

Figure 1. Israel and the church

Figure 1 illustrates the situation up to Acts 2:36. After this, however, things changed rather rapidly for the Christian community as a result of Peter's sermon.

Because Luke compressed his history of the early church, the reader of Acts has very little sense of chronology between events. Peter's address to the crowd, for example, is covered in twenty-three verses (Acts 2:14-36) that take the average person no more than two minutes to read. In all likelihood, however, the entire Pentecost event, including Peter's sermon, covered the better part of an entire day and involved considerably more dialogue than Luke recorded. Luke indicates this in Acts 2:40, where Peter "testified with many other arguments" *(diemartyrato)* as he exhorted the Israelites to be saved. "Testified," writes Everett Harrison, "suggests a further witness of a strong and penetrating nature, whereas 'exhorting' indicates repeated appeals to come to the point of decision."[48] No doubt this included additional information on the meaning of repentance, baptism in Jesus' name and the reception of the Holy Spirit (Acts 2:38).

As a history (albeit condensed) of the early church, Acts provides an invaluable bridge between the Gospels and the letters of Paul. It contributes to our understanding of the relationship between Jesus' teaching and the development of early Christian doctrine and world evangelism. In many ways, Acts is not strictly an "Acts of the Apostles," insofar as it deals with so few of the apostles. Peter is the central figure in the first twelve chapters, while the rest of the book is devoted primarily to Paul. For this reason, it has been suggested that Acts should be called "The Acts of the Holy Spirit," because the word *spirit (pneuma)* occurs seventy times in Acts, nearly 20 percent of the total usage of *pneuma* in the New Testament. This emphasis confirms Luke's conviction that it is the Spirit who is the power behind expansion of the church from Jerusalem to Rome.

In the prologue to his Gospel (Lk 1:1-4), Luke indicates that he used *written records* ("since many have undertaken to set down an orderly account of the events that have been fulfilled among us . . . I too decided, after investigating everything carefully from the very first, to write an orderly account") as well as *oral reports* ("[accounts] handed on to us by those who from the beginning were eyewitnesses and servants of the word") for his history. Since this prologue is intended to cover both of Luke's writings, it is natural to assume that some information in Acts was derived from eyewitnesses as well. This means that Luke would have studied some written sources, contacted a number of individuals throughout the Mediterranean world and used his own experiences while traveling with Paul (note the "we" sections in Acts 16:10-16; 20:5-15; 21:1-17; 27:1—28:16) to write his history of the early church.

Theologically, it appears that the theme of "fulfillment" mentioned in the prologue to Luke's Gospel *(plērophoreō)* is Luke's way of informing his readers (initially, Theophilus) that he is focusing on "divine accomplishments" and not simply narrating past events. Luke selects certain prophetic promises and shows how they have been fulfilled through the nation of Israel, the life of Jesus and

---

[48]Everett Harrison, *Acts: Expanding the Church* (Chicago: Moody Press, 1975), pp. 63-64.

now the continuation of that ministry through the church, God's missionary community.

Luke's theological purpose, therefore, determines the selectivity of his material. He omits references about the emergence of the church in such places as Galilee, Egypt, Mesopotamia and northern Asia Minor (regions mentioned in 1 Pet 1:1); he repeats certain events, such as Paul's conversion (three times), the continual rejection of the gospel by the Jews (Acts 2:23, 36; 4:10-11; 5:30; 7:51-53; 13:27-29) and Paul's deliberate turning from the Jews to the Gentiles and his successful reception among them (Acts 13:46-47; 18:5-7; 28:23-28) but omits other events in Paul's life found in his letters; he writes an "Acts of the Apostles" but focuses only on Peter and Paul.

Much of this makes sense if one grants that Luke's theological history was determined by his desire to write about the "events that have been fulfilled among us." Geographically, his aim was to show how the gospel was taken from Jerusalem to Rome. Hence, Jerusalem epitomizes the center of God's chosen people, the Jews, with their temple and law. Rome, on the other hand, epitomizes the nations without the law, the world center of the Gentiles. Even though Luke wrote about the emergence of the church through Paul's missionary activity in many places between Jerusalem and Rome (see part three), one senses his feeling of accomplishment when he writes, "And so we came to Rome" (Acts 28:14). Paul's successful missionary activity to the Gentiles was a fulfillment of God's plan to include them in the history of salvation (note prophetic fulfillment in Acts 2:17-21 = Joel 2:28-32; and Acts 15:16-18 = Amos 9:11-12).[49]

When commentators refer to Acts as an "apology" (from the Greek *apologia*, "a defense, apology," or *apologeomai*, "to speak in one's defense"), they affirm that Luke sought to convince Theophilus that Christianity was a legal and valid religion *(religio licita)* within the empire. Years ago, B. H. Streeter referred to Acts as *"the first of the Apologies.* It is a forerunner of that series of 'Defences of Christianity,' addressed to reigning emperors and members of the Imperial House, which constitutes the larger part of the surviving Christian literature of the second century."[50]

This approach to Acts helps us understand why Luke was so concerned to defend Christianity from outside attacks (primarily from the Jews), including in his narrative ten trials, two mob scenes and four deliberate investigations. Paul's

---

[49]For sources related specifically to this topic, see the bibliography in Witherington's commentary and references in Joel B. Green and Michael C. McKeever, *Luke-Acts and New Testament Historiography* (Grand Rapids, Mich.: Baker, 1994).

[50]B. H. Streeter, *The Four Gospels* (London: Macmillan, 1961), p. 539.

speech during his defense before the Jews in Jerusalem sums up Luke's motif rather succinctly: "I have in no way committed an offense against the law of the Jews, or against the temple, or against the emperor" (Acts 25:8), and Paul's imprisonment in Rome ended without a conviction, a profound way of acknowledging that Rome vindicated Paul personally and the movement he represented.

What we have from Luke, then, are documents from a historian-theologian who wrote a life of Jesus and a history of the early church to meet the needs of first-century believers. However, it is sometimes difficult to determine whether some of his information describes the earliest period of the church (c. A. D. 35-60) or the time he was writing Luke-Acts (c. the mid 80s). Although many scholars disagree on this point, Ralph P. Martin's understanding of Luke's approach in writing a history of the early church seems appropriate:

> Luke wrote in the 80s, but he told his story using sources which are trustworthy for the 40s and the 50s of the first century. His task was pastoral and proclamatory, namely, to recall his contemporaries to the church's ministry in the apostolic age. He was a second-generation pastor harking back to a first-generation model. By using the past history of the church as material, he meant to recall the church of his own day to apostolic norms and ministry, and in particular, to apostolic zeal in outreach based on a fresh experience of the dynamism of the Holy Spirit.[51]

The following chapters on the emergence of the church will provide several opportunities to examine the cogency of this conclusion.

---

[51]Ralph P. Martin, _New Testament Foundations,_ rev. ed. (Grand Rapids, Mich.: Eerdmans, 1994), 2:66-67.

3

THE GEOGRAPHICAL EXPANSION, NUMERICAL GROWTH & DIVERSITY OF THE EARLY CHURCH

P art one provided brief information about the geographical regions surrounding Jerusalem that is important for understanding the history of the Jewish people and locating the public ministry of Jesus as presented in the Gospels. The geographical expansion of the church includes these regions but also moves far beyond into other areas of the Roman Empire.

There are a number of ways to portray the expansion of the church as outlined by Luke in the book of Acts. The most obvious, and the one around which Luke developed his history, is recorded in Acts 1:8: "you will be my witnesses in Jerusalem, in all Judea and Samaria, and to the ends of the earth." In many ways, what began in Jerusalem had a rippling effect similar to tossing a pebble into a pond: the ripples expand in a series of concentric circles (see figure 2). The geographical divisions within the text include

☐ Acts 1:15—8:3: Jerusalem

☐ Acts 8:4—11:18: Judea, Samaria, Galilee and the coastal regions

☐ Acts 11:19—14:28: Antioch and Paul's first missionary journey

☐ Acts 15:36—21:16: Lands around the Aegean

☐ Acts 21:17—28:31: Jerusalem to Rome

It is also possible to see the church developing around the personalities of Peter and Paul:

☐ Acts 1—12: Peter's mission (Jerusalem to Antioch)
☐ Acts 13—28: Paul's mission (Antioch to Rome)

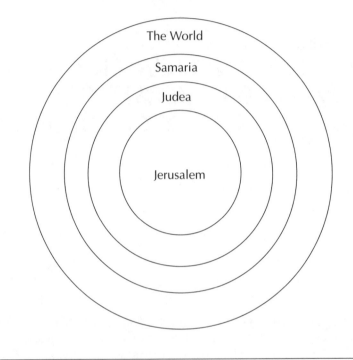

Figure 2. Outline of Acts 1:8

Admittedly, other names are mentioned, but with the possible exception of Stephen, they do not occupy the center stage as do Peter and Paul. Michael D. Goulder, who takes note of geographical outlines and recurrent literary patterns, suggests a different outline:[1]

☐ Apostolic Section: Acts 1:6—5:42
☐ Diaconal Section: Acts 6:1—9:31
☐ Petrine Section: Acts 9:32—12:24
☐ Pauline Section: Acts 12:25—28:31

C. H. Turner offered a creative proposal at the beginning of the twentieth century.[2] He identified six divisions in Acts, each ending with a summary state-

---

[1]Michael D. Goulder, *Type and History in Acts* (London: SPCK, 1964).
[2]C. H. Turner, "Chronology of the New Testament," *Dictionary of the Bible,* ed. J. Hastings (New York: Scribner's, 1905), 1:421. This approach is utilized by Floyd V. Filson in *Three Crucial Decades* (Richmond: John Knox Press, 1963), pp. 12-13.

ment that could be Luke's way of saying, "I do not have the time or space to tell you everything, but I want you to know that the church was progressing rapidly and successfully." The divisions and summary statements include

☐ Acts 1:1—6:7: "The word of God continued to spread; the number of the disciples increased greatly in Jerusalem, and a great many of the priests became obedient to the faith."

☐ Acts 6:8—9:31: "Meanwhile the church throughout Judea, Galilee, and Samaria had peace and was built up. Living in the fear of the Lord and in the comfort of the Holy Spirit, it increased in numbers."

☐ Acts 9:32—12:24: "But the word of God continued to advance and gain adherents."[3]

☐ Acts 12:25—16:5: "So the churches were strengthened in the faith and increased in numbers daily."

☐ Acts 16:6—19:20: "So the word of the Lord grew mightily and prevailed."

☐ Acts 19:21—28:31: "He [Paul] lived there [Rome] two whole years at his own expense and welcomed all who came to him, proclaiming the kingdom of God and teaching about the Lord Jesus Christ with all boldness and without hindrance."

Although these summary statements are useful within the larger scheme of things, they do not capture the main idea that Luke's selectivity was determined by the "purposes" discussed earlier. True, the word of God grew mightily and churches were multiplied and strengthened, but the growth of the church as a whole is subordinate to Luke's main theme of showing how the gospel spread from Jerusalem to Rome. These cities are the two geographical foci around which the book of Acts is structured.

3.1. Jerusalem (Acts 1:15—8:3)

There is no way of knowing how many people were present in Jerusalem on the day of Pentecost. Many pilgrims from the Diaspora came to celebrate this festival, so the resident population increased significantly.[4] Luke's concern at this point was not numerical exactness but geographical representation. Even though the text indicates that the Jews present were residents (Greek *katoikein*, "to dwell, reside, settle down") in Jerusalem, some, such as the "visitors *(epidēmountes)* from Rome", were clearly pilgrims.[5] Luke proba-

---

[3]Within this section one notes another summary statement at Acts 11:21, which describes growth in Antioch: "The hand of the Lord was with them, and a great number became believers and turned to the Lord."

[4]Ben Witherington III estimates between 180,000 and 200,000 (*The Acts of the Apostles* [Grand Rapids, Mich.: Eerdmans, 1998], p. 157).

[5]Commentators such as F. F. Bruce, James Dunn, David Williams and Ben Witherington III

bly mentioned Rome because this was the direction his narrative would take. It is possible, though speculative, that these "visitors" who witnessed Pentecost and heard the gospel in Jerusalem returned to Rome and established a church there (see 3.7.8.1).

It is also not possible to know where the Pentecost event took place. Luke mentions the "room upstairs" (Acts 1:13), which accommodated the 120 persons gathered to reflect upon the ascended Lord and to elect a replacement for Judas (Acts 1:15-26). The gathering at "one place" on the day of Pentecost is not specified, but since it included more than the 120, it must have been a location that could accommodate more people, even though Luke mentions "the entire house (_oikos_) where they were sitting" (Acts 2:2).

The "house" may refer to the temple or the temple area (note Lk 2:49, where "my Father's house" is a synonym for temple), although one would expect Luke to have mentioned that if it were intended. "Somewhere along the line," notes Witherington, "the event migrates to the temple precincts, the only place such a crowd could or would likely be congregated, but Luke does not explain the sequence, only the events."[6] Peter would have addressed the crowd from the same location (Acts 2:14-36). The image of Peter standing and raising his voice to address the crowd (Acts 2:14) suggests an outdoor location, such as Solomon's Portico, where further events took place (Acts 3:11-26; 5:12).

From the gathering in the "room upstairs" and Solomon's Portico (Acts 1:13; 3:11), there are a number of movements around the city, especially back and forth between homes and the temple area (Acts 2:46; 3:1-3). Certainly the baptism (immersion) of three thousand converts (Acts 2:41) required some movement to pools such as Bethesda or Siloam. Additional witnessing by Peter and John continued in the temple area (Acts 5:42) and homes throughout the city (Acts 4:1-12, 23; 5:42; on 5:42, note the NRSV footnote, "from house to house"). We are not sure if the apostles operated from some kind of headquarters or central location. Stephen's confrontation with certain Hellenists from the "synagogue of the Freedmen" took place before the council (Acts 6:9, 13, 15), but his martyrdom appears to have been a public execution witnessed by more people. The lack of apostolic support at this point is puzzling, since Stephen's theology does not appear to differ from the apostles'.

---

have different opinions whether the residents are permanent or pilgrims. For more extensive discussion, see Wolfgang Reinhardt, "The Population Size of Jerusalem and Numerical Growth of the Jerusalem Church," in _The Book of Acts in Its Palestinian Setting,_ ed. Richard Bauckham, BAFCS 4 (Grand Rapids, Mich.: Eerdmans, 1995), pp. 237-65. Estimates on the number of pilgrims on feast days go as high as one million people (p. 262).
[6]Witherington, _Acts,_ p. 132.

The ensuing persecution of the church all but ends Luke's concern with the Jerusalem church for the moment. Although he mentions this center again on several occasions, the most important events include Paul's visit (Acts 9:26), Peter's report to the "mother" church (Acts 11:1-18), the death of James (son of Zebedee) and the imprisonment of Peter by Herod Agrippa I (Acts 12:1-4), the Jerusalem Council (Acts 15:1-35) and additional visits by Paul (Acts 11:29-30; 12:25; 18:22), including his final trip and arrest (Acts 21:1—23:22). With the persecution of the church in Jerusalem (see comments on Acts 8:1, below), Luke turns to the expansion of the gospel into Samaria and the coastal regions (Acts 8:4—11:18).

Nearly all commentators agree that, when considering Luke's numbers, we must not ignore the Greek comparative particle "about" *(hōsei)*, meaning that these are approximations not to be taken literally. James Dunn reminds us, "Numbers in ancient historians tended to be more impressionistic (or propagan-distic) rather than to provide what we today would regard as an accurate accounting."[7] Nevertheless, we have no reason to doubt that this initial phase of the church attracted many people. In addition to the "about" 120 (Acts 1:15) and the "about" three thousand (Acts 2:41), Luke also refers to a total number of "about" five thousand (Acts 4:4).[8]

In spite of Luke's proclivity to approximate numbers, it would be difficult to believe that only men are meant in Acts 4:4. Five thousand men plus the many women who had joined the church would raise the total number considerably. Is it possible that membership in the church approximated 10 percent of the total population of Jerusalem? Even at a smaller rate of growth, one has to admit that Christianity was highly successful in attracting Jerusalem Jews to its movement. A sizable number, however, remained unconvinced that they should repent, be baptized and identify with the community that confessed Jesus as the Messiah.

Readers of Acts may form the impression that all the events mentioned in Acts 2—7 transpired within a very short period of time. Part of this is due to the way Luke condenses historical information (one can read these chapters within a span of several minutes). The reality is that Pentecost (c. A.D. 30) and Paul's conversion (c. A.D. 33) were separated by a period of approximately three

---

[7]James D. G. Dunn, *The Acts of the Apostles* (Valley Forge, Penn.: Trinity Press International), p. 34.

[8]The NRSV omits the Greek text's "number of men" *(andros)*, meaning male as distinct from women. On combinations of "men *and* women," see Acts 5:14; 8:3, 12; 9:2; 17:12; 22:4. In response to critics of Luke's numerical reliability, Wolfgang Reinhardt offers the following observation: "Thus critical research, in contradiction to predominant (largely uncritical) opin-ion, arrives at the conclusion that the Lukan figures need not be unhistorical at all and can in fact be dependent on reliable tradition" ("Population Size of Jerusalem," p. 265).

years.[9] It would have taken at least this long for the church to reach and baptize so many people and to establish its identity through its teaching, ritual (breaking of bread) and liturgy (prayers). Likewise, the animosities between unbelieving Jews and the apostles (primarily Peter and John in Acts 4:1-22; 5:17-41), Stephen (Acts 6:8—8:1) and members of the church (Acts 12:1-19; cf. 1 Thessalonians) took time to fester before they erupted into martyrdom and a wholesale persecution of the church.

Luke's brief account of the persecution of the church leaves a lot to the reader's imagination. The "all" (pantes) who were scattered in Acts 8:1 must refer to a significant number and not literally every last member of the church "except the apostles."[10] Still, it is not clear who was doing the persecuting and why. Given the earlier persecution of Stephen (a Hellenistic-Jewish Christian) by Jerusalem Jews, it is possible that these Jews continued to attack the church at large, including Hellenistic Christians, since it appears from Acts 11:20 that the Hellenists are the ones scattered to other regions of the empire.[11] However, one should not forget that Saul, a Hellenistic Jew, was the major leader of this persecution.

We do not know why "the apostles" were spared at this time. Ben Witherington suggests that it was due to respect for the pillars of the church.[12] But it appears obvious that there is more here than ecclesiastical esteem. Of the twelve apostles, Peter was the major player up to this point. John accompanied him but did not say a word. James, although mentioned in Acts 12:17, did not emerge as a prominent figure in Acts until his role in the Jerusalem Council (Acts 15:1-35) and later during Paul's last visit to Jerusalem (Acts 21:17-26). There he appears to be the leading figure in the church, perhaps even acting

---

[9]On the chronology of Jesus, see Harold W. Hoehner, "Chronology," DJG, p. 122; on Paul, Loveday C. A. Alexander, "Chronology of Paul," DPL, pp. 120-23; Stanley E. Porter, "Chronology, New Testament," DNTB, pp. 201-8. Ben Witherington follows the dating proposed by K. Lake, which places Pentecost in A.D. 30 and Paul's conversion around A.D. 33, thus allowing three years between Acts 1 and 8 (Acts, pp. 81-86). For further discussion on the chronology of Paul, see below.

[10]Acts 9:26 mentions "disciples" (mathētai) in the Jerusalem church. Martin Hengel and Anna Maria Schwemer write, "This is one of Luke's pieces of carelessness or exaggerations. Historically, presumably only the Jewish-Christian 'Hellenists' were driven out, while the tribulation passed by the 'Hebrews' and the group of their leaders" (Paul Between Damascus and Antioch: The Unknown Years [Louisville: Westminster John Knox, 1997], p. 137). See also, C. K. Barrett, Acts, 2 vols. (Edinburgh: T & T Clark, 1994), 1:391.

[11]See Richard Bauckham, "James and the Jerusalem Church," in Bauckham, ed., Palestinian Setting, pp. 428-34; F. F. Bruce, The Book of the Acts, rev. ed., NICNT (Grand Rapids, Mich.: Eerdmans, 1992), pp. 162-63; Dunn, Acts, p. 104; Craig C. Hill, "Hellenists, Hellenistic and Hellenistic-Jewish Christianity," DLNTD, pp. 463-67.

[12]Witherington, Acts, p. 278 n. 330.

with the authority of a bishop. Could it be that the local Jewish authorities (the Sanhedrin) and Hellenistic conservatives saw the apostles as representing a segment of the early church that could coexist peaceably with Judaism?

Even though the apostles proclaimed Jesus as the Messiah and called on the Jews to repent from their sins and hardness of heart and to be baptized, they criticized neither the law nor the temple. In fact, they continued to worship in the temple as well as in homes (Acts 2:46; 3:1-4). They referred to Scripture in terms of fulfilled prophecy (Acts 3:21: "the time of universal restoration that God announced long ago through his holy prophets"); they saw their mission as forming the true Israel, not a new Israel. The apostles avoided persecution at this time because they were not perceived as a threat to the status quo and because the Jerusalem church continued to be quite Jewish in nature and practice.

3.2. Judea, Samaria, Galilee and the Coastal Regions (Acts 8:4—11:18)

This expansion of the church began with the persecuted believers who were driven out of Jerusalem after Stephen's martyrdom and ended with the church being established in Antioch, Syria. This section of Acts is significant for several reasons.[13] First, it describes the stage of expansion that Luke envisioned in Acts 1:8: the church moving beyond Jerusalem to Judea and Samaria. Second, it depicts how the church shifted from a rather rural movement in the smaller communities of the provinces to the large cosmopolitan center of Antioch, which at this time was the third largest city in the Greco-Roman world (after Rome and Alexandria). Third, it demonstrates how God (the Spirit) gradually broke down religious, social and ethnic barriers, enabling Christianity to move out of its Jewish context and embrace people on the fringes of Judaism, including Gentiles. Fourth, it affirms that by the time Christianity became established in Antioch, believers had their own identity as "Christians" (Acts 11:26), signifying that they were no longer just regarded as followers of "the Way" (Acts 9:2; 18:25; 19:9, 23; 24:14, 22), a "sect [*hairesis*] of the Nazarenes" (Acts 24:5) or some other religious movement (Acts 24:14; 28:22).[14]

This section of Acts also describes (1) the ministry of the evangelist Philip in Samaria and Judea (Acts 8:5-40); (2) the conversion and early missionary activity of Paul in areas around Tarsus and Damascus (Syria and Cilicia), including a

---

[13]See Martin Hengel, "The Origins of the Christian Mission," in *Between Jesus and Paul* (Philadelphia: Fortress, 1983), pp. 46-64; Eckhard J. Schnabel, "Mission, Early Non-Pauline," *DLNTD*, pp. 752-75.

[14]See the important discussion of *hairesis* by Steven Mason, who argues: "An essential element of Luke's strategy to unite Christianity and Judaism is his portrayal of the church as a Jewish *philosophical school* alongside the Pharisees and Sadducees" ("Sadducees, Pharisees and Sanhedrin," in Bauckham, ed., *Palestinian Setting*, p. 153).

brief visit to Jerusalem (Acts 9:11-30); (3) Peter's travels, which took him (and John) briefly to Samaria (Acts 8:14-25) but then alone to the coastal cities of Joppa, Lydda and Caesarea (Acts 9:32—11:18); and (4) the dispersion of other persecuted Hellenists to the regions of Phoenicia, Cyprus, Cyrene and Antioch (Acts 11:19-29). All this took place within a time period of approximately twelve to thirteen years (c. A.D. 33-46).

3.2.1. The Ministry of Philip (Acts 8:4-40). Philip was one of "the Seven" who, like Stephen, was elected to distribute food to the Hellenistic widows. However, he became an "evangelist" in the early church instead (Acts 21:8; not to be confused with Philip the apostle mentioned in Luke 6:14; Acts 1:13). Philip's first mission was to "the city of Samaria,"[15] where his preaching, healing miracles and exorcisms attracted a large following, including a Jewish magician named Simon (see 1.2.4). The net result of Philip's ministry was that many Samaritans believed and were baptized "in the name of Jesus" (Acts 8:12). In a slight departure from the pattern in Acts 2:38 (belief-baptism-Holy Spirit) Luke has Peter and John coming from Jerusalem to lay hands on these baptized believers so that they might receive the Holy Spirit. It is possible that Luke wanted the church in Samaria to be linked to or unified with the mother church in Jerusalem and did not intend to imply that the Holy Spirit can only be transmitted through some rite of confirmation by the apostles.

Since Philip remains the main character in the narrative, Luke simply dismisses Peter and John by means of another typical summary: "Now after Peter and John had testified and spoken the word of the Lord, they returned to Jerusalem, proclaiming the good news to many villages of the Samaritans" (Acts 8:25). One wishes Luke had elaborated upon the duration and success (or failure) of this brief mission.

A second phase of Philip's ministry took place on a "wilderness road" between Jerusalem and Gaza, an ancient city near the coast on the southern border of Judea (Acts 8:26-39). Here Philip encountered an Ethiopian eunuch, a treasurer of Candace, queen of the Ethiopians. Although the eunuch may have been in Jerusalem on the queen's business, the text focuses on his religious quest. He probably was a God-fearer who used this opportunity for a pilgrimage to Jerusalem. We do not know how he happened to obtain a manuscript of the Old Testament (at least the book of Isaiah), because such copies were both

_____

[15]The text includes the article "the" *(tēn)*, implying a main or major city of Samaria, such as Sebaste (ancient Samaria) or Neapolis (ancient Shechem). Although external evidence strongly supports the article (see Bruce M. Metzger, *A Textual Commentary on the Greek New Testament,* 2nd ed. [New York: American Bible Society, 1994], pp. 355-56), most commentators believe that Luke had the Samaritan people in mind rather than any one specific city.

rare and expensive. At any rate, the Spirit directed Philip to the eunuch and gave him an opportunity to explain Isaiah 53:7-8 christologically. Philip continued with more "good news about Jesus" (Acts 8:35), which included the necessity of water baptism, probably along the pattern established in Acts 2:38 and 8:16. After this brief encounter Philip was swept off by the Spirit to the town of Azotus (north of Gaza), where he continued to preach to other towns in the region between Azotus and his final stop in Caesarea (Acts 8:40).

At this point Luke interrupts his narrative of the church's expansion in Judea and Samaria by returning to Saul (see Acts 8:3) and his relentless campaign to persecute the church (9:2: "any who belonged to the Way"). The first account of Saul's conversion/commission and early missionary activity (Acts 9:4-30) functions as Luke's introduction to the person who will become the leading personality of the early church. Here Luke sees the opportunity to bring Saul "on stage" before returning to Peter's missionary activities and his summary statement in Acts 9:31: "Meanwhile the church[16] throughout Judea, Galilee, and Samaria had peace and was built up. Living in the fear of the Lord and in the comfort of the Holy Spirit, it increased in numbers."

A number of questions arise from the way Luke understands the geographical relationship between the territories of Galilee, Samaria and Judea in his Gospel (Lk 17:11): "On the way to Jerusalem Jesus was going through the region between Samaria and Galilee" *(dia meson Samareias kai Galilaias)*.[17] Hengel dismisses most critics by noting that ancient writers such as Strabo, Pliny the Elder, Tacitus, and the like also lacked geographical precision when describing Judea and Palestine. Maps were not readily available to the public, and the military and political leaders guarded those that were produced. Hengel also observes that "Luke does not always use the term Judea in the same sense," nor can we assume that he, "the Greek Luke," ever visited the regions of Galilee, Judea, Samaria and the Jordan valley: "Luke is much more concerned for a clear pattern than for geographical exactitude."[18]

Luke's lack of precision on geographical details does not destroy the reality of the spread of the gospel to these regions. Although he mentions Galilee in

---

[16]Commentators continue to speculate on Luke's use of the singular "church" *(ekklēsia)* rather than the plural "churches" to describe the number of Christian communities in these regions. Paul, for example, refers to the "churches" *(tais ekklēsiais)* in Judea (Gal 1:22; 1 Thess 2:14). This feature may be due to Luke's desire to portray a church that was unified even though it was spread out geographically (see Bruce, *Acts*, p. 196).

[17]I. Howard Marshall notes that *"dia meson* could mean 'between,' and may simply be a Hellenistic form of the more correct idiom. If so, a journey along the border between Samaria and Galilee is meant" *(Luke,* NIGTC [Grand Rapids, Mich.: Eerdmans, 1978], p. 650).

[18]Hengel, *Between Jesus and Paul*, pp. 97-99. Rainer Riesner, "Archeology and Geography," *DJG,* esp. on Luke, pp. 45-46.

Acts 9:31, he does not refer to any Christian communities there. Since, for Luke, Galilee is significant as the place where Jesus began his mission (Acts 10:37; 13:31), Luke is not implying that there were no Christian communities in this area until the Hellenistic mission. His silence about churches in Galilee could simply mean that they were not important to his story of the church.

Interestingly, Philip's mission appears to be the first departure from Jesus' instructions in Matthew 10:5-6: "Go nowhere among the Gentiles, and enter no town of the Samaritans, but go rather to the lost sheep of the house of Israel." In other words, Luke uses the stories about Philip to illustrate the transition of the church's mission from Jews to Gentiles even before Saul's conversion and commission to be the apostle to the Gentiles (Acts 9:15; 13:46; 18:6; 22:21; Rom 11:13; Gal 2:7). The Samaritans could be called "semi-Jews" on the periphery of Judaism; the Ethiopian treasurer probably was a Gentile God-fearer or proselyte on his way home from a pilgrimage to Jerusalem; and the cities of Gaza, Azotus and Caesarea had a mixed population with probably more Greek than Jewish people.[19] The radical nature of Philip's ministry, especially to the Ethiopian eunuch, is astutely observed and described by F. Scott Spencer:

> Once again Philip proves to be a boundary-breaking pioneer. Geographically, he extends the gospel not only to the Judean coastal plain but also toward the eunuch's Ethiopian homeland, situated at "the ends of the earth" in Greco-Roman thought (Homer _Odys._ 1.22-24; Strabo _Geog._ 17.2.1; cf. Acts 1:8; Ps 68:31). Ethnically, Philip evangelizes a black African, Jewish-sympathizing Gentile ("God-fearer"). Socially, Philip's witness spans two poles. On the one hand he advises an elite government official _(dynastēs)_, the queen's treasurer (Acts 8:27). On the other hand, however, he reaches out to a castrated male _(eunouchos)_, who, despite his interest in Judaism, would have been regarded according to traditional law as impure and disgraceful, forever cut off from the covenant community (Lev 21:18-20; Deut 23:1; Josephus _Ant._ 4.8.40 §290-91; Philo _Spec. Leg._ 1.324-5). Within this scenario Philip's identification of Jesus with the shorn and scorned figure of Isaiah 53 becomes especially relevant.[20]

Next to Jerusalem, Caesarea was the second most important city in Palestine. It is safe to assume that a number of churches may have emerged in the city and sur-

---

[19]See Hengel, _Between Jesus and Paul,_ pp. 112-13. It is difficult to harmonize this phase of Philip's mission with the statement in Acts 11:19 that the scattered Hellenists "spoke the word to no one except Jews." Certainly Philip and others did not hesitate to speak to Gentiles during this time. One suspects that this may be Luke's way of "saving" the Gentile mission for Paul, even though he admits that some Hellenists also witnessed to Hellenists/Greeks (Acts 11:20) and were instrumental in founding the church in Antioch.

[20]F. Scott Spencer, "Philip the Evangelist," _DLNTD,_ p. 930. For further reference, see Spencer's monograph, _The Portrait of Philip in Acts: A Study of Roles and Relations,_ JSNTSup 67 (Sheffield: JSOT, 1992).

rounding towns between the time of Philip's first visit as an evangelist and Paul's trial and imprisonment some twenty-three to twenty-four years later. Caesarea eventually became the permanent residence of Philip and his four prophesying daughters (Acts 21:8).[21] Paul's contact with Caesarea included his departure from there to Tarsus after his conversion (Acts 9:30); a stop on his way back from Asia Minor (Ephesus) to Jerusalem (Acts 18:22); a more extensive stop and visit with Philip, his daughters and probably other believers (Acts 21:8-16); and then his two-year imprisonment before his final journey to Rome (Acts 23:23—26:32).

In addition to Peter's experiences in Caesarea (Acts 10), early church history testifies to the continuity and significance of the Christian community in Caesarea. Origen (c. 185-254), the Alexandrian biblical exegete and scholar who resided in Caesarea around A.D. 231, established a famous school and library and completed his Hexapla, an elaborate edition of the Old Testament in six parallel columns. Jerome (c. 340-420) also studied there and consulted the Hexapla when he was working on the revision of the Latin Bible that eventually resulted in the Vulgate around A.D. 400. Eusebius (c. 260-340) became the bishop of Caesarea and, as the result of his writings (esp. *Ecclesiastical History*), became known as "the father of church history."[22] These later events suggest that there probably was a vigorous Christian community in Caesarea during the first century.

3.2.2. The Ministry of Peter (Acts 9:32—11:18). It is difficult to know how much time elapsed between Philip's mission, Saul's conversion and the beginning of Peter's "tour of inspection"[23] among a number of coastal Christian centers. Luke does not indicate how and when these people became Christians. Some, we may suppose, had been disciples of Jesus; others probably were fugitives from the persecution of the church in Jerusalem. Still others may have been the direct fruit of

---

[21]It is possible to take Luke's comment in Acts 21:8 simply as a piece of information regarding the retirement of this early Christian evangelist. Nevertheless, Hengel's comments on the verse within the perspective of Luke's narrative are intriguing: "Through these precise details, with the title evangelist and the reference to the nucleus of the Seven, Luke puts the representative of the Christian community in Caesarea at a certain distance from that of Peter and the twelve apostles and then from Jerusalem represented by James and the elders, and from the communities in Judea dominated by Jerusalem (cf. 11.1)" (*Between Jesus and Paul,* p. 114).

[22]Arthur G. Patzia, *The Making of the New Testament* (Downers Grove, Ill.: InterVarsity Press, 1995), p. 21. On the dubious patristic and Gnostic traditions concerning Philip, see Spencer, "Philip the Evangelist," p. 931.

[23]A term used to describe Peter's mission by such scholars as Barrett, *Acts,* 1:484; Bruce, *Acts,* p. 197; Hans Conzelmann, *Acts of the Apostles* (Philadelphia: Fortress, 1987), pp. 76, 476; Ernst Haenchen, *The Acts of the Apostles* (Philadelphia: Westminster Press, 1971), p. 338; and Hengel, *Between Jesus and Paul,* p. 111. A different approach is taken by some scholars who rearrange Luke's chronology and suggest that Peter fled to these regions after his escape from prison in Jerusalem (Acts 12:1-19) and only returned to Jerusalem when it was safe to do so after the death of Herod Agrippa. See the discussion by Joshua Schwartz, "Peter and Ben Stada in Lydda," in Bauckham, ed., *Palestinian Setting,* pp. 392-93.

Philip's evangelization in this area. Either way, "Peter went here and there among all the believers" before he came to the "saints *[tous hagious]* living in Lydda" (Acts 9:32), to a paralytic (probably a Jewish Christian) named Aeneas and to the disciples *(hoi mathētai)* in Joppa (Acts 9:38), which included a woman disciple (Acts 9:36, feminine form *mathētria*) named Tabitha (Aramaic) or Dorcas (Greek, both meaning "deer" or "gazelle"). Figure 3 traces Peter's itinerary.

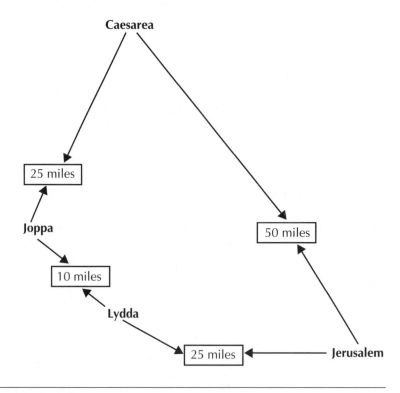

Figure 3. Peter's itinerary

Luke provides no details about the purpose, nature and extent of Peter's stay in Joppa with Simon the tanner (Acts 9:43). It is somewhat surprising that Peter would reside with an individual whose vocation was considered both unpleasant and unclean.[24] Perhaps this is simply an innocuous and insignificant fact; on the other hand, one wonders if Luke is preparing the reader for Peter's next episode with Cornelius, a Roman centurion, where he squarely faced the issue of clean

---

[24]For rabbinic judgments on this vocation, see Barrett, *Acts,* 1:486-87; Witherington, *Acts,* p. 333.

and unclean foods (see esp. Acts 10:9-16).

Lydda (Old Testament Lod; later Diospolis) and Joppa are approximately ten miles apart. Most commentators feel that by this time these coastal cities had a mixed population of Greek and Jewish citizens. Martin Hengel emphasizes the Jewish nature of the two towns, which confirms for him that Peter was remembered primarily as an apostle to the circumcised (Gal 2:7).[25] However, if one recognizes the non-Jewish (that is, Greek) populace of these villages, one could conclude that Luke is deliberately showing how the gospel is extending beyond Judaism.

The events recounted in Acts 10:1-48 leave no doubt that Luke intended readers to understand that this was a decisive step "in the expansion of Christianity into the non-Jewish world." By way of a vision on a rooftop in Joppa, God taught Peter that all foods are clean (Acts 10:9-16; note the repetition of this experience in Acts 11:4-14). Later, when Peter finally met Cornelius in Caesarea, he affirmed that Jews and Gentiles can fellowship together because no persons are profane or unclean (Acts 10:28-43). This was a radical reversal of all that Peter had been taught, believed and practiced as an orthodox Palestinian Jew.[26]

In his sermon to the Gentiles in Caesarea—sometimes referred to as "the Gentile Pentecost"—Peter affirmed the universality of the gospel: all nations can receive the forgiveness of sins (Acts 10:34-43). With events and words reminiscent of Acts 2, Peter witnessed the conversion of the Gentiles, their reception of the Holy Spirit and their baptism in the name of Jesus (Acts 10:44-48).

That the Gentiles could become members of the church through faith and baptism was a significant development in the expansion of Christianity into the non-Jewish world. The importance of this event is reiterated in the account of Peter's return to Jerusalem and his report to the believers there (Acts 11:1-18). Luke repeats the events described in Acts 10:1-48 and then reports that the Jerusalem church confirmed that it was all according to God's plan: the Gentiles are in! The next question—how Gentile and Jewish Christians relate to each other—will become the focus of discussion at the Jerusalem Council (Acts 15:1-35) as well as a major topic in some of Paul's letters, particularly Galatians and Romans.

For Luke, Acts 11:1-18 effectively ends Peter's missionary activity.[27] His par-

---

[25]Hengel, *Between Jesus and Paul,* pp. 116-17.

[26]Dunn appropriately titles this section "The Conversion of Peter," in *Acts,* pp. 134-40.

[27]The additions in the Western text of the Greek New Testament at Acts 11:2 include: "Peter, therefore, for a considerable time wished to journey to Jerusalem; and having called to him the brethren and having strengthened them [he departed], speaking much throughout the country [and] teaching them; he [lit., who] also went to meet them and reported to them the

ticipation in the Jerusalem Council is the last time he is mentioned in Acts. After Peter's release from prison (Acts 12:1-17), the text simply indicates that Peter "left and went to another place" *(eis heteron topon)*. Apart from considerable scholarly speculation on this "place,"[28] the only biblical accounts locate Peter in Antioch, where he is presented as a missionary to "the circumcised" (Gal 2:7-8), possibly accompanied by his wife (1 Cor 9:5). Peter's (Cephas) prestige in Corinth could be due to (undocumented) travels to this area or to the existence of followers from previous contacts (1 Cor 1:12; 3:22). Traditions also claim that he died as a martyr in Rome around A.D. 64 during the reign of Nero (see Jn 21:18-19; 1 Pet 5:1; *1 Clem.* 5.1—6.1).

Luke's abrupt dismissal of Peter leaves the reader somewhat baffled, unless one appreciates his literary creativity and purpose. Peter may have sought refuge from Herod, but Luke is ready to move on to the next phase of the emergence of the church, which involves the apostle Paul. Soon Paul becomes the central actor and dominates the rest of the book.

3.3. The Early Activity of Paul (Acts 9:20-30; Gal 1:17-21).

Readers of Acts are left with some gaping holes in Paul's life from the time he is introduced as a witness of Stephen's martyrdom (Acts 7:58) and persecutor of the early church in Jerusalem (Acts 8:1, 3) until his appearance in Antioch as a coworker with Barnabas.[29] Luke carefully records Paul's religious experience and baptism (Acts 9:1-19; cf. 22:6-21; 26:12-23) as well as his introduction to believers in Damascus by Ananias (Acts 9:10-19), a "devout man according to the law and well spoken of by all the Jews living there" (Acts 22:12; Ananias was not one

---

grace of God. But the brethren of the circumcision disputed with him saying . . ." For comments, see Metzger, *Textual Commentary,* pp. 337-38.

[28]Explanations for "place" include (1) that Luke simply did not know or have any way of finding out; (2) another house in Jerusalem; (3) that he withdrew from the territories of Herod's reign to some safe place; (4) Antioch; (5) Rome; (6) Asia Minor; (7) that Acts 12:17 should precede Paul's earlier missionary tour, so that the "places" are Lydda, Joppa and Caesarea; (8) that the word implies Peter's heavenly abode. The "he" in Acts 12:19 refers to Herod and not Peter going to Caesarea. For some specialized bibliography see Bruce, *Acts*, p. 239 n. 22.

[29]Unless quoting from a text, I will use the name *Paul* to refer to the apostle even before Luke changes it in Acts 13:9: "But Saul, also known as Paul." This probably is Luke's way of saying that the Roman *cognomen* is more appropriate for Paul's ministry in the Greco-Roman world (a better theory than that which claims that Luke borrowed it from the name of the proconsul, Sergius Paulus, in Acts 13:7). As a Roman citizen, "Paul would have had three names—*praenomen, nomen gentile,* and *cognomen*—of which Paullus was his *cognomen.* It is probably a mere coincidence that Luke should first designate him by his Roman name in a context where another Paullus figures. The apostle's *praenomen* and *nomen gentile* have, unfortunately, not been preserved; the *nomen gentile* would probably have given some indication of the circumstances in which his family acquired Roman citizenship" (Bruce, *Acts,* p. 249 n. 25).

of the persecuted fugitives from Jerusalem). After a brief preaching mission (Acts 9:20-22) Paul escaped from Jewish opponents in Damascus (Acts 9:23-25) and made a hasty trip to Jerusalem, where he met Barnabas and other "disciples" (Acts 9:26-27). Here a brief theological confrontation with certain Hellenists generated enough danger to his life that he was sent from Jerusalem to Caesarea and then off to his hometown of Tarsus (Acts 9:28-30). From Luke's account, one has no way of knowing how many years elapsed between these events.

Instead of narrating what Paul did in Tarsus, Luke jumps ahead to report that Barnabas summoned him to Antioch (Acts 11:25-26), where they served the church together "for an entire year" (Acts 11:26), made a quick trip with a famine-relief offering to "believers in Judea" (Acts 11:27-30) and then returned to Antioch with John Mark (Acts 12:25). The rest of Acts focuses on the missionary journey of Paul and Barnabas to Cyprus and the southern regions of Asia Minor (Acts 13:1—14:28), Paul's role in the Jerusalem Council (15:1-35), his Aegean ministry (Acts 15:36—20:38), his final return to Jerusalem (Acts 21:1-26), his arrest in Jerusalem and trial in Caesarea (Acts 21:27—26:32) and his final voyage to Rome for imprisonment and trial (Acts 27:1—28:31).

Although one wishes that Luke had provided more details about Paul's ministry and the expansion of the church, apparently such information did not fall within the author's purpose. The reader's frustration, however, is compounded when we compare Acts with additional information in Paul's letters, particularly Galatians. Here Paul refers to certain events following his conversion, such as three years in Damascus and the regions of Arabia (Gal 1:17), a quick fifteen-day visit to Cephas and James in Jerusalem (Gal 1:18) and then a sojourn into "the regions of Syria and Cilicia" (Gal 1:21). Fourteen years elapsed before Paul returned to Jerusalem to participate in the Jerusalem Council (Gal 2:1-14; see Acts 15:1-35).[30]

---

[30]For further reading on Pauline chronology, see Jürgen Becker, *Paul: Apostle to the Gentiles* (Louisville: Westminster John Knox, 1993), esp. ch. 2, "Chronological Questions on the Life of the Apostle," pp. 17-32; Raymond E. Brown, *An Introduction to the New Testament* (New York: Doubleday, 1997), pp. 428-37; Hengel and Schwemer, *Paul Between Damascus and Antioch*, pp. xi-xiv; Robert A. Jewett, *A Chronology of Paul's Life* (Philadelphia: Fortress, 1979); Richard N. Longenecker, *Galatians* (Dallas: Word, 1990), pp. lxxii-lxxxviii; Longenecker, *The Road from Damascus: The Impact of Paul's Conversion on His Life, Thought and Ministry* (Grand Rapids, Mich.: Eerdmans, 1997); Rainer Riesner, *Paul's Early Period: Chronology, Mission Strategy, Theology* (Grand Rapids, Mich.: Eerdmans, 1998), pp. 3-32; Calvin Roetzel, *Paul: The Man and the Myths* (Columbia: University of South Carolina Press, 1998), pp. 179-83; Paul Trebilco, "Itineraries, Travel Plans, Journeys, Apostolic Parousia," *DPL*, pp. 446-56; Ben Witherington III, *The Paul Quest* (Downers Grove, Ill.: InterVarsity Press, 1998), pp. 327-31; Witherington, *Acts*, pp. 81-86, 430-38, 449-49. J. Louis Martyn refers to the production of so many chronologies as almost a "subspecialization" in New Testament scholarship (*Galatians* [New York: Doubleday, 1998], p. 180). This is one of the few commentaries with a reasonably extended discussion on this period of Paul's life (see pp. 180-86).

What is one to make of these so-called silent or hidden years of Paul's life? Most commentators on Galatians 2 or Paul's life are content to note without much elaboration that Paul was moving about the regions of Syria and Cilicia proclaiming the gospel and connecting with existing congregations. In spite of the plethora of "chronologies" attempting to clarify and harmonize Acts and Galatians, little attention was given to Paul's activity between A.D. 36 and 48/49 until the publication of Martin Hengel and Anna Maria Schwemer's *Paul Between Damascus and Antioch: The Unknown Years*[31] (see figure 4).

While some scholars may question certain aspects of the authors' reconstruction of these "unknown years," it is difficult to hide one's enthusiasm for their creativity and erudition. Above all, one comes to appreciate the fact that these were very formative and productive years for the apostle Paul and the early church.

A.D. 33-36 (3 years)	A.D. 36-39/40 (3 years)	A.D. 39/40-48/49 (8-9 years)
Paul's conversion (Acts 9; Gal 1)	Paul's missionary activity in Tarsus and Cilicia (Acts 9:30; 11:25; Gal 1:21)	Paul joins Barnabas in Antioch (one year; Acts 11:26), but with additional activity in the city and the regions of Syria and Phoenicia
Paul in Damascus and Nabatean kingdom (Gal 1:17)		
Paul's brief (fifteen-day) visit to Peter and James in Jerusalem (Acts 9:26-30; Gal 1:18-19)		first missionary journey to Cyprus, Cilicia, southern Galatia (Acts 13:1-14:28)
		journey to Jerusalem for the Apostolic Council

Figure 4. Hengel and Schwemer's chronology of Paul's "unknown years"

Some key insights from Hengel and Schwemer's reconstruction are as follows.

3.3.1. The Damascus Church. The Christian community in Damascus was probably founded by Jewish-Christian Hellenists who had fled Jerusalem during the persecution following Stephen's martyrdom and not by "itinerant" followers of Jesus from Galilee. These Hellenists began their mission in the synagogues, appealing primarily to the Gentiles (God-fearers) who were attracted to Judaism. When Paul resided in Damascus, he met with a group of disciples (Acts 9:19b) and personally began his own ministry of proclamation *(kēryssō)* to Jews

---

[31]This is an impressive tome of 530 pages and 1,584 footnotes. See also Martin Hengel, "The Attitude of Paul to the Law in the Unknown Years Between Damascus and Antioch," in *Paul and the Mosaic Law*, ed. James Dunn (Grand Rapids, Mich.: Eerdmans, 2001). Figure 4 is a personal summary of Hengel and Schwemer's discussion.

and Greek sympathizers (Acts 9:20-22). Eventually these early Christian missionaries formed "small conventicles" of followers where messianic doctrines and Christianity "apart from the law" were taught.[32]

Paul's message was successful and controversial enough to irritate certain Jews into plotting his death (Acts 9:23). Paul escaped only through the resourcefulness of his fellow believers, who lowered him over the wall in a basket (Acts 11:25; 2 Cor 11:32-33). One suspects that Paul had numerous contacts with the Damascus church between A.D. 37 and 47/48 (see Gal 1:17 and discussion below).

3.3.2. Paul's Ministry in Damascus. Paul resided approximately three years in Damascus and Arabia—that is, the Nabatean Kingdom—before he was forced to flee for his safety because of political and religious tensions (Acts 9:23-25; 2 Cor 11:32).[33] His time was spent primarily as an active missionary and not in isolation, solitude and meditation, as sometimes is assumed by commentators (note the use of "proclaiming" *[euangelizetai]* in Gal 1:23). In fact, Hengel and Schwemer suggest that much of Paul's theology regarding God's plan of salvation-history for the Jews under the new covenant was developed in this area so rich in Israel's history.[34] In Damascus, Paul preached in the synagogues with the hope of reaching his own people with the gospel, even though it became apparent that most of his success was with the God-fearers (Gentiles) in the synagogues.

3.3.3. Paul in Jerusalem. Paul's brief fifteen-day visit to Jerusalem, where he conferred with Peter and James (Gal 1:18-20; cf. Acts 9:26-30 for a slightly different version), was a significant event because "The 'missionary loner' now wanted to make contact with the head of the group of the Twelve and the spokesman of the young Jesus community in the Holy City."[35] Although this visit was an opportunity to become personally acquainted with these two apostles, it primarily enabled Paul to gather valuable information about Jesus and the significance of his life, teaching and death. Jesus stood "at the centre of the conversations," and it is quite possible that some of the traditions Paul "received" and later "handed on" to his communities (see, e.g., 1 Cor 11:23-25; 15:3-9; 1 Thess 1—5) came from this visit.[36] The

---

[32]Hengel and Schwemer, *Paul Between Damascus and Antioch,* pp. 85-88.

[33]For discussion on Arabia/the Nabatean Kingdom, see ibid., pp. 106-26.

[34]Ibid., pp. 110-26.

[35]Ibid., p. 133.

[36]Ibid., p. 147. There is no doubt that a significant amount of Paul's knowledge about the Christian faith and life came from fellow believers in worshiping communities that he visited. Paul became a student of the faith before he became a teacher of the faith: "We need to remember that during Paul's formative years as a Christian—and even after—he was part of a worshipping and teaching church. His contacts with the believers in Damascus, Tarsus, Antioch and Jerusalem exposed him to the ideas and practices of early Christianity. Thus it was natural that as an apostle of Christ he would accept such traditions and pass them on through his teaching and preaching" (Patzia, *Making of the New Testament,* p. 74).

brevity of time should not detract from its significance in the formation of Paul's theology, which eventually would find fuller expression in his letters.

3.3.4. Paul in Tarsus. Luke's silence about Paul's stay in Tarsus is puzzling, and we simply have to accept the fact that either Luke did not have any information, did not consider it necessary or expected the reader to presuppose the obvious, namely, that Paul certainly proclaimed the gospel in his hometown of Tarsus and the region of Cilicia for three years (A.D. 36-38/40). Through Paul's preaching, Christian communities were established in Tarsus, neighboring cities and the surrounding areas. Most of these Christian communities consisted of converted Jews or Gentiles (God-fearers) who began their religious quest in the synagogues.[37]

The significance of Hengel and Schwemer's account is twofold: first, it reminds us that Paul was actively engaged in mission after his conversion and did not merely sit around waiting for another heavenly vision. His success in Tarsus may have been the main reason Barnabas felt that he was just the right person for the new challenge in Antioch; second, we can appreciate the fact that Paul's missionary activity began before his call to Antioch, his first visit to Asia Minor with Barnabas and further expansion around the Aegean.[38] These six years were exceedingly significant for the emergence of the church as well as for Paul's theological development and maturity.

3.4. The Church in Antioch (Acts 11:19—13:3; Gal 2)

> Now those who were scattered because of the persecution that took place over Stephen traveled as far as Phoenicia, Cyprus, and Antioch, and they spoke the word to no one except Jews. But among them were some men of Cyprus and Cyrene who, on coming to Antioch, spoke to the Hellenists also, proclaiming the Lord Jesus. (Acts 11:19-20)

Mention of "those who were scattered" refers back to the persecution of believers in Acts 8:1 following Stephen's martyrdom. The arrival of the Christian Hellenists in Antioch was roughly concurrent with Paul's ministry in Tarsus, that is, around A.D. 36.

Phoenicia, the coastal territory between Samaria and Syria, includes such important cities as Ptolemais (Acco), Tyre and Sidon. Since Jesus had contact with the people of this region during his ministry (Mt 15:21; Mk 3:8; 7:24, 31; Lk 6:17), one would assume that some individuals remembered his words and deeds, though

---

[37]Hegel and Schwemer, *Paul Between Damascus and Antioch,* pp. 171-72.

[38]Hengel and Schwemer note that there was a continuous Christian presence in Tarsus, even though the city "vanishes from Christian missionary history for about 200 years" (ibid., pp. 156-57). Note Eusebius's reference to Helenus, bishop of Tarsus in Cilicia, around A.D. 250 (*Hist. Eccl.* 6.46.3).

it exceeds the evidence to think of a remnant "Jesus movement" in this region.

There is nothing at this stage in the narrative of Acts to indicate where and who established these churches. All we know is that later, when Paul, Barnabas and other delegates journeyed to the Jerusalem Council, they traveled through Phoenicia, "reported the conversion of the Gentiles, and brought great joy to all the believers" in this region (Acts 15:3). When Paul returned to this area on his way to Jerusalem near the end of his ministry, he spent seven days with disciples in Tyre (Acts 21:3-4) and one day with believers in Ptolemais (Acts 21:7). One gets the impression that there was a rather substantial, closely knit and concerned community of believers in Tyre (see Acts 21:4-6).

The island of Cyprus lies approximately sixty miles off the coast of Syria. Although not particularly large (one hundred miles long and sixty miles wide), it became a major seafaring commercial center because of its rich copper deposits. Barnabas, an early convert to Christianity, leader of the church in Jerusalem and later missionary companion of Paul, was a native of Cyprus (Acts 4:36), as were some other early disciples (Acts 11:20; 21:16). Paul and Barnabas traveled across the island (from Salamis to Paphos) on their first missionary journey (Acts 13:4-13). After the split between Paul and Barnabas over John Mark, Barnabas and John Mark returned to the island (Acts 15:36-40). We do not know whether Mnason, "an early disciple" from Cyprus now living in or near Caesarea, became a believer in his homeland or in Judea (Acts 21:16). Cyrenian believers are also mentioned in Antioch (Acts 11:20; 13:1), although we have no early records of Christian communities there (see Acts 2:10; 6:9; cf. Mk 15:21 and par.).[39]

One wishes Luke had said more about the churches that were started in these as well as other areas of the Roman Empire. Martin Hengel, among others, reminds us that we do not hear anything from Luke "about the founding of communities in Egypt, Cyrenaica, northern and eastern Asia Minor, Armenia, East Syria, the Parthian kingdom or Italy."[40] Either Luke was unaware of certain developments, or he realized that it was humanly impossible to write a complete history of the church. However, it is more likely that Luke focused on events that met the theological and apologetic criteria for which he was writing. It certainly appears that "all roads lead to Paul" at this point; that is, Luke

---

[39]Alanna Nobbs, "Cyprus," in *The Book of Acts in Its Graeco-Roman Setting,* ed. David W. J. Gill and Conrad Gempf, BAFCS 2 (Grand Rapids, Mich.: Eerdmans, 1994), pp. 279-89.

[40]Martin Hengel, *Acts and the History of Earliest Christianity,* trans. John Bowden (Philadelphia: Fortress, 1980), p. 109; Hengel and Schwemer, *Paul Between Damascus and Antioch,* pp. 259-60. In the following pages I will limit the discussion of the regions/provinces into which Christianity came to issues that are significant for the spread of the gospel and the founding of the churches. Footnote references will point to literature that can be consulted for additional information.

selected, orchestrated and recorded events that brought Paul back to center stage.

Antioch, the capital city of Syria, was founded by Seleucus I around 300 B.C. and named after his father, Antiochus. Because of its strategic location on the Orontes River, it quickly established itself as a major commercial center. After Rome and Alexandria, it was the third most populous city in the empire (estimates range from 300,000 to 500,000; Josephus *J.W.* 3.2.4 §29).[41] Part of its rich ethnic and cultural diversity included a significant number of Jews.[42]

Apparently many Gentiles were attracted to the Jewish synagogues in Antioch and became either proselytes or God-fearers. Hence Josephus writes: "they [the Jews] were constantly attracting to their religious ceremonies multitudes of Greeks, and these they had in some measure incorporated with themselves" (*J.W.* 7.3.3 §45). Nicolaus, who was elected as one of the Seven, is mentioned as "a proselyte of Antioch" (Acts 6:5). If "Hellenists" means "Greeks" (Acts 11:20), then the "great number [who] became believers and turned to the Lord" (Acts 11:19-21) probably came from this God-fearing group who were attracted to Judaism for a variety of reasons (such as Judaism's belief in monotheism, worship and ethical standards).[43]

The success of the gospel among the Greeks in Antioch caught the attention of the Jerusalem leaders, who quickly dispatched Barnabas to look into the situ-

---

[41]See Raymond E. Brown and John P. Meier, *Antioch and Rome* (New York: Paulist, 1982); Jerome Crowe, *From Jerusalem to Antioch: The Gospel Across Cultures* (Collegeville, Minn.: Liturgical Press, 1997); Irina Levinskaya, "Antioch," in *The Book of Acts in Its Diaspora Setting,* BAFCS 5 (Grand Rapids, Mich.: Eerdmans, 1996), pp. 127-35; Lee Martin McDonald, "Antioch (Syria)," *DNTB,* pp. 34-37; John R. McRay, "Antioch on the Orontes," *DPL,* pp. 23-25; Robyn Tracey, "Syria," in Gill and Gempf, eds., *Graeco-Roman Setting,* pp. 223-78; David John Williams, "Antioch on the Orontes," *DLNTD,* pp. 53-55. All these sources have excellent bibliographical references to more extensive studies on Antioch.

[42]Josephus refers to the Jewish populace several times (*Ant.* 12.3.1 §§119-24; *J.W.* 7.3.3 §43) but does not give a number. Estimates range from 22,000 to 65,000 (see Williams, "Antioch on the Orontes"; McRay, "Antioch on the Orontes"). See also Wayne A. Meeks and Robert A. Wilken, *Jews and Christians in Antioch in the First Four Centuries of the Common Era* (Missoula, Mont.: Scholars Press, 1978), pp. 2-13.

[43]Scholars are divided on the correct reading of the text. *Hellēnistas* normally means "Hellenists" and refers to Greek-speaking Jews or perhaps anyone who used the Greek language. The variant *Hellēnas* refers to Greeks (or Gentiles). *Hellēnistas* has the best textual support, but most commentators feel that the context requires the meaning of "Greeks" to set it apart from "Jews" in Acts 11:19. A later copyist wanted to make sure this was understood by inserting *Hellēnas*. For a brief history of the textual issues, see Metzger, *Textual Commentary,* pp. 340-42. In commentaries, compare Barrett, *Acts,* 1:550-51; Bruce, *Acts,* p. 223; Dunn, *Acts,* p. 154; David J. Williams, *Acts* (Peabody, Mass.: Hendrickson, 1990), p. 207; Witherington, *Acts,* pp. 240-47.

ation.[44] Luke does not state any reason for this, but presumably it fits into his scheme of having all expansion ministries accountable to "the mother church" in some way. Barnabas ("son of encouragement") must have won the respect and confidence of the leaders in Jerusalem in order to be entrusted with this task. Since it was he who had earlier introduced the converted Paul to the apostles (Acts 9:27), one wonders if this is a subtle way for Luke to get him to Antioch and reconnect with Paul, as Acts 11:25-26 indicates.

In addition to the success of the gospel in Antioch (Acts 11:21, 24), several other factors made this an important transition in the life of the church. First, Antioch emerged as the most significant center of Christianity after Jerusalem. In fact, it was the first major city of the ancient world in which Christianity gained a foothold. Here is part of Luke's projection of the spread of the gospel "to the ends of the earth" (Acts 1:8). Christianity moved out of the bosom of the mother church and the surrounding areas of Judea, Samaria and Galilee and became established in a major Hellenistic city. In many ways, this was the first major move in taking the gospel to another culture.[45]

Luke's account is simply the first stage of Antiochene Christianity, involving such personalities as Barnabas, Paul, Peter and James. John Meier, along with other commentators, believes that the second-generation church is mirrored in the Gospel of Matthew. Although not all scholars concur, there are many compelling reasons to connect Matthew's community and Gospel with Antioch.[46] The third generation arose after A.D. 100 and possibly is reflected in the *Didache,* a late first or early second century document, as well as in the letters of Ignatius, bishop of Antioch before his martyrdom in Rome around A.D. 107.[47]

---

[44]On "success" in Antioch, note Luke's phrases: "a great number *[arithmos]* became believers" (Acts 11:21); "a great many people" (*prosetethē ochlos hikanos,* Acts 11:24:); "taught a great many people" (*didaxai ochlon hikanon,* Acts 11:26). Hengel and Schwemer wisely remind us that "all of this did not happen in a few months, but needed time to mature, i.e., some years. Moreover, Luke's indications of success are highly exaggerated—as numbers often are in ancient historians. The number of occasional listeners may, however, have been substantially greater. If there were around one hundred baptized Christians in Antioch after three or four years, that was already quite a lot. There is great uncertainty about the numerical success of the earliest Christian missionaries precisely because of Luke's exaggerated figure, so it is also difficult for us to imagine the reality of these first Gentile Christian communities, which are so alien to us" (*Paul Between Damascus and Antioch,* pp. 203-4).

[45]Hence the significance of Crowe's subtitle: *From Jerusalem to Antioch: The Gospel Across Cultures.*

[46]For a recent, comprehensive discussion, see Donald A. Hagner's introduction in *Matthew 1-13,* WBC (Dallas: Word, 1993), pp. lxv-lxxvii.

[47]See Brown and Meier, *Antioch and Rome,* pp. 45-86; Hengel and Schwemer, *Paul Between Damascus and Antioch,* pp. 21-23. On Ignatius, see Eusebius, *Hist. Eccl.* 3.22; 32.36. Matthew's focus on Peter has led many commentators to suggest that this apostle played a significant role in Antiochene Christianity. According to B. H. Streeter, Peter "is the supreme Rabbi

After the death of Ignatius, Antioch continued to play a significant role in the church even though Syriac Christianity spread and flourished to the eastern parts of the province, such as Edessa. Some important literature emerging from Syria includes Tatian's *Diatessaron,* a late second-century harmony of the Gospels (*dia tessarōn*, literally, "through four," that is, the four Gospels), and the Peshitta, an early Syriac version of the Bible.[48] These events testify to a vibrant church in Antioch during the first century.

Second, early Christianity in Antioch represented a major phase in the spread of the gospel to the Gentiles. As we saw, this movement began earlier on a smaller scale through the missionary activity of Philip and Peter in the coastal regions and of Paul in Syria and Cilicia before he came to Antioch. However, ministry in Antioch did not involve the deliberate shift in missionary strategy (taking the gospel exclusively to Gentiles) that characterizes Paul's later activity (see Acts 9:15; 13:46; 18:6; 22:21; 26:20; 28:28; Rom 11:13; 15:16; Gal 2:8-9; Eph 3:8).

Paul and Barnabas continued their witness in the synagogues of Antioch, reaching both Jews and Gentile sympathizers (God-fearers) with the gospel. "The new development which Antioch brought," according to Hengel and Schwemer, is "that for the first time the gospel was preached in a real metropolis, with numerous synagogues, not least on the periphery of the city and in its suburbs."[49] These authors also speculate that Greek and Jewish believers probably moved out of the synagogues and formed their own "house communities" or "messianic conventicles," not unlike those in centers such as Tarsus and Rome.[50] Here they were at liberty to develop their own identity and to worship and promote a gospel "free from the law," which soon led to conflicts within the early church (see below and 3.10.2).

---

in whom resides the final interpretation . . . of the New Law given to the New Israel . . . by Christ" (*The Four Gospels* [London: Macmillan, 1961], p. 515). No wonder the church in Antioch eventually claimed Peter as it first bishop.

[48]David Bundy, "Christianity in Syria," *ABD* 1:970-79; Everett F. Harrison, *The Apostolic Church* (Grand Rapids, Mich.: Eerdmans, 1985), pp. 183-89; Scott W. Sunquist, "Syria, Syrian Christianity," *DLNTD*, pp. 1150-53. On textual issues, Bruce M. Metzger, *The Early Versions of the New Testament* (Oxford: Clarendon, 1977), esp. pp. 3-98.

[49]Hengel and Schwemer, *Paul Between Damascus and Antioch,* p. 196.

[50]Ibid., pp. 196-97. Jürgen Becker writes, "Since the boundary between the God-fearers and those outside the synagogue was fluid, it happened in Antioch—no doubt for the first time in early Christianity—that members of the Christian church, who until then were always a group within the synagogal fellowship, introduced the Christian faith to residents of the city who previously had not even had a loose relationship with Judaism. Thus God-fearers who had become Christians could have approached their relatives about their new faith or perhaps exploited occupational contacts. If God-fearers could be baptized without being first circumcised, then the uncircumcised in general could also be baptized, especially if they also accepted the part of the Christian message that Jews did not need to accept anew, that is, if they abandoned the pagan cult and adopted Jewish-Christian monotheism (1 Thess 1:9) and thus assimilated themselves to the God-fearers known to the synagogue" (*Paul,* p. 86).

Third, it was in Antioch "that the disciples were first called 'Christians'" (Acts 11:26). Although some dispute remains about certain aspects of the term Christian, a fair consensus exists on the following: (1) the precise origin and meaning of Christian is obscure and may precede Luke's use here; (2) *Christianous* is a Latin formation; (3) this was not a self-designation but was given by outsiders who observed that the believers were followers/adherents of Christ, "Christus-people," who differed from Jews in worship, theology and attitude toward the law; (4) believers may have referred to themselves as Christians before it was recorded in the second century by Ignatius (cf. Ign. *Eph.* 11.2; Ign. *Rom.* 3.2; Ign. *Magn.* 3.4; Ign. *Pol.* 7.3; Ignatius uses "Christianity" in Ign. *Rom.* 3.3; Ign. *Phil.* 6.1; Ign. *Magn.* 10.3). Similarly, the other two uses in the New Testament are not self-designations but attributed to those who follow Christ (Acts 26:28; 1 Pet 4:16); and (5) although the term distinguished disciples from unbelievers (Jews and Gentiles), it was not intended or used as an ethnic label. It was more a sociological term describing how believers were perceived, much like other terms, such as disciples, believers, brothers, saints, followers of "the Way," and so forth.

A fourth factor that made this an important transition in the life of the church was Paul's introduction to believers in the Antioch church. Barnabas, who met Paul in Jerusalem shortly after his conversion (Acts 9:27-30), remembered that Paul had returned to Tarsus (Acts 9:30). It is possible that Barnabas and Paul were in contact with each other during this time so that Barnabas was well aware of Paul's ministry.[51] But Barnabas needed assistance with the rapidly growing Christian community (house churches) in Antioch. This city, with its large ethnic mix, would be an ideal place for this converted Hellenistic Jew and theologian.

Luke's comment that Barnabas and Paul worked together for "an entire year" (Acts 11:26) is misleading because their association with each other in Antioch and the regions of Syria and Phoenicia, and their journey to Cyprus and southern Asia Minor (Acts 13:1—14:28), actually spanned eight to nine years (A.D. 39/40-48).[52] The litany of hardships recorded in 2 Corinthians 11:23-29 could include some of the injustices and persecutions Paul experienced during this time, especially the beatings with lashes and rods by the Jews (2 Cor 11:24-25). Adolf Schlatter even suspects that some of the "many" shipwrecks may have

---

[51]Hengel and Schwemer, *Paul Between Damascus and Antioch,* p. 178.
[52]Thus Hengel and Schwemer refer to the one-year as "enigmatic," suggesting that Luke wanted to indicate the interval before the visit of Agabus and subsequent visit of Paul and Barnabas to Jerusalem. After one year elapsed, Paul and Barnabas visited other cities in northern Syria and founded communities there (*Paul Between Damascus and Antioch,* pp. 222-23).

occurred off the coast of Syria between Tarsus and Antioch.[53]

Fifth, the church leadership at this point consisted of prophets and teachers. The gift of prophecy was part of the apostolic church, so it is not surprising to see prophets here. Unfortunately, we do not know why or how many came from Jerusalem to Antioch, because Luke singles out only one, Agabus, and records his prediction of the famine in Judea (Acts 11:28). The phrase, "Agabus stood up," suggests that the prophecy probably was given within the context of a gathering of believers, as further described in Acts 13:2-3.

Teaching was an important function of Barnabas and Paul's one-year ministry with the believers in Antioch (Acts 11:26). Later Luke indicates a kind of prophetic and teaching office within the church (Acts 13:1). Since there does not appear to be any distinction between the two, it is reasonable to assume that the five individuals mentioned, including Barnabas and Paul, were recognized as possessing both gifts. There is no reason why the same person could not prophesy and teach. Here C. K. Barrett astutely notes that "the distinction between the two may have been a matter of manner rather than content."[54] The other three persons (Simeon, Lucius and Manaen) illustrate the interesting mix of individuals who were attracted to Christianity and became leaders in the church. After a period of prophecy, fasting and prayer, Barnabas and Paul were commissioned for a missionary journey that took them into many previously unevangelized areas of Asia Minor.

Sixth, Antioch was the place where a serious theological controversy developed in the church over the authority of the Jewish law for the Gentiles. Initially, this was not a problem for leaders of the Jerusalem church, for when they heard about the success of the gospel in Antioch following Stephen's martyrdom, they sent Barnabas to monitor the events and were satisfied to leave him there to proclaim the gospel (Acts 11:19-30). It appears that the Gentiles (God-fearers) who became believers were not numerically large enough or separated from the synagogue completely enough to alarm the church in Jerusalem.

However, a number of significant events happened in subsequent years (c. A.D. 33-48/49) to change the situation. Paul joined Barnabas in Antioch, and for eight to nine years they succeeded in winning Gentiles to the faith and forming Christian communities in such places as Syria, Cyprus, Cilicia and Galatia—communities not attached to the synagogue. In essence, Paul was preaching a "law-free" gospel, insisting that salvation/justification was based on "faith in

---

[53]Adolf Schlatter, *The Church in the New Testament Period,* trans. Paul P. Levertoff (London: SPCK, 1955), p. 111.

[54]Barrett, *Acts,* 1:602. This appears to be the case with Judas and Silas in Jerusalem, who are recognized as "leaders" (*hēgoumenous,* Acts 15:22; from Greek *hēgeomai,* "to lead, rule") as well as "prophets" (Acts 15:32).

Jesus Christ" and not "works of the law" (Gal 2:16-17). Gentiles, claimed Paul, do not come to faith in Christ through the law. They also are not required to follow Jewish customs.

The success of Paul and Barnabas's ministry to Gentiles and the growth of Gentile churches created problems. First, some zealous Jewish Christians (Judaizers) came to Antioch and disturbed the believers by insisting that Gentiles had to follow the law of Moses (Acts 15:1-2: "Unless you are circumcised according to the custom of Moses, you cannot be saved"). Second, success with the Gentiles precipitated the Apostolic Council in Jerusalem around A.D. 48 to discuss such issues in more detail. Paul and Barnabas traveled to Jerusalem for this meeting to represent their views before such apostolic leaders as Peter, James and the elders of the assembly. After a lengthy debate in which all parties had an opportunity to present their views (Acts 15:1-18; see Gal 2:1-10), the council endorsed Paul's gospel to the Gentiles but requested that they respect certain Jewish customs and food laws (Acts 15:19-21). This decision was recorded in a letter and supposedly delivered to the church in Antioch (Acts 15:22-35; Paul does not mention the letter in Galatians, which was written c. A.D. 54-55).

Paul's account of the Apostolic Council in Galatians 2:1-14 sheds more light on the event. He refers to "false believers secretly brought in" to "spy" on and disrupt the proceedings (Gal 2:4-5; these may be the believers whom Luke identifies as the Pharisees who promoted circumcision and obedience to the law of Moses in Acts 15:5). Paul also refers to another time when Peter and representatives of James (Gal 2:12) visited Antioch and were caught up in a controversy over table fellowship between Jewish and Gentile believers. When Peter and Barnabas withdrew from this fellowship because they feared judgment from the "circumcision faction" (Gal 2:12), Paul chastised them for their duplicity and hypocrisy (Gal 2:13-14).

One wonders whether this encounter with Barnabas played into Paul's decision to break their partnership before launching into the Aegean mission. Luke only refers to the sharp disagreement between Paul and Barnabas over John Mark. Paul did not want this former deserter as a missionary colleague (Acts 15:36-40). However, he certainly would not have wanted Barnabas either unless Barnabas could fully endorse and participate in Paul's mission to the Gentiles.

It is interesting to note that from this point on, Antioch did not play any significant role in Paul's life, even though Luke records a "token" stopover in Antioch several years later (Acts 18:22). Apart from the discussion in Galatians 2, Antioch is not mentioned again, nor does it appear in any of Paul's other letters. This may simply imply that Paul's work in that area was completed and that he wanted to move into new, unevangelized territory.

This does not mean that there was a serious split between Jerusalem and Antioch that divided the early church. It is true that differences, controversies and practices varied from place to place and between Jewish and Gentile Christians, but the church remained united in its confession of the one Lord Jesus Christ and the truth of the gospel delivered by the apostles and prophets. It was content to celebrate its unity in the midst of diversity (see 3.10). The most profound expression of this unity emerges later in the letter to the Ephesians.

Although we jumped ahead in the narrative to discuss the controversies in Antioch and the Jerusalem Council, we need to return to Acts 13:4, where Luke narrates how the gospel was taken to other regions of the world (see Acts 1:8). But there is more to the transition from Syria to Asia Minor than geographical expansion. C. K. Barrett expresses Luke's plans well in his comments on this section:

> This short paragraph marks a major departure in Luke's story. Up to this point, contacts with Gentiles (one might almost say, missionary activity in general) have been almost fortuitous. Philip was dispatched along an unusual road not knowing that he would encounter an Ethiopian eunuch reading Scripture; Peter was surprised by the gift of the Holy Spirit to an uncircumcised and unbaptized Gentile; the missionaries to Antioch did not set out with the intention of evangelizing Gentiles. Here, however, though the initiative is still ascribed to the Holy Spirit (v. 2), an extensive evangelistic journey into territory in no sense properly Jewish (though there was a Jewish element in the population, as there was in most parts of the empire) is deliberately planned, and two associates of the local church are commissioned to execute it.[55]

We now turn to the geographical expansion traditionally referred to as Paul's first missionary journey.[56]

3.5. The Mission of Paul and Barnabas (Acts 13:4—14:28)

On their way to Asia Minor, Paul and Barnabas made a brief missionary excursion to the island of Cyprus. Since Barnabas was a Cypriot (Acts 4:36), it seems natural that he desired to evangelize his native land. Luke records contact in Salamis and Paphos, the two largest cities and important seaports. The land journey of approximately 150 miles "through the whole island" (Acts 13:6) no doubt provided other opportunities to proclaim the gospel, though nothing is recorded in Acts. The significant events in this narrative include (1) the encounter with the Jewish magician Bar-Jesus/Elymas (see 1.2.4); (2) the con-

---

[55]Barrett, *Acts,* 1:598-99; see also 2:ci-civ.

[56]Raymond E. Brown rightly observes that neither Luke nor Paul thought of specific missionary journeys, nor would they know what we are talking about today. Rather, these terms "*are only a convenient classification developed by students of Acts*" (*Introduction to the New Testament,* p. 431, emphasis in original).

version of Sergius Paulus, the Roman proconsul; and (3) Luke's identification and use of Saul's Roman name, Paul. Some years later Barnabas and John Mark returned to Cyprus, where they possibly engaged in further evangelization and follow-up work (Acts 15:39).

Map 2. Paul and Barnabas's mission

In the ancient world Asia was the name given to modern-day Asia Minor—the entire peninsula bound by the Black Sea on the north, the Aegean Sea on the west, the Mediterranean Sea on the south and Syria on the east (also known as Anatolia, i.e., modern Turkey)—and to a province within that area (along the Aegean coast). At times there is some ambiguity with the two terms in Acts, leaving the reader wondering whether Luke meant the province or the entire area (see Acts 19:27; 21:27; 24:19; 2 Cor 1:8). Other provinces included Cappadocia, Cilicia, Galatia, Lycia, Pamphylia and Bithynia-Pontus.

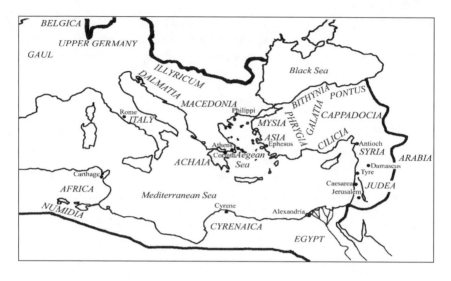

Map 3. Roman provinces

On this journey Paul and Barnabas covered certain regions of the provinces of Galatia, Pamphylia and Pisidia, including such major cities as Perga, Pisidian Antioch, Iconium, Lystra, Derbe and Attalia. This mission probably took place during A.D. 47/48. There were several important components to this early missionary thrust.

First, Paul visited the synagogues (there is no mention of synagogues in Lystra and Derbe), where he had opportunities to proclaim the gospel to Diaspora Jews and Gentile sympathizers ("[those] who fear God," Acts 13:16; "devout converts to Judaism," Acts 13:43). The synagogal sermon in Pisidian Antioch, which bears striking similarities to Peter's sermon in Jerusalem, resulted in the general rejection of the gospel by the Jews and acceptance by the Gentiles. The statement "we are now turning to the Gentiles" (Acts 13:46) is repeated in Acts18:6 (see also Acts 28:23-28).

Second, this was Paul's first recorded missionary encounter with pagan ideas about God and local religion (see 1.2.4). Although the inhabitants of Lystra and Derbe initially were attracted to and awed by a healing miracle, their reaction enabled Paul and Barnabas to clarify their own humanity and to call upon the listeners to abandon their idolatry ("these worthless things," Acts 14:15) and to turn to the living God who created all things.

Third, the proclamation of the gospel allowed Paul and Barnabas to establish churches in this area of the empire. Although it is difficult to determine the success of the mission, one must take Luke's summary statement in Acts 13:49 seriously ("the word of the Lord spread throughout the region"), implying that there were "disciples" in Lystra and in Derbe (Acts 14:20-21).

Fourth, Paul's actions revealed his pastoral care for new converts and churches. Instead of proceeding to Tarsus from Derbe, Paul and Barnabas decided to retrace their steps for the purpose of strengthening, encouraging and consolidating the churches (see also Acts 15:36). In order to ensure stability in leadership, Paul appointed "elders" *(presbyteroi)* in each congregation. Then the mission ended with the journey back to the "sending church" in Antioch, where Paul and Barnabas reported their success among the Gentiles (Acts 14:26-28).

Fifth, this mission took a physical toll on Paul. The persecutions (Acts 13:50) and stoning to the point of death (Acts 14:19) were traumatic experiences, so much so that they are mentioned again in 2 Timothy 3:10-11: "Now you have observed my teaching, my conduct, my aim in life, my faith, my patience, my love, my steadfastness, my persecutions and suffering the things that happened to me in Antioch, Iconium, and Lystra. What persecutions I endured!"

It also is likely that the litany of hardships recorded in 2 Corinthians 11:23-29 includes experiences from this mission, especially danger from "rivers" and "bandits" (2 Cor 11:26). Many commentators refer to the floods and robbers of the Pisidian highlands and the physical rigor of traversing some very rough terrain.[57] William Ramsay suspects that Paul's "physical infirmity" (Gal 4:13) may have been malaria, caught in the low-lying territory near Perga.[58] Others suggest that the infirmity was some kind of eye affliction (myopia) that affected Paul's ministry (Gal 4:15; 6:11),[59] especially in Galatia.[60]

3.6. Revisiting the Churches of Asia Minor (Acts 15:36—16:6)

Approximately one year expired between Paul and Barnabas's return to Antioch from their missionary journey in Asia Minor (14:21-28) and their decision to revisit these

---

[57]Williams, *Acts,* pp. 230-31; Riesner, *Paul's Early Period,* pp. 281-86.

[58]William Ramsay, *St. Paul the Traveler and Roman Citizen* (New York: Putnam, 1904), pp. 94-97.

[59]So Dunn, *Acts,* p. 179: "The best guess we can hazard is that Paul had some serious ailment, affecting particularly his eyes (Gal. 4.13-15), which made it necessary for him to abandon the heat of the coastal plain for the cooler air of the high country."

[60]Scholars who hold to the "Southern Galatian theory" believe that Paul wrote Galatians to the churches founded during this mission. For arguments on the Galatian church(es), see most introductions to the New Testament or commentaries on Galatians. See also G. Walter Hansen, "Galatia," in Gill and Gempf, eds., *Graeco-Roman Setting,* pp. 377-96.

churches (Acts 15:36).[61] During this interim time, they were active in the church as teachers proclaiming "the word of the Lord" (Acts 15:35). Their time in Antioch was interrupted by participation in the Apostolic Council (Acts 15:1-35), where the legitimacy of Paul's mission to the Gentiles was the main item on the agenda.

Acts 15:36 implies that Paul had nothing more in mind than revisiting and strengthening (Acts 15:41) the churches founded in Asia Minor during his earlier mission with Barnabas. The call to a mission beyond that region, into Europe, came by way of a miraculous vision (Acts 16:6-10). That vision would occupy the next seven to eight years of Paul's life (approximately 49/50-57/58), taking him to provinces and cities around the Aegean Sea (Acts 16:11—20:38).

Readers of Acts are not prepared for the sudden turn in Paul and Barnabas's relationship, a partnership of eight to nine years (39/40-48/49). The dispute, or sharp disagreement (Acts 15:39), over the suitability of including John Mark on the journey led to a dissolution of the partnership: Barnabas took John Mark and returned to Cyprus; Paul selected Silas, a leader and prophet from Jerusalem who, along with Judas, had accompanied Paul and Barnabas back to Antioch from the Jerusalem Council (Acts 15:22, 32). Paul probably became acquainted with Silas along the way and observed Silas's brief ministry in Antioch (Acts 15:32: "Judas and Silas, who were themselves prophets, said much to encourage and strengthen the believers").

On the basis of Galatians 2:13, one suspects that Paul and Barnabas also had strong theological differences regarding Paul's law-free gospel and table fellowship with Gentiles ("even Barnabas was led astray by their hypocrisy"). Apart from a brief and perhaps token stopover in Antioch later in his ministry, Paul no longer had any meaningful contact with the church. Nor does he mention Antioch in any of his letters. Many scholars suspect that he may have severed his relations with the church because, under pressure from Jerusalem, they reverted to a more Jewish and legalistic version of the gospel.[62]

On this mission Paul also added another member to his team. Timothy, a resident of Lystra, was a Jew by birth ("the son of a Jewish woman," Acts 16:1) and a believer from some previous contact with the gospel. One wonders if Paul and Barnabas had a role in his conversion as well as those of Timothy's mother and grandmother (see 2 Tim 1:5: "a faith that lived first in your grandmother Lois and your mother Eunice"). Paul's choice of Timothy began a long and affectionate relationship between the two that ended only

---

[61]Most chronologies place this journey 47-48, the Jerusalem Council 48-49 and the next journey 49-50/52.

[62]See, e.g., Dunn, _Acts,_ pp. 212-13. Further evaluation of this incident can be found in E. P. Sanders, "Jewish Association with Gentiles and Galatians 2:11-14," in _Studies in Paul and John,_ ed. Robert T. Fortuna and Beverly R. Gaventa (Nashville: Abingdon, 1990), pp. 170-88.

at Paul's death (1 Cor 4:17; Phil 2:22; 1 Tim 1:2).

Since Paul was prevented by the Holy Spirit from evangelizing in Asia (Acts 16:6), he moved west and then northward through the regions of Phrygia and Galatia. Although scholars dispute the location of these territories, as well as the correct translation of the Greek "through the region of Phrygia and Galatia" *(tēn Phrygian kai Galatikēn chōran)*,[63] it is reasonable to assume that "Phrygian-Galatia" is meant and not the northern regions of Galatia.[64]

The journey now took Paul to Mysia, a region in northwest Asia Minor. No reasons are given why the "Spirit of Jesus" prevented Paul from moving northward to Bithynia—and possibly into Pontus as well. Surely it is enough to be directed by the Spirit. However, suggestions that Paul wanted to preach only in unevangelized areas and "not build on someone else's foundation" (Rom 15:20) may also be a factor, since we know of earlier Jewish-Christian churches in Pontus.[65] Paul likely went to Troas because it was the main seaport for travel from Asia to Macedonia. Although Luke is silent here, it is conceivable that Paul founded a church at Troas (see Acts 20:6-12; 2 Cor 2:12-13; 2 Tim 4:13). The narrative describing the journey from Troas to Philippi takes on a personal flavor with the first of several "we" passages in Acts, implying that Luke personally accompanied Paul and, for the first time, was an eyewitness to the story.[66]

3.7. The Aegean Mission (Acts 16:11—20:38)

Rather than divide the next seven to eight years of Paul's life into two separate missionary journeys (Acts 15:36—18:18; 18:23—21:16), it seems better to speak of Paul's Aegean mission. Earlier I noted Raymond E. Brown's comment on the artificiality of these divisions. James Dunn is even more emphatic when he notes that the divisions are based on a "misperception and a misnomer." "What we actually have," continues Dunn:

> is the account of a sustained mission around the coasts of the Aegean Sea. Luke presents it as a coherent and integrated unit. It has a clear beginning: the mission was entered upon with all the marks of divine prompting ([Acts]16:6-9). And it has a clear end: that period of mission, as indeed Paul's whole period of unrestrained

---

[63]Barrett, *Acts,* 2:766-70; Riesner, *Paul's Early Period,* pp. 281-91. Note the references to Galatia and Phrygia (Acts 18:23) and the "interior regions" (Acts 19:1), all probably in southern Galatia and Asia.

[64]So Riesner, *Paul's Early Period,* p. 285; G. Walter Hansen, "Galatia," p. 378.

[65]Riesner (*Paul's Early Period,* pp. 291-92) notes the following evidence: pilgrims from Pontus were in Jerusalem at Pentecost; Aquila was from Pontus (Acts 18:2); the churches in the "Dispersion" (1 Pet 1:1) could have been founded by an earlier (?) Petrine mission; and Pliny the Younger's reference in *Ep.* 10.96.

[66]See Acts commentaries for discussion of the "we" passages. A useful summary is available in Witherington, *Acts,* pp. 480-86.

missionary work, is climaxed and concluded with a speech which has all the appearance of Paul's last will and testimony ([Acts] 20:18-35).[67]

Tied into Dunn's reasoning is the separation of Paul from the Antiochene community and the likelihood that he considered himself an independent missionary.

3.7.1. The Church in Philippi (Acts 16:11-40; Phil 1—4).

Luke makes two significant comments about Philippi, a city originally built and fortified by Philip of Macedon around 358 B.C.: it was a "leading city of the district of Macedonia" and "a Roman colony" (Acts 16:12). Its location on the Egnatian road (_via Egnatia_), the main east-west route across Macedonia connecting Rome and the eastern provinces, made it an important center for military and commercial enterprises.

Map 4. Paul's Aegean mission

[67]Dunn, _Acts,_ p. 212.

The formation of the Christian community in Philippi is recorded in three stages. First, in the absence of a synagogue, Paul discovered a "place of prayer" *(proseuchēn)* by the River Gangites, where a number of women gathered, probably to worship, pray and fellowship (Acts 16:13, 16). Since it appears that Philippi did not have a permanent synagogue, it is doubtful that they possessed scrolls of the Law and Prophets to read. Some of the leadership for this gathering may have come from Lydia, a businesswoman from Thyatira, who is identified not only for her wealth and social status but as a "worshiper of God" *(sebomenē ton theon*, a Gentile who worshiped the biblical God). As a result of Paul's teaching, Lydia was converted ("opened her heart" to the gospel) and was baptized, along with her household, by Paul. As far as we know, she was the first convert in Europe. Presumably Paul and Silas met with this group several times and Lydia was not the only woman to embrace the gospel. Perhaps Euodia and Syntyche were participants in this prayer group as well (Phil 4:2).

The second stage in the formation of a Christian community in Philippi involved an encounter with a slave girl with a gift of "fortune-telling," which earned her owners considerable money (Acts 16:16-21; see 1.2.4). Paul exorcised her evil spirit, and thus a pagan religious practice was subordinated to the Most High God of Christianity. In this pagan context, the "Most High God" probably referred to Zeus, the most important god of the Greek pantheon. Anger and hatred against Paul and Silas erupted when the owners of the slave girl realized that their source of revenue had just disappeared. Because of their false accusations and general prejudice, Paul and Silas were severely beaten with rods and imprisoned (Acts 16:19-23).

The imprisonment of Paul and Silas led to the third stage in the formation of a Philippian Christian community (Acts 16:25-39). The most striking events were the disposition of Paul and Silas, "praying and singing hymns" (Acts 16:25), and an odd earthquake. The latter was strong enough to loosen the prisoners' chains, open the cells and partially destroy the building yet did not injure any of the prisoners. Just as strange, for unknown reasons but to the jailer's relief, the prisoners decided not to bolt for freedom. The jailer was so overcome by these events that he requested spiritual assistance from Paul and Silas, asking, "Sirs, what must I do to be saved?" (Acts 16:30).

One suspects that there is more to the story than is recorded. The jailer simply may have been frightened by the quake and realized that his two prisoners had some divine power. On the other hand, he may have been listening to the prayers and songs and discussed Christianity with Paul and Silas earlier. In either case, the missionaries did not question his sincerity but responded (in Luke's conversion language) with the basic message or formula of belief and baptism (see Acts 2:38), stating, "Believe on the Lord Jesus, and you will be saved" (Acts 16:31, 34). This was followed by another household baptism.

At this point, the magistrates became embarrassed and concerned that they had unlawfully beaten and imprisoned Roman citizens. Thus, a quick apology preceded their ultimatum that Paul and Silas leave the city. On their way out, the two battered missionaries visited Lydia's house—by now probably the first house church in Philippi—to offer encouragement to the believers and then headed out toward Thessalonica.

From Luke's account of these events, one forms the impression that the stop in Philippi was eventful (exorcism, beating, imprisonment, earthquake, apology from city magistrates) but not very productive for the church, with only two recorded conversions and household baptisms. However, we must not forget that Luke has abbreviated the story and chosen to narrate certain events that fit into his theological agenda.

We learn much more about the Philippian church from the letter that Paul wrote to these believers a number of years later.[68] Here we read that these believers had a special place in Paul's heart and memory: they had partnered with him in sharing the gospel by continuing to evangelize the city and teach new converts after his departure (Phil 1:5); they had supported Paul's ministry financially in Thessalonica (Phil 4:16) and possibly Corinth (2 Cor 11:9); they had contributed generously to the offering for the saints in Jerusalem (2 Cor 8:1-5); and they had sent one of their own members, Epaphroditus, to minister to Paul in prison (Phil 2:25; 4:18).

True, there were some problems in the church when Paul wrote his letter. Paul recalled his suffering and shameful treatment (1 Thess 2:2); he was aware of outsiders (Judaizers) attempting to enslave the church to a law-abiding gospel (Phil 3:2-16) and of libertines attempting to free the gospel from its moral constraints (Phil 3:17-21); he knew of inner tensions arising from selfishness, conceit and pride (Phil 2:2-4) and of Euodia and Syntyche's fractured relationship (Phil 4:2). In response, Paul found it fitting to appeal to the "mind [of] Christ Jesus" in one of the most profound christological hymns in the entire New Testament (Phil 2:5-11).[69]

In spite of this, we have no reason to doubt Paul's sincerity when he writes: "my brothers and sisters, whom I love and long for, my joy and crown, stand firm in the Lord in this way, my beloved" (Phil 4:1). Even in prison Paul expressed his desire to visit the church again (Phil 1:26; 2:24).

---

[68]The date of composition depends on one's view of Paul's imprisonment. If he was imprisoned in Ephesus, he wrote it around 55-56; if Caesarea, around 58-60; if Rome, around 61-63. See R. Brown, *Introduction to the New Testament,* p. 484.

[69]Ralph P. Martin, *A Hymn of Christ: Philippians 2:5-11 in Recent Interpretation and in the Setting of Early Christian Worship* (Downers Grove, Ill.: InterVarsity Press, 1997).

Some of the credit for the growth and character of this church probably belongs to Lydia and Luke. Although Lydia may have traveled back and forth from Thyatira, Acts 16:40 implies that she had a home in Philippi. Luke, who joined Paul, Silas and Timothy in Troas, probably remained in Philippi (the "we" section stops here) while the team moved on to Thessalonica. No doubt Luke played a major role in this congregation. Many commentators suspect that he is the "loyal companion" to whom Paul appeals in Philippians 4:3.

3.7.2. The Church in Thessalonica (Acts 17:1-9; 1 and 2 Thess). Paul and Silas made their journey from Philippi to Thessalonica (about 100 miles) along the *via Egnatia,* stopping overnight in Amphipolis and Apollonia without, apparently, taking any opportunity to proclaim the gospel in these cities. Either there were no synagogues there or the missionaries were intent on reaching Thessalonica as quickly as possible because it was a significant and populous city (the capital of Macedonia) that offered more opportunities for preaching. Some scholars suspect that Paul already had his eyes on Rome and would have traveled west if the circumstances in Thessalonica had not forced him south.[70] Could this be the meaning behind Romans 1:10 ("that by God's will I may somehow at last succeed in coming to you") and Romans 15:23 ("I desire, as I have for many years, to come to you")?

Paul began his Thessalonian ministry in the synagogue and for "three sabbaths" (that is, at least three to four weeks) interpreted the gospel to Jews, devout Greeks *(sebomenoi)* and leading women (Acts 17:2-4).[71] The initial results of Paul's labors were encouraging, for some individuals from each group were persuaded by Paul's teaching and "joined" the missionaries, probably in forming a Christian community apart from the synagogue. Jealousy among certain Jews, however, created a mob scene that quickly led to anarchy, false accusations and arrest. The disdainful accusation, "Those people who have been turning the world upside down have come here also" (Acts 17:6), refers to upsetting the status quo.[72] In this case the Jews wanted to convince the city authorities that Paul and Silas were a threat to the established order of the empire.

It appears that Paul and Silas spent roughly three weeks in the city ("three sabbath days") before they were forced out. If true, this would leave very little time for further preaching, teaching and opportunities to solidify the new con-

---

[70]Riesner, *Paul's Early Period,* p. 295. Yet Acts 19:21 is the first mention of Paul's commitment to travel to Rome.

[71]The frequent mention of women in the cities of Macedonia should be noted. See Bruce, *Acts,* p. 323: "Macedonian women had a well-earned reputation for their independence and enterprising spirit."

[72]Greek *anastatoō,* "to agitate, unsettle, incite a revolt" (see Acts 21:38).

verts into a church. However, Paul's letter(s) about his ministry to this congregation suggests a longer time period.[73]

First, Paul and Silas "set up shop" as leather workers in the city. This took time, but it provided an explicit example of labor and toil, proof that accusations about their "freeloading" were false (see 1 Thess 1:5; 2:9; 2 Thess 3:8).

Second, certain phrases imply a teaching ministry beyond the synagogue, which suggests that Paul spent three sabbaths with Jews in the context of the synagogue before he moved on to work with his converts. This seems likely from the claims that the Thessalonians "learned from us how you ought to live and . . . know what instructions we gave you" (1 Thess 4:1-2), which imply a rather substantial paraenesis. In addition, certain exhortations could be reminders of concerns that Paul had shared with them in person, such as to love (1 Thess 3:12; 4:10), to encourage and build up one another (1 Thess 5:11), to abstain from immorality (1 Thess 4:3) and to strive for holiness (1 Thess 4:1, 7). Even Paul's preaching (1 Thess 1:5) would have followed the pattern of early Christian kerygma.

Third, Paul may have assisted in the appointment of leaders. Although the terms elders *(presbyteroi)* and overseers *(episkopoi)* are not used, the Thessalonians are admonished "to respect" and "esteem" those who "have charge of you in the Lord" (1 Thess 5:12-13). Perhaps Aristarchus and Secundus, two Thessalonians who joined Paul several years later in Macedonia, were part of this leadership (Acts 20:4).

Fourth, Paul commended the Thessalonians for their witness: "For the word of the Lord has sounded forth from you not only in Macedonia and Achaia, but in every place your faith in God has become known"(1 Thess 1:8). Even granting a bit of Pauline hyperbole, this verse shows that the Thessalonians understood enough of the gospel to share with others.

3.7.3. The Church in Berea (Acts 17:10-15). Concern for Paul and Silas's safety in Thessalonica led the believers to usher them out of the city under cover of darkness (Acts 17:10). Upon their arrival in Berea, Paul and Silas followed the traditional pattern of heading for the synagogue, where they found a "receptive" (Acts 17:11) group of Jews eager to study the Scriptures. The Greek word *eugenesteroi* in Acts 17:11 usually means "well born" or "nobility of origin." In this context it probably implies "a more noble attitude."[74] C. K. Barrett

---

[73]The oldest preserved letter of Paul is 1 Thessalonians, written c. 50/51 from Corinth, a few months after leaving Thessalonica. On the authorship of 2 Thessalonians, see R. Brown, *Introduction to the New Testament,* and other introductions and commentaries. Even if it is Pauline, 2 Thessalonians does not contribute much toward reconstructing Paul and Silas's visit there.

[74]So Joseph A. Fitzmyer, *The Acts of the Apostles* (New York: Doubleday, 1997), p. 597.

understands Luke to mean "that the Beroean Jews allowed no prejudice to prevent them from giving Paul a fair hearing."[75] Paul welcomed this spirit of openness and was able to interpret the Scriptures on a daily rather than sabbath schedule (Acts 17:11). Unfortunately, a contingent of angry and frustrated Jews from Thessalonica succeeded in interrupting Paul's seminar and forced him to head further south to Athens (Acts 17:13-15).

If we read between the lines (as we must with Luke) it is reasonable to conclude that there was more to Paul's ministry in Berea than is documented. Luke indicates that many Jews believed, "including not a few Greek women and men of high standing" (Acts 17:12). In addition to their conversion to Christianity, they were probably baptized and received additional instruction in the faith. The fact that "believers" (implied from the Greek *adelphos,* "brothers") took Paul under their wing suggests that Paul had enough time in Berea for a personal relationship to develop with his coworkers and converts. In addition, Timothy and Silas may have had a brief ministry with the church before leaving to rejoin Paul in Corinth (Acts 18:5). In the end, the church in Berea survived, for several years later a Berean named Sopater joined Paul's party in Macedonia (Acts 20:4).

3.7.4. The Gospel in Athens (Acts 17:16-33). Although this is one of the most important passages in Acts, one looks in vain for any discussion of a church in Athens. The reason for this is simple: there is no biblical or extrabiblical evidence that a church was established in Athens during the first century. How (and why) is it that this prestigious city, so famous as the intellectual capital, architectural wonder and philosophical center of the Greco-Roman world, could be without a church? While one may reason the same for other cities that Paul visited (such as Troas and Berea), there is at least more evidence supporting the likelihood of Christian communities of some kind in those situations.

With Athens, however, there is little evidence in Acts 17:16-32 and nothing in Paul's letters, apart from one reference confirming that he and Timothy had been there (1 Thess 3:1-2). Even the most critical scholars of this account concede that there is a historical core to Luke's narrative. Separating Paul and Luke, however, is a difficult and even unrewarding enterprise.

How are we to interpret Paul's experience in Athens? Basically, there appear to be three approaches among scholars. First, some are extremely skeptical about its historicity and attribute all of the speech to the creative genius of Luke.[76] An intermediate position sees the speech written by Luke but emanating from the Christian community rather than Paul. Thus C. K. Barrett writes, "It

---

[75]Barrett, *Acts,* 2:817.
[76]Analyzed and documented carefully by Barrett, *Acts,* 2:824-26.

might be a little better to say that Luke was not in a position to recount something that he had himself heard but used what had come to be the accepted Christian approach to Gentiles. It is very doubtful whether he was correct in ascribing this approach to Paul."[77] Others, however, concede Luke's creativity but keep Paul in the picture as well. For example, David J. Williams explains, "It does come to us now in Lukan accents, but we may accept it as essentially Paul's."[78] Scholars taking the third approach conclude that there is nothing here that Paul was incapable of articulating, once we acknowledge that this was a unique occasion for Paul to address the pagan world and to "meet people where they were" intellectually and spiritually (a position usually drawn from Paul's statement in 1 Cor 9:19-23).

The account in Athens begins with Paul "waiting" for Timothy and Titus to join him from Berea (Acts 17:16). However, since Paul was not the type of person to "wait around," he immediately headed for the synagogue, where he found Jews and "devout persons" *(sebomenoi)* with whom to "argue" *(dialogizomai,* "to discuss, reason, question"). From there he moved to a public arena, the agora (marketplace), following the methods of ancient and contemporary philosophers and orators. His first encounter was with Epicurean and Stoic philosophers, who found him somewhat amusing and his arguments about Jesus and the resurrection confusing and strange.

Paul moved from the agora and specifically engaged members of the Areopagus, an authoritative institution in Athens responsible for legal, political, educational and religious issues. The council *(Areios Pagos)* took its name from the Hill of Ares ("Mars Hill"), on which they originally met. When Paul stood "in front" of (literally, in the midst or middle of) them, they probably were meeting in a special section of the agora.[79]

Since Paul was appealing to a unique audience, his speech dealt with "natu-

---

[77]Ibid., 2:825.

[78]Williams, *Acts,* p. 300

[79]Bruce expresses the opinion of most commentators at this point: "At the time with which we are dealing it held its ordinary meetings in the Royal Colonnade *(stoa basileios)* in the northwest corner of the Agora" *(Acts,* p. 331). David Gill adds, "Imagine him standing in the Stoa Poikile, the setting for his disputations. He would have been able to view at least two of the structures connected to the worship of the emperor: in front of him in the Agora, the temple of Ares, and beyond that on the skyline, the temple of Roma and Augustus. Moreover to his right, the Stoa of Zeus Eleutherios may have housed the imperial cult in the Agora. The agora itself was the site for numerous dedications to the imperial family. Many of the thirteen small altars dedicated to Augustus, with implications for his divinity, were found in the agora area. A statue base of Livia (as Julia Augusta) was found to the east of the Metroon in the Agora and this linked her with the deity Artemis Boulaia. This cult may have been located in the so-called South-west temple" ("Macedonia," in Gill and Gempf, eds., *Graeco-Roman Setting,* p. 444; see also J. R. C. Cousland, "Temples, Greco-Roman," *DNTB,* pp. 1186-88).

ral" rather than "revealed" theology. On this occasion, a history of the old covenant would not have made much sense. In Joseph Fitzmyer's words, Paul's speech mirrors rather "the reaction of a Jewish Christian missionary confronted with Greco-Roman culture, Greek intellectual curiosity, and pagan piety. It reflects a mild line of Hellenistic Jewish missionary propaganda, viz., God's forbearance of paganism, but it is christianized at the end of it."[80] Nor is there any indication that Paul used traditional kerygmatic or paraenetic material on this occasion.

Acts 17:32-35 records three results to the speech: some listeners "scoffed," presumably over the implausibility of the doctrine of the resurrection; some delayed their response, desiring to hear more from Paul on another occasion; and some joined Paul as "believers," including Dionysius the Areopagite and a woman named Damaris.[81]

Although it is difficult to imagine Paul not solidifying this small group into a Christian community and appointing some kind of leadership, there is nothing in the text to indicate this took place. Even baptism, so crucial in Luke's pattern of Christian initiation, is missing. Later Paul referred to "the household of Stephanas" rather than Dionysius and Damaris as his first converts in Achaia (1 Cor 16:15). The rapid transition from Athens to Corinth (Acts 18:1) and Paul's critique of wisdom and knowledge in Corinth (e.g., 1 Cor 1:17—2:16) should not, however, be interpreted to imply that his mission in Athens was a failure.

3.7.5. The Church in Corinth (Acts 18:1-17; 1 and 2 Corinthians). Although this brief passage in Acts (Acts 18:1-17) describes the establishment of the church in Corinth, it does little to inform us about the significant and tumultuous relationship that Paul had with this congregation. [82] For that, we must consult 1 and 2 Corinthians, the longest letters written to any of the churches that Paul founded.

Luke's sequence of events is rather straightforward and uneventful. First, Paul met Aquila and Priscilla, two tentmakers (literally "leather workers," *skēnopoioi*) from Rome. They had been expelled when the Roman emperor Claudius (41-54) ordered all Jews to leave Rome in 49 because they had apparently been involved in certain domestic disturbances (Suetonius *Claudius* 25.4). Paul joined them in their shop, and together they carried on their trade.

Second, Paul continued his witness in the Jewish synagogue, seeking to convince Jews and Greeks (supposedly God-fearers) that "the Messiah was Jesus"

---

[80]Fitzmyer, *Acts*, pp. 601-2. For a good outline of the speech see pp. 601-2.

[81]There is no historical warrant for the tradition recorded in Eusebius (*Hist. Eccl.* 3.4.11; 4.23.3) that Dionysius became the first bishop of Athens.

[82]Even though there may have been several house churches in Corinth I will use the singular *church* when referring to the believers in Corinth.

(Acts 18:4-5). This eventually resulted in Jewish rejection of the gospel (Acts 18:12), and, as with Jews elsewhere, Paul denounced their contumacy and moved on to the Gentiles (Acts 18:6).

Third, Paul had more success with the gospel once he separated from the synagogue. His first coverts included Titius Justus, a "worshiper *[sebomenos]* of God," and Crispus, an "official of the synagogue [who] became a believer . . . together with all his household" (Acts 18:7-8). According to Luke, many other Corinthians "became believers and were baptized" (Acts 18:8). One must consult Paul's correspondence to the church to know that, in addition to Titius Justus and Crispus, new converts included Gaius, the household of Stephanas (1 Cor 1:14-16) and probably Fortunatus and Achaicus (1 Cor 16:17). Paul's "vision" that he should remain in Corinth to continue preaching and teaching the gospel resulted in a continuous and settled ministry for eighteen months (Acts 18:11). His later correspondence with the church is a useful commentary on the nature of the church in Corinth as well as the church in general.

The arrival of Silas and Timothy from Macedonia was a significant event in Paul's ministry. Paul had left them behind in Thessalonica to care for that church when he abruptly departed for his safety. They brought reports (possibly even a letter) from the church to Paul in Corinth. It was during this time (probably c. 51) that Paul wrote 1 Thessalonians as an apostolic response to the Thessalonian church (note the salutation in 1 Thess 1:1: "Paul, Silvanus, and Timothy, To the church of the Thessalonians"). Since Silvanus (Silas) and Timothy are mentioned several times in the Corinthian letters, they probably played an important part in the life of the church during these eighteen months (see 1 Cor 4:17; 16:10; 2 Cor 1:1, 19).

From Acts we do not know whether Paul continued his trade as a leather worker with Aquila and Priscilla the entire time. Later, when Paul wrote 2 Corinthians, he responded to accusations about his financial affairs by referring to the generosity of the Macedonian churches (2 Cor 8:1) and by noting that his "needs" (financial?) were "supplied by the friends who came from Macedonia" (2 Cor 11:9), namely, Silas and Timothy. Did Paul have enough financial support that he could devote himself full time to the ministry? His words of gratitude to the Philippian church suggest such a possibility (see Phil 4:14-15).

Fourth, the Roman authorities were once again indifferent to Jewish accusations against Christians. Gallio, the proconsul of Achaia, passed their charges off as an internal dispute and had no interest in becoming involved. Once again Rome regarded Christianity either as a legitimate sect of Judaism or as a *religio licita* in its own right within the empire (see 2.5.3).[83]

---

[83]Fitzmyer writes, "The proconsul treats it as if it were but a form of Judaism, which already had been accorded tolerance in the Roman empire" (*Acts,* p. 619).

After eighteen months (probably the fall of 50 to the spring of 52), Paul decided to return to Syria, a journey that included stops in Cenchreae, Ephesus (where he left Priscilla and Aquila), Caesarea, Jerusalem and Antioch (Acts 18:18-23). The fact that Paul returned to Antioch and spent time there (Acts 18:22-23) indicates, at least from Luke's perspective, that the rupture between Paul and Antioch may not have been as permanent as some commentators suggest. On the other hand, this may have been the time when Paul had the confrontation with Peter recorded in Galatians 2:11-14.[84]

Paul began his journey back to Ephesus (where, God willing, he promised Aquila and Priscilla to return [Acts 18:21]) by revisiting churches that he had established earlier in Galatia and Phrygia, "strengthening all the disciples" (Acts 18:23). The "interior regions" (Acts 19:1) probably include other provinces in Asia Minor. By the time he reached Ephesus, approximately one year must have elapsed (52-53).

Corinth, the capital of Achaia, was an important Roman city in Paul's day. Its geographical setting on the Isthmus of Corinth enhanced its value as a seaport on the Mediterranean for naval, political and commercial interests. This, as well as the celebration of the Isthmian games, brought a wide variety of people from various social ranks to the city. Religiously it was pluralistic, exhibiting a diverse melange of shrines and temples, including one to Aphrodite on the Acro-Corinth. Like most seaports, it was noted for its immorality. Hence "to Corinthianize" became synonymous with all sorts of immorality and sexual passions of the flesh.[85]

It appears that most of the converts in Corinth were Gentiles (1 Cor 7:12-20; 8:10; 12:2), although there were obviously a few Jewish believers as well. Many Gentiles probably came from the lower classes (1 Cor 1:26-28), including slaves (1 Cor 7:21-24; 12:13). Individuals such as Tertius, Gaius, Erastus (see Rom 16:22-23) and Sosthenes belonged to a higher social rank.[86]

Most of what we know about the internal life of the Corinthian church comes from Paul's correspondence with the congregation (letters written

---

[84]So Hengel and Schwemer, *Paul Between Damascus and Antioch,* p. xiii; Schlatter, *Church in the New Testament Period,* pp. 159-61. Barrett simply makes the following comment: "It is easy to guess, impossible to prove, that Paul was occupied in straightening out tangled relations with the church"(*Acts,* 2:881).

[85]According to William Barclay, Corinth "had a reputation for commercial prosperity, but she was also a by-word for evil and immoral living. The very word *korinthiazesthai,* to live like a Corinthian, had become a part of the Greek language, and it meant to live with drunken and immoral debauchery" (*The Letters to the Corinthians* [Edinburgh: St. Andrews Press, 1958], p. 3). Jerome Murphy-O'Connor rightly suggests that such descriptions were "fabrications," and that "in reality Corinth was neither better or worse than its contemporaries" (*ABD:* 1:1135-36; "The Corinth That Saint Paul Saw," *BA* 47 [1984]:152).

[86]See Ben Witherington III, "The Social Level of Paul and His Converts," in *Conflict and Community in Corinth* (Grand Rapids, Mich.: Eerdmans, 1995), pp. 19-35.

between 53 and 56 from Ephesus and Macedonia). From them we can construct a series of personal and literary exchanges that not only reflect the editorial activity of a later collector of Paul's epistles but also shed light on the internal dynamics of this Christian community.[87]

From the evidence in 1 Corinthians, we can conclude the following: (1) Paul's first letter, dealing with "sexually immoral persons" (1 Cor 5:9) apparently reached the church but was lost.[88] (2) Paul received a letter from the Corinthians (1 Cor 7:1), possibly carried by the delegation of Stephanas, Fortunatus and Achaicus (1 Cor 16:17-18), but it was also lost. (3) The church communicated with Paul through a report from "Chloe's people" (1 Cor 1:11; perhaps also 1 Cor 11:18), most likely representatives of a church family (1 Cor 1:11). (4) In response to the oral and written exchanges from the congregation, Paul wrote a second letter from Ephesus (our 1 Corinthians, c. 56/57). (5) Paul sent Timothy, who was traveling throughout Macedonia, to Corinth with oral instructions. In time he returned to Ephesus with a discouraging report about the hostility of false apostles toward Paul (1 Cor 4:17-19; 16:10-11).

Evidence from 2 Corinthians adds several more pieces to the puzzle: (6) Paul made a brief but "painful visit" (2 Cor 2:1-2), during which he was personally wronged by a church member, then returned to Ephesus without any apparent reconciliation (2 Cor 12:21). (7) Paul wrote a third letter (delivered by Titus), a harsh and sorrowful letter written "out of much distress and anguish of heart and with many tears" (2 Cor 2:3-4, 9) but which had the desired effect of correcting some errant behavior and attitudes (2 Cor 7:8-14).[89] (8) Titus brought encouraging news about the church to Paul in Macedonia (2 Cor 7:5-7, 14-16). (9) While in Macedonia, Paul wrote a fourth (conciliatory) letter.[90] Here Paul

---

[87]Patzia, _Making of the New Testament,_ pp. 78-88. Most commentators reconstruct these events in some form or another. In addition to commentators, see Becker, _Paul,_ pp. 161-63; R. Brown, _Introduction to the New Testament,_ pp. 511-58; John C. Hurd, _The Origins of 1 Corinthians,_ 2nd ed. (Macon, Ga.: Mercer University Press, 1983); Charles B. Puskas, _The Letters of Paul_ (Collegeville, Minn.: Liturgical Press, 1993), pp. 52-58; Calvin Roetzel, _The Letters of Paul,_ 4th ed. (Louisville: Westminster John Knox, 1998), pp. 83-96.

[88]Some authors contend that it is partially preserved in 2 Cor 6:14—7:1 (see R. Brown, _Introduction to the New Testament,_ p. 515).

[89]Perhaps the essence of this letter is recorded in 2 Corinthians 10—13 (Roetzel, _Letters of Paul,_ pp. 84, 93). For further explanations, see R. Brown, _Introduction to the New Testament,_ pp. 548-51.

[90]Written c. 57, this letter contained most of 2 Corinthians, such as 2 Cor 1:1—6:13; 7:2—9:15. According to R. Brown (_Introduction to the New Testament,_ p. 543), "this letter was to be carried by Titus (and two other brothers) as part of a continued mission to raise money at Corinth for Paul to take back to Jerusalem (8:6, 16-24)." Roetzel considers 6:14—7:1 an "insertion," thus not part of the original 2 Corinthians (_Letters of Paul,_ p. 94).

specifically encouraged the Corinthians to support Titus's efforts to complete their contribution to the collection for Jerusalem with the same generosity as the church in Macedonia (2 Cor 8:1-24). (10) Paul visited the Corinthians for a "third time" (2 Cor 12:14; 13:1-2) to receive the offering for the poor before his final trip to Jerusalem (1 Cor 16:1-6).

The problems addressed in these letters are illuminating from two perspectives: first, they provide a snapshot of the struggles that the church faced in an idolatrous and immoral pagan society; second, they reveal Paul's correctives to these issues and his explanations on the nature of Christian life, community, worship and apostolic integrity.

Paul admits that he came to Corinth "in weakness and in fear and in much trembling" (1 Cor 2:3). His relationship with the church was filled with tensions, disappointments and concerns, but there were many reasons to celebrate the founding of a church in such an important city. At this point the famous words by Charles Dickens seem appropriate:

> It was the best of times, it was the worst of times, it was the age of wisdom, it was the age of foolishness, it was the epoch of belief, it was the epoch of incredulity, it was the season of Light, it was the season of Darkness, it was the spring of hope, it was the winter of despair.[91]

In many ways Paul echoes these sentiments when he implies that Corinth was the best of churches and the worst of churches, both wise and foolish, embracing belief and skepticism, experiencing periods of darkness and of light; prompting hope and despair.

Eighteen months of preaching and teaching enabled Paul to see his earlier vision from the Lord fulfilled ("there are many in this city who are my people," Acts 18:10). Here Jürgen Becker cautiously asks: "Can we reckon with fifty to a hundred Christians for the time when Paul left Corinth in A.D. 52?"[92] Such a number would have required several house churches: one in Aquila and Priscilla's home (1 Cor 16:19) and probably another one with Titius Justus (Acts 18:7).

Several indications in the New Testament suggest church growth beyond the city. In Paul's greeting in 2 Corinthians he writes, "To the church of God that is in Corinth, including all the saints throughout Achaia" (2 Cor 1:1), a statement that implies the existence of other congregations with whom his letters would be shared. In Romans, Paul commends "our sister Phoebe, a deacon [diakonos] of the church at Cenchreae" (Rom 16:1). It is quite likely that through Paul's ministry and the outreach of the Corinthian church, "many new communities

---

[91]Charles Dickens, *A Tale of Two Cities* (Boston: Ginn, 1906), bk. 1, chap. 1.
[92]Becker, *Paul,* p. 147.

were established throughout the Peloponnese and to the north."[93]

Not much is known about the Corinthian church after the first century, apart from Clement's first letter ("The Letter of the Church of Rome to the Church of Corinth"), written about A.D. 96. In his introductory comments to this letter, Cyril Richardson writes, "The same factious spirit that Paul had encountered there had once again provoked serious dissension."[94] Hence Clement refers to quarrels, impetuous and headstrong fellows (*1 Clem.* 1.1), young men revolting against older ruling presbyters (*1 Clem.* 3.3; 44.6; 47.6; 57.1), as well as to conflicts over the recognition of certain spiritual gifts, knowledge and lifestyles (see *1 Clem.* 21.5; 38.2; 48.5-6; 57.2—58.2). There is no way of knowing whether Clement's exhortations for peace, humility, unity and obedience to their leaders had any positive effect on the church of his day.

3.7.6. The Church in Ephesus (Acts 18:24—20:38). Several reasons account for Ephesus's significance in the ancient world, making it a strategic city in which to start a Christian church. First, it was well located and wealthy. Ephesus was a port city on the mouth of the Cayster River in western Asia Minor, situated at the crossroads of several important land routes. All this made it the most important center of international trade in the region.[95] Its significance as a port city waned as alluvial (silt) deposits regularly filled the harbor.

A second foundation of Ephesus's significance was its culture. As the capital city of the Roman province of Asia, it became the site of many major buildings, such as a stadium, library, agora, harbor gate, temple of Apollo, *prytaneion* (town hall), baths and gymnasiums. "Through her buildings," notes Paul Trebilco, "the citizens of Ephesus expressed the greatness of the city."[96] Among all these structures, two stood out for their beauty and prominence: the theatre, capable of seating 20,000 to 25,000 people for performances; and the temple of Artemis (or Diana, her Roman name). This magnificent temple was one of the "seven wonders" of the ancient world. Archaeologists estimate that it covered an area 300 feet by 108 feet and had approximately 120 columns, each 60 feet

---

[93]Clinton E. Arnold, "Centers of Christianity," *DLNTD*, pp. 148-49. From the New Testament we note such cities as Knossos, Gortyna and Nicopolis on the island of Crete (Tit 1:5), Illyricum (Rom 15:19) and Dalmatia (2 Tim 4:10). Lee M. McDonald mentions a number of other possible locations in "Christianity in Greece," *ABD* 1:961-65.

[94]Cyril Richardson, *Early Christian Fathers*, LCC 1 (Philadelphia: Westminster Press, 1958), p. 34.

[95]There are many helpful and thorough descriptions of Ephesus beyond those found in major commentaries on Acts. See esp. Helmut Koester, ed., *Ephesos: Metropolis of Asia*, HTS 41 (Valley Forge, Penn.: Trinity Press International, 1995); Levinskaya, *Diaspora Setting*, pp. 137-48; Paul Trebilco, "Asia," in Gill and Gempf, eds., *Graeco-Roman Setting*, pp. 302-11.

[96]Trebilco, "Asia," pp. 306-7. For brief descriptions of some of these and other structures, see Richard E. Oster Jr., "Ephesus," *ABD* 2:542-49.

high. This made it four times larger than the Parthenon in Athens. The first temple (called the Artemision), originally constructed in the sixth century B.C., was destroyed around 350 B.C. but rebuilt again with similar dimensions. Throughout history it also served as a treasure house (bank) and asylum for fugitives and runaway slaves.[97] The temple became less important with the advent of Christianity and was burned by the Goths in A.D. 262.

Religion was the third element of Ephesus's significance. Although the Ephesians had loyalties to many gods and practiced numerous cults, the worship of Artemis stood out front and center.[98] Luke recognizes the Ephesians' strong devotion and passion by noting that, even though many pilgrims came to Ephesus from "all Asia and the world" (Acts 19:27), the residents proudly considered themselves the "temple keeper *(neōkoros)* of Artemis, whose statue "fell from heaven" in some supernatural way (Acts 19:35). Perhaps their comment on the divine origin of the statue was their response to Paul's condemnation of idolatry, that "gods made with hands are not gods" (Acts 19:26). It is no wonder that the crowds acclaimed Artemis's greatness ("Great Artemis of the Ephesians!") when they felt invaded and threatened by Christianity (Acts 19:28, 34).[99]

Both Artemis's reputation and the economic interests of the silversmiths who earned a living making shrines and statues to her were at stake here (Acts 19:23-27). Luke also refers to Jewish exorcists and magicians who seemed to have quite a lucrative trade until Paul exposed their evil practices and succeeded in having many of them renounce their folly, burn their books and turn to the Lord (Acts 19:11-20). The seven sons of the Jewish high priest named Sceva, muses Dunn, "sound . . . something like a circus act, and that is probably how they should be regarded."[100]

Although Luke's record of events in Ephesus is rather extensive (Acts 18:19-21; 19:1-41), he gives little information about the nature and life of the church during Paul's three-year ministry there (Acts 20:31). When one removes the section on miracles (Acts 19:11), magic (Acts 19:12-20) and malevolence from the devotees of Artemis (Acts 19:23-41), we are left with a condensed but nevertheless helpful version of events from which to construct the emergence of the church in Ephesus.

---

[97]Trebilco, "Asia," pp. 324-26.

[98]Arnold writes, "Epigraphic, numismatic and literary evidence reveals that the people of Ephesus worshiped up to fifty different gods and goddesses" ("Centers of Christianity," p. 147).

[99]Since there is no verb in the Greek, one suspects that the phrase "Great Artemis" or "Great Artemis of the Ephesians" was a stock religious utterance (so William Ramsay, *The Church in the Roman Empire* [Grand Rapids, Mich.: Baker, 1954], pp. 135-39).

[100]Dunn, *Acts*, p. 259. On magic, syncretism, exorcisms, etc., see part one, as well as Josephus (*Ant.* 8.2.5 §§42-49) on Jewish exorcisms.

3.7.6.1. The Founding of the Church in Ephesus. Since there appears to have been a significant number of Jews in Ephesus (see Josephus *Ant.* 14.10.12 §§225-27; 16.6.7 §§172-73), one would expect that there were one or more synagogues in the city.[101] Paul's first brief visit to Ephesus with Aquila and Priscilla took him to a synagogue where he had a "discussion" (*dialegō*) with the Jews (Acts 18:19). It appears that Aquila and Priscilla (and later Apollos) continued a mission among the Jews as well (Acts 18:24-28). When Paul returned to Ephesus (Acts 19:1-8), he spent three rather intense months in the synagogue ("spoke out boldly, and argued persuasively about the kingdom of God") before Jewish opposition forced him to find another venue for his evangelization. It appears reasonable to conclude from Luke's pattern elsewhere that the earliest members of the church consisted of converted Jews, God-fearers and Greeks. At this stage one probably could describe it as a Jewish-Christian congregation. It is interesting to note that Luke never explicitly attributes the founding of the church in Ephesus to Paul.

3.7.6.2. Apollos (Acts 18:24-28). Before Paul returned to Ephesus, Aquila and Priscilla encountered Apollos, an Alexandrian Jew who appears on Luke's stage rather unexpectedly by beginning an aggressive evangelistic campaign among the Jews in the synagogue. Luke presents him as a bold, eloquent and enthusiastic (literally "fervent in spirit" *[zeōn tō pneumati]*) speaker who was very knowledgeable in the Scriptures, that is, the Old Testament (Acts 18:24-28). The only problem was that Apollos did not have a complete picture of the gospel and what is involved in becoming a believer.

In spite of considerable scholarly research, Apollos remains a rather enigmatic figure in early Christianity. Apparently he was exposed to teachings about Jesus ("he had been instructed in the Way of the Lord") but had no awareness of Pentecost and the early-church practice of baptism in the name of Jesus. This suggests that the complete story of the church had not reached Egypt by the time he left.[102] Aquila and Priscilla recognized this "omission" in his message and so explained "the Way of God to him more accurately" (18:26), an expression that implies at least Christian baptism.[103]

Apollos's zeal led him to seek out a place of ministry in Achaia (probably

---

[101]Paul Trebilco, *Jewish Communities in Asia Minor,* SNTSMS 69 (Cambridge: Cambridge University Press, 1991).

[102]On Egyptian Christianity, see references in Bruce, *Acts,* p. 359, n. 71 and comments below.

[103]It is possible to interpret spirit (*pneuma*) here as the Holy Spirit, implying that he was a "full" Christian on Luke's terms. So Dunn: "For Luke here again it is the coming of the Spirit which is the central and most crucial factor in conversion-initiation and in Christian identity"(*Acts,* p. 251).

Corinth).[104] The church in Ephesus encouraged his move and even wrote a letter of recommendation to the church in Corinth, where he had considerable success witnessing to the Jews "that the Messiah is Jesus" (Acts 18:27-28). This is the last we hear of Apollos from Luke. Paul, however, mentions Apollos several times in 1 Corinthians as one of the teachers in the congregation (see 1 Cor 1:12; 3:4-6, 22; 4:6) and concludes that letter by acknowledging that he has encouraged Apollos to visit the Corinthian congregation again (1 Cor 16:12).

3.7.6.3. The Disciples of John the Baptist (Acts 19:1-7). While Aquila and Priscilla were dealing with Apollos, Paul was making his way back from Antioch to Ephesus through the "interior regions" of Asia Minor, a shorter and more direct route through the inland parts of Asia Minor rather than the regular trade routes of the Lycus and Meander Valleys. Upon his arrival he met twelve "disciples" *(mathētai)* who apparently were believers ("Did you receive the Holy Spirit when you became believers?" [*ei pneuma hagion elabete pisteusavtes*, literally, in the process/act of believing]). But these disciples had only been baptized into John the Baptist's baptism, a baptism of repentance without the accompanying Holy Spirit (Acts 19:4). So Paul baptized them "in the name of the Lord Jesus" and laid hands on them. As a result, they received the Holy Spirit and broke out in "tongues" and prophetic utterances (Acts 19:5-6).[105]

Given Luke's theology of Christian initiation, especially the relationship between faith, baptism and the Holy Spirit, it seems reasonable to argue that he considered John's disciples believers in some sense but had them rebaptized because they had not received the Holy Spirit, an essential component of Christian baptism in Luke's theology.[106] It is interesting to note that this is the only record of a rebaptism in the New Testament. Since there is no evidence that any of Jesus' disciples were rebaptized "in the name of Jesus," one might assume

---

[104]F. F. Bruce reminds us that in the Western text Apollos "was invited to do so by some Corinthians who made his acquaintance in Ephesus" (*Acts,* p. 360). If true, we should not conclude that these individuals formed a special allegiance to Apollos, as others apparently did to Cephas, Jesus and Paul (see 1 Cor 1—4; Bruce, *Acts,* p. 361).

[105]See the discussion of Christian initiation and baptism in 5.9. This passage is no less puzzling than the previous one concerning Apollos and raises all sorts of questions: Who were these disciples anyway? When and where were they baptized into John's baptism? What were they doing in Ephesus? Why did they need Christian baptism and Apollos did not? What is the relationship between baptism, the reception of the Holy Spirit, speaking in tongues and prophecy? How do these events relate to other passages where Luke talks about Christian initiation? Apart from the major commentaries, see C. K. Barrett, "Apollos and the Twelve Disciples of Ephesus," in *The New Testament Age: Essays in Honor of Bo Reicke*, ed. William C. Weinrich (Macon, Ga.: Mercer University Press, 1984), pp. 29-39; Ernst Käsemann, "The Disciples of John the Baptist in Ephesus," in *Essays on New Testament Themes* (London: SCM Press, 1964), pp. 136-48.

[106]On the possession of the Spirit in Paul, see Rom 8:9; 1 Cor 12:13; Gal 3:2-3.

that the gift (baptism) of the Holy Spirit at Pentecost was adequate in their case. These twelve disciples, however, must have left Jerusalem for Ephesus before Pentecost and thus were unaware of what had happened.[107] Apollos, it appears, was not rebaptized because he possessed the "spirit," even though it is unlikely that he was present in Jerusalem during Pentecost.

It is difficult to harmonize certain events in this passage with Luke's other accounts of Christian initiation. Ernst Käsemann, therefore, suggests that we interpret this narrative within the wider perspective of Luke's theology. Luke, as noted earlier, wrote his history of the beginning of the church from a later perspective (possibly c. 85), when the church had to be extremely careful about admitting any "fringe" movements into its fellowship. "The living context of the passage," affirms Käsemann, "is the reception of ecclesiastical outsiders into the _Una sancta catholica._"[108] In other words, Luke's point is that these disciples were incorporated into mainstream Christianity: a legitimate apostle laid hands on them, and they manifested the reception of the Holy Spirit through tongues and prophecy.

3.7.6.4. Paul's Ministry in Ephesus (Acts 19:8—20:1). Paul's attempt to evangelize the Jews ended in frustration over their obduracy and slander ([they] "spoke evil of the Way before the congregation"), so he took his disciples and moved to a different location in Ephesus, where he remained for two years (Acts 19:8-10).[109] The "lecture hall of Tyrannus" _(tē scholē Tyrannou)_ was a private room for lectures owned or used by Tyrannus, and Paul either rented it or had it donated for his ministry. The Western Greek text (D) expands Luke's statement that Paul "argued daily _[kath hēmeran dialegomenos]_" by adding "from eleven o'clock in the morning to four in the afternoon," the normal siesta time in Mediterranean countries. If true, Paul may have practiced his trade as a leather worker during normal working hours and then lectured in the hall when people were free to come and listen (note Acts 20:34: "You know for yourselves that I worked with my own hands to support myself and my companions").

Paul's confrontations with the Jewish magicians, devotees of Artemis and city politics (see 1.2.4) reveal that his time in Ephesus was filled with danger,

---

[107]For the existence and continuation of a group (sect?) belonging to John the Baptist, see Charles H. H. Scobie, "The Baptist Sect," in _John the Baptist_ (Philadelphia: Fortress, 1964), pp. 187-202. There is a glimpse of John's movement in the Fourth Gospel as well (see Jn 4:1-2).

[108]Käsemann, "Disciples of John the Baptist in Ephesus," p. 141.

[109]Williams may be correct in noting that even before this breach with the synagogue the believers were holding separate meetings (_Acts_, p. 331). Most likely they met in Aquila and Priscilla's home. Since Luke does not allude to any conflicts between Jewish and Gentile Christianity, one "presupposes the independence of the Ephesian church from the synagogue" (Becker, _Paul_, p. 152).

distress and discouragement. Other than Luke's summaries in Acts 19:10 ("all the residents of Asia, both Jews and Greeks, heard the word of the Lord") and 19:20 ("the word of the Lord grew mightily and prevailed"), we are not given details about Paul's ministry or the nature and organization of the church. We do learn some of this information from Paul's later farewell meeting with the Ephesian "elders" at Miletus before his final departure for Jerusalem (Acts 20:18-35).[110]

3.7.6.5. The Significance of Ephesus. *In Paul's ministry.* Even though Luke never explicitly attributes the founding of the Ephesian church to Paul, this important city became a strategic center for Paul's mission to the Gentiles. After Paul had ministered there for three years, it also signified the termination of his Aegean ministry (Acts 20:25-38).

At the conclusion of 1 Corinthians, Paul sends greetings to that congregation from the "churches of Asia," including Aquila and Priscilla and the believers who were meeting in their house in Ephesus (1 Cor 16:19). When Luke writes that during Paul's ministry in Ephesus "all the residents of Asia, both Jews and Greeks, heard the word of the Lord" (Acts 19:10), he is intentionally using hyperbolic language (see also Acts 19:26). Still, it is true that the church had its most significant growth during this period, a time when Paul did not engage in any travel. His missionary strategy changed from the itinerant "man on the go" to a settling down in one place. His ministry became characterized by winning converts through his teaching and then depending upon them and his coworkers to begin churches in surrounding communities of Asia. Paul seems very optimistic about this policy when he writes to the Corinthians that he will remain in Ephesus because "a wide door for effective work has opened to me" (1 Cor 16:9).

Timothy and Erastus had been dispatched to Macedonia earlier (Acts 19:22). Then, near the completion of his Ephesian ministry, Paul made a brief trip to Macedonia and Achaia (Acts 20:3), accompanied by such colleagues as Sopater, Aristarchus, Secundus, Gaius, Timothy, Tychicus and Trophinius (Acts 20:4). No doubt others, such as Titus, were actively establishing churches and teaching believers as well.

Paul experienced considerable joy and personal satisfaction in Ephesus over the spread of the gospel and the emergence of churches, but he also experienced troubles that took a heavy toll on his life. While fighting against the magicians and followers of Artemis (1 Cor 15:32: "I fought with wild animals at Ephesus"), he was also dealing with conflicts in the Corinthian church. Some of the hardships may have included at least one of several imprisonments (2 Cor

---

[110]For a discussion on the historicity of this speech, see Stephen E. Fowl, "Paul and Paulinisms in Acts," *DLNTD,* pp. 883-87.

11:23) and additional affliction in Asia (2 Cor 1:8). Although the activities mentioned in his speech to the Ephesian elders were a broad description of his entire ministry (see 4.6), there is no doubt that his ministry in Ephesus included Jewish opposition, working his trade, teaching "from house to house" and shepherding believers (Acts 20:19-20).

One of the greatest tributes to Paul comes from the pen of one of his later admirers, Clement of Rome:

> Paul showed how to win the prize for patient endurance. Seven times he was in chains; he was exiled, stoned, became a herald [of the gospel] in East and West, and won the noble renown, which his faith merited. To the whole world he taught righteousness, and reaching the limits of the West he bore his witness before rulers. And so, released from this world, he was taken up into the holy place and became the greatest example of patient endurance. (*1 Clem.* 5.6-7)

Given the strategic geographical location of Ephesus as a commercial and cultural center, it is not difficult to envision how the gospel could have spread from there to surrounding communities (see figure 5). According to Pliny the Younger's letter to Trajan in A.D. 112, a similar growth took place in other provinces of the Empire: "For this contagious superstition [Christianity] is not confined to the cities only, but has spread through the villages and rural districts" (*Ep.* 10.96).[111]

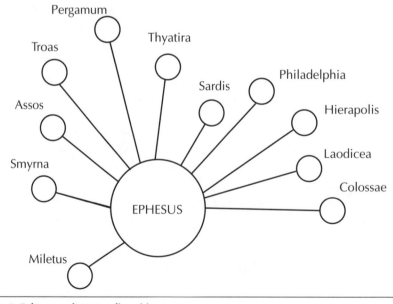

Figure 5. Ephesus and surrounding cities

[111]For additional comments and interpretation, see Trebilco, "Asia," esp. pp. 311-56.

Epaphras is a good example of someone who came to Ephesus, heard Paul's teaching, became a believer and took the gospel to his community. The internal evidence in the letter to the Colossians shows that Epaphras was the first convert to proclaim the gospel in that city (Col 1:7). A similar case could be made with surrounding communities and other individuals. The churches established in Laodicea and Hierapolis (Col 4:13) probably followed a pattern similar to that in Colossae. Philemon and his wife Apphia, residents of Colossae, hosted a church in their house (Philem 1-2). In addition to Paul's colleagues mentioned earlier, the apostle also greeted Mark, Onesimus, Jesus/Justus, Luke, Demas, Nympha and believers in her house (Col 4:7-17; Philem 23).

The Pastoral Epistles. The so-called Pastoral Epistles of 1 and 2 Timothy have traditionally been connected with Ephesus. Scholars claiming that they are genuine letters of Paul develop a scenario (admittedly from silence) that, after Paul's first Roman imprisonment of two years (Acts 28:16, 30), he was released and continued to visit churches in places such as Macedonia (1 Tim 1:3), Crete (Tit 1:5), Nicopolis (Tit 3:12), Miletus (2 Tim 4:20) and Ephesus (1 Tim 1:3; 3:14; 4:13; 2 Tim 1:15-18; 4:19). During this time of freedom he wrote a letter to Timothy in Ephesus (1 Timothy) and to Titus in Crete (Titus). Around A.D. 67 Paul was once again arrested, imprisoned in Rome and wrote another letter to Timothy (2 Timothy) before being beheaded by Nero around A.D. 67/68. Nothing is known about Paul's trip to Dalmatia, a coastal region of ancient Illyricum along the Adriatic Sea (2 Tim 4:10), or his winter in Nicopolis (Tit 3:12).

These letters reveal that the church in Ephesus was being threatened by a wide variety of false teachings and practices, particularly relating to Jewish legalism and early Gnosticism. Hence Paul warned Timothy about these heresies and instructed his colleague to correct the errors through sound teaching and the appointment of bishops and deacons to church leadership.[112]

The Epistle to the Ephesians. This letter presents a similar problem to that of the Pastorals. If it is genuinely Pauline, it was probably written along with other captivity epistles (Philippians, Colossians, Philemon and the Pastorals) before Paul's death. Textual analysis of Ephesians 1:1 (the best manuscripts omit "in Ephesus" as the destination) has led many scholars to conjecture that the epistle was intended as a circular letter to a number of churches in Asia emphasizing

---

[112]All major commentaries on the Pastoral Epistles and New Testament introductions deal with the issues of the Pauline authorship of these letters. For a brief analysis, see E. Earle Ellis, "Pastoral Letters," *DPL,* pp. 661-62; Witherington, *Acts,* pp. 85-86. If the letters are deutero-Pauline, they give us a picture of the church in Ephesus toward the end of the first century rather than around A.D. 67. For this, the insights of B. H. Streeter ("The Church in Asia," in *The Primitive Church, Studied with Special Reference to the Origins of the Christian Ministry* [New York: Macmillan, 1929], pp. 101-15), remain stimulating and useful.

unity between Jewish and Gentile believers in the church (particularly Eph 2:11-22).[113]

The Churches of Revelation. It is reasonable to assume that, in addition to the churches in Ephesus and Laodicea, the other five churches of Asia mentioned in Revelation 2—3 (Smyrna, Pergamum, Thyatira, Sardis, Philadelphia) also were started during this period of Paul's ministry. The issues in these churches that the book of Revelation addresses developed between their founding in the late fifties and the mid-nineties, when the Apocalypse was written. The church in Ephesus is commended for its good works, toil, endurance, orthodoxy, patience and indefatigability, but it is called back to repent and remember its first love (Rev 2:2-4). The comments to the other churches reflect concerns relating to indifference and false teaching, and they are summoned to repent and be faithful (Rev 2—3).

The Johannine Community. Although scholars debate issues of authorship related to the Johannine corpus (Fourth Gospel, 1-3 John, Revelation), most agree that this correspondence emerged from a "Johannine school," "community" or "circle" consisting of a number of house churches in and around Ephesus.[114] Early church traditions locate John's ministry in Asia, specifically in Ephesus. Eusebius refers to John's mission and death in Ephesus (*Hist. Eccl.* 3.1.1) and provides an extended passage on his ministry (*Hist. Eccl.* 3.23), with information coming from Irenaeus and Clement of Alexandria. According to Irenaeus, for example, John, "the disciple of the Lord . . . published the Gospel, while he was residing at Ephesus in Asia" (Irenaeus *Haer.* 3.1.1), where he continued to live until the time of Trajan (*Haer.* 3.3.3). [115] Given the prominence of Ephesus and the traditions of John connected with it, it was natural that John's tomb would be located in this significant city.

It is somewhat ironic that the traditions of John's connections with the Ephesian church have almost completely eclipsed the significance of its ear-

---

[113]This theme appears to describe a situation of the church after the apostle's death. For suggestions, see Arthur G. Patzia, *Ephesians, Colossians, Philemon,* NIBCNT 10 (Peabody, Mass.: Hendrickson, 1990), esp. pp. 121-44.

[114]See Thomas Johnson, *1, 2 and 3 John,* NIBC (Peabody, Mass.: Hendrickson, 1993), pp. 4-5. Besides similar comments in major commentaries, other useful studies include Raymond E. Brown, *The Community of the Beloved Disciple: The Life, Loves and Hates of an Individual Church in New Testament Times* (New York: Paulist, 1979); F. F. Bruce, "St. John at Ephesus," *BJRL* 60 (1977-1978): 339-61; Oscar Cullmann, *The Johannine Circle* (Philadelphia: Westminster Press, 1975); R. Alan Culpepper, *The Johannine School* (Missoula, Mont.: Scholars Press, 1975); J. Louis Martyn, *History and Theology in the Fourth Gospel* (Nashville: Abingdon, 1968).

[115]Although Helmut Koester argues for a Syrian or Palestinian provenance of the Fourth Gospel, he acknowledges its significance for Irenaeus when it reached Asia Minor in the second century ("Ephesos in Early Christian Literature," in Koester, ed., *Ephesos,* pp. 135-40).

liest leader, the apostle Paul. There is "almost nothing at Ephesus to remind us of the great apostle whose ministry made the city so memorable in the history of Christianity."[116] One notable exception, however, is Ignatius's letter *To the Ephesians,* written on his way to martyrdom in Rome. In the letter he assumes that the believers know about Paul and his ministry: "You have been initiated into the [Christian] mysteries with Paul, a real saint and martyr, who deserves to be congratulated. When I come to meet God may I follow in his footsteps, who in all his letters mentions your union with Christ Jesus" (Ign. *Eph.* 12.2).

3.7.7. Churches in the Dispersion (1 Pet).

3.7.7. Churches in the Dispersion (1 Pet). The First Epistle of Peter begins with a salutation: "To the exiles of the Dispersion in Pontus, Galatia, Cappadocia, Asia and Bithynia" (1 Pet 1:1). As noted earlier, some of these Roman provinces were reached with the gospel during Paul's missionary activities. Peter's letter acknowledges the existence of churches in these territories but includes regions not mentioned in Luke's history or Paul's epistles. How, when, and by whom did the gospel arrive in these other geographical areas?

In reality, there is no concrete or undisputed evidence to help us with these questions. As far as we know, neither Peter nor any other apostles evangelized in these regions. One plausible explanation is that some residents from these regions were present in Jerusalem at Pentecost (see Acts 2:9, which lists Cappadocia, Pontus and Asia), heard Peter's sermon, believed, were baptized, returned home and began establishing churches.

According to John K. Elliott's research, by the end of the first century, this area probably included as many as 8.5 million people, including one million Jews and perhaps eighty thousand Christians.[117] If Elliott is correct, it is phenomenal to think of so many believers in one region in such a short period of time. How could such a large number of people be evangelized and so many churches be established so quickly?[118] Is this why Pliny writes, "This conta-

---

[116]Edwin Yamauchi, *New Testament Cities in Western Asia Minor* (Grand Rapids, Mich.: Baker, 1980), p. 111.

[117]John K. Elliott, *A Home for the Homeless: A Sociological Exegesis of 1 Peter, Its Situation and Strategy* (Minneapolis: Fortress, 1990), p. 63 and p. 91 n. 14; see also his "Peter, First Epistle of," in *ABD* 5:273. Unfortunately, Elliott does not provide any original sources for his figures (see 3.9 for further discussion of numerical estimates).

[118]This "time factor" is one of the compelling reasons for a late dating of the letter. Hence Elliott argues that "time must be allowed for the development of Christian communities throughout the provinces. . . . Time must also be allowed for the popularization and spread of the nomenclature 'Christian' from Antioch . . . Caesarea . . . and Rome to the interior of Asia Minor" (*Home for the Homeless,* p. 87).

gious superstition has spread not only through the cities, but also throughout the villages and rural areas" (*Ep.* 10.96.9)?

Since 1 Peter was written as a circular letter, most commentators suggest that the provinces are listed in the order that a courier would have taken. Peter Davids, for example, speculates that "if a person landed on the Black Sea coast of Pontus . . . he would travel southeast, crossing into Galatia and then Cappadocia . . . swing west back across a piece of Galatia into Asia . . . north into Bithynia, departing by sea from Nicomedia, Heraclea, or Amastris, or perhaps traveling through Chalcedon and on across the Bosphorus on the way back to Rome."[119]

As an encyclical, 1 Peter speaks about the Christian life in general rather than addressing a local congregation, such as we find in Paul's letters. Its classification, therefore, as one of the catholic, general, or universal letters is certainly fitting. Internal evidence suggests that the congregations were largely converted Gentiles (1 Pet 1:14, 18; 2:9-10, 25; 3:6; 4:3-4) facing internal struggles and outward oppression familiar to Christians throughout the Roman world at that time (1 Pet 5:9). The specific references to trials and persecutions (1 Pet 1:6-7; 3:14; 4:12-19) are no guarantee that the churches were being systematically persecuted by the authorities.[120] Since society in general was hostile to the faith, believers were to live out their convictions with respect and love to everyone, including the emperor (1 Pet 2:17). When they were accused of wrongdoing (1 Pet 2:12; 3:15-16; 4:15-16), they were to respond with good conduct and sound words (1 Pet 3:13-17) instead of open aggression and hostility.

The recipients of the letter were "visiting strangers" (*parepidēmoi*, NRSV "exiles," 1 Pet 1:1; 2:11) and "resident aliens" (*paroikoi*, NRSV "aliens," 1 Pet 2:11; see also 1 Pet 1:17), literally foreigners who live alongside (*para*) the home (*oikos*) of other people. As was true with Jews in the Diaspora, these believers were scattered among unbelievers (pagans) and hence away from their heavenly home. Neither the word "church" (*ekklēsia*) or Paul's metaphor of "the body" appears in this epistle. Rather, the believers are designated as "a chosen race, a royal priesthood, a holy nation, God's own people" (1 Pet 2:9) for whom Christ is the shepherd and guardian of their souls (1 Pet 2:25; 5:4).

On the strength of Elliott's analysis, it appears that the majority of these churches were "household communities" (see 1 Pet 4:17), that is, "domestic

---

[119]Peter Davids, *The First Epistle of Peter* (Grand Rapids, Mich.: Eerdmans, 1990), p. 8.

[120]Pliny's correspondence with Trajan appears to confirm this observation (see *Ep.* 10.96-97). For a useful sequence of this material, consult J. Ramsey Michaels, *1 Peter*, WBC 49 (Waco, Tex.: Word, 1988), pp. lxiii-lxv.

pockets of Christians dispersed across the landscape of Asia Minor."[121] That they were known as "Christians" (1 Pet 4:16) suggests an identity not unlike believers in Antioch (Acts 11:26). Other groups singled out for instruction include "free people" (1 Pet 2:16), wives of non-Christian husbands (1 Pet 3:1-6), husbands of Christian wives (1 Pet 3:7), elders (1 Pet 5:1-5) and "younger" converts *(neōteros)* who should "accept the authority of the elders" (1 Pet 5:5). Beyond the existence of "elders," nothing specifically can be determined about the organization and structure of the church. Attempts to understand and interpret 1 Peter from a liturgical perspective have not been convincing.

There is no unanimity among scholars on questions of authorship or date of composition. Those who attribute the epistle to Peter obviously date it before his martyrdom in Rome sometime between A.D. 65-67; if it is pseudonymous, dates range anywhere between A.D. 69-96. Most holding to the latter position believe that the letter comes from a Petrine school or circle of Peter's associates in Rome (1 Pet 5:13: "Babylon," meaning Rome). Either way, we are able to reconstruct a fairly good picture of the churches in this area without debating critical issues.

3.7.8. The Churches in Rome.

3.7.8.1. The Founding of the Church.
It is disappointing (and unfortunate) that we know nothing about the origin of the church in Rome. How is it that Luke the historian, who crafts his story of the early church around the two foci of Jerusalem and Rome, fails to mention how Christianity first reached the capital of the Roman Empire, a city of approximately one million people? How is it that Paul can write his most significant letter *(Hauptbrief)* to the churches in Rome ("To all God's beloved in Rome, who are called to be saints," Rom 1:7), a letter that includes such a profound statement of his gospel, and yet not refer to the proclamation of the gospel that started the church? How ironic that we have no record of the origin of the church in a city that eventually became the center of early Christianity.

Of course there are several theories about the founding of the church in Rome. The most common explanation is that the "visitors from Rome, both Jews and proselytes" who were present in Jerusalem on Pentecost (Acts 2:10) were converted and took the gospel back to Rome as early as A.D. 40. Another possibility is that many of Paul's (and other missionaries') converts from the eastern Mediterranean mission made their way to Rome and began meeting as

---

[121]Elliott, *Home for the Homeless,* p. 64. Elliott draws upon the insights of several reliable studies that compare the development of Christianity to other sectarian movements. See Robin Scroggs, "The Earliest Christian Communities as Sectarian Movement," in *Christianity, Judaism and Other Greco-Roman Cults,* ed. Jacob Neusner (Leiden: E. J. Brill, 1975), pp. 1-23; for additional references, see Elliott, *Home for the Homeless,* p. 96; Rodney Stark, *The Rise of Christianity* (Princeton, N.J.: Princeton University Press, 1966).

local congregations. At any rate, the saying that "all roads lead to Rome" certainly included the migration of believers to the capital. Perhaps Aquila, a native of Pontus (Acts 18:2), was one of many such individuals.[122]

3.7.8.2. The Nature of the Church. If the church in Rome began with Jewish converts returning from Jerusalem, it seems likely that the first church in Rome began as a "sect" of Judaism within the context of the synagogue. According to various computations, scholars estimate that there were approximately 40,000 to 50,000 Jews resident in Rome during the first century A.D. and that they were divided into "a number of district synagogues (at least eleven) rather than gathered as a single community."[123]

This loose organizational structure may have facilitated the growth of the church as well. Thus Wolfgang Wiefel notes:

> The loose structure . . . provided an essential prerequisite for the early penetration of Christianity in Rome. The multitude of congregations, their democratic constitutions, and the absence of a central Jewish governing board made it easy for the missionaries of the new faith to talk in the synagogues and to win new supporters. Permission for missionaries to remain in the autonomous congregations could only be revoked if the governing body considered exclusion to be necessary and enforceable. However, since Rome had no supervising body, which could forbid any form of Christian propaganda in the city, it was possible to missionize in various synagogues concurrently or to go successively from one to the other. It is likely that the existence of newly converted Christians alongside the traditional members of the synagogue may have led to increased factions and even tumultuous disputes.[124]

---

[122]Here Joseph Fitzmyer's reconstruction is suggestive: "Most likely the Christian community in Rome began not under any direct evangelization of the area, as it did in parts of the eastern Mediterranean, but through the presence of Jewish Christians and Gentiles associated with them who came to live there and went about ordinary tasks and secular duties. Slaves brought to Rome, merchants who came from other parts of the empire, and other individuals probably carried the Christian gospel there. Neither the Letter to the Romans nor the Acts of the Apostles alludes to any initial evangelization of Rome by a particular missionary, but Paul does send greetings to Andronicus and Junia, whom he recognizes as 'my fellow countrymen' and 'outstanding among the apostles' (16:7) and who may have been among such Jewish Christians who originally came from Jerusalem. The community undoubtedly also grew by the gradual immigration of Christians themselves, who traveled to the capital during the 40s via the Jewish diaspora" (*Romans*, AB 33 [New York: Doubleday, 1993], p. 30). See also James Dunn, *Romans 1-8*, WBC 38A (Dallas: Word, 1988), pp. xliv-liv.

[123]Andrew Clark, "Rome and Italy," in Gill and Gempf, eds., *Graeco-Roman Setting*, p. 466. See also Brown, *Introduction to the New Testament*, pp. 561-62.

[124]Wolfgang Wiefel, "The Jewish Community in Ancient Rome and the Origins of Roman Christianity," in *The Romans Debate*, ed. Karl P. Donfried, rev. ed. (Peabody, Mass.: Hendrickson, 1991), p. 92. See also Brian M. Rapske, "Rome and Roman Christianity," *DLNTD*, pp. 1063-68; and Mark Reasoner, "Rome and Roman Christianity," *DPL*, pp. 850-55.

Perhaps such disputes precipitated the emperor Claudius's expelling the Jews from Rome in A.D. 49 (Acts 18:2). Most commentaries and studies of this edict interpret Suetonius's statement as follows: "[Claudius] expelled from Rome Jews who were making constant disturbances at the instigation of Chrestus" *(Iudaeos impulsore Chresto assidue tumultuantis Roma expulit)*.[125] Although the precise cause of such agitation between Jewish and Gentile converts is unknown, it very well could have been over issues of observing the law.[126] With the Jews gone, the Christian community broke completely with the synagogue and formed their own house churches. When the Jews were permitted to return, many Jewish Christians would have joined existing congregations, a move that led to internal tensions.

3.7.8.3. Paul's Letter to Rome. Most of our information about early Christianity in Rome comes from Paul's letter to the Romans, written from Corinth around A.D. 57/58.[127] First, Paul wrote to "all God's beloved" (Rom 1:7). This suggests a plurality of congregations meeting in different locations of the city, in house churches such as that of Aquila and Priscilla (Rom 16:5; see Rom 14—15; 16:10-11). It appears that during his imprisonment Paul also had some type of "house church" ministry (Acts 28:30-31). Second, the believers were predominantly Gentiles, with Jewish Christians in the minority. Hence the letter is full of references and allusions to Jews and Greeks and how, through God's grace, both groups are part of God's elect (Rom 1:16; 2:9-10; 3:9, 29; 9:24; 10:12). Third, there were tensions between Jewish and Gentile believers in the churches. Paul's appeal to the "strong" and the "weak" encouraged the Gentile majority to avoid behavior that, even though part of their charter of Christian freedom in matters of food and worship, could be offensive to their Jewish brothers and sisters (Rom 14:1—15:6).[128] Fourth, the church included different levels of Roman society (male and female, slave and free) and different nationalities. Of the twenty-five names mentioned in

---

[125]For further arguments and references, see Wiefel, "Jewish Community," pp. 92-94; Fitzmyer, *Romans,* pp. 30-32. "Chrestus" is taken to refer to Christ.

[126]Raymond Brown, with others, believes that Christianity in Rome was more devoted to Jewish law and customs (perhaps influenced by Peter and James) than were Paul's converts (Brown and Meier, *Antioch and Rome,* pp. 97-104).

[127]In addition to the commentaries, see the following specialized studies on the purpose of Romans: several essays in Donfried, ed., *Romans Debate;* James D. G. Dunn, *The Partings of the Ways: Between Christianity and Judaism and Their Significance for the Character of Christianity* (Philadelphia: Trinity Press International, 1991); L. Ann Jervis, *The Purpose of Romans,* JSNTSup 55 (Sheffield: JSOT, 1991); Francis B. Watson, *Paul, Judaism and the Gentiles. A Sociological Approach,* SNTSMS 56 (Cambridge: Cambridge University Press, 1986).

[128]Michael B. Thompson, "Strong and Weak," *DPL,* pp. 916-18; Thompson, "Stumbling Block," *DPL,* pp. 918-19.

Romans 16, some are Greek, some Roman, and others Jewish.

3.7.8.4. Paul in Rome. When Paul wrote his letter to the Romans, he expressed a wish to visit "all God's beloved in Rome" (Rom 1:7) on his way to begin a new mission in Spain (Rom 15:24, 28). No biblical documents record the realization of such a mission. All we know from Luke is that Paul was imprisoned (a form of house arrest) in Rome for a period of two years, during which he was able to meet people and continue his ministry of evangelism and teaching (Acts 28:30-31).[129]

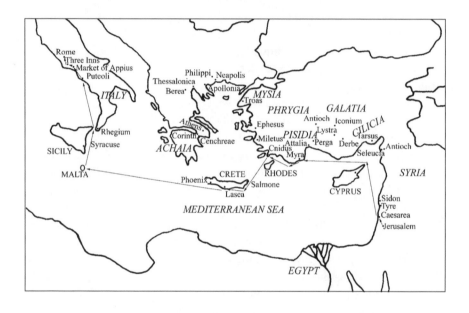

Map 5. Paul's journey from Jerusalem to Rome

The church fathers do not offer any helpful information on Paul's imprisonment. When Clement writes his eulogy of Paul, he mentions that the apostle "became a herald [of the gospel] in East and West, and won the noble renown which his faith merited. To the whole world he taught righteousness, and reaching the limits of the West he bore his witness before rulers" (*1 Clem.* 5.6-7). However, we have no way of knowing whether Spain is implied in the phrase

---

[129]Nothing is said about a release, further ministry, final arrest and martyrdom. This theory is an "argument from silence," usually proposed by scholars attempting to fit the Pastoral Epistles into Paul's ministry.

"limits of the West." Eusebius only records that Paul and Peter suffered martyrdom on the Ostian road about the same time (*Hist. Eccl.* 2.25.7-8).

3.7.8.5. Peter in Rome. Many legendary traditions detail Peter's relationship with the church in Rome. Some sources make him the founder of the church, while others simply identify him as one of the pillars.[130] Since neither Paul nor Luke intimates that Peter had any relationship with the church in Rome, there is no reason to think that he spent much time there before his martyrdom. No credible scholars today affirm that Peter is the founder of the church. Raymond E. Brown speaks for many when he writes:

> As for Peter, we have no knowledge at all of when he came to Rome and what he did there before he was martyred. Certainly he was not the original missionary who brought Christianity to Rome (and therefore not the founder of the church of Rome in that sense). There is no serious proof that he was the bishop (or local ecclesiastical officer) of the Roman church—a claim not made till the third century. Most likely he did not spend any major time at Rome before 58 when Paul wrote to the Romans, and so it may have been only in the 60s and relatively shortly before his martyrdom that Peter came to the capital.[131]

There also is no record of Peter's activities during the time he may have been in Rome.

3.7.8.6. Rome and Early Christianity. In addition to Paul's letter to the Romans, there are several other documents associated with the church in Rome.

Mark. Scholars who reconstruct the origin of this Gospel often locate it in Rome. Many identify Mark as the John Mark mentioned in Acts (Acts 12:25; 15:36-41; see Col 4:10; 2 Tim 4:11; Philem 24; 1 Pet 5:13) and cite a comment by Eusebius that Papias regarded the apostle Peter as Mark's informant (*Hist. Eccl.* 3.39.15; see also 2.15; 6.14.6)[132]

1 Peter. As mentioned earlier, scholars who take this as a genuine letter of Peter explain that "Babylon" (1 Pet 5:13) is a veiled reference to Rome and thus argue that the epistle was written by the apostle Peter from Rome around 60-63.

Hebrews. Even though scholars continue to debate the authorship, date and destination of Hebrews, virtually everyone admits that it is an anonymous letter written either from Alexandria, Jerusalem or Rome. A growing number favor Rome for its origin and destination. Reasons for this include the final greeting in the letter (Heb 13:23-24: "I want you to know that our brother Timothy has been set free; and if he comes in time, he will be with me when I see you. Greet

---

[130]Fitzmyer (*Romans*, pp. 29-30) has a concise listing of such sources.
[131]Brown and Meier, *Antioch and Rome*, p. 98.
[132]In addition to commentaries, see in Brown and Meier, *Antioch and Rome*, pp. 191-201.

all your leaders and all the saints. Those from Italy send you greetings") and the fact that the epistle was well known in Rome by the end of the first century (attested by *1 Clement* and the *Shepherd of Hermas*). If, as many believe, Hebrews was written in the 80s, we have, notes Brown, "an insight into the ongoing struggles of a Christian community that proved to be one of the most important in the history of Christianity."[133]

Revelation. This book, written just before the turn of the first century, includes much imagery applicable to Rome (Babylon). In the words of Brian Rapske:

> Babylon is the "great city" (Rev 16:19; 18:10, 16, 19, 21) seated on "seven hills" (Rev 17:9) and "the waters" which are "peoples, multitudes, nations and languages" (Rev 17:1, 15). It is the political power which holds kings and nations in thrall (Rev 17:2, 18; 18:3, 9), the great parasite to which vast goods and wealth go (Rev 18 passim). Babylon is the prostitute; morally corrupt and a corrupter (Rev 14:8; 17:5; 18:2). It is the place where the blood of the apostles, prophets and saints has been shed (Rev 17:6; 18:20, 24). John calls for believers to "come out of" or disassociate themselves from the city's sins (Rev 18:4).[134]

Apostolic Fathers. Sources such as *1 Clement* and Ignatius's letter *To the Romans* provide further insights into the nature of the church in Rome and its place among other churches in Italy. Some valuable information also comes from the *Shepherd of Hermas* and the *Didache,* two documents written somewhere near the turn of the first century.

In addition to Rome, we must not overlook another Christian community in Italy that Paul visited on his way to prison. Luke notes that, during a brief stop at the seaport of Puteoli, Paul and his party "found believers" and spent seven days with them (Acts 28:13-14). Then, when believers from Rome heard that Paul was arriving, some traveled the thirty to forty miles on the Appian Way to the Forum of Appius and Three Taverns (Acts 28:15). There is no way of knowing how the church in Puteoli began or whether there were churches in these and other towns and cities of Italy at this time.

3.8. The Church in Egypt

Since there is no evidence of any local congregations in specific towns or cities in Egypt in the first century, it is common to speak of Christianity in Egypt as "Alexandrian Christianity." Most students of religion know about the significance of Alexandria, with its large Jewish population, the translation of the

---

[133]Brown, *Introduction to the New Testament,* p. 701.
[134]Rapske, "Rome and Roman Christianity," p. 1067; on Babylon as Rome in 1 Peter and Revelation, see Alan J. Beagley, "Babylon," *DLNTD,* pp. 111-12.

Hebrew Scriptures into Greek (Septuagint) and the works of Philo, a Hellenistic Jew who sought to interpret the Old Testament by utilizing Greek philosophy and allegorical exegesis (see 1.2.2). Some New Testament scholars believe that Hebrews was written in Alexandria because it has so many theological and exegetical affinities with the writings of Philo.

"It is one of the ironies of history," notes William Petersen, "that although Christianity in the west is defined by such African luminaries as Clement of Alexandria, Origen, Tertullian, Cyprian and Augustine, its introduction to and the earliest development on that continent remain hidden."[135] The late tradition that credits Mark the Evangelist as the first missionary to establish a church in Alexandria (Eusebius, *Hist. Eccl.* 2.16) is fictitious.

There are several significant references to Egypt in the book of Acts. People from "Egypt and the parts of Libya belonging to Cyrene" are mentioned in Luke's roll call of nations at Pentecost (Acts 2:10); the synagogue of the Freedmen in Jerusalem includes Cyrenians and Alexandrians (Acts 6:9); and the baptism of the Ethiopian eunuch by Philip confirms another contact between Christianity and North Africa (Acts 8:26-40).

Luke also mentions that Apollos was a "native of Alexandria" who had some knowledge of Christianity but who required further instruction from Priscilla and Aquila (Acts 18:24-26). The Western text (D) includes the additional note at Acts 18:25 that Apollos "had been instructed in his own country in the word of the Lord." This addition, according to Bruce Metzger, "implies that Christianity had reached Alexandria by about A.D. 50. Whether the statement of the Western reviser depends upon personal knowledge or is based on inference, the implication no doubt accords with historical fact."[136] Birger Pearson, a leading expert on Egyptian Christianity, suggests that some of the persecuted Hellenists from Jerusalem after Stephen's martyrdom (Acts 8:1) may have been responsible for bringing the gospel to Alexandria.[137] Many scholars have noted "significant similarities" between Stephen's speech and the *Epistle of Barnabas,* "the oldest Christian document from Alexandria that we possess."[138]

---

[135]William Petersen, "North African Christianity," *ABD* 1:965-66.

[136]Metzger, *Textual Commentary,* p. 466.

[137]See Birger A. Pearson, "Christians and Jews in First-Century Alexandria," *HTR* 79 (1986): 206-16; Pearson, "Earliest Christianity in Egypt," in *The Roots of Egyptian Christianity,* ed. Birger A. Pearson and James E. Goehring (Philadelphia: Fortress, 1986); Pearson, "Christianity in Egypt," *ABD* 1:954-60. See also Jonathan M. Knight, "Alexandria, Alexandrian Christianity," *DLNTD,* pp. 34-37.

[138]Clinton E. Arnold, "Centers of Christianity," *DLNTD,* p. 149. Pearson writes, "Something of the flavor of Jewish Christianity in Alexandria can be extrapolated from *Barnabas* and the *Gospel of the Hebrews*" ("Christianity in Egypt," *ABD* 1:659). Note also Eusebius *Hist. Eccl.* 2.17.2-3.

Although Christianity in Egypt began in Alexandria and had its most signifi-cant development in the catechetical school presided over by Clement and Ori-gen, there is little doubt that it spread to other parts of the country as well, especially along the coastal regions of the Roman frontier, to places such as Cyrene.[139] However, there is no way of knowing how extensively it spread nor how many churches existed by the end of the first century. An examination of the apocryphal and Gnostic literature that emerged from Alexandria suggests that Egyptian Christianity was anything but monolithic.

3.9. Summary

From the preceding survey we are able to identify several significant fea-tures about the early church. First, by A.D. 100 the gospel had spread to nearly all Roman provinces and regions. Arranged alphabetically, these include Achaia, Asia, Bithynia, Cappadocia, Cilicia, Crete, Cyprus, Dalma-tia, Egypt, Galatia, Illyricum, Italy, Macedonia, Mysia, Pamphylia, Phrygia, Pisidia, Pontus and Syria. To this list one can also add the coastal areas of Palestine and Samaria. Up until approximately A.D. 50, the two foci were Jerusalem and Antioch; during the next fifty years the focus shifted to Ephe-sus and Rome.[140]

Most of our attention naturally focused on the missionary travels of the apos-tle Paul because he was such a key figure in the expansion and theology of the early church. It is estimated that Paul traveled nearly ten thousand miles during his career, utilizing all available modes of transportation.[141] An individual could cover approximately fifteen to twenty miles a day on foot, twenty-five to thirty-five by horse or a wheeled conveyance and one hundred miles by ship, depending on the winds.[142] The mileage figures in figure 6 by sociologist Rod-ney Stark utilize commonly traveled sea routes from Jerusalem to various cities of the Roman Empire and give us a visual representation of distances covered by Paul on some of his journeys.

Second, the expansion of the church was mainly an urban rather than a rural phenomenon. Although some Christian communities emerged in rural areas and smaller town and villages, missionaries targeted the major urban centers in

---

[139]W. Petersen, "North African Christianity," 1:967.

[140]See Brian S. Rosner, "The Progress of the Word," in *Witness to the Gospel*, ed. I. Howard Marshall and David Peterson (Grand Rapids, Mich.: Eerdmans, 1998), pp. 215-23.

[141]See Ronald. F. Hock, *The Social Context of Paul's Ministry: Tentmaking and Apostleship* (Philadelphia: Fortress, 1990), p. 27; Wayne A. Meeks, *The First Urban Christians* (New Haven, Conn.: Yale University Press, 1983), pp. 16-23.

[142]Meeks, *First Urban Christians*, p. 18; Brian M. Rapske, "Roman Empire, Christians and the," *DLNTD*, pp. 1061-62.

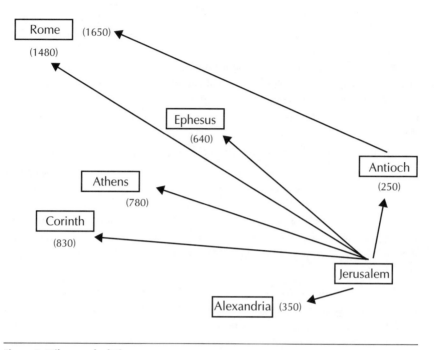

Figure 6. Mileage calculations

each region. Rodney Stark lists twenty-two Greco-Roman cities mentioned in the New Testament with populations ranging between 30,000 (Athens) and 650,000 (Rome). The major cities in Paul's mission included Rome (650,000), Ephesus (200,000), Antioch (150,000), Corinth (100,000), Damascus (45,000) and Athens (30,000)[143] Even though Stark omits centers with a population estimated below 30,000, we know of churches in other important cities, such as Philippi, Thessalonica and the seven churches of Revelation. These centers, in turn, became catalysts in spreading the gospel and establishing churches in neighboring towns and rural areas.

There is no way of knowing how many churches or how many Christians there were by the end of the first century. Luke's figure of five thousand believers just in Jerusalem (although some may have come from surrounding regions) following Pentecost is one of his numerical summaries, probably meaning a considerable number (see 3.1), and Pliny's letter to Trajan (A.D.

---

[143]Stark, *Rise of Christianity,* pp. 131-32; see Meeks, *First Urban Christians,* pp. 10-16; Schnabel, "Mission, Early Non-Pauline," pp. 757-58.

112), which mentions the spread of Christianity (Pliny refers to Christianity as a "superstition") throughout villages and rural districts, provides no numerical help either.[144]

Numerical estimates by archaeologists, sociologists, church historians and missiologists vary considerably. Rodney Stark, for example, uses his sociological insights to suggest that there were no more than 7,530 believers by the end of the first century.[145] At the other extreme, missiologist Robert T. Glover writes, "On the basis of all the data available it has been estimated that by the close of the apostolic period the total number of Christian disciples had reached half a million."[146] Perhaps the truth lies somewhere in between and probably closer to Stark's figures. It is easier to embrace Stark's projection of the growth of Christianity from A.D. 100 to the time of Constantine (c. 306-337), when the number of Christians approximated six million. Thus Christians numbered close to 10 percent of the population of the Roman Empire, estimated at sixty million by the beginning of the fourth century.[147]

Third, the church moved out of the synagogue into self-identifiable communities or house churches. Even though the missionaries of the church never gave up evangelizing Jews, Christians formed a separate identity in Jerusalem (Acts 2:38-47), Antioch (Acts 11:26) and other communities in Paul's mission.

Fourth, the spread of the church throughout the empire was a combination of divine and human elements: divine in the sense that all of this was possible only by God's initiative and providence; human in the sense that the Holy Spirit called, empowered and enabled individuals such as Peter, Philip, Stephen, Paul, Timothy, Lydia, Priscilla, Aquila and a host of other believers mentioned

---

[144]Bo Reicke suggests that there may have been as many as 80,000 Christians in Asia Minor alone around A.D. 100 and approximately 320,000 in the entire Roman empire (*The New Testament Era* [Philadelphia: Fortress, 1968], pp. 302-4). Robert Wilken is much more conservative when he writes, "The total number of Christians within the empire was probably less than fifty thousand, an infinitesimal number in a society comprising sixty million" (*The Christians As The Romans Saw Them* [New Haven, Conn.: Yale University Press, 1984], p. 31).

[145]Stark, *Rise of Christianity*, pp. 4-13.

[146]Robert T. Glover, *The Progress of World-Wide Missions* (New York: Harper, 1960), p. 18.

[147]Stark, *Rise of Christianity*, table, p. 7. Sixty million is a fairly unanimous estimate among historians. Biblical scholars differ on their estimates for individual cities. Brad Blue suggests that there were approximately 30,000 believers in Rome by A.D. 250 and about one hundred members in first-century Corinth ("Acts and the House Church," in Gill and Gempf, eds., *Graeco-Roman Setting*, pp. 127, 175 n. 219). Other estimates for Corinth range between thirty to fifty members (see Robert Banks, *Paul's Idea of Community*, rev. ed. [Peabody, Mass.: Hendrickson, 1994], p. 42; and Jerome Murphy-O'Connor, *St. Paul's Corinth*, GNS 6 [Collegeville, Minn.: Liturgical Press, 1983], pp. 153ff.).

in the New Testament to take the gospel to the ends of the earth (Mt 28:19-20). "Christianity," concludes Stark,

> did not grow because of miracle working in the marketplaces (although there may have been much of that going on), or because Constantine said it should, or even because the martyrs gave it such credibility. It grew because Christians constituted an intense community, able to generate the "invincible obstinacy" that so offended the younger Pliny but yielded immense religious rewards. And the primary means of its growth was through the united and motivated efforts of the growing numbers of Christian believers, who invited their friends, relatives, and neighbors to share the "good news."[148]

3.10. Diversity in Early Christianity and the Partings of the Ways[149]

3.10.1. Diversities in Early Christianity. Just as scholars acknowledge a diversity of "Judaisms" in the first century, many also identify diversities within early Christianity.[150] This reality forms the thesis of James Dunn's book *Unity and Diversity in the New Testament* (first published in 1977), where he identifies four different types or strands of early Christianity that appear in New Testament literature: Jewish Christianity, Hellenistic Christianity, apocalyptic Christianity and early Catholicism. Since he does not see these as separate or mutually exclusive categories, it is useful to illustrate them with overlapping circles (see figure 7).

What is significant to note here is that early Christianity could embrace such

---

[148]Stark, *Rise of Christianity,* p. 208.

[149]The following comments are a brief and simplified discussion of serious scholarly research and dialogue throughout the history of New Testament scholarship, particularly during the last decade. My main purpose is to identify some of the issues in the early church and to show the effects of that struggle. For further reading, see Raymond E. Brown, "Not Jewish Christianity and Gentile Christianity but Types of Jewish/Gentile Christianity," *CBQ* 45 (1983): 74-79; James D. G. Dunn, *Unity and Diversity in the New Testament,* 2d ed. (Philadelphia: Trinity Press International, 1990); Dunn, *Partings of the Ways;* James D. G. Dunn, ed., *Jews and Christians: The Partings of the Ways A.D. 70-135* (Grand Rapids, Mich.: Eerdmans, 1999); Craig A. Evans, "Christianity and Judaism: Partings of the Ways," *DLNTD,* pp. 159-70; L. Goppelt, *Apostolic and Post-Apostolic Times* (Grand Rapids, Mich.: Baker, 1970); Donald A. Hagner, "Jewish Christianity," *DLNTD,* pp. 579-87; Craig C. Hill, "Hellenists, Hellenistic and Hellenistic-Jewish Christianity," *DLNTD,* pp. 462-69; I. Howard Marshall, "Palestinian and Hellenistic Christianity: Some Critical Comments," *NTS* 19 (1972-1973): 271-87; John Reumann, *Variety and Unity in New Testament Thought* (Oxford: Oxford University Press, 1991); Gottfried Schille, "Early Jewish Christianity," *ABD* 1:935-38; Stephen G. Wilson, "Jewish-Christian Relations 70-170 C.E.," *ABD* 3:834-39. All these sources have excellent bibliographies that encompass a wide range of scholarship.

[150]For example, Jewish Christianity, Gentile Christianity, Hellenistic Christianity, Palestinian-Jewish Christianity, Hellenistic-Jewish Christianity, Hellenistic-Gentile Christianity, Pauline Christianity, Galilean Christianity, and so forth.

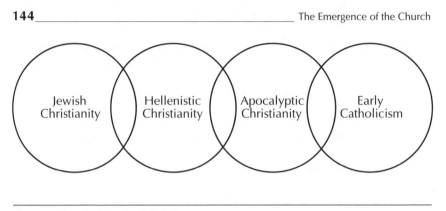

Figure 7. Diversity in early Christianity

diversity as long as it retained an essential unity with respect to the person of Christ.[151] Unfortunately, according to Dunn, there were developments in each of these categories where "acceptable diversity falls over into unacceptable diversity."[152] For Jewish Christianity it was Ebionism; for Hellenistic Christianity, Gnosticism; for apocalyptic Christianity, Montanism; and for early Catholicism, rigid ecclesiastical institutionalism.[153] Although each of these movements is represented in the literature, our focus will be on Jewish and Gentile Christianity.

Another valuable but somewhat different contribution to this discussion comes from Raymond Brown and John Meier, who prefer to speak of "varying types of 'Jewish/Gentile Christianity' " rather than separating the two.[154] I summarize their observations and comments diagrammatically but with the confession that this does not do full justice to the authors' insights (see figure 8).

The effect of these two interpretations is basically the same: early Christianity was characterized by considerable diversity.[155] This reality confirms what I have affirmed repeatedly throughout this study: the churches of the first century varied in their theology and praxis. The church was a dynamic phenomenon; there was no one divine pattern of organization, leadership, worship, and the like, so any desire to "get back to the New Testament church" must deal with this reality and ultimately ask, "To which church should we return?"

---

[151]See Dunn, _Unity and Diversity,_ pp. 235-366.

[152]Ibid., p. 265.

[153]Ibid., pp. 365-66.

[154]Brown and Meier, _Antioch and Rome,_ pp. 2-8. See also Brown, "Not Jewish Christianity and Gentile Christianity."

[155]In _Unity and Diversity,_ Dunn lists all the New Testament documents that show traces of Jewish Christianity (p. 265) and Hellenistic Christianity (p. 308).

Group IV	Group III	Group II	Group I
Jewish/Gentile Christianity	Jewish/Gentile Christianity	Jewish/Gentile Christianity	Jewish/Gentile Christianity
no Torah observance required	no Torah observance required	partial Torah observance (sabbath, food, laws)	full observance to Mosaic law
no abiding significance in Jewish cults, feasts, etc.	1 Cor 8: believers not required to abstain from foods	moderately conservative	Gentiles must become Jews
Hellenists more radical than Paul	Paul opposes Cephas (Gal 2:11, 13); Paul separates from Barnabas (Acts 15:39)	James and Peter (Acts 15; Gal. 2); men of James (Gal 2:11-14)	"circumcised believers" (Acts 11:2); "sect of the Pharisees" (Acts 15:5); "thousands of believers . . . among the Jews . . . zealous for the law" (Acts 21:20)
Stephen: disdain for Temple and Law(?)	"freedom from the law" (Gal 3:10-13)	association with the Jerusalem apostles	"false believers" (Gal 2:4)
John: separates Jesus from the Law—"your law," "their law"; temple destroyed	Torah observance not always abandoned completely (e.g. Paul)		"dogs . . . evil workers. . . . mutilate the flesh" (Phil 3:2)
Hebrews			

Figure 8. Summary of Brown and Meier

3.10.2. Partings of the Ways. This section will reiterate and briefly summarize some of the factors that led to the separation of early Christianity from Judaism and the split between Jewish and Gentile Christianity by the end of the first century.

Throughout this book I have reiterated that the early believers who formed the first Christian communities saw themselves as the true or renewed Israel of God within first-century Judaism (part two and figure 9).[156] They interpreted the Christ-event, particularly the resurrection and God's gift of the Spirit on the day of Pentecost, as the fulfillment of Old Testament prophecies and as events that marked them off as the eschatological people of God. Hence they remained in Jerusalem, continued to participate faithfully in cultic activities, studied their Scriptures and continued to proclaim that Jesus is the promised Messiah (Acts 1—5).

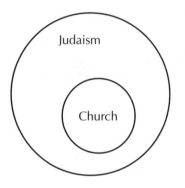

Figure 9. Partings of the ways: Phase 1

Most of the Jewish Christians in and around Jerusalem would fall into Group I on the Brown and Meier figure. They remained faithful to the Torah but were challenged by various threats to their theology and practice (see below). This type of Jewish Christianity survived most of these threats, including the destruction of Jerusalem in A.D. 70. Here tradition suggests that most Jewish believers fled to Pella in the Transjordan and continued a form of Judaism that may eventually have degenerated into some of the identifiable Jewish Christian sects (Ebionites, Nazoreans, and Elkesaites).[157] While there may have been a slight revival of Jewish Christianity in Jerusalem after A.D. 70, most scholars believe that by the end of the second Jewish revolt led by Bar Kokhba (132-135),

---

[156]The idea for these circles is adapted from Donald J. Selby, "Introduction to the New Testament," in _Introduction to the Bible_, ed. Donald J. Selby and James K. West (New York: Macmillan, 1971), pp. 328-30.

[157]So Hagner, "Jewish Christianity," pp. 584-85; H. Lichtenberger, "Syncretistic Features in Jewish and Jewish-Christian Baptism Movements," in Dunn, ed., _Jews and Christians,_ pp. 85-97; Wilson, "Jewish-Christian Relations 70-170 C.E.," 3:835.

"Christian and Jew were clearly distinct and separate."[158]

As we read through Acts we quickly realize that the relationship between Jewish Christianity and Judaism changed quite rapidly after Pentecost (see figure 10). From Luke's account we learn that not all the Jews in Jerusalem responded favorably to Peter's sermon to repent and be baptized. Many of them were not convinced that Jesus was the Jewish Messiah or that these new believers constituted the true Israel. Jewish unbelievers were offended by a number of events.

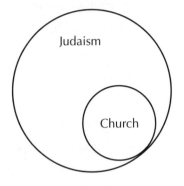

Figure 10. Partings of the ways: Phase 2

First, they resented (1) Peter's interpretation of certain portions of their Scripture, which implicated them in the death of Jesus of Nazareth (Acts 2:22-23; 3:12-15); (2) Peter's affirmation of Jesus' exaltation to the "right hand of God" (Acts 2:29-36; 3:17-26); and (3) Peter's insistence that repentance and baptism in the name of Jesus Christ were the only way for salvation (Acts 2:37-40; 3:19-26; 4:10-12).

Second, they were offended by Peter and John's power to heal a lame man "in the name of Jesus" and the apostles' audacity to present him publicly within the temple area (Acts 3:1-10).

Third, the Jewish leaders resented the attention that Peter and John received for this miracle from the populace in Jerusalem and their persistence in proclaiming the gospel (Acts 4:1-22). A power struggle soon emerged over the issue of authority. Members of the Jewish hierarchy—priests, captain of the temple, Sadducees, rulers, elders, scribes, Ananias the high priest and other members of the high priestly family (Acts 4:1-6)—questioned Peter's right to heal and preach (Acts 4:7: "By what power or by what name did you do this [heal]?"). The apostles were interrogated, threatened, imprisoned and flogged (Acts 4:18-

---

[158]Dunn, *Partings of the Ways,* p. 35. See also Evans, "Christianity and Judaism," p. 165.

31; 5:17-33, 40-41). Only the wise intervention of Gamaliel spared their lives and prevented a terrible persecution of the apostles and believers at this time (Acts 5:33-39). Animosities increased to the extent that a severe persecution arose against the church in Jerusalem, with Saul acting as one of the leading henchmen (Acts 8:3; 9:1-2). The Jewish leaders also endorsed Herod's murder of James and the imprisonment of Peter (Acts 12:1-5). The net result was that Jewish Christianity moved toward the periphery of Judaism.

During a third phase of development we can identify a number of reasons that explain why Jewish Christianity continued to move away from Judaism and why Gentile Christianity emerged (see figure 11).

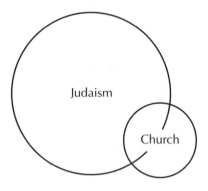

Figure 11. Partings of the ways: Phase 3

First, the rituals of Christian initiation (repentance, water baptism and reception of the Holy Spirit), the christological interpretation of the Old Testament, additional meetings in homes for the purpose of worship, celebrating the Lord's Supper, and the like began to give Jewish Christianity an identity separate from Judaism, because Christianity replaced some familiar and established patterns.

Second, tension between "Hellenists" and "Hebrews" over the distribution of food to their widows helped to identify two separate groups of Jewish Christians in Jerusalem (Acts 6:1-6).

Third, Stephen's speech, particularly his comments on the significance of Christ's death and his critique of the temple, precipitated his martyrdom and a subsequent persecution of likeminded Hellenistic believers (Acts 6:8—8:4).

Fourth, the spread of the gospel to the Samaritans and their inclusion into the early church was an affront to Jews and Jewish Christians (Acts 8:4-25).

Fifth, the conversion and baptism of the Ethiopian eunuch initiated a person into the Christian faith who previously was prohibited from entering "the assembly of the LORD" (Deut 23:1).

Sixth, Peter's visit with Cornelius, his vision and the conversion of the Gentile expanded the Christian mission to non-Jews and broke down existing food laws (Acts 9:32—11:18).

Seventh, Paul's experience on the Damascus road created suspicion and mistrust among the Jews of Jerusalem and Judea (Acts 9:26-30).

Eighth, in Antioch Paul developed his theological independence from the leaders in Jerusalem, and through that, members of the church were identified as "Christians," that is, a group distinct from Judaism rather than a sect of Judaism (Acts 11:26).

Ninth, Paul's confrontation with Peter and James at the Jerusalem Council and the council's subsequent endorsement (though qualified) of his mission to the Gentiles led to an ever-widening gap between Jewish and Gentile believers (Acts 15:1-35; Gal 2).

Tenth, Paul's theological development of a law-free gospel, asserting that Gentiles are saved by "faith in Jesus Christ" and not "by works of the law" (Gal 2:15-16 and other passages in his letters), threatened the more conservative Jewish Christians and led to provocation from Judaizers (see Brown and Meier, Groups II and III).[159] In essence, Paul argued that the law has no enduring validity for either Jew or Gentile because it has been superseded by faith in Jesus Christ. More and more, Paul became a victim of Jewish misunderstanding, hatred and persecution (Acts 9:23-25). Luke's accounts document repeated rejection of Paul's gospel, harassment of Paul and his coworkers, and several types of persecution, including his arrest in Jerusalem (see Acts 13—23; 2 Cor 11:24-29).

In phase 4 (see figure 12) we see the final results of the seeds of separation that

---

[159]The entire debate on Paul and the law during the last twenty-five years goes beyond the task here but is well documented. For further reading, see James D. G. Dunn, "Works of the Law and the Curse of the Law (Galatians 3:10-14)," *NTS* 31(1985): 523-42; Dunn, *Jesus, Paul and the Law* (Louisville: Westminster John Knox, 1990); James D. G. Dunn, ed. *Paul and the Mosaic Law* (Grand Rapids, Mich.: Eerdmans, 2001); Donald A. Hagner, "Jewish Christianity," *DLNTD*, pp. 579-87; Hans Hübner, *Law in Paul's Thought* (Edinburgh: T & T Clark, 1984); H. Räisänen, *Paul and the Law* (Tübingen: J. B. C. Mohr, 1983); E. P. Sanders, *Paul and Palestinian Judaism* (Philadelphia: Fortress, 1977); Sanders, *Paul, the Law, and the Jewish People* (Philadelphia: Fortress, 1983); Thomas Schreiner, "Works of the Law," *DPL*, pp. 975-79; Krister Stendahl, "The Apostle Paul and the Introspective Conscience of the West," *HTR* 56 (1963): 199-215; Frank Thielman, *From Plight to Solution: A Jewish Framework for Understanding Paul's View of the Law in Romans and Galatians*, NovTSup (Leiden: E. J. Brill, 1989); Thielman, "Law," *DPL*, pp. 529-42; Thielman, *The Law and the New Testament: The Question of Continuity* (New York: Crossroad, 1999); Stephen Westerholm, *Israel's Law and the Church's Faith* (Grand Rapids, Mich.: Eerdmans, 1988); Westerholm, *Paul and the Law: A Contextual Approach* (Downers Grove, Ill.: InterVarsity Press, 1994).

were sown throughout the first century between Jewish Christianity and Judaism as well as Jewish and Gentile Christianity. Much of what was happening took place as internal polemical debates between Jews and Jewish Christians over matters of the law. While most Jews may have been comfortable with a Group I or II (Brown and Meier) type of Jewish Christianity, problems arose with the more liberal perspectives shared by Groups III and IV (Brown and Meier).

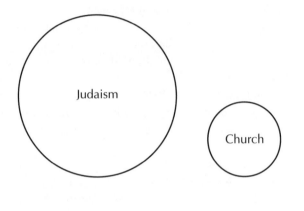

Figure 12. Partings of the ways: Phase 4

To a large extent, the conflicts centered on Paul's doctrine of a gospel free from the law as opposed to a commitment to the law held by the more conservative Jewish Christians (Judaizers). This set up an obvious polarity between Jewish Christians and unbelieving Jews. According to Donald Hagner, Jewish Christians "had to defend themselves against Jewish charges of disloyalty to the religion of Israel, abandonment of the law, and affiliation with an alien (if not pagan) religion whose membership was mainly Gentile."[160]

Evidence for this tension goes far beyond anti-Pauline polemics. Scholars have noted many references to hostility and persecution between Jewish Christians and the synagogue (unbelieving Jews) in the Gospels (see Mt 10:17; 23:34; Mk 13:9; Lk 21:12; Jn 9:22; 12:42; 16:1-4; note also Rev 2:9; 3:9).[161] The *Birkat ha-Minim* ("cursing of the heretic") was introduced as a specific attempt to drive Christians out of the synagogue (see 1.2.1.9).

[160]Hagner, "Jewish Christianity," p. 581.
[161]Evans, "Christianity and Judaism," pp. 159-70; Hagner, "Jewish Christianity," pp. 579-87; Schille, "Early Jewish Christianity," 1:935-38; Wilson, "Jewish-Christian Relations 70-170 C.E.," 3:834-39. These references represent brief accounts of research on the subject (see their bibliographies for more information).

During this time there was continual development of a Christian theology that repeatedly questioned and reinterpreted what James Dunn calls the "four-fold foundation" or "four pillars" on which the various forms of first-century Judaism were built: (1) monotheism; (2) election; (3) the covenant, focused on the Torah; and (4) the land, focused on the temple. Most of Dunn's book deals with the tensions between Judaism and early Christianity over these issues and how Christianity's reformulation of these cherished beliefs became "unaccept-able to mainstream Judaism."[162] The end result was that in the second century, "Jews began to regard Christianity as idolatry and heresy; Christians began to view Judaism in terms of apostasy and obduracy."[163]

By way of conclusion, however, two observations about Jewish Christianity are important: first, it was largely replaced by the Gentile-Christian church, which now claimed to be the true Israel; second, rabbinic Judaism triumphed within the Palestinian-Jewish communities.[164]

During this time of geographical expansion and theological self-definition, the church was also going through a process of institutionalization.[165] Thus, we turn now to examine several aspects of the church that emerged during the first century from the time of its inception as a rather loosely organized charismatic community to a more structured association of believers.

---

[162]Dunn, *Partings of the Ways,* p. 35.

[163]Evans, "Christianity and Judaism," p. 167.

[164]To quote Philip S. Alexander, "Jewish Christianity was finally destroyed between the upper and nether millstone of triumphant Gentile Christianity and triumphant Rabbinism" ("'The Parting of the Ways' from the Perspective of Rabbinic Judaism," in Dunn, ed., *Jews and Christians,* p. 24). See also William S. Campbell, "Church as Israel, People of God," *DLNTD,* pp. 204-19.

[165]See Derek J. Tidball, "Social Setting of Mission Churches," *DPL,* pp. 883-92 and his useful bibliography.

4

THE EMERGENCE
OF MINISTRY,
LEADERSHIP &
CHURCH ORDER
IN THE EARLY CHURCH

Many scholars acknowledge that it is difficult to determine the nature of early-church leadership, government, order and ministry from the New Testament literature, and in spite of a voluminous amount of research, there is little consensus among scholars on these topics. Perhaps this accounts for the existence of so many different (and often irreconcilable) church groups and denominations on these matters. Nevertheless, as Kevin Giles observes, "All too many Presbyterians, Roman Catholics, Anglicans and Pentecostals, just to take four examples, find their church order and no other endorsed by the NT."[1]

A number of understandable reasons account for this situation. First, the literature that deals with these topics, both in the New Testament and the early church fathers, is incomplete and ambiguous, thus inviting a variety of interpretations and suppositions.[2] Second, scholars approach the text with different pre-

---

[1]Kevin N. Giles, "Church Order, Government," *DLNTD*, p. 220.
[2]Unfortunately, the study of leadership in the early church is one of those areas characterized more by *eisegesis* (reading *into* the text) than *exegesis* (discovering the meaning *out* of the text). Far too often we come to the text with our contemporary presuppositions and practices of leadership and church order, hoping to substantiate what we already believe. True, there are times

suppositions and methodologies. Robert Banks expresses this reality with respect to church order and government when he writes:

> During the last half-century Paul's teaching and practice regarding how the Christian communities were ordered and led has undergone frequent investigation. (1) Exegetical work on Paul has rediscovered the charismatic dimension in Paul's approach to church order, developed a more contextual understanding of his approach and emphasized the indigenous leadership of his communities. (2) Socio-historical and sociological investigation of Paul has explored connections between Paul's church and other first-century institutions, authority and power, charisma and its routinization. In addition feminist perspectives on Paul have discussed the role of women in ministry in the light of a cultural analysis of his writings.[3]

Third, scholars begin their investigation of the New Testament at different points. Some follow the canonical order of the text and proceed from the Gospels through the book of Revelation. Others approach the text chronologically, believing that one must begin with Paul, the earliest writer, and then continue with texts that were written after his death. Any approach is critical, because it determines how the material is used to reconstruct the early church. For example, it makes a big difference if we attribute the ecclesiology in Matthew to an audience around A.D. 85 or to the historical Jesus around A.D. 33-34. The approach to Acts is no less problematic. Here is a document, probably written in the mid-eighties, supposedly telling the history of the early church between A.D. 34-64 but possibly reflecting practices of the church from Luke's time, which he projected back to the beginning of the Christian movement (e.g., Acts 20:17-38).

This chapter will examine the New Testament concepts of church leadership and ministry and test two of the working hypotheses mentioned in the introduction, namely, "early Catholicism" and "diversity." The definition of early Catholicism, when applied to church structure, leadership, and the like, claims that the church began as a charismatic community but took on the markings of an institution by the end of the first century. By definition, a charismatic community supposedly operates under the direct influence of the Holy Spirit and its members exercise their spiritual gifts *(charismata)* for the "common good," that is, for

---

when we discover a truth that makes us reexamine our beliefs and change our practices, but on most occasions we become more dogmatic and unwilling to change, believing that change is a sign of accommodation or a breach of trust with tradition. Today we are more tempted to change our ecclesiology for social, psychological and physical reasons rather than as a result of scriptural teaching. For example, a believer may switch from a high liturgical type of church to one more charismatic (or vice versa) simply because of the style rather than any theology of worship.
[3]Robert Banks, "Church Order and Government," *DPL,* p. 131.

the sake of the body of believers (see discussion below and figure 13 below on Rom 12:6-8; 1 Cor 12:8-10, 27-28). According to 1 Corinthians 12:28 and Ephesians 4:11, the Spirit "gave" certain *leaders* to the church (apostles, prophets, evangelists, pastors/teachers), although they were not regarded as superior to other members of the congregation. The early church believed that the Spirit was given to all believers and was active in the lives of all God's people (see Rom 12:11; 1 Cor 2:4, 12-13; 12:7; Gal 3:5; 5:18, 22; 1 Thess 5:19-21).

Signs of a more "institutionalized" church are evident in the Pastoral Epistles, where specific leaders and offices are prominent. That is, Timothy was formally installed into his office through a type of ordination: "the laying on of hands" by the apostle Paul and the "council of elders/presbyters" (2 Tim 1:6; 1 Tim 4:14; see also 1 Tim 5:22). Titus, who may have had a similar appointment, is charged to "appoint elders" in the churches on the island of Crete (Tit 1:5). This type of human appointment, as well as the lengthy qualifications laid out for the offices of bishops (1 Tim 3:1-7; Tit 1:7-9), deacons (1 Tim 3:8-13) and elders (1 Tim 5:17-22), surpasses anything found in the early letters of Paul and puts church leadership on a trajectory that leads to continuing institutionalization in the threefold office of bishop, elder and deacon in the following centuries (see 4.11).[4]

4.1. Apostles

Luke ends his Gospel with two brief postresurrection appearances of Jesus. The first appearance was to two of his followers on the road to Emmaus, where, in the intimate fellowship of a meal, Jesus affirmed the reality of his resurrection and reinforced the fact that all the events of his life were the fulfillment of Scripture (Lk 24:13-35). The second was Jesus' appearance to the eleven disciples and "their companions" in Jerusalem, where he again revealed himself as the resurrected Lord, enlightened their minds to understand the fulfillment of Scripture (Lk 24:44-47) and promised that they soon would be "clothed with power from on high" (Lk 24:49). After the ascension near Bethany, the group returned to Jerusalem with new hope and joy.

These events provide an important segue to the book of Acts, where Luke begins his story of the emergence of the church. In a *final* postresurrection appearance to his disciples, Jesus reaffirmed his promise to bestow the Holy Spirit upon them so that they would be empowered to be his witnesses to "the ends of the earth" (Acts 1:8; see Lk 24:48-49). The group that witnessed this ascension near the mount called Olivet (we are not certain how many were

---

[4]Hans von Campenhausen develops this in *Ecclesiastical Authority and Spiritual Power in the Church of the First Three Centuries* (Peabody, Mass.: Hendrickson, 1997), pp. 149-292.

present) returned to the "room upstairs" in Jerusalem where they had been stay-ing and there joined other believers, including Jesus' family, a number of women and other believers (Acts 1:1-15).

The first item on the agenda at this gathering was to replace Judas with Matthias and thus reconstitute the group to its original number and signifi-cance (see 2.5.2). However, nothing further is mentioned about his ministry in the early church. In fact, of all the Twelve, only Peter played a major role in the leadership of the early church. The James who emerged later to become the head elder of the Jerusalem church was James the Lord's brother, not James the apostle. The latter was killed by Herod (Acts 12:1-2), but unlike the case with Matthias, he was not replaced in order to keep the number of apos-tles at twelve.

The term *apostle* is commonly used to designate the twelve individuals whom Jesus chose to be his specific followers, learners (disciples) and commis-sioned envoys, or messengers called to proclaim the gospel (Mt 10:2; Mk 3:14; Lk 6:13; Acts 1:2).[5] The noun *apostle (apostolos)* is derived from the Greek verb *apostellō,* which means "to send or commission." Hence in the New Testament apostles are individuals serving as missionaries or preachers of the gospel. Sev-eral scholars suggest that the term has parallels to the *šāliaḥ* (someone commis-sioned; an agent representing an individual or cause) found in late rabbinic literature. Thus Paul W. Barnett suggests that Jesus took this concept, "applied it first to himself as 'the one *sent* by God' and then, by extension, to those who were *sent* by him first to Galilee and then to the Gentiles."[6]

---

[5]Only Matthew refers to "twelve disciples" (*mathētēs,* Mt 10:1; 11:1; 20:17; cf. 28:16). Although *mathētēs* can refer to the Twelve, it is used more frequently and consistently to describe a larger circle of Jesus' followers and members of the early church in Acts (see Robert P. Meye, "Disciple," *ISBE* 1:947-48). For additional reading, see Paul W. Barnett, "Apostle," *DPL,* pp. 45-51; Hans-Dieter Betz, "Apostle," *ABD* 1:309-11; Colin G. Kruse, "Apostle," *DJG,* pp. 27-33; Kruse, "Apostle, Apostleship," *DLNTD,* pp. 76-82; Kruse, *New Testament Models for Ministry: Jesus and Paul* (Nashville: Nelson, 1984); Karl H. Rengstorf, "ἀποστέλλω κτλ," *TDNT* 1:398-447; William C. Robinson, "Apostle," *ISBE* 1:192-95; Erich von Eicken, Helgo Lindner, Dietrich Müller and Colin Brown, "Apostle," *NIDNTT* 1:126-37. All these authors list additional valuable sources in their bibliographies. For a succinct overview, see Ralph P. Mar-tin, "Patterns of Ministry," in *The Family and the Fellowship* (Grand Rapids, Mich.: Eerdmans, 1979), pp. 56-75; and J. B. Lightfoot's timeless section on "The Christian Ministry" in his com-mentary *St. Paul's Epistle to the Philippians* (London: Macmillan, 1898), pp. 181-269.

[6]Barnett, "Apostle," p. 47; see also Kruse, "Apostle," pp. 29-30. After a detailed discussion of current approaches Kruse concludes: "there is a strong case for claiming that the idea of the Christian apostolate originated with Jesus and that he understood it in a way similar to that reflected in the use of *šālah/apostellō* terminology in the OT. This in turn means that Jesus' understanding of the apostolate has close affinities with that of the function of the *šāliaḥ* reflected in the rabbinic writings" (p. 29). These views generally follow those of Karl H. Reng-storf's article in *TDNT.* Dietrich Müller, on the other hand, disagrees with the *šāliaḥ* interpreta-

Although the idea of sending for the purpose of preaching the gospel is the primary meaning in the New Testament, we shall see that the apostles performed other functions as well.

4.1.1. Apostles in Luke-Acts. Luke's definition of an apostle is unique in limiting the title to disciples of Jesus who witnessed the resurrected Lord (Acts 1:21-22).[7] In the first half of Acts, Luke equates _apostles_ with the Twelve (Acts 6:2; note also Lk 6:13: "he called his disciples and chose twelve of them, whom he also named apostles") and indicates that they were the first leaders of the Jerusalem church (Acts 1:2; 2:37, 42-43; 4:33, 35-37; 5:2, 12, 18, 27-32, 40; 6:6; 8:1, 14, 18; 9:27; 11:1; 14:4; 15:2-23; 16:4).

These references to apostolic leadership in the early church depict a wide variety of functions and responsibilities. In addition to preaching, teaching and performing miracles (Acts 2:42-43; 4:33; 5:12), the apostles distributed aid to the needy (Acts 4:35, 37; 5:2), approved and anointed "the Seven" (Acts 6:6), authenticated the mission to Samaria (Acts 8:14) and to the Gentiles (Acts 11:1, 18), received the converted Saul (Acts 9:27; 15:4) and participated in the Jerusalem Council (Acts 15:1-35). Acts 16:4 is the last time the Twelve are mentioned by Luke. Their identity as a special group ceases even though certain functions of their ministry continue with other individuals.[8]

4.1.2. Apostles in Paul's Letters. As noted above, except in one case (Acts 14:4, 14) Luke limits the concept of apostleship to Jesus' twelve disciples. The Twelve are recognized as the leaders of the early church until Paul and Barna-

---

tion. No doubt he expresses the sentiments of many scholars on this issue when he writes, "We are forced by the perplexing multitude of attempts at a solution to the conclusion that the darkness that lies over the beginnings of the primitive Christian apostolate can no longer be illuminated with certainty. In any case, if we take the growth of the canon seriously, we shall have to recognize that the concepts of the apostolate vary in the various NT writings. However we try to understand these various conceptions in their historical setting, we cannot avoid hypotheses. That does not free us from the duty of choosing the most probable of these, and of constantly checking and questioning it anew" ("Apostle," _NIDNTT_ 1:134).

[7]The one exception is his reference to Paul and Barnabas as apostles (Acts 14:4, 14). It appears that even though Luke regarded the twelve in a unique way and with a special function to fulfill, he saw Paul and Barnabas as servants who were commissioned by the church for missionary work. There is no transfer of authority to Paul and Barnabas nor are they considered successors of the twelve apostles. See the helpful analysis by John A. Kirk, "Apostleship Since Rengstorf," _NTS_ 21 (1974-75), pp. 261-64. Dietrich Müller argues that Luke attributed apostleship to the Twelve _after_ and not before the time of Paul, thus making the twelve apostles "guarantors of the legitimate tradition" (_NIDNTT_ 1:135). This, however, does not imply any form of apostolic succession, for Müller writes that the New Testament "never betrays any understanding of the apostolate as an institutionalized church office, capable of being passed on" (p. 135).

[8]See David L. Bartlett, _Ministry in the New Testament_ (Minneapolis: Fortress, 1993), esp. pp. 115-23.

bas begin their mission to the Gentiles. When we turn to Paul's letters, however, we see a different and more expansive concept of the term in two different ways. First, Paul is absolutely clear and adamant that he is called by God to be an apostle; second, some of Paul's coworkers and fellow believers also are designated as apostles.

Paul's personal claim stems from his encounter with the risen Christ (a christophany) on the road from Jerusalem to Damascus (Acts 9:1-9; see also Acts 22:6-21; 26:12-18). For Paul, this event is as meaningful and valid as the experience of the twelve apostles. Thus, while defending his apostleship to the Corinthians, he writes: "Am I not free? Am I not an apostle? *Have I not seen Jesus our Lord?* Are you not my work in the Lord?" (1 Cor 9:1; italics added). This is emphasized again in the creedal statements of 1 Corinthians 15:3-8:

> For I handed on *(paradidōmi)* to you as of first importance what I in turn had received: that Christ died for our sins in accordance with the scriptures, and that he was buried, and that he was raised on the third day in accordance with the scriptures, and that he appeared to Cephas, then to the twelve. Then he appeared to more than five hundred brothers and sisters at one time, most of whom are still alive, though some have died. Then he appeared to James, then to all the apostles. Last of all, as to one untimely born, he appeared also to me.[9]

In this passage Paul emphasizes his experience of the resurrected Lord along with the other witnesses mentioned. In some ways he could be considered the "thirteenth" apostle because he meets Luke's criteria for the Twelve. Paul makes a similar point in Galatians when he clarifies that his call and appointment were from God and not "human authorities" (Gal 1:1).

Paul is equally adamant about his call and commission as an apostle to the Gentiles when he corresponds with the churches he founded (see Rom 1:1, 5; 11:13; 1 Cor 1:1; 2 Cor 1:1; Gal 1:1; Col 1:1). A similar claim is repeated in the letters to Timothy and Titus, where Paul's call and authority as an apostle are recognized and where he is presented as the guarantor of Christian faith and practice (1 Tim 1:1; 2:7; 2 Tim 1:1, 11; Tit 1:1; see also Eph 1:1; 3:1-6).[10]

---

[9]Barnett suggests that the phrase "last of all" implies a finality of such appearances: "Paul is able to go on to say 'I am the least of the apostles . . . by the grace of God I am [an apostle]' because the apostles are a group limited in number. He can say that he is the 'least of the apostles' since he is, in reality, the 'last' apostle to whom the Lord 'appeared'" ("Apostle," p. 48). One doubts, however, that Paul meant that there were no apostles *after* him (contra Barnett, "Apostle," p. 50).

[10]Hans-Dieter Betz observes that Paul does not refer to himself as an apostle in his early letters (the prescript of 1 Thessalonians, Philippians and Philemon), suggesting that it first appears in Gal 1:1, then in subsequent letters when others challenge his apostleship ("Apostle," *ABD* 1:310).

Not every witness of the risen Lord became an apostle (e.g., the five hundred in 1 Cor 15:6). But elsewhere Paul either mentions explicitly or implies that there are other apostles in the church besides himself and the Twelve (1 Cor 9:5; 15:7). In Romans 16:7 he mentions that his relatives Andronicus and Junia are "prominent among the apostles." By implication the list could include Sosthenes (1 Cor 1:1), Apollos (1 Cor 4:9, though Paul refers to Apollos and himself in 1 Cor 3:5 as "servants" [diakonos]), Barnabas (1 Cor 9:5-6; Gal 2:8-9; explicit in Acts 14:4, 14), Timothy (1 Cor 16:10, 1 Thess 2:7), Silvanus (1 Thess 1:1; 2:7) and some "other apostles" not mentioned by name (1 Cor 15:7).

On several occasions the NRSV translates apostolos as "messenger," suggesting that someone like Epaphroditus (Phil 2:25), Titus and other "brothers" (2 Cor 8:23) were not on the same level as the apostles and thus not members of the apostolate. The fact that Paul mentions apostles *first* in his list of church leaders indicates that this is the highest gift of ministry and that probably many other apostles were working in the early churches (1 Cor 12:28; see also Eph 4:11).[11] But being first on the list does not imply hierarchical structure of any kind. These are spiritual gifts for building up the body of Christ (ekklēsia) in unity and maturity (Rom 12:3-8; 1 Cor 12—14; Eph 4:11-16). Paul nowhere gives the impression that his position sets him apart or exalts him above others in the church. He does, however, believe that his apostleship gives him authority to reprimand, admonish and discipline his congregation (see 2 Cor 13:1-10).

To sum up the discussion to this point, one can make the following observations with respect to apostles: (1) The idea or concept goes back to Jesus' call and commission of twelve disciples to be witnesses to the gospel. (2) In Acts, Luke portrays the leadership of the Twelve in the early church as a continuation of the ministry they began with the earthly Jesus. (3) Paul repeatedly affirms his call and commission as a legitimate apostle to the Gentiles on equal standing with the Twelve. (4) Since apostles are one of God's appointed ministries for the church, we must assume that a significant number of indi-

---

[11]Still, it is worth noting that in the seventy-nine times apostolos is used in the Greek New Testament, the noun refers almost exclusively to the Twelve and to Paul. When Heb 3:1 designates Jesus "the apostle and high priest," it conveys the idea that Jesus is the one sent by God (see Heb 1:1-2) to represent God to his people. John uses apostolos only once in his Gospel (Jn 13:16) with the connotation of "messenger" but develops his story of Jesus as the one sent (apostellō) by God into the world (Jn 3:16-17, 34; 5:36-38; 6:29, 57; 7:29; 10:36; 11:42; 17:1-25; 20:21; see also 1 Jn 4:9-10, 14). John equates Jesus' disciples with the Twelve (Jn 6:67, 70-71; 20:24) but avoids calling them apostles. For other New Testament references to apostle, see Eph 3:5; 4:11; 1 Pet 1:1; 2 Pet 1:1; 3:2; Jude 17; Rev 2:2; 18:20; 21:14.

viduals served in this capacity, even though New Testament writers do not refer to them by name.[12]

4.1.3. The Ministry of Apostles. As already noted, the primary function of an apostle was to be a witness to the gospel. This was true of the Twelve, although they performed additional ministries in the early church. The same could be said of Paul, who repeatedly emphasized that he was called as an apostle to take the gospel to the Gentiles (Rom 1:1, 5; 11:13; Gal 2:8; see also Acts 9:15; 22:21; 26:20). His primary ministry as an apostle was that of a preacher, missionary or even evangelist (1 Cor 1:17; 2:1-5; 9:16-17; 15:11; 2 Cor 5:19-20).

In attempting to discern the functions and authority of an apostle in the New Testament we must be careful not to make Paul the normative apostle or to make any particular church (e.g., Jerusalem, Corinth or Ephesus) the normative church. Paul was unique among the apostles, and all his churches had unique characteristics and needs. Hence the role of the apostles and their functions were determined primarily by the needs of specific churches. Unfortunately, we know very little about the activities of apostles other than Paul. But if Paul can serve as a model, we may assume that other apostles functioned in areas of doctrine, discipline and administration in the local churches.

In addition to Paul's preaching and evangelistic activity, he was also engaged in teaching, solving congregational and personal problems, disciplining and admonishing certain members, performing administrative tasks, healing, and praying for his congregations. In other words, "he wore many hats." As a teacher and prophet his responsibility was to clarify the mysteries of God both orally and in writing (Rom 16:25-26; 1 Cor 2:15; 4:1; Eph 3:1-6). But he also had to expose false apostles whose demeanor and teaching did not conform to the truth of the gospel. When he exposed "false apostles" (2 Cor 11:13) or the "super-apostles" (2 Cor 11:5; 12:11) in Corinth, he wrote that "the signs of a true apostle were performed among you with utmost patience, signs and wonders and mighty works" (2 Cor 12:12; see also Rom 15:18-19).[13]

Another component of Paul's ministry was the delegation of authority to other individuals. As noted earlier, some were apostles, but a far larger number

---

[12]Floyd V. Filson make the following astute observation: "It is remarkable . . . that most of the leaders in the history [of the church] are not numbered among the Twelve. If we ask what persons take an active and influential role, there are six who stand out. This 'big six' includes Peter, Barnabas, Stephen, Philip, Paul, and James the brother of Jesus. Only one of these six was a member of the Twelve" (*Three Crucial Decades* [Richmond: John Knox Press, 1963], p. 14).

[13]Bengt Holmberg believes that Paul's influence as the founder of certain churches "transformed every aspect of their existence: spiritual, intellectual, ethical and social" (*Paul and Power: The Structure of Authority in the Primitive Church As Reflected In the Pauline Epistles* [Lund: CWK Gleerup, 1978], p. 72).

can be categorized as brothers, companions, coworkers, coprisoners, fellow soldiers, and the like.[14] There is no evidence in the New Testament that Paul personally appointed apostles. Apostles always are by God's appointment; they are one of God's spiritual gifts to the church. Their authority, including Paul's, comes from the Lord and is recognized by, not imposed upon, the church.

The same is true of the spiritual gifts that God gives to church members. Thus Paul encouraged his readers to acknowledge these gifts within the context of the church (Rom 12:3-8; 1 Cor 12; Eph 4:11-16). On several occasions, "the apostle" specifically referred to such relationships in his letters. For example, he exhorted the Thessalonians "to respect those who labor *[kopiaō]* among you, and have charge of you *[proistēmi]* in the Lord and admonish you" (1 Thess 5:12).[15] We do not know who authorized these individuals to work in the church or who gave them this authority. Were they apostles, or did they possess a different spiritual gift?

A similar situation emerges with Paul's commendation of Stephanas and members of his household to the Corinthians: "I urge you to put yourselves at the service *[hypotassō]* of such people, and of everyone who works and toils with them . . . for they refreshed my spirit as well as yours. So give recognition *[epiginōskō]* to such persons" (1 Cor 16:16-18). This appears to be a simple case of Paul the apostle requesting (not legislating) that the spiritual gifts of Stephanas and some members of his household be acknowledged in the church. It does not appear that these individuals had any specific title or office.

Recently, certain scholars have connected local congregational leadership to the head of the household where the church met. Such could be the case with Stephanas as well as with Prisca and Aquila (Rom 16:3-5; 1 Cor 16:19) and Philemon and Apphia (Philem 1-2). Hence David Bartlett writes:

> While the evidence is not conclusive . . . it is likely that the Pauline churches, for all their equality in the Spirit, nonetheless reflected something of the social structure of their time. Heads of households and of house churches were quite likely those Christians who were wealthy enough to house and feed Paul or other missionaries on their visits to Hellenistic towns. Along with that patronage quite likely went a certain authority. And it would not be surprising if those who had positions of leadership in a household, a guild, or a community were acknowledged as having particular authority in the church as well.[16]

---

[14]E. Earle Ellis, "Paul and His Co-Workers," *NTS* 17 (1971): 437-52, lists thirty-six individuals in various categories.

[15]Romans 16:2 uses *prostatis*, the nominal form of *proistēmi*, for Phoebe, translated in the NRSV as "benefactor." Timothy almost appears as a "surrogate" apostle for Paul to the believers in Philippi (see Phil 2:19-22).

[16]Bartlett, *Ministry in the New Testament*, p. 41; see also Colin Kruse, "Ministry," *DPL*, pp. 603-4.

However, there is no way of knowing with certainty if and how the apostles related to this type of structure.

There appear to have been several significant developments in the concept of *apostles* during the postapostolic writings of the New Testament and the early church fathers. The author of the Pastorals, for example, appeals to Paul's apostolic authority "as the preeminent guarantor of right Christian tradition" in order to combat the rising threats of false teaching and doctrine in the postapostolic church (see esp. 2 Tim 1:11-14).[17]

During the postapostolic age, when heresy, apostasy and schism threatened to destroy the church, it became necessary to appeal to the apostles, the apostolic faith and apostolic authority. This trend is noticeable, not only in the Pastorals, but also in Ephesians, which mentions that the church is "built upon the foundation of the apostles and prophets" (Eph 2:20; also Eph 3:5 and 2 Pet 3:2: "Remember the words spoken in the past by the holy prophets, and the commandment of the Lord and Savior spoken through your apostles"). John's image of the eternal city describes this same foundation of the "twelve apostles of the Lamb" (Rev 21:14). The trajectory toward apostolic authority continued into the second and third centuries with the composition of the Apostles' Creed and the publication of such documents as The Apostolic Rule of Faith, The Apostolic Canon of Scripture and The Apostolic Office.[18]

Several observations emerge from a study of this later literature: (1) Most writers of these documents refer to Paul but are aware of other apostles; (2) there is a development of the threefold offices of bishop, elder and deacon already present in the Pastorals; (3) there appears to be considerable overlapping in the functions of apostles, teachers, prophets, bishops and elders (presbyters); (4) there is no specific mention of "apostolic succession" until the late second century, although *1 Clement* 44.2 may imply that possibility. Colin Kruse provides a succinct summary at this point:

> It may be said in very general terms that within the NT literature under consideration, the emphasis falls upon the function of apostles as witnesses of the resurrec-

---

[17]Bartlett, *Ministry in the New Testament,* p. 159.

[18]Could this be why Acts is called "The Acts of the Apostles"? Acts first appears as a separate work under this title around A.D. 150, after the Gospel of Luke became part of the fourfold Gospel collection (see Arthur G. Patzia, *The Making of the New Testament* [Downers Grove, Ill.: InterVarsity Press, 1995], p. 90). For a brief discussion of *apostle* in the writings of the early apostolic fathers, including useful bibliographic references, see Giles, "Church Order, Government," pp. 224-26; Colin G. Kruse, "Ministry," *DLNTD*, pp. 744-75; Kruse, "Apostle, Apostleship," pp. 80-82. The documents examined by these authors include the *Epistle of Barnabas, 1 Clement, Didache,* the epistles of Ignatius, Polycarp's *To the Philippians, 2 Clement,* and *Shepherd of Hermas.*

tion and preachers of the gospel of Jesus Christ. In one place the Twelve are portrayed as the foundations upon which the church is built and in another as the authoritative transmitters of the tradition. In the writings of the apostolic fathers the emphasis upon apostles as preachers is also found, but this is supplemented variously by emphases upon their role as examples in the matter of godly living and perseverance in face of persecution, upon ways in which true and false apostles/prophets may be distinguished, and upon the apostles' role in appointing bishops and presbyters in the church, all of which reflect the concerns of the post-apostolic church.[19]

4.2. Prophets

There is no denying that prophets and the gift *(charisma)* of prophecy were a significant component of leadership in the early church. Paul listed this ministry second in his triad of church leaders (apostles-prophets-teachers, 1 Cor 12:28). Luke saw the fulfillment of Joel's prophecy at Pentecost as the universalization of God's Spirit, ushering in a new age of prophetic activity (Acts 2:17-18). Ephesians identifies prophets as one of God's "gifts" to the church; they, along with the apostles, form the foundation of the church (Eph 2:20; 3:5).[20] Some New Testament books, such as 2 Peter, Jude and 1 John, reveal a strong concern to expose and rid the church of *false* prophets, and the author of Revelation intended his book to be understood as a prophecy (Rev 1:3; 22:7, 10, 18-19).

It is difficult to describe prophetic activity from the New Testament, which never clearly defines the office and function. Some scholars argue that New Testament prophecy needs to be limited to persons with supernatural revelations of the Spirit in dreams and visions that lead to periodic oracular utterances.[21] Agabus, for example, predicted a famine "by the Spirit" (Acts 11:28) and enacted Paul's arrest in Jerusalem (Acts 21:10-11). When Paul addressed the Ephesian elders, the Holy Spirit forewarned him about future problems that

---

[19]Kruse, "Apostle, Apostleship," p. 82.

[20]Apostles and Prophets are two separate groups, not "apostles who are prophets" (see Best, *Ephesians*, pp. 281-84; O'Brien, *Ephesisans*, pp. 214-16).

[21]See, e.g., David E. Aune, *Prophecy in Early Christianity* (Grand Rapids, Mich.: Eerdmans, 1983); Gerhard Dautzenberg, *Urchristliche Prophetie: Ihre Erforschung, ihre Voraussetzungen im Judentum und ihre Struktur im ersten Korintherbrief* (Stuttgart: Kohlhammer, 1975). Other valuable studies on prophecy include J. R. C. Cousland, "Prophets and Prophecy," *DNTB*, pp. 830-35; E. Earle Ellis, *Prophecy and Hermeneutic in Early Christianity* (Grand Rapids, Mich.: Eerdmans, 1978); Kevin Giles, "Prophecy, Prophets, False Prophets," *DLNTD*, pp. 970-77; Gerald F. Hawthorne, "The Role of Christian Prophets in the Gospel Tradition," in *Tradition and Interpretation in the New Testament: Essays in Honor of E. Earle Ellis*, ed. Gerald F. Hawthorne and Otto Betz (Grand Rapids, Mich.: Eerdmans, 1987); Hawthorne, "Prophets, Prophecy," *DJG*, esp. "Jesus as Prophet," pp. 640-41; Max Turner, *The Holy Spirit and Spiritual Gifts: Then and Now* (Carlisle: Paternoster Press, 1996); Turner, *Power from on High* (Sheffield: Sheffield Academic Press, 1996).

he and the church would face (Acts 20:23-30). The believers in Tyre advised Paul ("through the Spirit") not to go to Jerusalem because they knew the fate that awaited him (Acts 21:4). Paul also spoke of those who receive a "revelation" (1 Cor 14:30) and possess prophetic powers to "understand all mysteries and all knowledge" (1 Cor 13:2; see also 2 Pet 1:20-21). Nevertheless, not everyone possessing the Spirit was a prophet. Stephen and Philip, for example, were "full of the Spirit and wisdom" but are not identified as prophets. In terms of Christian initiation, there is only one occasion in Luke where the reception of the Holy Spirit manifests itself in prophecy (Acts 19:6).

Most scholars, on the other hand, define prophecy more broadly and note that it took on many forms in the early church. The individuals that Luke identifies by name in Antioch were prophets *and teachers* (Acts 13:1-2). Their ministry of exhorting, strengthening and guiding believers was more pastoral than prophetic in nature (Acts 11:23; 13:1-2, 15-16; 15:32). Luke also identifies Philip's daughters as possessing the "gift of prophecy" (Acts 21:9), but Scripture does not record anything about their activity. As far as we know, they did not play any leading role as prophets in the early church.[22]

Although listed among the prophets in Acts 13:2, Paul never referred to himself as a prophet nor claimed to possess the spiritual gift of prophecy (though it is perhaps implied in 1 Cor 14:6 and at Timothy's call to ministry and ordination, 1 Tim 1:18; 4:14). Nevertheless, there are several similarities between his call and commissioning *as an apostle* and that of a prophet in the early church.[23]

A prophet or prophecy is one of the spiritual gifts that Paul acknowledges (Rom 12:6; 1 Cor 12:10, 28; see Eph 4:11; 1 Tim 4:14; 2 Pet 1:20-21) and encourages believers to cultivate and practice within the church (1 Cor 14:1, 5, 39; see also 1 Thess 5:20). As with all the spiritual gifts, prophecy is given to believers for "upbuilding and encouragement and consolation" (1 Cor 14:3; see also 14:31). These functions are not unlike those attributed to the five prophets in Antioch (Acts 13:1-2). Some prophecy is similar to preaching and teaching and could be possessed by a number of different leaders in the church. It

---

[22]In some cases certain prophets were itinerant, that is, traveled from place to place. The general impression from Paul, however, is that they were attached to one congregation. Bengt Holmberg notes, "The wandering of prophets was a hypothesis of von Harnack based on *Didache*, which has now lost general approval" (*Paul and Power,* p. 97 n. 7).

[23]Compare the language of his call in Gal 1:15-16, for example, with Is 49:1, 5 and Jer 1:5. See Craig Evans, "Prophet, Paul As," *DPL*, pp. 762-65; Kevin Giles, *Patterns of Ministry Among the First Christians* (Melbourne: Collins-Dove, 1989), p. 138; Martin Hengel and Anna Maria Schwemer, *Paul Between Damascus and Antioch: The Unknown Years* (Louisville: Westminster John Knox, 1997), p. 237.

appears likely that *the same person could be an apostle, a prophet and a teacher.*

Mention of prophetic activity in the Pastorals is limited to Timothy's call and ordination (1 Tim 1:18; 4:14). In these letters there is no manifestation of the charismatic gifts or prophetic activity, both of which had been so prominent in the early church, especially in Corinth. The impression one receives from the Pastorals is that order, structure and other offices and roles of leadership have replaced the Lukan and Pauline models. Kevin Giles expresses this change when he writes: "The more the church became institutionalized, the less free expression of charismatic gifts, and prophecy in particular, were encouraged."[24] This trend continued into the postapostolic age, as the prophetic voice was slowly silenced until it was resurrected by a late second-century apocalyptic movement known as Montanism.[25]

4.3. Teachers

Of the approximately sixty references to the Greek word *teacher (didaskalos)* in the New Testament, forty-four occur in the Gospels as references to Jesus. By all accounts, he is recognized as the Teacher. Many references refer specifically to some kind of instruction Jesus gave to his disciples, to the crowds or to Jewish religious authorities. In a number of cases, preaching *(kēryssō)* and teaching *(didaskō)* were part of the same event; in other cases they are used interchangeably (for example, Mt 4:23; 9:35; 11:1; Mk 1:39; 7:36; 16:20; Lk 4:18, 44). A similar relationship between preaching and teaching is found in Acts (Acts 4:2; 5:42; 15:35; 28:31; see also Col 1:28: "whom we proclaim, warning *[nouthetountes]* everyone and teaching everyone").

It is no overstatement to claim that teaching was one of the most important ministries of the church. What is unclear, however, is whether there actually was an identifiable and permanent office of "teacher." Luke refers to five individuals in Antioch (including Paul and Barnabas) as "prophets *and teachers*" (Acts 13:1), and Paul includes "teachers" in his triad of church leaders (1 Cor 12:28; see also Rom 12:7). Ephesians joins "pastors and teachers" together (there is no separate Greek article for "teachers"), thus suggesting shared responsibilities (Eph 4:11). References to Paul as "a teacher" (1 Tim 2:7; 2 Tim 1:11) simply confirm Paul's calling as an apostle *and* teacher. Although Paul was an itinerant apostle-teacher in many ways, it appears that most teachers

---

[24]Giles, *Patterns of Ministry,* pp. 142-43; see also his "Prophecy, Prophets, False Prophets," pp. 974-76.

[25]This is not to imply that there was no prophetic activity or acknowledgment of prophets during this time. For additional references and commentary see Giles, *Patterns of Ministry,* pp. 143-45; Giles, "Prophecy, Prophets, False Prophets," pp. 975-76.

were connected with local congregations and taught within the context of worship services.

The situation in the early church clearly involved prophetic teachers (Acts 13:1-2), pastor-teachers (Eph 4:11) and, in Paul's case at least, an apostle-teacher. Other references to teachers in the New Testament (Gal 6:6; Heb 5:12; Jas 3:1) simply refer to the function of teaching rather than a specific "teaching office." The early church undoubtedly had many believers involved in teaching ministries (Mt 28:19; Acts 15:35; 18:27-28; Rom 15:14; Col 3:16), including women (Acts 18:24-28; Rom 16:7; 1 Cor 11:5; 12:28; Eph 4:11; Tit 2:3). The "egalitarian" nature of the early church (that is, no division or status among believers) and the indwelling of the Holy Spirit enabled *all* believers to share in this ministry according to their ability to comprehend and communicate the gospel.[26]

Nevertheless, we should note that teaching is an important responsibility for the leaders who emerge in the postapostolic church. A bishop *(episkopos)* must be "an apt teacher" (1 Tim 3:2), a requirement more fully defined in Titus 1:9, where a bishop is to have "a firm grasp of the word that is trustworthy in accordance with teaching, so that he may be able both to preach with sound doctrine and to refute those who contradict it." Elders *(presbyteros)* also are summoned to "labor in preaching and teaching" (1 Tim 5:17). The emphasis on teaching "sound doctrine" in the Pastorals is necessitated by the emergence of many false teachers who were corrupting the word of God and leading believers astray (1 Tim 1:10; 6:3; 2 Tim 1:13; 2:14-18; 3:1-9; 4:3; Tit 1:9; 2:1; 3:9-11).[27]

4.4. Evangelists

The few references to "evangelists" in the New Testament do not indicate how their ministry of proclamation *(euangelizō)* differed from others who preached *(kēryssō)* and taught *(didaskō)* the word of God. Philip, one of the Seven (Acts 6:5), is identified as "Philip the evangelist" (Acts 21:8), presumably because of his itinerant mission to Samaria (Acts 8:4-40) and the coastal regions of Palestine before he settled in Caesarea.[28]

---

[26]Giles, *Patterns of Ministry*, p. 113; so also Banks, "Church Order and Government," pp. 131-37. Note the discussion on women and leadership at 4.9.

[27]Teachers are occasionally mentioned in some postapostolic literature, but nothing there indicates a separate or specific office. See the useful summary and references by Giles, *Patterns of Ministry*, p. 113.

[28]Later tradition relocates Philip and his four "prophetic daughters" in Ephesus, where he also died and was buried (*Hist. Eccl.* 3.31.2-5; 5.24.2). For connections between Philip and early Gnosticism, see F. Scott Spencer, "Philip the Evangelist," *DLNTD*, p. 931.

In 2 Timothy 4:5, Timothy is exhorted to "do the work of an evangelist" and to carry out his "ministry" (diakonia) fully. On the basis of what we know of early-church leadership, it is reasonable to conclude that Timothy's ministry included the proclamation of the gospel but did not limit him to this role. This probably is another example where the responsibilities of apostle, prophet and teacher overlap.

The inclusion of "evangelists" for building up the church (Eph 4:11-12) is puzzling and has no parallels in the other lists where the charismata are mentioned (Rom 12:6-8; 1 Cor 12:4-11, 28). One associates their role more with the beginning of the church than its maturity, but, as Andrew T. Lincoln suggests, "their mention here could be that the churches in Asia Minor, which are being addressed, were not founded directly by Paul but by just such people, co-workers and followers of Paul who continued this type of missionary activity."[29]

4.5. Deacons

The office of "deacon" is difficult to reconstruct from the New Testament texts for a number of reasons. First, the Greek verb diakonein is used to describe a variety of functions such as "to wait at table," "to provide or care for," "to administer" and "to serve."[30] The Gospels use the verb often for people serving or providing for Jesus during his earthly ministry (Mt 8:15 par. Mk 1:31; Lk 4:39; Mt 27:55; Lk 17:8; Jn 12:2, 26). Jesus himself epitomized this virtue as "the Son of Man [who] came not to be served [diakonēthēnai] but to serve [diakonēsai], and to give his life a ransom for many (Mt 20:28 par. Mk 10:45; see also Lk 22:27). These same ideas and functions appear in the rest of the New Testament (see Acts 6:2; 2 Cor 8:19-20; 1 Tim 3:10, 13; 2 Tim 1:8; Philem 13; Heb 6:10; 1 Pet 1:12; 1 Pet 4:10-11).

Second, the verbal form and meaning of this Greek word implies that anyone involved in a diakonia performs some kind of ministry, task or service (see Lk 10:40; Acts 1:25; 6:1, 4; 21:19; Rom 11:13; 12:7; 15:31; 1 Cor 16:15; 2 Cor 4:1; 5:18; 6:3; 8:4; 9:12-13; Eph 4:12; Col 4:17; 1 Tim 1:12; 2 Tim 4:5, 11; 1 Pet 4:10-11; Rev 2:19).[31] Paul's list of gifts (charismata) to the church includes

---

[29]Andrew T. Lincoln, Ephesians, WBC (Dallas: Word, 1990), p. 250. Gerhard Friedrich writes: "The evangelists continue the work of the apostles. They are not just missionaries, for, as [euangelion] is congregational as well as missionary preaching . . . , so the leader of the community can also be called [euangelistēs] (2 Tm. 4:5). His task is [kērussein ton logon] (2 Tm. 4:2)" ("εὐαγγελίζομαι," TDNT 2:737).

[30]See Hermann W. Beyer, "διακονέω, διακονία, διάκονος," TDNT 2:81-93; K. Hess, "Serve," NIDNTT 3:544-49.

[31]This is not a complete list of all the occurrences of diakonia.

"varieties of services" *(diaireseis diakoniōn)*. The gifts in Ephesians 4:11-12 are given to equip all the saints "for the work of ministry" *(eis ergon diakonias)*. The same idea is present in 1 Peter 4:10-11:

> Like good stewards *[oikonomoi]* of the manifold grace of God, serve *[diakonountes]* one another with whatever gift *[charisma]* each of you has received. Whoever speaks must do so as one speaking the very words of God; whoever serves *[diako nei]* must do so with the strength that God supplies, so that God may be glorified in all things through Jesus Christ.[32]

Third, any person involved in *diakonia* is a *diakonos* (deacon). Thus, the one "waiting at table" is the "waiter at a meal" (Jn 2:5, 9). In most cases the NRSV translates *dia konos* as "servant" or "minister." Nevertheless, the noun *deacon* is attributed to Phoebe, a leader in the church at Cenchreae (Rom 16:1), as well as to a specific group of leaders in the church at Philippi (Phil 1:1) and at Ephesus (1 Tim 3:8, 10, 12-13). The New Testament identifies Paul and some of his coworkers, such as Tychicus (Eph 6:21; Col 4:7), Epaphras (Col 1:7) and Timothy (1 Tim 4:6), as deacons. In fact, if all believers are deacons because of the service they render, then who are *the deacons* belonging to a specific office, and when did this office originate?

The question of origin is difficult to trace. An older and common interpretation held that the office began with the election of the Seven in Acts 6:1-6, a group of Greek-speaking Jews (Hellenists) appointed and ordained by the Twelve as almoners.[33] The difficulty with this approach is that the Seven are never called deacons and two of them (Stephen and Philip) were involved as *diakonoi* of "the Word," much like the Twelve. Since we do not hear about this group (the Seven) again, it is likely that their function was "taken over by the elders shortly afterward (Acts 11:27-30)."[34]

Philippians 1:1 appears to be the earliest reference to a group of individuals identified as "deacons." Nothing, however, is said about their number, qualifications, appointment or responsibilities. Some commentators suggest that they may have been responsible for the *diakonia* of collecting and sending the monetary gift to Paul in prison (Phil 4:15-19).[35] Others wonder whether Euodia, Syn-

---

[32]On this text Giles suggests, "We are probably observing here an early functional differentiation of the ministries that would later be formalized in the office of bishop and deacon" (*Patterns of Ministry*, p. 54). While possible, it seems more likely that the passage simply means that one gift leads to speaking, such as teaching, and another one to serving.

[33]See Donald Hagner, "Seven, The," *ISBE* 4:426-27.

[34]Kruse, "Ministry," *DLNTD*, p. 742; see also Giles, "Church Order, Government," p. 222.

[35]Beyer, "[διακονέω]," 2:90; Ralph Martin, *Family and the Fellowship*, p. 62. For further discussion, see Gordon Fee, *Paul's Letter to the Philippians* (Grand Rapids, Mich.: Eerdmans, 1995), pp. 66-71; Peter T. O'Brien, *The Epistle to the Philippians* (Grand Rapids, Mich.: Eerdmans, 1991), pp. 46-50.

tyche, the "loyal companion" (*syzygos,* fellow-worker, companion), Clement and other "co-workers" in the church may be part of this group (Phil 4:2-3).[36] This would suggest more of a function than an office, not unlike Stephanas, whom Paul commends for his service *(diakonia)* to the converts in Achaia (1 Cor 16:15), or those involved in the *diakonia* of collecting money for the church in Jerusalem (2 Cor 8:4, 19; 9:1, 12-13).

Another approach seeks to correlate the offices of bishops and deacons with leadership in Jewish synagogues, which included a ruler *(archisynagōgos)* and an assistant *(hypēretēs).* Since the early Christians met in homes, Kevin Giles, for example, suggests that the *episkopos* would be "the host of the church" and the *diakonoi* "respected senior members of house churches who gave themselves in the service of other Christians."[37] According to this view, bishops were the overseers in the church, and deacons served as their assistants.

The office of deacon seems to have been well established by the time the Pastorals were written, because 1 Timothy has an extensive list of qualifications for persons in this position (1 Tim 3:8-13):

> Deacons likewise must be serious, not double-tongued, not indulging in much wine, not greedy for money; they must hold fast to the mystery of the faith with a clear conscience. And let them first be tested; then, if they prove themselves blameless, let them serve as deacons. Women likewise must be serious, not slanderers, but temperate, faithful in all things. Let deacons be married only once, and let them manage their children and their households well; for those who serve well as deacons gain a good standing for themselves and great boldness in the faith that is in Christ Jesus.

Although nothing is said about their function, it is reasonable to assume that they were assistants to the bishops whose qualifications are specified earlier (1 Tim 3:1-7).[38] In the middle of these standards, readers should note that women are included in this office as well as men. Given the recognition of Phoebe as a deacon (Rom 16:1), it seems more reasonable to interpret the

---

[36]Bartlett, *Ministry in the New Testament,* p. 43; Massey H. Shepherd Jr, "Deacon," *IDB* 1:786.

[37]Giles, *Patterns of Ministry,* p. 60, as well as pp. 31-32, 37-38; also in his "Church Order, Government," p. 223; Bartlett, *Ministry in the New Testament,* pp. 177-78; Beyer, "[δια–κονέω]," 2:90-91.

[38]Giles reasons that the best way to explain the functions of deacons is with household imagery and domestic structure: "In the extended church-family, the *diakonoi* were those who also attended to the practical needs of members. They were the servants of the community" (*Patterns of Ministry,* p. 40). It is somewhat surprising that there is no mention of deacons in Titus when bishops are discussed (Tit 1:7-9). Could this mean that there were no deacons in the churches of Crete?

phrase "women likewise" to mean women deacons rather than wives of male deacons.[39]

The numerous references to deacons in the postapostolic literature indicates that this office continued into the second century with many of the same qualifications mentioned in 1 Timothy.[40]

4.6. Bishops

Of all the variations of meaning attached to the Greek verb *skopeō* (to be concerned about, to watch out for, pay attention, etc.), only four references in the New Testament with the prefix *epi (episkopeō, episkopē, episkopos, episkeptomai)* refer to a leader of a community (Acts 20:28; Phil 1:1; 1 Tim 3:2; Tit 1:7). Jesus is designated "the shepherd [*poimena*] and guardian [*episkopos*] of your souls" (1 Pet 2:25).[41] A number of other references indicate that care and oversight were the responsibility of all members in the early church (see Mt 25:36; Acts 6:3; 15:14, 36; Heb 12:15; Jas 1:27). But the question we face is: When did such ministry become the function of a special office in the emerging church?

The earliest reference—if we take the account as chronologically accurate—is Acts 20:17-38, Paul's address to the Ephesian "elders" *(presbyteroi)*.[42] The speech includes some reflections of his apostolic ministry and concerns for his welfare as he travels to Jerusalem. But Paul also predicts that the Ephesian church will face serious external and internal threats to its theology and unity (Acts 20:29-31). Thus he exhorts the elders: "Keep watch over yourselves and over all the flock, of which the Holy Spirit has made you overseers [*episkopous*], to shepherd [*poimainein*] the church of God that he obtained with the blood of his own Son" (Acts 20:28).[43] One could reasonably conclude that this

---

[39]See comments and suggestions in Gordon Fee, *1 and 2 Timothy, Titus,* NIBCNT (Peabody, Mass.: Hendrickson, 1988), pp. 88-89; George W. Knight III, *The Pastoral Epistles,* NIGTC (Grand Rapids, Mich.: Eerdmans, 1992), pp. 170-72. In Pliny the Younger's letter to Trajan, he mentions that he tortured "two female slaves who were called deacons" (*Ep.* 10.97).

[40]Since this material falls beyond the scope of this book, students may wish to consult the extensive list provided by Shepherd, "Deacon," 1:786 and the brief but useful discussion by Giles in *Patterns of Ministry,* pp. 62-64.

[41]There is a textual problem in 1 Peter 5:2, where the NRSV includes "oversight" in the text but draws attention to its omission in some manuscripts. See Bruce M. Metzger, *A Textual Commentary on the Greek New Testament,* 2nd ed. (New York: American Bible Society, 1994), pp. 625-26.

[42]This comment is made in response to Bartlett's discussion of Acts 20:17-38, which he thinks is a post-Pauline literary creation of Luke (*Ministry in the New Testament,* pp. 154-55 and 132-33). See further comments below.

[43]The combination of *overseer* and *shepherd* is reminiscent of 1 Pet 2:25, where Jesus is the shepherd *(poimena)* and guardian *(episkopos)*. Here one values the observation of Lothar Coenen, who notes "that the titles of offices in the NT are essentially titles that apply to Christ in the first instance" (*NIDNTT,* "Bishop," 1:191).

passage equates elders with bishops. On the other hand, "oversight" could simply be a *function* of the elders.[44]

As noted earlier, Philippians 1:1 ("bishops and deacons") may identify bishops as leaders and overseers of the house churches in the community. The same interpretation for bishops as house-church leaders is possible in the Pastorals. This idea is reinforced by the requirement that a bishop "must manage his own household well. . . . if someone does not know how to manage his own household, how can he take care of God's church?" (1 Tim 3:4-5).

The primary difference between Philippians 1:1 and the Pastorals is the detailed list of qualifications for the office of bishop (1 Tim 3:1-7; Tit 1:7-9). The list in 1 Timothy begins by stating that "whoever aspires to the office of bishop"—that is, whoever desires to oversee the church—"desires a noble task" (1 Tim 3:1). But this "noble task" requires certain qualifications:

> Now a bishop must be above reproach, married only once, temperate, sensible, respectable, hospitable, an apt teacher, not a drunkard, not violent but gentle, not quarrelsome, and not a lover of money. He must manage his own household well, keeping his children submissive and respectful in every way—for if someone does not know how to manage his own household, how can he take care of God's church? He must not be a recent convert, or he may be puffed up with conceit and fall into the condemnation of the devil. Moreover, he must be well thought of by outsiders, so that he may not fall into disgrace and the snare of the devil. (1 Tim 3:2-7)

> For a bishop, as God's steward, must be blameless; he must not be arrogant or quick-tempered or addicted to wine or violent or greedy for gain; but he must be hospitable, a lover of goodness, prudent, upright, devout, and self-controlled. He must have a firm grasp of the word that is trustworthy in accordance with the teaching, so that he may be able both to preach with sound doctrine and to refute those who contradict it. (Tit 1:7-9)

What is striking about the exhortation to Titus is that he is mandated (Tit 1:5-6) to appoint "elders" *(presbyterous)* who meet certain requirements. But then the text moves directly to describe the qualifications of a bishop. Here, as in Acts 20:17, 28, one is tempted to conclude that elders and bishops are one and the same.[45] This does not appear to be the case in 1 Timothy, which lists elders separately (1 Tim 5:17-19).[46] Yet it is quite clear that the responsibilities of bish-

---

[44]So Giles, *Patterns of Ministry,* p. 81.

[45]See detailed discussion in Martin Dibelius and Hans Conzelmann, *The Pastoral Epistles,* trans. P. Buttolph and Adela Yarbro, ed. H. Koester, Hermeneia (Philadelphia: Fortress, 1972), pp. 54-57.

[46]No office is mentioned in 2 Timothy. Rather, Timothy is instructed to be a faithful, true and courageous interpreter and defender of the faith (see 2 Tim 1:8, 13; 2:1-2, 14-16, 22-25; 3:14-17; 4:1-2).

ops, elders and deacons overlapped considerably.

From the extant evidence it is possible to conclude that, at the time the Pastorals were written, bishops were overseers of local house churches and were assisted by a group of individuals identified as deacons. These offices are also mentioned in the *Didache* (15.1), *1 Clement* (42.4-5) and *Shepherd of Hermas* (9.27.1). There is no hint of any monarchical episcopacy until the time of Ignatius, who is the first church leader to imply such a position (Ign. *Eph.* 6.1; Ign. *Trall.* 3.1; Ign. *Smyrn.* 9.1) and the first to bear witness to a threefold order: bishop, presbyter and deacon (Ign. *Magn.* 6.1; Ign. *Trall.* 2.2-3; 3.1; Ign. *Smyrn.* 8.2).[47]

4.7. Elders

All major historical, textual and etymological studies of the Hebrew noun *zāqēn* (elder) discuss its various usages: (1) to refer to an elderly person; (2) to indicate persons with some official status acting as representatives or officials at community functions; and (3) to identify certain members of judicial bodies, such as a "council of elders" and the Sanhedrin.[48]

The Greek *presbyteros* (elder) also has multiple uses in the New Testament. First, it refers to an elderly or senior person (Acts 2:17; 1 Tim 5:1-2; Philem 8; 1 Pet 5:5; possibly 1 Pet 5:1, which begins "now as an elder [*presbyteros*] myself and a witness of the sufferings of Christ"; cf. also Tit 2:2-3).

Second, *presbyteros* applies to certain Jewish authorities ("elders," "elders of the people" and the "traditions of the elders") who often joined the scribes, priests and Pharisees in opposition to Jesus' ministry (see, e.g., Mt 16:21; 21:23; 26:3, 47, 57; Mk 7:3, 5; 8:31; 14:43; Lk 9:22; 20:1; 22:52). This same group of individuals also opposed the preaching and mission of the early church (Acts 4:5, 8, 23; 6:12; 23:14; 25:15; cf. Acts 22:5).

Third, the term identifies a group of *Jewish Christians* who were involved in the leadership of the early church in Jerusalem along with the apostles. This is particularly evident during the Jerusalem Council (Acts 15:2, 4, 6, 22-23; 16:4) and in the organizational structure of the Jerusalem church under the leadership of James (Acts 21:18).[49] These elders received the famine relief offering that

---

[47]Note Giles, *Patterns of Ministry,* p. 47, but also the comment in *1 Clem.* 44.2. See also Giles, "Church Order, Government," pp. 224-25; Coenen, "Bishop," 1:192; Geoffrey W. Bromiley, "Bishop," *ISBE* 1:518.

[48]For additional reading, see Günther Bornkamm, "πρέσβυς κτλ," *TDNT* 6:651-83; Coenen, "Bishop," *NIDNTT* 1:192-201; Charles F. Fensham, "Elder in the OT," *ISBE* 1:53-54; Giles, *Patterns of Ministry,* pp. 71-77; Grant R. Osborne, "Elder," *DJG,* pp. 201-3; R. Alastair Campbell, *The Elders: Seniority Within Earliest Christianity* (Edinburgh: T & T Clark, 1994).

[49]Giles thinks that Luke depicts James as the leader ("president") of this group of elders: "In this scene James appears as a typical Jewish *archōn* or *gerousiarchēs*, the prototype of the later

Paul and Barnabas had raised and sent to the Jerusalem church (Acts 11:30), indicating, at least at this point, that they had some kind of administrative function in the early church. "It may well be," observes Bartlett, "that by implication these Judean Christian elders function for the Christian community as the elders of the Jews function for them."[50] One wonders what happened to the Seven who appear in Acts 6, since they (except Stephen and Philip) are not mentioned after their appointment. Did the Hellenists benefit from this offering? And who carried out the distribution? Unfortunately, Luke is silent on such matters.

A "council of elders" *(tou presbyteriou)* participated in the ordination of Timothy to the ministry (1 Tim 4:14: "Do not neglect the gift that is in you, which was given to you through prophecy with the laying on of hands by the council of elders"). Given the Palestinian context of this "council," one would expect such an event to have taken place in Jerusalem. However, Luke does not mention this event in Acts, and as far as we know, Timothy only worked in the Greco-Roman world. This leaves Ephesus as the logical place for the council.

Finally, *presbyteros* also refers to a council of twenty-four heavenly elders in the book of Revelation (Rev 4:10; 5:5-6, 8, 11, 14; 7:11, 13; 11:16; 14:3; 19:4). Here it is unclear whether the council is a counterpart to the office of elders on earth.[51]

None of the above information explains the origin and development of Christian *eldership.* The first mention of elders outside of Jerusalem occurs in Acts 14:23, where Paul and Barnabas appointed elders in "each church" they visited on their inaugural missionary journey (Derbe, Lystra, Iconium and Antioch in Pisidia; perhaps also in Perga, Acts 14:25). This reference—and event—in Acts 14:23 raises many questions, since it is the only account in Acts of Paul personally appointing elders (nor does Paul mention elders in any of his undisputed letters).[52] Were these elders modeled after those in Jerusalem? Were their

---

monarchical bishop—a bishop who rules over a geographically circumscribed community. This use of the word *episkopos* is first found in the writings of Ignatius" ("Church Order, Government," p. 222).

[50]Bartlett, *Ministry in the New Testament,* p. 130.

[51]See Coenen, "Bishop," 1:200; Giles writes: "All one can say is that the book of Revelation bears witness to a council of heavenly elders, twenty-four in number, which *could* indicate that at least sometimes a council of elders in an earthly setting was as numerous as this" (*Patterns of Ministry,* p. 84).

[52]There is no easy solution to these two observations. One could just take them at face value and move on. But many interpreters struggle with these issues and look for clarity within Luke's historical and theological method. James D. G. Dunn answers the apparent "historical anomaly" at Acts 14:23 by concluding: "It looks, then, as though Luke, both here and in 20.17, has either assumed the presence from the first of a practice and church structure which had become more common in his own day (the procedures of 13.3 were more 'charismatic'), or he has made more formal the sort of commendation of mature individuals such as we find in 1 Thess. 5.12-13 and 1 Cor. 16:15-18. Either way it tells us something of the character and

responsibilities purely administrative? Did they have any role in public worship?

Some answers may come from the only other reference to Christian elders in Acts, where they *may* be equated with bishops (Acts 20:17-28, see 4.6). Kevin Giles rejects this correlation and suggests that the Ephesian elders simply are "a fairly large number of senior Christians to whom the overall care of the flock is entrusted."[53] But we have no idea when, how or by whom these elders were appointed or how their functions and authority compared with those in Jerusalem.

The most striking development in Christian eldership occurs in the Pastorals:

> Do not speak harshly to an older man *[presbyterō]* but speak to him as to a father, to younger men as brothers, to older women as mothers, to younger women as sisters—with absolute purity. (1 Tim 5:1-2)

> Let the elders who rule well be considered worthy of double honor, especially those who labor in preaching and teaching. . . . Never accept any accusation against an elder except on the evidence of two or three witnesses. As for those who persist in sin, rebuke them in the presence of all, so that the rest also may stand in fear. In the presence of God and of Christ Jesus and of the elect angels, I warn you to keep these instructions without prejudice, doing nothing on the basis of partiality. Do not ordain anyone hastily, and do not participate in the sins of others; keep yourself pure. (1 Tim 5:17, 19-22)

> I left you behind in Crete for this reason, so that you should put in order what remained to be done, and should appoint elders in every town, as I directed you: someone who is blameless, married only once, whose children are believers, not accused of debauchery and not rebellious. (Tit 1:5-6)

Amid all the intricacies of exegesis and interpretation, several possibilities emerge: (1) that elderly men and women were to be honored and respected by the Christian community (1 Tim 5:1-2; Tit 2:2-3); (2) that not all "elderly" men and women were elders, belonging to a council of elders with specific responsibilities of church leadership; and (3) *either* that bishops and elders were coequal and interchangeable (Tit 1:5, 7) *or* that bishops were chosen from the body of elders.[54]

---

objectives of Luke as a historian—a readiness to read the traditions he had from the founding period in a way which brought out the harmony of the early churches and the settled pattern of their organization from the first (cf. 11.30; James 5:14)" (*The Acts of the Apostles* [Valley Forge, Penn.: Trinity Press International, 1996], p. 193). David Bartlett takes a similar approach on Acts 20:17-38 (see 4.6). Bartlett is convinced that this passage "certainly represents Luke's picture of the appropriate role of elders in his own time" by using Paul as the "model elder" (*Ministry in the New Testament,* p. 132; cf. p. 154).

[53]Giles, *Patterns of Ministry,* p. 81.

[54]Kevin Giles, for one, takes the second alternative, concluding that the bishop "is an elder chosen to 'oversee' or manage a house-church" (ibid., p. 89; see also, his conclusions on pp. 95-97).

In 1 Peter 5:1-5 the author refers to himself as an elder and goes on to exhort fellow elders to lead their communities with enthusiasm and humility: "I exhort the elders among you to tend the flock of God that is in your charge, exercising the oversight [episkopountes], not under compulsion but willingly, as God would have you do it—not for sordid gain but eagerly. Do not lord it over those in your charge, but be examples to the flock" (1 Pet 5:1-3). Many thoughts in this passage are reminiscent of Acts 20:17-35.[55]

The epistle of James, which is generally understood as a document written to Jewish Christians, recognizes an order of elders that may have close affinities with Jewish elders. The role of elders in this setting is pastoral in nature, since it involves prayer and anointing for healing, participation in prayer and confession of individual sins and, together with other members, the restoration of wayward members (Jas 5:19-20).

The author of 2 and 3 John simply introduces himself as "the elder," without any explanation or qualifications.[56] If the author truly is an "elder" within the parameters we have discussed, he appears to have taken on the role of an authority figure warning his community about apostasy and insubordination and encouraging believers to demonstrate love and hospitality toward each other. In this, he also epitomizes the role of apostle, bishop and pastor.

When one moves beyond the New Testament into the postapostolic period, the literature includes a number of useful references to the office and role of elders.[57] Thus Clement writes from Rome to correct a power play in the Corinthian church, where a group of young men succeeded in deposing the ruling elders (e.g., _1 Clem._ 3.3; 44.6; 47.6; 54.2; 57.1). In Ignatius's letters, elders are mentioned "in association with bishops and the deacons," as a "council of elders" replacing the council of the apostles. The elders are "to be obeyed and respected by the community," although they are subject to the bishop, whose authority now extends beyond the local church to the wider Christian community. In the writings of Polycarp and Hermas, elders assume more of a pastoral role to their congregations.[58]

---

[55]"In both cases the elders are responsible for 'the flock' (_poimnion_), they give oversight (_episkopein_) and the work entrusted to them is of a general pastoral nature" (Giles, _Patterns of Ministry,_ p. 82).

[56]There is much speculation on his identity, and numerous alternatives have been suggested. Many of them are summarized by Giles (_Patterns of Ministry,_ p. 90) and discussed in substantial commentaries on these epistles, most notably the writings of Raymond E. Brown.

[57]The following comments are a brief summary of the useful research by Giles, _Patterns of Ministry,_ pp. 90-93.

[58]See references in ibid., p. 92-93.

4.8. Pastors

Ephesians 4:11 ("The gifts he gave were that some would be . . . pastors and teachers") is the only place in the New Testament where the noun *poimēn* (shepherd) is used as a title for a church leader (the English *pastor* is derived from the Latin *pastor,* "shepherd"). The absence of the article before *teachers (tous de poimenas kai didaskalous)* in the verse suggests that the two categories are identical; that is, the author may be thinking of pastors who teach (or teaching pastors) and assume that teaching is the pastors' most important activity. However, in Ephesians 2:20 "apostles and prophets" are governed by one article *(tōn apostolōn kai prophētōn)* even though they form two separate groups. In other New Testament writings the ministry of teachers is presented separately from other leaders as well (see 4.3).

On this basis it appears reasonable to think of these ministries as two groups, but with overlapping functions rather than a rigid separation between the two.[59] A pastor's responsibilities to a congregation would involve nurture, care and guidance (using the shepherding imagery) *as well as teaching.* "Perhaps," notes John R. W. Stott, "one should say that, although every pastor must be a teacher, gifted in the ministry of God's Word to people (whether a congregation or groups of individuals), yet not every Christian teacher is also a pastor."[60]

Undoubtedly this pastoral ministry comes from the application of the shepherd imagery that characterized Jesus' relationship with his disciples. Jesus is "the good shepherd" who knows, guards and cares for his sheep (Mt 9:36; 18:12-14; Mk 6:34; Lk 15:3-7; Jn 10:11-18).[61] Later the church regarded Jesus as the "great" (Heb 13:20) and "chief" (1 Pet 5:4) shepherd of the church. On several occasions the elders *(presbyteroi)* of the church are exhorted to be shepherds who oversee *(episkopeō)* the flock of God (Acts 20:28; 1 Pet 5:2). We see here the same overlapping of functions that were noted of other church leaders (see 4.6). From all appearances in the New Testament, the terms *bishop, elder* and *pastor* represent the same office and ministry.

In many ways, the New Testament presents the apostle Paul as a living example of this spiritual gift. He was obviously one of the greatest teachers in the early church, but he also functioned as a pastor to his coworkers and congregations (see Rom 16; 1 Thess 2:11). Pastoral care, however, becomes a ministry for all believers as they are exhorted to care for one another (1 Cor 12:25),

---

[59]See discussion in Peter T. O'Brien, *The Letter to the Ephesians* (Grand Rapids, Mich.: Eerdmans, 1999), pp. 300-1; Ernst Best, *Ephesians* (Edinburgh: T & T Clark, 1998), pp. 392-93.

[60]John R. W. Stott, *The Message of Ephesians,* Bible Speaks Today (Downers Grove, Ill.: InterVarsity Press, 1979), pp. 163-64.

[61]On shepherd imagery and metaphors in the Old and New Testaments, see Joachim Jeremias, "ποιμήν κτλ," *TDNT* 6:485-502; Erich Beyreuther, "Shepherd," *NIDNTT* 3:564-69.

bear one another's burdens (Gal 6:1-2) and encourage, build up, teach and admonish one another (e.g., 1 Cor 12:7; Eph 4:12; Col 3:16; 1 Thess 5:11; 1 Pet 4:10).[62]

4.9. Women

In current scholarship, the subject of the role of women in ministry and leadership in the early church has generated considerable debate and emotion.[63] Although time and space do not permit a detailed examination and critique of all the issues and materials, most of the literature tends to support the following general principles.

First, since the ancient Near Eastern cultures were patriarchal in nature, it was natural for Judaism to restrict the roles of women in society and to reflect those roles in its literature (Old Testament and rabbinical traditions). Second, most societies encompassed by the Greco-Roman world were also patriarchal in structure, but the roles of women varied in different parts of the empire. Third, Jesus gave women a new dignity as persons in society, and even though he selected only men as his disciples, many women became his followers and, on occasion, ministered to his physical needs (see Lk 8:1-3; 10:38-42; 23:49,

---

[62]See Paul Beasley-Murray, "Pastor, Paul As," _DPL,_ pp. 654-58.

[63]The secondary literature—specialized monographs, articles and sections in commentaries— is voluminous. The "selected" references here reflect sources relevant to the topic of ministry in the church and not those that deal with roles of women in ancient cultures and the like. For additional reading, see David E. Aune, _Prophecy in Early Christianity and the Ancient Mediterranean World_ (Grand Rapids, Mich.: Eerdmans, 1983); Bartlett, _Ministry in the New Testament,_ pp. 177-78; Linda Belleville, _Women Leaders and the Church_ (Grand Rapids, Mich.: Baker, 2000); David L. Balch, _Let Wives Be Submissive: The Domestic Code in 1 Peter,_ SBLMS 26 (Chico, Calif.: Scholars Press, 1981); Gilbert Bilezikian, _Beyond Sex Roles: What the Bible Says About a Woman's Place in the Church and Family_ (Grand Rapids, Mich.: Baker, 1986); Stanley Grenz and Denise M. Kjesbo, _Women in the Church_ (Downers Grove, Ill.: InterVarsity Press, 1996); Paul K. Jewett, _Man As Male and Female: A Study in Sexual Relationships from a Theological Point of View_ (Grand Rapids, Mich.: Eerdmans, 1975); Craig S. Keener, _Paul, Women and Wives: Marriage and Women's Ministry in the Letters of Paul_ (Peabody, Mass.: Hendrickson, 1992); Keener, "Man and Women," _DPL,_ pp. 583-92; Keener, "Woman and Man," _DLNTD,_ pp. 1205-15; George W. Knight III, _The New Testament Teaching on the Role Relationship of Men and Women_ (Grand Rapids, Mich.: Baker, 1977); Richard C. Kroeger and Catherine C. Kroeger, _I Suffer Not a Woman: Rethinking 1 Timothy 2:11-15 in Light of Ancient Evidence_ (Grand Rapids, Mich.: Baker, 1992); Catherine C. Kroeger, "Women in the Early Church," _DLNTD,_ pp. 1215-22; C. Kroeger, "Women in Greco-Roman World and Judaism," _DNTB,_ pp. 1276-80; Alvera Mickelsen, ed., _Women, Authority and the Bible_ (Downers Grove, Ill.: InterVarsity Press, 1986); Aída B. Spencer, _Beyond the Curse: Women Called to Ministry_ (Peabody, Mass.: Hendrickson, 1989); David C. Verner, _The Household of God: The Social World of the Pastoral Epistles,_ SBLDS 71 (Chico, Calif.: Scholars Press, 1983); Ben Witherington III, _Women in the Earliest Churches,_ SNTSMS 59 (Cambridge: Cambridge University Press, 1988).

55-56; 24:1-10). Fourth, both men *and women* responded to the proclamation of the gospel in the early church, received the Holy Spirit (Acts 2:17-18, 37-38 [see Joel 2:28-32]), were baptized and regarded as equals with men in the worshiping communities throughout the empire (Acts 5:14; 8:3, 12; 9:2-3; 17:4, 12; Gal 3:27-28).

Although many women believers remain anonymous in the New Testament (as do most men!), there is enough evidence in Luke-Acts and the Epistles to indicate that a significant number were involved in various ministries. For example, Mary the mother of Jesus and other "women" prayed after Jesus' ascension (Acts 1:14); Mary the mother of John Mark appears to have been a leader of one of the early Christian groups, her house being used for church meetings (Acts 12:12: "where many had gathered and were praying"); Dorcas (Greek for Tabitha) was "a disciple *[mathētria]* . . . devoted to good works and acts of charity" (Acts 9:36-41); Lydia's household served as a gathering place for the early believers in Philippi (Acts 16:12-15, 40); in Thessalonica (Acts 17:4) several "leading women" responded to the gospel, as did other Greek women in Berea (Acts 17:12); Damaris was converted in Athens (Acts 17:34); Priscilla and her husband Aquila became significant leaders of the church in several different locations (Acts 18:18, 26; Rom 16:3; 1 Cor 16:19; 2 Tim 4:19).[64] Luke also refers to Philip's prophetic daughters as if this was a natural ministry for them (Acts 21:8-9). It is worth noting that the two house churches specifically mentioned in Acts are in homes of women (Mary in Acts 12:12; Lydia in Acts 16:11-15).

Paul, likewise, refers to a number of women involved in ministry. If Jesus had "twelve" apostles, could one say that Paul had "seven" women as his fellow workers? The seven mentioned in connection with the Roman church are Prisca, that is, Priscilla (Rom 16:3), Mary (Rom 16:6), Junia (Rom 16:7),[65] Tryphaena, Tryphosa, Persis (Rom 16:12) and Julia (Rom 16:15). Other women mentioned by Paul include Phoebe in Cenchreae (Rom 16:1-2), Chloe (1 Cor 1:11-17), Euodia and Syntyche (Phil 4:2-3), Nympha (Col 4:15) and Apphia (Philem 2). Both Paul and the author of Revelation acknowledge the existence of female prophets in the early church, and, even though they are singled out for different reasons, there is nothing in the text to indicate that their *ministry* was in question. In Corinth, their conduct disrupted the worship service; in Thyatira, Jezebel was spouting false prophecies (see Rev 2:20-29).

---

[64]Luke lists Priscilla before Aquila, "apparently indicating that her ministry and influence are more forceful than his" (C. Kroeger, "Women in the Early Church," *DLNTD,* p. 1217).

[65]Note the textual variant "Junias" (masculine) and discussion in commentaries as well as Metzger, *Textual Commentary,* pp. 475-76.

The overall impression from Luke's and Paul's perspective is that women played a significant role in the life, ministry and leadership of the early church.[66] However, two texts appear to give a different impression and continue to be a source of debate in the contemporary church:

> women should be silent in the churches. For they are not permitted to speak, but should be subordinate, as the law also says. If there is anything they desire to know, let them ask their husbands at home. For it is shameful for a woman to speak in church. (1 Cor 14:34-35)

> I desire, then, that in every place the men should pray, lifting up holy hands without anger or argument; also that the women should dress themselves modestly and decently in suitable clothing, not with their hair braided, or with gold, pearls, or expensive clothes, but with good works, as is proper for women who profess reverence for God. Let a woman learn in silence with full submission. I permit no woman to teach or to have authority over a man; she is to keep silent. For Adam was formed first, then Eve; and Adam was not deceived, but the woman was deceived and became a transgressor. Yet she will be saved through childbearing, provided they continue in faith and love and holiness, with modesty. (1 Tim. 2:8-15)

In matters of interpretation, it is best to follow the basic hermeneutical principle that "a text without a context is a pretext." Here, this means that since Paul elsewhere affirms women in ministry there must be some specific contextual reasons for his comments in these passages. Thus it seems better to see this as a specific situational-cultural-historical problem rather than a theological one. Both passages contain the prohibitions that they do because of certain unacceptable behavior on the part of some women. In Corinth, women are encouraged to pray and prophesy (1 Cor 11:4-5). However, because women in that setting were often less educated than men, they were, in certain circumstances, not to disrupt the worship services with incessant questions but to learn from their husbands at home.

Several solutions have emerged among commentators on this text: (1) some take it as an absolute, universal and eternal prohibition for women in ministry;[67] (2) some argue that this is an interpolation into the text by a later redactor;[68] (3) E. Earle Ellis explains both of these passages as "preformed traditions" that

---

[66]Wife-husband relationships are discussed in 1 Peter 3:1-7, but not in the context of worship.

[67]A theory generally espoused by George W. Knight III in *The New Testament Teaching on the Role Relationship of Men and Women* (Grand Rapids, Mich.: Baker, 1977).

[68]For discussion, see Gordon Fee, *The First Epistle to the Corinthians,* NICNT (Grand Rapids, Mich.: Eerdmans, 1987), pp. 699-708. A major challenge to the interpolation theory is presented by E. Earle Ellis, who claims that this passage is an example of a "preformed tradition" (*The Making of the New Testament Documents* [Leiden: E. J. Brill, 1999], pp. 426-34).

belong in the text and fit the context of the letters[69]; (4) others conclude that Paul is addressing the specific problem of women disrupting the worship service. Here Craig Keener judiciously notes that Paul provides both a short-range and a long-range solution that addresses the specific problem without universalizing it. The "short-range" solution was that women were to stop interrupting the service with a lot of questions; the "long-range" solution was that they receive instruction from their husbands at home.[70]

Keener takes a similar approach to the problems addressed in 1 Timothy 2:8-15. Here, in Ephesus, women were not only to dress tastefully and modestly (1 Tim 2:9-10)—that is, different from pagan women—but also to learn "in silence" and to have no teaching ministry in the church or authority over men (1 Tim 2:11-12). (There is value and support in seeing the idea as women "seizing authority" or being "domineering" in the church—the same actions that Paul would disapprove in men.) As in the Corinthian passage, the short-range solution was for women not to take ruling positions as teachers in the church because they lacked adequate knowledge. They were, rather, to learn at home (the long-range solution).[71] Leaders in the early church sought to reform certain societal structures of the first century without repudiating those values, but at a pace that would not create suspicion and misunderstanding.

4.10. Anonymous Leaders and Spiritual Gifts

The preceding discussion of specific leaders and ministries in the early church noted several references to what may be called unspecified or unidentified leaders in the church. Thus Paul reminds the Thessalonian church that certain individuals "have charge" (*proistamenous*) over them in the Lord and are responsible for admonishing the members (1 Thess 5:12). The same root is used to denote Phoebe as a "benefactor" (*prostatis*) in the church at Cenchreae (Rom 16:2) and the diligent "leader" mentioned in Romans 12:8.[72]

Hebrews mentions "leaders" (*hēgoumenōn*) several times without identifying or equating them with any of the terms or offices that we know from our study of the New Testament (Heb 13:7, 17, 24; see also Heb 6:10). A different word is

---

[69]Ellis, *Making of the New Testament Documents*, pp. 82-83; 426-34.

[70]Keener, "Man and Women," *DPL*, p. 590. For expanded discussion, see his *Paul, Women and Wives.*

[71]Keener, "Man and Women," pp. 509-10; see also Kroeger and Kroeger, *I Suffer Not a Woman;* David M. Scholer, "1 Timothy 2:9-15 and the Place of Women in the Church's Ministry," in Mickelsen, ed., *Women, Authority and the Bible,* pp. 193-219. See also Fee, *1 and 2 Timothy, Titus,* pp. 70-77; Ben Witherington III, "Women (NT)," *ABD* 957-61; Witherington, *Women in the Earliest Churches.*

[72]This word is translated "manage" when used as a qualification for the office of bishops and deacons (1 Tim 3:4, 5, 12).

used for "leadership" in the list of spiritual gifts (*kybernēsis*, 1 Cor 12:28; sometimes translated "administration," that is, one with the ability to hold a leading position in the church). There are also some "co-workers" who are not mentioned by name (Phil 4:3; Col 4:11) as well as the "brother who is famous among all the churches for his proclaiming the good news . . . [who] has also been appointed *[cheirotoneō]* by the churches to travel with us" (2 Cor 8:18-19).

From this and other insights from the New Testament we may assume that there was a significant cadre of unclassified individuals actively engaged in various ministries of the early church according to their spiritual gifts (*charismata*; see figure 13).[73]

1 Cor 12:8-10	1 Cor 12:28-30	Rom 12:6-8	Eph 4:7-11
wisdom (*sophia*)	apostles (*apostolos*)	prophecy (*prophēteia*)	apostles (*apostolos*)
knowledge (*gnōsis*)	prophets (*prophētēs*)	ministry (*diakonia*)	prophets (*prophētēs*)
faith (*pistis*)	teachers (*didaskalos*)	teaching (*didaskalia*)	evangelists (*euangelistēs*)
healing (*iama*)	deeds of power (*dynamis*)	exhortation (*paraklēsis*)	pastors/teachers (*poimēn didaskalos*)
miracles (*dynamis*)	healing (*iama*)	generosity (*haplotēs*)	
prophecy (*prophēteia*)	assistance (*antilēmpsis*)	leadership (*proistēmi*)	
discernment of spirits (*diakriseis pneuma*)	leadership (*kybernēsis*)	compassion (*eleos*)	
tongues (*glōssa*)	tongues (*glōssa*)		
interpretation of tongues (*hermēneia glōssa*)			

Figure 13. The spiritual gifts

Unfortunately, we do not know how, where and under what circumstances most of these individuals contributed to the church. Some ministries, such as

[73]See appropriate sections in Robert Banks, *Paul's Idea of Community,* rev. ed. (Peabody, Mass: Hendrickson, 1994); E. Earle Ellis, *Pauline Theology: Ministry and Society* (Washington, D.C.: University of America Press, 1997), pp. 26-52.

teaching, exhorting, leading, serving, assistance and giving, probably were regular components of all congregations. We are less certain when it comes to the practice of healing, miracles, prophecy, tongues and the interpretation of tongues. As mentioned earlier, we must be careful not to make the Corinthian church, where most of these so-called spectacular gifts are listed, normative for all churches in the first century.[74] Nevertheless, as Hans von Campenhausen reminds us, *all* gifts are important in Paul's theology of the Spirit:

> All Christians have received the Spirit, and thus become "spiritual" men and women. For Paul, without the Spirit there is no being a Christian, and no spiritual life. On the other hand, he definitely does not regard unity in the Spirit as implying "equality". For him it is of the essence that the underlying unity of the Spirit which has been given to all is made concretely effective in the multiplicity of different gifts bestowed on different people. Paul knows of no operation of the Spirit that is formless, universal, and indiscriminately interchangeable. One man has received this gift, another that; and the life of the Church is to be found only in the continual interplay of a variety of spiritual capacities, which complement one another, and which precisely in this way reveal the fullness and harmony of the Spirit of Christ.[75]

4.11. Concluding Comments

We began this section on ministry and leadership in the early church with two assumptions in view: (1) that the early church developed from an early charismatic style of ministry to a more regulated and ordered one, a concept sometimes identified as "early Catholicism"; and (2) that a considerable diversity of leadership and ministry was evident in the churches of the first century. Both of these hypotheses appear to be valid, even though some issues need further exploration. From this study, however, one can offer the following summary conclusions.

First, the New Testament presents certain church leaders as gifted *individuals* because they were endowed with the "gifts of the Spirit." This group included apostles, prophets, teachers, evangelists and pastors/teachers (1 Cor 12:28; Eph 4:11). Other leaders in the early church (primarily deacons, elders and bishops) possessed the Spirit along with all believers (see Rom 8:1-17; Gal 3:1-14; 5:16-26), but they are not listed among those who received the *charismata*.

Second, individuals with specific charismatic gifts and whose functions dif-

---

[74]Apart from Acts, 1-2 Corinthians and Revelation, prophecy is mentioned as a spiritual gift or phenomenon only in Rom12:6 and healing in Jas 5:13-16 ("signs and wonders" as the sign of a true apostle are cited in 2 Cor 12:12). Believers are encouraged in 1 Pet 4:10-11 to use their spiritual gifts (*charismata*) in "speaking" (*laleō*) and "serving" (*diakoneō*). See Max Turner, *The Holy Spirit and Spiritual Gifts Then and Now* (Carlisle: Paternoster Press, 1966).

[75]Von Campenhausen, *Ecclesiastical Authority and Spiritual Power*, p. 57.

fered from the leaders or offices mentioned above carried out some of the ministries of the early church.

Third, the functions of leaders varied among the first-century churches. In other words, people with the same title performed different ministries or roles in different localities.

Fourth, rather than promoting distinct and self-contained roles, the early church made room for a variety of functions. The picture of leadership is much more like a series of interlocking and overlapping circles than a row of separate entities (see figure 14).

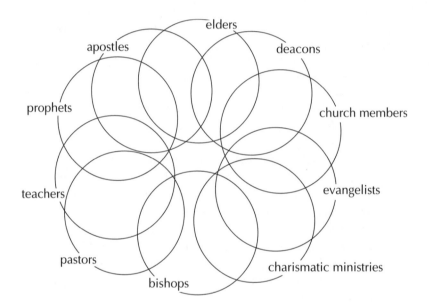

Figure 14. Overlapping roles and ministries

Fifth and last, the church moved from an early charismatic basis of ministry in which all members of the congregations exercised their gifts to a place where leadership and ministry were solidified into several specific offices. This does not imply that members of the congregation no longer had any responsibilities to each other and society; it simply means that some ministries became the primary responsibility of certain leaders—a development that eventually resulted in the threefold apostolic offices of deacons, elders and bishops by the second century A.D.

5

WORSHIP
IN THE EARLY CHURCH

T he challenge of writing about worship in the early church is not unlike the work of a detective gathering pieces of evidence to solve a crime or a person attempting to assemble a complicated jigsaw puzzle. Paul Bradshaw describes the task of a "liturgical historian" as someone locating a series of dots on a large sheet of paper and then attempting to connect them into some meaningful configuration.[1]

There are a number of significant "clues" or "dots" scattered throughout the New Testament that enable us to understand and appreciate various aspects of early Christian worship. For example, we know that the believers met in homes that were large enough to accommodate approximately twenty-five to forty people and that during these meetings they listened to teachers, studied the Scriptures, prayed, sang hymns, baptized new believers, celebrated the Lord's Supper and fellowshiped with each other (Acts 2:42, 46; 1 Cor 11:23-34; 14:26; Eph 5:19-21; Col 3:16-17; Jas 5:13-19).

There are many components of worship and liturgy embedded throughout the New Testament in the form of confessions, creeds, hymns, doxologies, baptismal instruction, eucharistic formulas, and the like. The task of the following discussion will be to identify such components and then suggest how they *may* have been used within the context of early Christian worship. Beyond those

---

[1]Paul Bradshaw, *The Search for the Origins of Christian Worship* (New York: Oxford University Press, 1992), p. 56.

components we have very little data: there are no extant sermons, hymn books, orders of worship, liturgies or developed catechisms within the New Testament to make the task easier.

5.1. Preliminary Considerations

The following discussion takes a number of methodological principles into consideration. First, I work from the premise that there was no archetypal form or original blueprint of worship prescribed for the early church in Jerusalem or subsequent churches. Believers in Jerusalem and in other predominately Jewish communities may have adopted—and adapted—certain Jewish elements of worship into their own. But even here scholars are divided on the church's loyalty to or detachment from the worship of Israel.[2] Recent studies have raised many uncertainties about our knowledge of first-century Judaism and challenged long-standing assumptions of the relationship between Judaism and early Christianity (see 1.2.1 and 3.10). Some of the churches founded by Paul with connections to the synagogue may have adopted some Jewish forms of worship, but the historical development of Christian worship needs to be explored within the setting of the Greco-Roman world as well.[3] There is no evidence that Paul ever felt compelled to standardize worship according to some divine blueprint.

Second, we must question the view that there was a consistent development—a linear trajectory—from Jewish Christian to Christianity in the Greco-Roman world or from worship in the first century to succeeding centuries. There simply are too many variations, inconsistencies and uncertainties in early Christian literature to make this assumption. We must also expose the danger of of interpreting the New Testament documents from later church literature. David Aune acknowledges that there is "a marked tendency to read early, fragmentary evidence anachronistically in the light of later, more detailed accounts of liturgical practice."[4]

At the same time, however, we should not dismiss all early church literature

---

[2]See, e.g., Bradshaw, *Search for the Origins*, pp. 2-29; Gerhard Delling, *Worship in the New Testament*, trans. Percy Scott (London: Darton, Longman & Todd, 1962), pp. 1-14.

[3]See Larry W. Hurtado, *At the Origins of Christian Worship* (Grand Rapids, Mich.: Eerdmans, 2000).

[4]David. E. Aune, "Worship, Early Christian," *ABD* 6:974. Such documents usually include the *Didache*, Hippolytus's *Apostolic Tradition* (written around A.D. 215 in Rome) or sections from *1 Clement*, Justin's *Apology* and Tertullian's *Apology*. Ralph P. Martin appropriately notes that this trap "exposes the readers to a false impression that Christian worship developed in a linear fashion, and that we can trace the lines of development with unbounded confidence" ("Worship and Liturgy," *DLNTD*, p. 1225). See also "Ten Principles for Interpreting Early Christian Liturgical Evidence" in Bradshaw, *Search for the Origins*, pp. 56-79.

as anachronistic or invaluable. The *Didache,* which many scholars date between the mid-sixties to the second century A.D., is a good example of "evolved literature" that details liturgical practices and church structure in Syria and thus may have some affinity with the Christian communities addressed in the Gospel of Matthew and the letter of James.[5] A similar observation can be made for Hippolytus's *Apostolic Tradition,* which documents liturgical life and activity of some churches in Rome in the early third century A.D. It is quite possible that this work reflects *some* traditions and practices that go back to the first century.

Third, we need to avoid a trend among some biblical commentators toward "pan-liturgism," commonly defined as the tendency to interpret certain New Testament texts as liturgical documents, lectionaries, baptismal catechisms, and the like.[6] In most cases this is simply the fallacy of claiming too much from the liturgical language in a specific letter. Ephesians, for example, contains many allusions to baptism and employs baptismal theology to talk about new life in Christ. But this is quite different from claiming that it is a document written specifically to celebrate baptism in the church.[7]

Fourth, we must avoid the temptation to harmonize, which basically is an attempt to take all the pieces of liturgy throughout the New Testament in order to form one composite picture of worship in the early church. This procedure falsely assumes a basic unity of worship practices among the churches in the first century and overlooks the wide range of diversity that existed.

We must acknowledge that worship in the early church was a dynamic and living phenomenon rather than a static one. Hence different patterns of worship emerged as churches responded to pressures and needs in different geographical regions. Diversity or "pluriformity" rather than uniformity characterizes early Christian worship. When some say, "Let's get back to the New Testament church," they generally imply that God provided one divine and eternal model

---

[5]On the dating, provenance and value of the *Didache,* see Michael W. Holmes, "Didache, The," *DLNTD,* pp. 300-2; Robert A. Kraft, "Didache," *ABD* 2:197-98; and Kurt Niederwimmer, *The Didache* (Minneapolis: Augsburg Fortress, 1998). In spite of all the research on the *Didache,* there is very little unanimity among scholars on crucial issues. Robert Kraft summarizes the current state of affairs when he writes: "It is no wonder that, more than a century after its resurrection, the *Didache* continues to frustrate those who try to fit it into a neat and consistent picture of early Christian history and thought" (*ABD* 2:198).

[6]On "pan-liturgism" see Bradshaw, *Search for the Origin,* pp. 30-34; James Dunn, *Unity and Diversity in the New Testament,* 2d ed. (Philadelphia: Trinity Press International, 1990), pp. 141-43; Martin, "Worship and Liturgy," p. 1224; and C. F. D. Moule, *Worship in the New Testament* (Richmond, Va.: John Knox Press, 1961), p. 3. For attempts to interpret 1 Peter and Ephesians liturgically, see major commentaries on these epistles.

[7]See a brief critique of this theory in Arthur G. Patzia, *Ephesians, Colossians, Philemon,* NIBCNT 10 (Peabody, Mass.: Hendrickson, 1990), pp. 131-33.

of worship from which we have departed and to which we should return. A fitting response to such an appeal is: Which church? Should we return to the church in Jerusalem? Antioch? Ephesus? Corinth? Rome? Our current patterns of worship would be quite different if we adopted a Jerusalem (probably more Jewish Christian) rather than a Corinthian (Hellenistic charismatic) model.

5.2. The Context of Early Christian Worship

The worship of the early church emerged within the matrix of Judaism around the two foci of temple and synagogue.[8] The *temple* was the dwelling place of God and the site where sacrifices, daily prayers and seasonal festivals took place (Ex 29:38-43; Josephus *Ant.* 14.4.3 §§64-68). For the most part, Jesus honored the traditions of his faith and participated in religious life with his family and disciples (see Mt 21:23; Lk 2:49; Jn 2:13-17; 4:22; 7:2-8; 10:22-23), although there is no indisputable evidence in the Gospels that he personally offered sacrifices in the temple during his public ministry. The temple court also provided a public forum for his preaching ministry (Lk 19:47-48; 21:37-38). Nevertheless, Jesus was critical of traditions that valued performance more than an inner relationship to God and a concern for humanity (Jn 4:21-24; see also Mt 9:13; 12:7; 23:1-28; Mk 2:15-17, 23-28; 3:1-6; Lk 15:1-2). His frequent conflicts with the scribes and Pharisees of his day indicate how he sought to challenge certain traditions during his ministry. The cleansing of the temple before his arrest and trial is his most significant and symbolic attempt to reform the temple cult (Mt 21:12-16 and parallels).

Since the first Jewish believers saw themselves as a reform movement *within* Judaism (the *true,* not a *new,* Israel), it is not surprising that disciples such as Peter and John went to the temple at the "hour of prayer" (Acts 3:1), taught and preached in its precincts (Acts 2:46; 3:8; 5:20-21, 42; see also Lk 24:53) and continued to live as Jews in every way.[9] The first serious and negative critique of

---

[8]See the earlier discussion in 1.2.1.8-9 and 3.1. This is not meant to discount or minimize the significance of Jewish homes, where domestic responsibilities included religious instruction, observance of food laws, preparation for the sabbath, etc. (see Eduard Lohse, "σάββατον κτλ," *TDNT* 7:15-16).

[9]David Peterson suggests that Peter and John probably participated in the burnt offerings and incense as well ("The Worship of the New Community," in *Witness to the Gospel,* ed. I. Howard Marshall and David Peterson [Grand Rapids, Mich.: Eerdmans, 1998], pp. 378-79). One suspects, however, that their early understanding and interpretation of Jesus' atoning death for their sins as proclaimed in the kerygma soon made this unnecessary (see Acts 5:31; 10:43; 13:38). Thus Stephen C. Farris comments: "The Temple is a convenient and appropriate place for worship but, inasmuch as the sacrificial system is no longer valid in the new age inaugurated by the life, death . . . and resurrection of Jesus Christ, it is not an essential place for worship of the God of Israel" ("Worship," *DJG,* p. 892).

the physical temple came in Stephen's speech (Acts 6:13—7:53), which was less an attack on the temple itself than on the attitude that gave permanency to it. Stephen "is asserting that the promise to Abraham finds its ultimate fulfillment not in the law as given to Moses nor in the temple but in Jesus to whom everything in the OT points."[10] Nevertheless, some Jewish Christians in Jerusalem, under the leadership of James, may not have abandoned their loyalty to the temple until its destruction in A.D. 70 (see Acts 21:26; 24:18).

As already noted (1.2.1.9), the synagogue was another major institution in the public and religious life of the Jews during the first century A.D.[11] However, while Jewish believers continued an association with the temple, Luke is silent about any contact with the synagogues in or around Jerusalem. One surmises that the house gatherings of the early believers replaced the synagogal meetings by providing similar opportunities and structures of Christian worship and fellowship. Contacts with the synagogue apart from Stephen and the "synagogue of the Freedmen" (Acts 6:9) were important in Paul's missionary activity only as opportunities to initiate the proclamation of the gospel and a model for Christian house churches in the Greco-Roman world (see 3.7).

Relatively little is known about the *specifics* of synagogal worship before the codification of the Mishnah toward the end of the second century A.D. However, there is enough available information to conclude that a typical first-century synagogue service included the following: (1) an opening invocation of praise and congregational responses; (2) a section of prayers of thanksgiving, the reading of the Shema (see Deut 6:4) and the Eighteen Benedictions; and (3) a reading of selections from the Law and Prophets followed by an exposition or homily.[12] Some of these items are noticeable in Luke's account of Jesus' visit to the synagogue in Nazareth (Lk 4:16-30) and Paul's in Pisidian Antioch (Acts 13:14-15).[13]

Christianity began as a reform movement within Judaism, retained many

---

[10]Peterson, "Worship of the New Community," pp. 378-79.

[11]On the temple and synagogue, Moule admits that "it has always been tempting to find already there the two components of Christian worship—the Sacraments, corresponding to the Temple, and 'the Word,' corresponding to the non-sacrificial, non-sacramental synagogue, with its strong element of reading and instruction" (*Worship in the New Testament,* p. 7). For a critique of this approach, see Oscar Cullmann, *Early Christian Worship,* trans. A. Stewart Todd and James B. Torrance (London: SCM Press, 1953), pp. 27-28.

[12]For more details see Bradshaw, *Search for the Origins,* pp. 1-29; Bruce Chilton and Edwin Yamauchi, "Synagogues," *DNTB,* pp. 1145-53; Fredrick C. Grant, *Ancient Judaism and the New Testament* (London: Oliver & Boyd, 1960), pp. 39-57; Hurtado, *At the Origins,* pp. 31-36; Martin, *Early Christian Worship,* pp. 24-27.

[13]There is nothing is the entire New Testament that could be considered a replica of synagogue worship; nevertheless, the Jewish nature of Luke's hymns (Lk 1:46-55, 68-79; 2:29-32), the development of prayer and the celebrations of the Passover are strikingly Jewish in nature.

Jewish beliefs and practices and quickly spread to distant regions of the Roman empire (see part three). When churches began with a nucleus of Hellenistic Jews in the Diaspora, they probably modeled some of their worship after the synagogue. But pagan (Gentile) converts had a different set of religious beliefs, loyalties and practices that shaped their faith. Such factors may account for the rather charismatic style of worship that characterized the church at Corinth (see 1 Cor 11—14) and possibly other Gentile congregations as well.

5.3. The Setting of Early Christian Worship (House Churches)

When the group of Jesus' followers returned to Jerusalem after his ascension from the Mount of Olives, they reassembled in a "room upstairs" (or "upper room," *hyperōon*) and began to pray and discuss the implications of what had taken place and how to move forward without the physical presence of their Lord (Acts 1:12-15; 2:2). Scholars speculate that this "upper room" is the same one where Jesus celebrated the Last Supper with his disciples (Mk 14:15) and that it was part of the house owned by Mary the mother of John Mark (Acts 12:12).[14] However, this was only one of several homes in Jerusalem where the early believers met for worship, study, fellowship and the sharing of goods (see Acts 2:42, 46; 5:42). When Saul began ravaging the early church in Jerusalem, he entered "house after house" in his attempt to eradicate this new movement (Acts 8:3).

There is no way of knowing how many homes were needed to accommodate the growing number of believers in Jerusalem, even if Luke's "about three thousand persons" (Acts 2:41) is not taken literally (see 3.1). Most rooms in an "average" home probably could not have accommodated more than thirty or forty people without spilling over into a courtyard of some kind. We also do not know who made their homes available for these Christian gatherings and who handled the administrative and logistical details.

Most reconstructions of the organizational structure of the early church agree that it was modeled after the synagogal pattern in Judaism *and* the household or *collegia* in the Greco-Roman world.[15] Given the close relationship

---

[14]F. F. Bruce, *The Book of the Acts,* rev. ed., NICNT (Grand Rapids, Mich.: Eerdmans, 1992), p. 40. According to Bradley B. Blue, these connections were not made until the fifth century ("Acts and the House Church," in *The Book of Acts in Its Graeco-Roman Setting,* ed. David W. J. Gill and Conrad Gempf, BAFCS 2 [Grand Rapids, Mich.: Eerdmans, 1994], p. 134).

[15]For additional reading, see Robert Banks, *Paul's Idea of Community,* rev. ed. (Peabody Mass.: Hendrickson, 1994), pp. 26-36; Stephen C. Barton, "Social Values and Structures," *DNTB,* pp. 1127-34; Bradley B. Blue, "The Influence of Jewish Worship on Luke's Presentation of the Early Church," in Marshall and Peterson, eds., *Witness to the Gospel,* pp. 473-97; Blue, "Acts and the House Church," pp. 119-22; Blue, "Architecture, Early Church," *DLNTD,* pp. 91-95;

between Judaism and early Christianity it is not surprising that church and synagogal assemblies had many similarities. We already noted this with respect to
worship and leadership. The same applies to places of worship. Many Jews
who made their homes available for synagogal meetings would have done the
same for the church when they became believers.[16]

The structure of the household had a significant impact upon early Christianity in the Hellenistic world. The household was a social unit that included
both the nuclear and extended family under the headship of the householder,
who had complete authority over all the members. In many cases such households included slaves, freedpersons, servants, laborers, business associates
and tenants. Some of these homes were used for gatherings of social, profes-
sional and religious clubs or guilds (*schola collegii*). The owner probably was
the leader of such meetings or at least was considered the benefactor or
patron.

When Brad Blue writes that "early Christianity expanded throughout the
Empire house by house," he captures well a significant principle of Paul's mission-

---

David A. deSilva, "Patronage," *DNTB*, pp. 766-71; deSilva, *Honor, Patronage, Kinship and
Purity: Unlocking the New Testament Culture* (Downers Grove, Ill.: InterVarsity Press, 2000);
E. Earle Ellis, *Pauline Theology* (Washington, D. C.: University of America Press, 1997), esp. ch.
5, "Pauline Christianity and the World Order," pp. 122-59; Floyd V. Filson, "The Significance of
the Early House Churches," *JBL* 58 (1939): 105-112; Rita H. Finger, *Paul and the Roman House
Churches* (Scottdale, Penn.: Herald Press, 1993); E. A. Judge, *The Social Pattern of the Christian
Groups in the First Century: Some Prolegomena to the Study of New Testament Ideas of Social
Obligation* (London: Tyndale, 1960); Judge, "The Social Identity of the First Christians," *JRH* 11
(1980), pp. 201-17; Craig S. Keener, "Family and Household," *DNTB*, pp. 353-68; Hans-Josef
Klauck, *Hausgemeinde und Hauskirche im frühen Christentum* (Stuttgart: Verlag Katholisches
Bibelwerk, 1981); Abraham J. Malherbe, "House Churches and their Problems," in *Social
Aspects of Early Christianity* (Baton Rouge: Louisiana State University Press, 1977), pp. 60-91;
Dan G. McCartney, "Household, Family," *DLNTD*, pp. 511-13; Wayne A. Meeks, *The First
Urban Christians: The Social World of the Apostle Paul* (New Haven, Conn.: Yale University
Press, 1983), pp. 75-77; Carolyn Osiek and David Balch, *Families in the New Testament
World: Households and House Churches* (Louisville: Westminster John Knox, 1997); J. M.
Peterson, "House-Churches in Rome," *VC* 23 (1969): 264-72; John Reumann, "One Lord, One
Faith, One God, but Many House Churches," in *Common Life in the Early Church*, ed. Julian V.
Hills (Harrisburg, Penn.: Trinity Press International, 1998), pp. 106-17; Peter Richardson,
"Architectural Transitions from Synagogues and House Churches to Purpose-Built Churches,"
in Hills, ed., *Common Life in the Early Church*, pp. 373-89; Philip H. Towner, "Households and
Household Codes," *DPL*, pp. 417-19.

[16]So Blue in "Acts and the House Church," p. 136: "Most synagogues were single rooms in
houses. Because the majority of the early believers were converts from Judaism and coupled
with the fact that the early community in Jerusalem included believers who were financially
solvent . . . it would not be inconsistent to propose that some of the Jewish believers had for-
merly opened their houses (or parts thereof) to the synagogue community. In turn, having
espoused the Christian faith, it would have been natural for these patrons to use the same
facilities as a gathering place for the Christian community."

ary strategy.[17] When Paul's attempts to evangelize the Jews in the synagogues of the Diaspora failed, he was forced to turn to the Gentiles. As we shall see, many of his first converts were entire "households," with the "heads" of each house probably becoming the benefactors or patrons of the church by offering their homes as meeting places. Such leaders probably would have taken responsibility for the weekly gatherings of fellowship, worship and the study of Scripture.

Some of the early converts to Christianity were God-fearers who were attracted to Judaism but had not become full proselytes. In Palestine, we have the example of Cornelius, a Roman centurion stationed in Caesarea, whom Luke describes as "a devout man who feared God *[eusebēs kai phoboumenos]* with all his household *[panti tō oikō]*; he gave alms generously to the people and prayed constantly to God" (Acts 10:2). As a result of Peter's vision and proclamation of the gospel (Acts 10:44-48) a number of Gentiles, including Cornelius' household, were saved and baptized (Acts 11:1-18, esp. v. 14). As noted earlier (part three), Peter opened the door of faith to the Gentiles. Luke appears to reinforce the significance of this event by repeating it to the Jewish believers and leaders in Jerusalem (Acts 11:1-18) and alluding to it again at the Jerusalem Council. Peter reminded the council members that God had obliterated certain legal distinctions between Jews and Gentiles and that salvation was by faith and not by keeping the law (Acts 15:7-11). Given Cornelius's piety, generosity and financial means, he no doubt opened his house to the believers in Caesarea. One wonders whether Philip's house in Caesarea was used in this way as well (Acts 21:8-10).

The majority of New Testament households and house churches were connected with Paul's ministry in some way. When Paul traveled to Philippi, two significant events took place: the conversion of Lydia, a businesswoman and God-fearer from Thyatira (Acts 16:11-15), after which she invited Paul to her home (Acts 16:15); and the conversion and baptism of the Philippian jailer, his family and his household (Acts 16:30-34). It is reasonable to believe that either one or both of these homes (or even some unknown home) became a house church in Philippi.

When Paul writes to "the church *[ekklēsia]* of God that is in Corinth" (1 Cor 1:2), the contemporary reader has no way of knowing that he is addressing the sum total of believers in a number of house churches in the city. Upon closer examination, however, we discover the *possibility* of seven assemblies (see 3.7.5).

First, there was the home of Aquila and Priscilla (or Prisca; Paul calls her Prisca, a common Latin name, but Luke prefers Priscilla). They were Jewish

---

[17]Blue, "Influence of Jewish Worship," p. 474.

converts who settled in Corinth when Claudius expelled a large number of Jews from Rome around A.D. 49/50 (Acts 18:2). Paul began his life in Corinth by moving into Aquila and Priscilla's home, where all of them carried on their trade as tentmakers. Most likely this was a type of storefront home that doubled as a work/retail outlet and domestic residence.

During Paul's eighteen-month stay in Corinth (Acts 18:11), this home must have been a significant place for proclaiming the gospel, teaching and gathering believers in worship. At the end of that time, Aquila and Priscilla moved on to Ephesus with Paul and started a house church there (Acts 18:18-19; see 1 Cor 16:19 and 2 Tim 4:19). Paul's greeting to "Prisca and Aquila" and "the church in their house" (Rom 16:3-5) implies that they returned to Rome, probably after Claudius lifted his edict against the Jews.

Second, Luke mentions Titius Justus, a "worshiper of God" *(sebomenou ton theon)*, whose house was next to the synagogue (Acts 18:7), and Crispus, an official *(archisynagōgos)* of the synagogue. The conversion and baptism of these individuals, including the "household" of Crispus (on his baptism, see 1 Cor 1:14) and "many" other Corinthians (Acts 18:7-11), indicates that there was a sizeable group of believers during Paul's eighteen-month ministry. No doubt the homes of Titius Justus or Crispus were utilized for church gatherings as well.

Third, Paul refers to the baptism of "the household of Stephanas" (1 Cor 1:16) as one of the first converts in Achaia (1 Cor 16:15a). The fact that he is commended so highly by Paul for his devoted service to the saints in Corinth (1 Cor 16:15b-16) leads one to suppose that he, too, may have hosted and led a house church in the city.

Fourth, there is also reference to "Chloe's people," a group of individuals who journeyed across the Aegean Sea from Corinth to Ephesus with the disturbing report about factions within the Corinthian church (1 Cor 1:11-17). Chloe's "people" may be a pseudonym for Chloe's household, which would have included members of her family and employees. Gordon Fee proposes that she "was a wealthy Asian . . . whose business interests caused her agents to travel between Ephesus and Corinth."[18] If true, her economic means and concern for the church suggest that she also may have had a significant role in one of the house churches.

Fifth, Paul names Gaius, one of three individuals he commends in the closing chapter of Romans, which he writes from Corinth. This explicit reference to Gaius (see 1 Cor 1:14 on his baptism by Paul) "who is host to me and to the whole church" (Rom 16:23) leaves little doubt that he was another benefactor of the church.

---

[18]Gordon Fee, *The First Epistle to the Corinthians*, NICNT (Grand Rapids, Mich.: Eerdmans, 1987), p. 54.

Sixth, Paul also sends greetings from Erastus, "the city treasurer," and another brother, Quartus (Rom 16:23). While Erastus may not have been one of Paul's fellow workers, his position gave him a higher social rank and economic status than most people, perhaps enough to make him another patron of a house church.

Seventh, Paul commends Phoebe, "a deacon" and "benefactor" (prostatis) or patron of the church at Cenchreae (Rom 16:1-2). From this "we may infer that Phoebe is an independent woman . . . who has some wealth and is also one of the leaders of a Christian group in the harbor town of Cenchreae."[19] Since Cenchreae was only seven miles from Corinth, the church probably was considered part of Corinth.

All this illustrates that "the church of God that is in Corinth" (1 Cor 1:2) and the "whole church" (holēs tēs ekklēsias) mentioned in Romans 16:23 consisted of several local house churches, each one somewhat different in its ethnic, social and economic mix of people. Paul's reference to "the church of God in Corinth" (1 Cor 1:2) and to the believers coming together "as a church" (gar synerchomenōn hymōn en ekklēsia, 1 Cor 11:18), along with the implication that Gaius was hosting the entire (holēs) church (Rom 16:23), suggest that there were occasions in Corinth when *all* the believers assembled.[20] This thesis helps to explain some of the fragmentation in Corinth with respect to church leadership, worship, morality and social status. Certain sections of Paul's correspondence to the Corinthians probably were sent to specific house churches that were encountering particular problems. In time, these letters were shared with other churches in the city and read at their worship services before a redactor collected and edited them into their current format as 1 and 2 Corinthians.[21]

The prior discussion of the founding and nature of the church in Rome concluded that it was a mixture of Jewish and Gentile believers who probably met separately in a number of different house churches (see 3.7.8). This historical reality created certain tensions and required a response from Paul to the effect that all believers should respect their ethnic, religious and social diversity and live together in unity (especially Rom 14:1—15:6).[22]

---

[19]Meeks, *First Urban Christians,* p. 60.

[20]See esp. Banks, *Paul's Idea of Community,* pp. 31-34; Klauck, *Hausgemeinde und Hauskirche,* pp. 34-41.

[21]On the Corinthian correspondence, see Calvin Roetzel, *The Letters of Paul: Conversations in Context,* 4th ed. (Louisville: Westminster John Knox, 1998), pp. 83-87; Arthur G. Patzia, *The Making of the New Testament* (Downers Grove, Ill.: InterVarsity Press, 1995), pp. 78-79.

[22]Commentators believe that this includes converted slaves, freedpersons, people with a higher social rank and Jewish converts. See, for example, James Dunn, *Romans 1-8,* WBC 38A (Dallas: Word, 1988), p. lii; Francis Watson, "The Two Roman Congregations: Romans 14:1-15:13," in *The Romans Debate,* rev. ed., ed. Karl P. Donfried (Peabody, Mass.: Hendrickson, 1991), pp. 203-15.

There is currently no accurate way to determine how many house churches existed in Rome. Most of the evidence appears in Romans 16, which contains Paul's greetings and commendations to a number of individuals.[23] Some of the named individuals were simply Paul's friends and coworkers, but when Paul names certain individuals and refers to "other" people in the same verse, he may have churches in mind. The possibilities include: (1) the house of Prisca and Aquila (Rom 16:3-5); (2) "those who belong to the family of Aristobulus" (Rom 16:10); (3) a group belonging "to the family of Narcissus" (Rom 16:11); (4) Asyncritus and other named individuals whom Paul knew personally *as well as* "the brothers and sisters who are with them" (Rom 16:14); and (5) Philologus, other acquaintances "and all the saints who are with them" (Rom 16:15).

In contrast to the situation in Corinth, it is unlikely that Paul envisioned this letter being read to a single gathering of *all* the house churches in the city. More likely it would have circulated from one house church to another so that all believers might hear it. The church at Rome did not operate like the Corinthian church. This, according to Robert Banks, explains the rather unusual greeting in Romans: "To all God's beloved in Rome, who are called to be saints" (Rom 1:7) instead of the "church" or "churches," as Paul writes in other letters (see 1 Cor 1:2; 2 Cor 1:1; Gal 1:2; 1 Thess 1:1; 2 Thess 1:1). Banks argues that since *ekklēsia* for Paul "cannot refer to a group of people scattered throughout a locality unless they all actually gather together, it is not possible for him to describe all the Christians in Rome as a 'church.' The 'whole church' of Rome never assembled in one place."[24]

Paul's letters to the Colossians and to Philemon refer to several house churches in the cities of Colossae, Hierapolis and Laodicea—communities evangelized by Epaphras. Although Epaphras "worked hard" in Hierapolis (Col 4:13), there is no evidence that Epaphras was successful in establishing a church there at this time.[25] With respect to Laodicea, Paul refers to a group "of brothers and sisters, and to Nympha and the church in her house" (Col 4:15). The natural reading of the text implies that two separate groups were meeting, one of them led by Nympha, the likely patron and leader.

Colossae appears to have had at least two house churches. A church in Philemon's house is mentioned explicitly (Philem 2). The existence of a second

---

[23]Here I concur with scholars who accept this chapter as genuinely belonging to Romans and not as a cover letter of a copy to the church in Ephesus. See most commentaries for discussion and esp. Harry Gamble, *The Textual History of the Letter to the Romans* (Grand Rapids, Mich.: Eerdmans, 1977).

[24]Banks, *Paul's Idea of Community,* p. 34; cf. Meeks, *First Urban Christians,* pp. 142-43.

[25]There is a tradition that Philip the evangelist and his daughters moved from Caesarea (see Acts 21:8) to Hierapolis around A.D. 70. Later (around A.D. 125), Papias became the bishop of the church in Hierapolis.

house church is based on the assumption that all the "saints and faithful brothers and sisters in Christ in Colossae" (Col 1:2) required additional homes for fellowship and worship.[26] Other house churches may be implied in situations where hospitality to itinerant teachers and evangelists is encouraged. In this situation the leaders of a house may have decided who should and should not be taken in (see Rom 12:13; Heb 13:2; 1 Pet 4:9; 3 Jn 5-10; *Did.* 11-12). Some commentators suggest that the salutation to the "elect lady and her children" (*eklektē kuria kai tois teknois,* 2 Jn 1) relates to a specific woman (rather than the church at large) who may have been a leader of a specific house church somewhere in the vicinity of Ephesus.[27]

History confirms that there were significant changes in the homes used as churches during the first three centuries A.D. Initially the church met in a home large enough to accommodate a small group of people. In some cases, according to the financial resources of the patron, a certain room may have been set aside and even redecorated to make it more appealing and comfortable. Brad Blue proposes that such renovations belong to a second stage of development (c. A.D. 150-250), and in this case, homes were identified as the *domus ecclesia.* A third stage (c. 250-313), "saw the introduction of larger buildings and halls (both private and public) before the introduction of basilical architecture by Constantine."[28]

5.4. The Components of Early Christian Worship
Before discussing life in the early church, it may be helpful to reflect on the role that Jesus' teaching had in this process.[29] Here we need to remember that the Gospels, as we have them today, were not written until thirty to fifty years *after*

---

[26]Colossians 4:16 is an interesting commentary on the circulation of Paul's letters among churches in close geographical proximity to each other: "And when this letter has been read among you, have it read also in the church of the Laodiceans; and see that you read also the letter from Laodicea." It is clear that the church in Laodicea was to receive and read Colossians, but "the letter from Laodicea" is a mystery. For suggestions that this was (1) a letter written from the church (or someone) in Laodicea to Paul; (2) the letter to the Ephesians; (3) the letter to Philemon; or (4) a letter of Paul to Laodicea that did not survive, see James D. G. Dunn, *Colossians and Philemon* (Grand Rapids, Mich.: Eerdmans, 1996), pp. 285-87; Peter T. O'Brien, *Colossians, Philemon,* WBC 44 (Dallas: Word, 1982), pp. 257-58.

[27]For a brief discussion, see Catherine. C. Kroeger, "Women in the Early Church," *DLNTD,* p. 1220.

[28]Blue, "Acts and the House Church," p. 125; see also his "Architecture, Early Church," pp. 91-95. Both articles contain valuable bibliographies on church structures and archaeology of this time period. Hans-Joseph Klauck quotes Porphyry, an early pagan critic (c. A.D. 232-303) as saying: "But even the Christians imitate the temple architecture and build enormous buildings *[megistous oikous]* in which they come together to pray, which they could instead do unhindered in their houses *[en tais oikiais]* since it is well known that the Lord hears from everywhere" (*Hausgemeinde und Hauskirche,* p. 74, personal translation).

[29]For more detailed discussion, see Patzia, *Making of the New Testament,* pp. 40-67.

the resurrection and ascension of Jesus and the founding of the church at Pentecost. This means that Paul's letters (and most of the New Testament books) were composed *before* the sayings of Jesus acquired their present literary form. It is a mistake to assume that the Gospels were written first based on the order of the books in the New Testament.

When Jesus gathered his twelve disciples, he communicated with them orally. Likewise, the crowds who heard him came without notebooks and left without paperback copies of "The Good News According to Jesus." They simply had to retain his message by applying it to their daily lives, memorizing it and retelling it. Learning by memorization may explain why Jesus used certain "forms" of teaching, such as parables and parallelism (*parallelismus membrorum*).

After Pentecost, the early Christians in Jerusalem continued to pass on the stories and sayings of Jesus in their preaching and teaching. When they were asked questions about Jesus, such as who he was, what he said, why he was crucified, what he thought of the Torah, where he went, and so on, they would rely upon their memory and the oral traditions that were passed on in their religious communities. The sayings that were retained and transmitted were those that met the missionary, preaching, apologetic and pastoral needs of the early church. Scholars often refer to this sociological setting as "the life setting of the church" (*Sitz im Leben Kirche*). As time passed, these "random" sayings of Jesus became more stereotyped and were organized into units ("forms"). The Evangelists (authors) eventually used these and other materials to write their stories (Gospels) about Jesus.

One of the reasons the Gospels were written was the need for an authoritative and unified record of Jesus' sayings for the church. As the church grew, it became necessary to teach and strengthen the believers. The stories and sayings of Jesus were treasured as tools for evangelism and instruction in the faith, not for their nostalgic value. New converts needed instruction in Christian doctrine and practice to understand the changes that had taken place in their lives so that they could accept the privileges and responsibilities of belonging to the body of Christ and face external threats to their faith.

Even though Paul probably knew quite a bit about Jesus, his letters contain very little information (see, e.g., Rom 1:3; 1 Cor 1:23; Gal 4:4; Phil 2:8) and express very little interest in Jesus' life, ministry and teaching.[30] Nevertheless, both he and the early church based their preaching and teaching on the realities of the Christ-event (life-death-resurrection-exaltation) as they began to witness to the world and to instruct believers.

According to Acts, the first converts to Christianity were Jews who responded to

---

[30]Partial quotations from Jesus appear in 1 Cor 7:10-11; 9:14; 11:23-25; 1 Thess 4:16-17; for echoes of Jesus' sayings, see Roetzel's list in *Letters of Paul*, pp. 73-74.

Peter's sermon by being baptized "in the name of Jesus" and receiving the Holy Spirit (Acts 2:37-38). At first this confession of Jesus as Messiah did not separate them from Judaism. The Jews simply acknowledged that Jesus was the fulfillment of God's promises to his covenant people and that they now constituted the true Israel. They did not see themselves as a separate movement outside Judaism, even though they were later identified as a sect (*hairesis;* see Acts 24:5, 14; 28:22). Thus it seemed natural that Peter and John would continue attending the temple for prayer and that priests and Pharisees would believe in the gospel (Acts 6:7; 15:5).

It gradually became obvious to those who had been baptized that they differed from unbelieving Jews and that a peaceful coexistence with their Jewish heritage was no longer possible at every level. Baptism was an initiatory rite that set Christian believers apart from Jewish brothers and sisters. Moreover, in addition to confessing Jesus as Messiah publicly, they soon met separately in homes to fellowship with each other, to reflect upon their faith and to celebrate the Lord's Supper (Acts 2:42: "They devoted themselves to the apostles' teaching and fellowship, to the breaking of bread and the prayers").[31] The formalization of their faith and practice put them on a collision course with Judaism that eventually led to a "Partings of the Ways."[32]

The previous section (part four) identified certain leaders in the early church and suggested some functions they performed. Now it is appropriate to expand that section by analyzing the preaching, teaching and administrative components of the early church that found their context within the worshiping community. Although most of our information comes from the letters of Paul, we realize that he is indebted to the early church for many early Christian traditions, creedal and doctrinal formulations, and paraenetic material. Paul expresses this indebtedness to his predecessors when he refers to material that he "received" (*paralambanō*) from the church and "delivered" (*paradidomi)* to his congregations (e.g., 1 Cor 11:23-25; 15:3-4).[33] It may be that 1 Corinthians

---

[31]Reference to "the prayers" (*tais proseuchais)* suggests some specific and possibly liturgical prayers following Jewish models.

[32]A phrase used by several scholars to describe the gradual separation of early Christianity from Judaism. See especially James D. G. Dunn, *The Partings of the Ways* (Philadelphia: Trinity Press International, 1991).

[33]R. Longenecker's summary following his investigation of confessional material is worth noting: "All that can be said historically is that probably most of the confessional materials identified above were formed earlier than Paul's major missionary letters, which are the earliest writings in the NT. And all that can be said religiously is that these early confessions evidently came about through the guidance of the Holy Spirit as the earliest Christians reflected on the work and person of Jesus of Nazareth and as they attempted to express their new faith in their particular circumstances of worship, instruction and witness" (*New Wine into Fresh Wineskins: Contextualizing the Early Christian Confessions* [Peabody, Mass.: Hendrickson, 1999], p. 26).

15:3-8 is the earliest example of preformed material, going back to the kerygma of the Jewish-Christian communities in Jerusalem and Antioch, where the cross and the resurrection were vital components of preaching.

5.4.1. Early Christian Preaching (kērygma) **and Teaching** (didachē). Martin Dibelius in Germany and C. H. Dodd in England were two notable scholars responsible for the earliest reconstructions of the content of the early church's preaching and teaching.[34] Both utilized speeches (sermons) from the book of Acts. Dibelius condensed the material under the topics of (1) salvation in Christ; (2) scriptural proofs; and (3) the call to repentance. Dodd, on the other hand, elaborated further by including the following elements:

1. the messianic age foretold by the prophets has arrived (Acts 2:16-21; 3:18, 24; 10:43; Rom 1:2);

2. the life, death and resurrection of Jesus marks the fulfillment of the messianic age (Acts 2:24, 31; 3:15; 5:30; 10:37-43; Rom 1:3-4; 4:24-25; 8:34; 1 Cor 15:3-4; 1 Thess 1:10);

3. by virtue of his resurrection, Jesus is the exalted Lord (Acts 2:33-36; 4:11; Rom 8:34; 10:9; Phil 2:9);

4. the presence of the Holy Spirit in the church is a sign of God's presence with his people (Acts 2:37-47; 4:31; 5:32; Rom 8:26-27; 1 Cor 12:1-11);

5. that Christ will return as Judge and Savior of the world (Acts 3:20-26; 10:42; 17:31; Rom 2:16; 1 Thess 1:10); and

6. the call to repentance includes an offer of forgiveness from sins and the reception of the Holy Spirit as a guarantee of salvation (Acts 2:38; 3:19; 10:43; 11:18; Rom 10:9).

Recent critics fault both Dibelius and Dodd on several counts: (1) for relying too heavily on the speeches of Acts to reconstruct the kerygma; (2) for making the kerygma too monolithic; and (3) for creating too sharp a distinction between preaching (kērygma) and teaching (didachē). Today it is more accurate to speak of "multiple kerygmas" (or kērygmata) and to acknowledge the diversity of early preaching.[35]

In fairness to Dibelius and Dodd, it must be said that they did not imply that all these ingredients were present every time apostles, evangelists, missionaries

---

[34]Martin Dibelius, *Die Formgeschichte der Evangelium*, Eng. trans., *From Tradition to Gospel*, trans. B. L. Woolf (New York: Charles Scribner's, 1965); C. H. Dodd, *The Apostolic Preaching and Its Developments* (London: Hodder & Stoughton, 1963). See also Robert Mounce, *The Essential Nature of New Testament Preaching* (Grand Rapids, Mich.: Eerdmans, 1960).

[35]See Peter H. Davids, "Homily, Ancient," *DNTB*, pp. 515-18; James Dunn, *Unity and Diversity*; Gordon P. Hugenberger, "Preach," *ISBE* 3:940-43; Robert H. Mounce, "Preaching, Kerygma," *DPL*, pp. 735-37; John B. Polhill, "Kerygma and Didache," *DLNTD*, pp. 626-29.

and other believers proclaimed the gospel. Presentations varied according to the different situations and needs of the hearers. Their studies simply affirm that the kerygma of the early church embodied certain theological truths that were shared with unbelievers.

Calvin Roetzel provides a creative reconstruction of the kerygmatic elements of Paul's preaching, which embodied "the good news that he proclaimed" (see, e.g., 1 Cor 15:1):

> Yahweh is God of the Jews, and through the Jews came his promises, the commandments, the prophets, and finally the Messiah. But Yahweh is not God of the Jews only. In past generations he has never left himself without witness among any people. Through his creation of the world and his gifts of rain and good harvest, God has shown his care for all people. But instead of the Creator, the Gentiles worshiped nature gods and local deities. God has decided to overlook the error and ignorance of the past and is once more making his appeal to all people, not just to Jews. His promise through Abraham was to all nations. Now in the last days that promise is being realized in Jesus the Christ who was crucified and whom God raised from the dead. Jesus will soon return to judge the world and collect all of his people. He will come from heaven with his angels in flaming fire; he will vindicate God's righteousness and punish those who reject God and the gospel. He will grant mercy and peace to all who believe in him. Those who accept his gospel will now taste the joys of the kingdom of God and enjoy deliverance from the present evil age. Repent, for the final days are at hand. Turn to God from the worship of idols. Be baptized into Jesus' death and rise up to walk in newness of life through the gift of the Holy Spirit. Be alert, watch, and wait for the return of the son of God.[36]

In broad terms, preaching could be defined as the initial presentation of the gospel by missionaries and evangelists to individuals, with salvation as the primary goal (Acts 5:42; 10:42; 16:10, 17; 17:23; 26:23; Rom 1:15; 10:14; 15:20; 1 Cor 1:17, 23; 9:16; 2 Cor 2:12; 4:5; Gal 1:16; 2:2; Col 1:28; 1 Jn 1:5). But preaching also contained some didactic material.[37] This is true in what we traditionally label as sermons in Acts by Peter (Acts 2:14-42), by Stephen (Acts 7:2-53) and by Paul in Pisidian Antioch (Acts 13:14-41), Lystra, Derbe and Iconium (Acts 14:1-18), Athens (Acts 17:22-31) and Thessalonica (1 Thess 1:9-10).[38] Philip's proclamation of "the word" and "the

---

[36]Roetzel, *Letters of Paul*, pp. 80-81.

[37]The Greek words *kērussō, euangelizō* and *katangellō* typically are translated into English as "preaching" or "proclaiming." The NRSV uses "preach" for *parakalein* in Tit 1:9 and for *en logō* in 1 Tim 5:17. See David S. Lim, "Evangelism in the Early Church," *DLNTD*, pp. 353-59.

[38]See Johannes Munck, "1 Thessalonians 1:9-10 and the Missionary Preaching of Paul," *NTS* 9 (1962-1963): 95-110; Gerhard Friedrich, "κῆρυξ κτλ," *TDNT* 3:683-718.

Messiah" (Acts 8:48) probably included the basic components of the *kerygma* as well.

The predominant word for "teaching" in the New Testament is *didaskō* (to teach). But other words, such as *noutheteō* (instruct, warn), *elenchō* (rebuke, reprove, condemn) and *parakaleō* (exhort, comfort) are used in the context of teaching as well. Timothy, for example, is told to "proclaim *[kēryssō]* the message . . . convince *[elenchō]*, rebuke *[epitimaō]*, and encourage *[parakaleō]*, with the utmost patience in teaching *[didachē]*" (2 Tim 4:2). On other occasions preaching and teaching take place in the same setting, thus implying that no major differentiation was made between the two (see Acts 5:42; Col 1:28; 1 Tim 4:13; 5:17; 2 Tim 4:2; Tit 1:9).

5.4.2. Early Christian Creeds and Confessions. The early church also expressed its faith by developing and using a variety of creeds and confessions.[39] Some are very concise, such as "Jesus is Lord" (Rom 10:9; 1 Cor 12:3), "Jesus is the Christ" (1 Jn 2:22; 5:1), "Jesus Christ has come in the flesh" (1 Jn 4:2) and "Jesus is the Son of God" (1 Jn 4:15; see Heb 4:14). Others, however, are more elaborate and indicate that the early church reflected more deeply on key realities of Christ, such as his death, burial, resurrection and exaltation (e.g., Rom 1:3-4; 4:24-25; 8:34; 1 Cor 15:3-5; Phil 2:6-11; Col 1:15-20; 1 Tim 3:16; 2 Tim 2:11-13; Heb 1:3; 1 Pet 3:18-22; Rev 15:3-4). The fact that some passages identified as hymns contain the most profound christological thought in the New Testament indicates how central Christ was in the church's preaching and worship.[40]

There are, to be sure, other creedal and creedal-type statements that could be added to this list.[41] However, these examples illustrate sufficiently that such creeds and confessions were very much a part of early Christian theology, that they were read or recited in worship services and that they became the basis for further doctrinal teaching in the church, especially as the church developed its understanding of the person and work of Christ.

5.4.3. Early Christian Hymnody. Music, at least in the form of singing,

---

[39]The literature on this subject is voluminous but extremely helpful in understanding this phase of early Christian worship. Richard Longenecker's *New Wine into Fresh Wineskins* is a recent attempt to summarize the history of scholarship, to analyze this material and to demonstrate how such confessions were contextualized in the early church. For further reading, see Ralph P. Martin, *Worship in the Early Church* (Grand Rapids, Mich.: Eerdmans, 1983), pp. 39-65; Martin, "Creed," *DPL*, pp. 92; Martin, *New Testament Foundations,* rev. ed. (Grand Rapids, Mich.: Eerdmans, 1986), 2:248-75; Wendy J. Porter, "Creeds and Hymns," *DNTB*, pp. 231-38; David F. Wright, "Creeds, Confessional Forms," *DLNTD*, pp. 255-60.

[40]Martin Hengel, "Hymns and Christology," in *Between Jesus and Paul* (Philadelphia: Fortress, 1983), pp. 78-96.

[41]Cited by Longenecker, *New Wine into Fresh Wineskins,* pp. 13-23.

formed another significant component of early Christian worship.[42] Worship assemblies mentioned in 1 Corinthians 14:26 include "a hymn, a lesson, a revelation, a tongue, or an interpretation." The worship setting in Corinth allows for the probability of fresh spontaneous hymns of praise by the congregation or even a "solo" on the analogy of glossolalia, where one person would speak in tongues or prophesy.[43] Such may have been the case with Paul and Silas when they were "praying and singing hymns *[proseuchomenoi hymnoun]* to God" in the Philippian jail (Acts 16:25). But it is also likely that they were drawing upon familiar hymns from their Jewish-Christian heritage rather than creating something entirely new.

Both Colossians (Col 3:16) and Ephesians (Eph 5:19) list psalms (*psalmois*), hymns *(hymnois)* and spiritual songs *(ōdais pneumatikais)* as parts of the hymnody. Nearly all scholars agree that it is impossible to differentiate between these three elements or to know how they relate to one another.[44] Most likely they are synonymous and thus describe the *total* range of singing that is prompted by the Spirit—that is, "as a description of the fullness and multiplicity of possible responses to the word that dwells in its richness among the faithful."[45] A. T. Lincoln strikes a nice balance on this point when he writes:

> The songs which believers sing to each other are spiritual because they are inspired by the Spirit and manifest the life of the Spirit. But spirituality should not

---

[42]Unfortunately, there are no extant hymnbooks from the first century. For useful studies, see Larry Hurtado, *At the Origins,* pp. 86-92; Robert J. Karris, *A Symphony of New Testament Hymns* (Collegeville, Minn.: Liturgical Press, 1996); Ralph Martin, "Hymns, Hymn Fragments, Songs, Spiritual Songs," *DPL,* pp. 419-23; Wendy J. Porter, "Music," *DNTB,* pp. 711-19; Julie L. Wu, "Liturgical Elements," *DPL,* pp. 557-60; Wu, "Liturgical Elements," *DLNTD,* pp. 659-65; Julie L. Wu and Sharon Clark Pearson, "Hymns, Songs," *DLNTD,* pp. 520-27. For discussion on the *Odes of Solomon* as a possible collection of late first-century Christian hymns, see James H. Charlesworth, ed., *The Old Testament Pseudepigrapha,* vol. 2 (Garden City, N.Y.: Doubleday, 1985).

[43]Fee, *First Corinthians,* p. 671.

[44]Thus Markus Barth and Helmut Blanke write: "The adjective *pneumatikos* (spiritual) probably refers not only to *ōdē* (song), after which it is positioned in the Greek sentence, but to all three substantives, and is placed after them for emphasis" (*Colossians,* AB 34B [New York: Doubleday, 1994], p. 428). For additional reading, see Gerhard Delling, "ὕμνος κτλ," *TDNT* 8:489-503; Delling, *Worship in the New Testament* (London: Darton, Longman & Todd, 1962) pp. 77-91; Dunn, *Colossians and Philemon,* pp. 235-41; A. T. Lincoln, *Ephesians,* WBC 42 (Dallas: Word, 1990), pp. 345-49; Eduard Lohse, *Colossians and Philemon* (Philadelphia: Fortress, 1971), pp. 151-53; O'Brien, *Colossians, Philemon,* pp. 208-10; Wu and Pearson, "Hymns, Songs," pp. 520-27. Most interpreters also concur that J. B. Lightfoot's attempt to differentiate between psalms, hymns and spiritual songs is based more on categories developed by Gregory of Nyssa in the fourth century than from the New Testament (*St. Paul's Epistles to the Colossians and to Philemon* [London: Macmillan, 1875]).

[45]Barth and Blanke, *Colossians,* p. 428; also commentaries by Bruce, Dunn and Lohse.

necessarily be identified with spontaneity, and all forms of Christian hymnody found in the early church are likely to have been in view, from liturgical pieces that had already established themselves in the church's worship . . . to snatches of song freshly created in the assembly.[46]

The above—albeit incomplete—list of hymns or hymnic portions of Scripture does not mean that these verses were utilized every time churches met for worship. Ralph Martin identifies a number of hymns that probably were composed for specific functions. These include: (1) sacramental hymns (Rom 6:1-10; Eph 2:19-22; Tit 3:4-7); (2) hymnlike meditations (Rom 8:31-39; 1 Cor 13; Eph 1:3-14); (3) confessional hymns (1 Tim 6:11-16; 2 Tim 2:11-13); and (4) hymns to Christ (Phil 2:6-11; Col 1:15-20; Heb 1:3).[47] Julie Wu concurs with this idea as she acknowledges the close relationship between hymnic and confessional materials and how both were "originally devised for evangelistic, cultic, apologetic purposes and carried didactic and hortative functions in their contexts."[48]

Wu's comments should not lead us to conclude that most hymns of the early church were standardized, not allowing for any musical freedom. The passages referenced earlier (1 Cor 14:26; Col 3:16; Eph 5:19-20) show that there were spontaneous expressions of praise to God in song and that the charismatic nature of the early church included singing praise "with the spirit" as well as "with the mind" (1 Cor 14:15). In other words, *singing was for praise and gratitude to God as well as for the instruction of believers.*[49]

Although the Pauline corpus provides most of the examples of early church hymnody, we have also noted hymnic sections in other New Testament letters, and one must remember that these letters were written to worshiping congregations. The opening hymn in Hebrews (Heb 1:3), the singing of praises as a "sacrifice" to God (Heb 13:15) and the striking references to a community gathered for worship, exhortation and instruction (Heb 3:12-13; 4:14; 5:11-12; 10:21-25; 12:12, 28; 13:1-25) are other examples. The epistle of James (especially Jas 5:13-19) illustrates a worshiping community that cheerfully sings songs (*psalletō*) of praise, administers healing through its elders, confesses its sins and prays for and restores one another. The hymnic passages embedded in 1 Peter (most notably 1 Pet 1:3-12, 18-21; 2:21-25; 3:18-22) address theological and practical issues that these Diaspora churches (see 1 Pet 1:1) were facing.

---

[46]Lincoln, *Ephesians*, p. 346.

[47]Martin, *Early Christian Worship*, pp. 39-52; Martin, "Hymns, Hymn Fragments, Songs, Spiritual Songs," pp. 421-22; Martin, *New Testament Foundations*, 2:263-68.

[48]Wu, "Liturgical Elements," *DPL*, p. 557; see also M. Alfred Bichsel, "Hymns, Early Christian," *ABD* 3:350-51.

[49]A significant point made by Luke Timothy Johnson, *Religious Experience in Earliest Christianity* (Minneapolis: Fortress, 1998).

The life setting *(Sitz im Leben)* of the liturgical elements and hymnic materials in Revelation is difficult to determine, for many of the hymns portray heavenly rather than earthly worship. However, since the letter was written to specific Johannine communities (the seven churches), the author utilized current hymnic material as a vehicle for praising God and communicating a message of encouragement, hope and comfort for his readers.[50]

There is further evidence of development in worship, liturgy, hymnody and the sacraments as the church moved into the postapostolic age. With respect to hymns, for example, Pliny the Younger reports to the emperor Trajan (c. A.D. 112) that Christians in his area were accustomed "to come together on a regular day before dawn to sing a song alternately to Christ as a god" *(Ep. 10.96.7)*. Additional references to hymns are found in the *Odes of Solomon* and the letters of Ignatius.[51]

5.4.4. Early Christian Paraenesis. This term *paraenesis* (also *parenesis*) is a technical word referring to New Testament ethical or moral exhortations that were given in the context of teaching or worship in the early church.[52] With careful study, it is possible to categorize different types of paraenetic materials that are scattered throughout the New Testament and suggest how they may have been used in the church. Whereas creeds, confessions and hymns largely served to clarify certain doctrines (What do we believe?), the paraenetic material was directed primarily toward the ethical life (How do we live?).[53]

Individuals who responded to the preaching of the gospel and became members of an early Christian community would need ethical instruction. Jewish Christians would already have some idea of the ethical life expected of them from their former life in Judaism and their knowledge of the Old Testament. But converts from the pagan Gentile world, on the other hand, had no (or very little) idea of what constituted Christian behavior. Thus it is not surprising that most of the paraenetic material is found in letters addressed to churches in the Greco-Roman world.

After conversion, new believers were instructed that their lives were transferred "out of darkness" and placed into God's "marvelous light" (1 Pet 2:9; cf.

---

[50]See Wu and Pearson, "Hymns, Songs," pp. 521-25; Martin, *Worship in the Early Church*, pp. 45-46.

[51]For additional reading, see David Aune, "Worship, Early Christian," *ABD* 6:976-82; Bichsel, "Hymns, Early Christian," 3:350-51; Martin, "Worship and Liturgy," pp. 1224-38; Wu and Pearson, "Hymns, Songs," pp. 525-26.

[52]The word is essentially a transliteration of the Greek noun *parainesis* (advice) and distinguished from the content of faith, where *catechesis* (*katēchēsis*) is used.

[53]For additional reading, see Philip Carrington, *The Primitive Christian Catechism: A Study in the Epistles* (Cambridge: Cambridge University Press, 1940); Roetzel, *Letters of Paul*, pp. 74-78; E. G. Selwyn, *The First Epistle of Peter* (London: Macmillan, 1947); Michael B. Thompson, "Teaching/Paraenesis," *DPL*, pp. 922-23; Michael J. Wilkens, "Teaching, Paraenesis," *DLNTD*, pp. 1156-59.

Acts 26:18; Rom 13:12; 2 Cor 4:6; Eph 5:8). They were reminded who they "once" had been as unbelievers and who they "now" had become in Christ (Rom 6:19; 11:30; Eph 2:2; 5:8; Tit 3:3-6; 1 Pet 2:10); they were exhorted to "put away" their former way of life (Eph 4:22, 31) and to "clothe" themselves with Christian virtues (Eph 4:24; Col 3:12, 14; 1 Pet 5:5). The constant refrain to watchfulness (1 Cor 16:13; Col 4:2; 1 Thess 5:6, 10; 1 Pet 5:8; Rev 3:2-3; 16:15) and steadfastness (1 Cor 16:13; Gal 5:1; Phil 1:27; 4:1; 1 Thess 3:8; 2 Thess 2:15) shows the concern the apostles had for all believers attempting to live out their new faith "in the household of God" (1 Tim 3:15) and the world (Phil 2:15; Col 2:20; Jas 4:4; 2 Pet 1:4; 1 Jn 2:15-16).[54]

Occasionally, some paraenetic material is simply presented in the form of brief "wisdom" sayings (1 Cor 15:33; 2 Cor 9:6; Gal 5:9; 6:7) or as more developed imperative clusters that focus on such Christian virtues as love, patience, thanksgiving, mutual affection, hospitality, generosity, and the like. Romans 12:9-13 serves as a good example of a passage with this focus:

> Let love be genuine; hate what is evil, hold fast to what is good; love one another with mutual affection; outdo one another in showing honor. Do not lag in zeal, be ardent in spirit, serve the Lord. Rejoice in hope, be patient in suffering, persevere in prayer. Contribute to the needs of the saints; extend hospitality to strangers.

Similar statements appear in Galatians 6:7-10 and Colossians 4:2-6.

There also are two major categories of paraenetic material in the Epistles. First, there are extensive lists or "catalogues" of vices and virtues, which set the parameters for the ethical life of the believer (Rom 1:29-31; Gal 5:19-23; Eph 5:3-5; Phil 4:8; 1 Pet 4:1-6).[55] The second are the so-called household rules or

---

[54]The imagery of "darkness and light," "clothing," and "once you were . . . now your are," may be part of early Christian baptismal language and catechism. Ephesians 5:14 ("Therefore it says, 'Sleeper, awake! Rise from the dead, and Christ will shine on you'") could be a possible baptismal formula (see Patzia, *Ephesians, Colossians, Philemon,* pp. 261-62).

[55]*Catalogue* is technical term used by some scholars for these passages, even though it is very unlikely that such "lists" or *Urkatalog* existed. George E. Cannon has shown that the terms used are general and familiar ones focusing on paganism, idolatry and heresy and are closely related to the Decalogue and Holiness Code of the Old Testament (*The Use of Traditional Materials in Colossians* [Macon, Ga.: Mercer University Press, 1983], ch. 3). For additional reading, see David L. Balch, "Household Codes," *ABD* 3:318-20; J. Daryl Charles, "Vice and Virtue Lists," *DNTB,* pp. 1252-57; Philip H. Towner, "Household Codes," *DLNTD,* pp. 513-20 (where he briefly discusses this teaching in some Apostolic Fathers [Clement, Ignatius, Polycarp, Barnabas] and the *Didache*); and "The Haustafel" in Ben Witherington III, *Women in the Earliest Churches* (Cambridge: Cambridge University Press, 1988), pp. 42-61. Additional *vices* in the New Testament include Mt 15:19 par. Mk 7:21-22; Rom 1:24, 26; 13:13; 1 Cor 5:10-11; 6:9-10; 2 Cor 12:20; Eph 4:31; 1 Tim 1:9-10; 6:4-5; 2 Tim 3:2-5; Tit 3:3; Jas 1:21; 1 Pet 2:1; Jude 8, 16; Rev 9:20-21; 21:8; 22:15. Additional *virtues* include Mt 5: 3-11; 2 Cor 6:6-7; Eph 6:14-17; Phil 4:8; 1 Tim 3:2-3; 6:11; Tit 1:7-8; Jas 3:17; 2 Pet 1:5-7.

duties (German *Haustafeln*) directed specifically to relationships in the household between wives and husbands, children and parents, and slaves and masters (Eph 5:22—6:9; Col 3:18—4:1; 1 Pet 2:18—3:7).

Obviously there are many more moral exhortations scattered throughout the New Testament than those listed above. Still, this discussion illustrates the point that teaching (*didachē*) was an essential component of Christian worship. New converts to Christianity received some instruction at the time they responded to the apostles' preaching and formed a Christian community in a city. Further instruction would be given by designated leaders in the church as well as in apostolic letters that were sent to particular congregations for public reading and further study during worship services (see Col 4:16; Eph 3:3-4).[56]

The Thessalonian correspondence provides material for reconstructing such a scenario (see discussion on Thessalonica at 3.7.2). These believers received their first instruction from the apostle Paul when the church was founded (1 Thess 4:2: "For you know what instructions we gave you through the Lord Jesus"). After Paul's departure, this responsibility continued with leaders in the church. Thus when Paul writes 1 Thessalonians, he exhorts church members "to respect those who labor among you, and have charge of you in the Lord and admonish you; esteem them very highly in love because of their work (1 Thess 5:12). Additional instructions and encouragement came in the form of Paul's letters (1 and 2 Thessalonians) to the church, which he expected to be read and studied at worship gatherings (1 Thess 4:18; 5:27; 2 Thess 3:14).

There are a number of places in Paul's letters where he assumes that believers have enough information about theology and ethics that he can simply allude to the principles that they learned, received and were taught when Paul first established certain churches. In Philippians, for example, Paul states: "Keep on doing the things that you have learned and received and heard and seen in me, and the God of peace will be with you" (Phil 4:9); in Colossians, Paul refers to the importance of teaching for Christian maturity (Col 1:28; 2:7); in Romans he reminds the church about the form of teaching they received in the past (Rom 6:17; 16:17); Ephesians mentions that believers learned about Christ (*emathete ton Christon*) and the Christian life by what they "heard" and "were taught" (Eph 4:20-22). The Pastoral Epistles also have many references to the importance in the early church of teaching. Timothy is reminded to "give attention to the public reading of scripture, to exhorting, to teaching" (1 Tim 4:13;

---

[56]Colossians 4:16 mentions "the letter from Laodicea." There is no genuine extant letter to the Laodiceans. Some scholars suggest that this could be the "letter to the Ephesians," which may have been written as a circular letter to the churches in Asia Minor (see discussion in Best, *Ephesians*, pp. 98-99). First Peter and possibly James were also circulated among the church in the regions to which they are addressed.

see also 1 Tim 4:16; 5:17; 2 Tim 1:13; 4:2), and Titus is encouraged to teach "sound doctrine" (Tit 2:1) with integrity and gravity (Tit 2:7).

As noted earlier, the formation of creeds and confessions in the early church were attempts to express certain foundational principles of the church's faith. That is, the church gradually developed a recognizable body of theological and ethical truths that characterized its faith and served as basic instructional material for its members in fundamental areas of their Christian life. Gradually, however, teachers and believers were able to employ certain "catch phrases" or "summary statements" that embodied the important truths of their preaching and teaching. Anyone with some maturity in the faith would understand what was meant by phrases such as "the gospel" (Rom 2:16; 16:25; 1 Cor 15:1-6; Phil 1:7, 27) or "the faith of the gospel" (Phil 1:27; cf. Eph 4:5; Col 2:6-8; 1 Tim 6:20-21), "the truth" (Col 1:5; 2 Thess 2:13; 2 Tim 2:18, 25; 4:4), "the word of life" (Phil 2:16), "sound doctrine" (2 Tim 4:3; Tit 1:9), "the words of the faith and of the sound teaching" (1 Tim 4:6), "the apostles' teaching" (Acts 2:42), "the [apostolic] traditions" (1 Cor 11:2; 15:1-8; Gal 1:9; Col 2:6; 1 Thess 4:1; 2 Thess 2:15) and "the form of teaching to which you were entrusted" (Rom 6:17).

With the exception of Acts 2:42, all these phrases are found in letters attributed to Paul. When the apostle Paul wrote his letters, he used such phrases to remind his readers of their heritage and thus to encourage them to remain faithful in times of doubt and apostasy.

5.5. Additional Liturgical Components and Expressions

In addition to such key elements as preaching, teaching and singing in worship, additional components were part of certain congregations and formed part of their worship experience.[57]

5.5.1. Prayer. When Luke describes the early Christian community in Jerusalem, he indicates that prayer was an important expression of their faith (Acts 2:42, 46; 3:1). This is not surprising given the significance of personal and corporate prayer in Judaism, as described in the Old Testament and practiced in temple and synagogue worship. Those who followed Jesus as disciples during his earthly ministry not only observed the importance of prayer in his personal life but were taught how they themselves were to pray (Mt 6:90-13; Lk 11:2-4).[58]

---

[57]Ralph Martin refers to one of these expressions as "the prayer-speech of the early belivers" (*Worship in the Early Church,* p. 34).

[58]See James D. G. Dunn, "Prayer," *DJG,* pp. 6127-24; J. L. Houlden, "Lord's Prayer," *ABD* 4:356-62; Joachim Jeremias, *The Prayers of Jesus* (Naperville, Ill.: Allenson, 1967).

Hence it is quite natural that his followers who met in the upper room after the ascension "were constantly devoting themselves to prayer" (Acts 1:14). Luke gives considerable attention to the role of prayer in the early church: first, he refers to the prayers of individuals such as Stephen (Acts 7:59), Saul (Acts 9:11), Peter (Acts 10:9; 11:15), Cornelius (Acts 10:30-31) and to Paul and Silas (Acts 16:25); second, he records time of corporate prayer among the believers when they selected Matthias (Acts 1:24), prayed for Peter's release from prison (Acts 12:5, 12), commissioned Paul and Barnabas (Acts 13:3), appointed elders in certain churches (Acts 14:23), and when Paul said farewell to the Ephesian elders (Acts 20:36) and the church in Tyre (Acts 21:5).

Paul's letters reveal that he constantly prayed for each congregation (Rom 1:9; 2 Cor 13:9; Eph 1:16-17; 3:16, 18; Phil 1:4, 9; Col 1:3, 9; 1 Thess 1:2; 3:10; 2 Thess 1:11; 2 Tim 1:3; Philem 4, 6) and encouraged people to pray for themselves (Rom 8:26; 12:12; 2 Cor 13:7; Eph 6:18; Phil 4:6; Col 4:2; 1 Thess 5:17; 1 Tim 2:1) and for his apostolic ministry (Rom 15:30; 2 Cor 1:11; Eph 3:3; 6:19-20; Phil 1:19; Col 4:3; 1 Thess 5:25; 2 Thess 3:1; Philem 22).[59] In the book of James prayer is encouraged for those who are suffering and sick (Jas 5:13-16), and in Revelation, "prayers" are a common feature of the saints who praise God (Rev 5:8; 8:3-4).

5.5.2. Abba. _Abba_ is the Greek transliteration of an Aramaic word _(abbā')_ used to address God as "Father," which, according to most interpreters, connotes familial intimacy and may have been used by small children to address their fathers.[60] Jesus used _abba_ during his agonizing prayer in the Garden of Gethsemene, praying, "Abba, Father, for you all things are possible; remove this cup from me; yet, not what I want, but what you want" (Mk 14:36). It appears likely that _abba_ was utilized on other occasions where the Greek "Father" _(patēr)_ occurs, including both Luke's (Lk 11:2) and Matthew's (Mt 6:9) version of the Lord's Prayer.[61]

Jesus' use of _abba_ in prayer conveys a sense of intimacy between himself

---

[59]In addition to these references where the word _prayer (proseuchomai)_ is used, there are many equivalent words indicating prayers such as _petition, invocation, supplication, thanksgiving,_ and _worship._ See the list by Michael J. Wilkins, "Prayer," _DLNTD,_ pp. 942-43, and discussion by W. Bingham Hunter, "Prayer," _DPL,_ pp. 725-34. Calling on or invoking "the name of the Lord" may well be another euphemism for prayer and worship (see Acts 2:21; 19:17; 22:16; Rom 10:13; 1 Cor 1:2; 2 Tim 2:19; Jas 5:14).

[60]See Joachim Jeremias, _The Prayers of Jesus_ (London: SCM Press, 1967), pp. 11-65; G. Kittel, "ἀββᾶ," _TDNT_ 1:6. Scholars continue to debate whether this is a term of endearment equivalent to the English "Daddy" or "Papa." For discussion, see James Barr, "Abba Isn't Daddy," _JTS_ 39 (1988): 28-47; Ben Witherington III, _The Christology of Jesus_ (Minneapolis: Fortress, 1990), pp. 216-21.

[61]The phrase "my Father" _(ho patēr mou)_ occurs thirty-nine times in the Gospels (NRSV).

and the Father. This would be true of his disciples as well, because they were brought into a new and intimate relationship with the Father through Jesus. *Abba* thus became a standard expression of this relationship in the worship services of the early Palestinian churches and was retained in Greek-speaking congregations as well. Thus Paul writes to the Roman believers, "For you did not receive a spirit of slavery to fall back into fear, but you have received a spirit of adoption. When we cry, 'Abba! Father!' . . . " (Rom 8:15). To the churches in Galatia he writes: "Because you are children, God has sent the Spirit of his Son into our hears, crying, 'Abba! Father!'" (Gal 4:6). The context of these two passages, according to Ralph Martin, suggests a setting of "public worship which, led by the spirit, was the occasion when believers confessed God as Father and received the assurance of their adoption into the divine family."[62]

5.5.3. The Lord's Prayer. Studies of the so-called Lord's Prayer generally conclude that this was a model prayer that Jesus gave to his disciples because he believed in the importance of prayer from his Jewish heritage and it identified those who followed Jesus apart from John the Baptist's disciples. Literary analysis suggests that Luke's version (Lk 11:2-4) is the oldest and that Matthew's rendition (Mt 6:9-13) is a development and adaptation of certain themes to make it more suitable for worship.[63]

Since we do not possess any explicit order of service from any first-century church, we have no specific proof that the Lord's Prayer was used in worship by the communities to whom the Evangelists were writing. However, the preservation and development of the prayer leads one to believe that the church may have used it regularly in much the same way that it used other sayings of Jesus. The same may be true of the congregations mentioned in Acts and the epistolary literature, where there are no explicit prayers approximating the style and content of the Lord's Prayer. The fact that the *Didache* instructs its readers to pray the Lord's Prayer three times a day "as the Lord bids us in his gospel" (*Did.* 8.2) confirms that the prayer had become an integral part of the worship services of some congregations. There is no way of knowing whether this was true in all the churches of the empire.

---

[62]Ralph P. Martin, *The Worship of God* (Grand Rapids, Mich.: Eerdmans, 1994), p. 35. Martin observes that this explicit utterance may have been used at the celebration of baptism or the recital of the Lord's Prayer (see also 1 Pet 1:17). His suggestion that the Lord's Prayer inspired the use of *abba* in Rom 8:15-17 and Gal 4:6, as well as Paul's prayers for the churches that invoke "the name of God as Father," certainly is tenable (ibid., p. 36).

[63]Such development is even more evident in the doxological ending found in several late manuscripts, which add "For the kingdom and the power and the glory are yours forever. Amen." For discussion, see Bruce M. Metzger, *A Textual Commentary on the Greek New Testament,* 2d ed. (New York: American Bible Society, 1994), pp. 13-14.

5.5.4. Amen. Amen (Greek *amēn*) is a literal transliteration of the Hebrew *'āmēn,* meaning certainty or affirmation in the sense of "so let it be!" In the Old Testament it is used to affirm curses (see Deut 27:15-26; Num 5:22) and specific actions of God (1 Kings 1:36; Neh 5:13; Jer 11:5; 28:6). It appears frequently as a doxology in the context of Israel's worship, as in 1 Chronicles 16:36: "'Blessed be the LORD, the God of Israel, from everlasting to everlasting.' Then all the people said 'Amen!' and praised the LORD" (see also Pss 41:13; 46:48; 72:19; 89:52; 106:48). The NRSV "God of faithfulness" in Isaiah 65:16 is literally "God of Amen," a meaning not unlike that attributed to Christ in Revelation 3:14: "And to the angel of the church in Laodicea write: The words of the Amen, the faithful and true witness, the origin of God's creation." Both biblical passages affirm that God and Jesus Christ remain eternally true and can always be relied upon.[64]

Since *amen* became a standard expression in Jewish synagogue worship, it is not surprising that most New Testament references are found in the context of worship as well. This is most noticeable in several categories: (1) benedictions (Rom 15:33; 1 Cor 16:24 [variant]; Gal 6:18; 1 Thess 3:13 [variant]; 2 Tim 4:18; Philem 25 [variant]; Heb 13:21; 1 Pet 5:11; 2 Pet 3:18; Jude 25); (2) doxologies (Rom 1:25; 9:5; 11:36; 16:27; Gal 1:5; Eph 3:21; Phil 4:20; 1 Tim 1:17; 6:16; 2 Tim 4:18; Rev 1:6; 7:12); and (3) prayers of thanksgiving and affirmation (1 Cor 14:16; 1 Pet 4:11; Rev 1:7; 7:12).

We can best appreciate the effectiveness of these liturgical components of worship when we remember that these letters were read aloud in worship settings in local house churches. Some passages suggest that the church already was familiar with these expressions; other phrases may have inspired a unified response from the congregation. This accounts for Paul's concern in the Corinthian church (1 Cor 14:16), where the practice of glossolalia (without an interpreter) would lead to disunity and confusion ("if you say a blessing with the spirit, how can anyone in the position of an outsider say the 'Amen' to your thanksgiving, since the outsider does not know what you are saying?").

5.5.5. Doxologies. Doxologies (from the Greek verb *doxazō,* "praise, honor, magnify, glorify") appear in the New Testament as short forms of exalted speech and affirmations in praise of God, either as concluding formulas to prayers and hymnic expressions or within larger doxological sections. They are not just random or stereotyped additions but are thoughtfully and purposefully inserted into the text at appropriate places to reinforce the authors' message.

Some doxologies appear in the form of "blessed be . . ." and thus resemble

---

[64]The sayings of Jesus in the Gospels where *amēn* is used (NRSV "truly") confirm his authority and truth (see Gerald Hawthorne, "Amen," *DJG,* pp. 7-8.)

the Jewish *Shemoneh Esre* (Eighteen Benedictions). New Testament examples include Romans 1:25 ("the Creator who is blessed forever! Amen"), Romans 9:5 ("God blessed forever. Amen"), 2 Corinthians 1:3 ("Blessed be the God and Father of our Lord Jesus Christ") and 2 Corinthians 11:31 ("The God and Father of the Lord Jesus [blessed be he forever!]"). The extensive eulogy in Ephesians (Eph 1:3-14) begins with the formula "Blessed be the God and Father of our Lord Jesus Christ" and then continues to enumerate the spiritual blessings that God has bestowed upon the believer. The author of 1 Peter also begins his section on the believers' inheritance with a similar doxology: "Blessed be the God and Father of our Lord Jesus Christ"(1 Pet 1:3).

Another doxological form utilizes temporal expressions to praise God. Phrases such as "to him be the glory forever" or simply "forever and ever" either stand alone or appear within the context of longer doxologies (e.g., Rom 11:33-36; 16:25-27; Gal 1:5; Eph 1:14; 3:21; Phil 4:20; 1 Tim 1:17; 6:16; 2 Tim 4:18; Heb 13:21; 1 Pet 4:11; 5:11; 2 Pet 3:18; Jude 25; Rev 1:6; 5:13; 7:12).[65]

5.5.6. Benedictions. New Testament benedictions are apostolic expressions of a wish that the hearers will experience God's gifts of grace and peace. Although the benedictions in the New Testament share a similar purpose to those in Jewish worship, they are "Christianized" in most cases by the addition of the phrase "the Lord Jesus Christ" to "God our Father." Thus, we have on many occasions the benediction "Grace to you and peace from God our Father *and the Lord Jesus Christ*" [italics added] (see Rom 1:7; 1 Cor 1:3; 2 Cor 1:2; Gal 1:3; Eph 1:2; Phil 1:2; Col 1:2; 1 Thess 1:1; 2 Thess 1:2; Philem 3).

In the Pauline corpus, the letters that begin with a benediction (or salutation) often end with one quite similar in content:

Beginning	Ending
Rom 1:7	16:20 (see also 15:5, 13, 33)
1 Cor 1:3	16:23
2 Cor 1:2	13:13
Gal 1:3	6:18
Eph 1:2	6:23-24 (see 3:20-21)
Phil 1:2	4:23 (see 4:9)
Col 1:2	4:18
1 Thess 1:1	5:28 (see 5:23)
Philem 3	25

---

[65]See Wu, "Liturgical Elements," *DPL*, pp. 557-58; Wu, "Liturgical Elements," *DLNTD*, p. 660; Peter T. O'Brien, "Benediction, Blessing, Doxology, Thanksgiving," *DPL*, p. 69.

This pattern does not appear in the other epistolary literature, where, as Julie Wu observes, "not every letter includes a benediction (e.g., Jas and 1 Jn) and, except for 1 Peter, each letter includes only one benediction, either at the beginning (1 Pet 1:2; 2 Pet 1:2; 2 Jn 3; Jude 2; Rev 1:4) or at the end (Heb 13:20-21, 25; 1 Pet 5:14; 3 Jn 15; Rev 22:21)."[66]

5.5.7. Maranatha. The Aramaic phrase *Marana tha* occurs only once in the New Testament (1 Cor 16:22) and in *Didache* 10.6, where it is translated "Our Lord, come." As such, it reflects a transliteration of the Aramaic *māranā tā* (an imperative) rather than *māran atā*, which would be translated either as "Our Lord has come" or, perhaps, "Our Lord will come," an eschatological prayer much like Revelation 22:20: "Come, Lord Jesus" *(erchou kyrie Iēsou).*[67]

In Corinthians 16:22 *maranatha* is connected with the preceding curse ("Let anyone be accursed *[anathema]* who has no love for the Lord. Our Lord come!"). Thus it could be directed against those who questioned Paul's teaching about a futuristic eschatology (cf. 1 Cor 1:7-8; 11:26; 15:50-54). Its use in *Didache* 10.6 is ambiguous. It could serve as a liturgical formula inviting the Lord to be present at the celebration of the Eucharist; or, if taken with the preceding exhortation to repent ("If anyone is holy, let him come; if not, let him repent. Our Lord come"), it emphasizes the eschatological judgment of the Lord.

Apart from these difficulties, however, the use of *maranatha* in these passages reveals two important truths about the early church. First, it takes us back to its Palestinian setting, where Aramaic was used and Jesus was referred to as *Mar* (Lord); second, it shows that a foreign term found its way into the liturgy of Greek-speaking churches (along with other terms such as amen, hosanna and hallelujah) and that it was used on certain occasions within the context of worship.

5.5.8. Hallelujah. Hallelujah (or Alleluia, Hebrew *halᵉlûyāh*) was used in Jewish worship as a standard expression of joy, praise and thanksgiving to God (see Ps 104—106; 111—13; 115—17; 135; 146—50). The Hellenistic (Greek-speaking) Jews simply transliterated the term into Greek in the Septuagint, as does the writer of the Apocalypse, where "Hallelujah" *(hallēlouia)* appears four times (Rev 19:1, 3, 4, 6). Julie Wu describes the context of the term in

---

[66]Wu, "Liturgical Elements," *DLNTD,* p. 660.

[67]Scholars are divided on how the Aramaic should be pointed and thus arrive at different interpretations of the phrase. For discussions on the linguistic and interpretive difficulties see Fee, *First Corinthians,* pp. 838-39; K. G. Kuhn, "μαραναθα," *TDNT* 4:466-72; Martin, *Worship in the Early Church,* pp. 32-33, 128, 131; Niederwimmer, *Didache,* pp. 161-64; Max Wilcox, "Maranatha," *ABD* 4:514; Julie Wu, "Liturgical Elements," *DPL,* pp. 559-60; Wu, "Liturgical Elements," *DLNTD,* pp. 662-63.

Revelation when she writes:

> Since "hallelujah" is mentioned only here, the writer's intention is also evident. In Revelation 19 "hallelujah" is placed at the last song of praise, shared by both celestial and human beings in exuberant response to God's sovereign judgment upon the evil (Rev 19:1, 3, 4) and his final victory (Rev 19:6). Just as the Hebrew Psalter closes with God's chosen people singing "hallelujah" (Ps 150 ends with this word), the Apocalypse also closes with the "hallelujah chorus," inviting the readers to join. The book closes on a high note. While reminding his readers to focus on God's power and sovereignty, the writer skillfully incorporates the familiar acclamation *hallelujah* to achieve his goal more effectively.[68]

Since this liturgical acclamation only appears in this one book, we have no way of knowing whether it was unique to John and thus unknown in other Christian communities. A similar uncertainty applies to the *Ter Sanctus* ("Thrice Holy") in Revelation 4:8: "Holy, holy, holy, the Lord God the Almighty, who was and is and is to come."[69]

5.5.9. Prayer and Fasting. On two occasions in Acts prayer and fasting are mentioned together: once when the church in Antioch commissions Paul and Barnabas for their missionary activity (Acts 13:2-3), and again when Paul and Barnabas appoint elders in some of the church (Acts 14: 23).[70] The two references in Acts may indicate that fasting had some value in Jewish Christian circles, but as far as we know, there was no fasting in the Gentile churches in the first century. The joyous celebration of the resurrected Lord in the Eucharist may be an indication that "feasting" rather than "fasting" was more appropriate for believers. Nevertheless, the textual variants (see Mt 17:21; Mk 9:29; 2 Cor 6:5; 11:27) indicate that fasting continued in some circles. Pre-Easter and prebaptismal fasts are prescribed in the *Didache* (8.1).

---

[68]Wu, "Liturgical Elements," *DLNTD*, p. 662.

[69]See Wu's helpful comments on this phrase in ibid., pp. 662-63. The exclamation "Hosanna" (from the Hebrew *hôšaʿ nāʾ*, meaning "save, I/we pray"), is found only in the Old Testament (see Ps 118:26) and in the Gospels, where it is used in the context of Christ's triumphal entry into Jerusalem (Mt 21:9; Mk 11:9, 10; Jn 12:13; see also Mt 21:15). It does appear in the *Didache* (*Did.* 10.6) in the context of other liturgical acclamations ("Maranatha" and "Amen"), suggesting that it now was used in worship as an expression of joy rather than as a plea for deliverance (Wu, "Liturgical Elements," *DLNTD*, 663).

[70]The addition of "fasting" *(nesteia)* in Acts 10:30 and in 1 Corinthians 7:5 does not have good textual support and probably was introduced to support asceticism. The translation of *nesteia* as "hunger" (NRSV) in 2 Corinthians 6:5 and 11:27 indicates the deprivation of food as one of the hardships that Paul endured and not a voluntary or deliberate act of fasting (see Metzger, *Textual Commentary,* pp. 330-31, 488).

5.6. The Time of Worship (The "Lord's Day")

Given the Jewish nature of early Christianity, it is not surprising that believers met for worship on the sabbath, according to their custom and reverence for the fourth commandment. Even though some of the congregational gatherings recorded in Acts 2 were daily, it is difficult to imagine that the sabbath was not observed and that the first believers saw a need to alter their custom of public worship.

It soon became apparent, however, that Christianity was heading in a different theological direction from Judaism and Jewish Christianity. Peaceful coexistence would soon be replaced by the "parting of ways," especially with the success of Paul's mission to the Gentiles and his theology of a law-free gospel.

We cannot determine from the New Testament if and when the church moved its worship from the sabbath to Sunday or whether this became a universal custom. One suspects that Jewish-Christian congregations continued to meet on the sabbath and the Gentile churches on Sunday. But there is no certainty on this matter. The "first day of the week" (the day of resurrection), when the Lord appeared to some of his disciples (Mt 28:1; Mk 16:2, 9; Lk 24:1; Jn 20:1, 19) was forever etched in their memory. The postresurrection appearance to the disciples on the Emmaus road (Lk 24:13) included the "breaking of bread," which I conclude was a form of the Lord's Supper (see 5.8). Jon C. Laansma rightly notes that even though an observance cannot be demonstrated from this passage, "the memory of Lord's Supper observance on that particular 'first day of the week' is fixed in tradition."[71]

Acts 20:7 refers to another gathering of believers (at Troas) on "the first day of the week" in order to "break bread." This seems to have become an established custom in Paul's ministry. In 1 Corinthians Paul instructs the believers to "put aside" money for the Jerusalem collection on "the first day of every week" (1 Cor 16:2). Here it is difficult to know whether the Corinthians were to do this privately or at a worship service on that day.

Revelation 1:10 is the only reference to the "Lord's day" in the New Testament (see also Rev 4:2). Most interpreters conclude that by the time Revelation was written readers would have taken this as "the first day of the week," Sunday. Variations on the use of this term occur in the _Didache_ (_Did._ 14.1), Ignatius

---

[71]Jon C. Laansma, "Lord's Day," _DLNTD_, p. 681. This is a helpful article on the issues involved that lists significant bibliographical material. See also Donald A. Carson, ed., _From Sabbath to Lord's Day_ (Grand Rapids, Mich.: Zondervan, 1982); Stephen Westerholm and Craig A. Evans, "Sabbath," _DNTB_, pp. 1031-35. Also important for its detail is David E. Aune, _Revelation 1-5_, WBC 52A (Dallas: Word, 1997). See his bibliography on Rev 1:9—3:22 on pp. 60-62 and commentary on 1:10, pp. 82-85.

(*Magn.* 9.1) and other early Christian literature.[72] There is little doubt, according to Laansma, that "by the turn of the first century it can be taken for granted not only that the weekly observance of Jesus' resurrection is customary but even that it can be referred to intelligibly in shorthand fashion (adjective only) as the Lord's (day)."[73] What could be more logical and fitting than for the church to set aside the first day of the week, the day of resurrection, as the distinctive day to celebrate their worship?

5.7. The Offering

There is no way to determine whether a collection of money was a regular part of the worship services in the early church. If it was not part of worship, how and when did the believers collect money to meet the financial responsibilities of the group and assist those in need? The New Testament has much to say about stewardship and principles of giving that should characterize and motivate every believer.[74] But most of these principles are developed in the context of Paul's effort to raise money destined for Jerusalem and not for local church needs. Nevertheless, Paul encourages believers in Rome to "contribute to the needs of the saints"(Rom 12:13). The ministry to "real widows" in the early church also implies some kind of financial assistance or support (*eparkeō,* 1 Tim 5:3-16).

5.7.1. The Sharing of Goods. On several occasions in Acts, Luke mentions that the *koinōnia* of the early believers included the common possession of property ("All who believed were together and had all things in common" [*eichon hapanta koina*]), "the sharing of goods" (Acts 2:44-45; 4:32—5:11). This practice—sometimes referred to as a type of early Christian communism—may imply that *all* the property of *all* believers was at the disposal of the entire church and that proceeds from the sale of such property went into a common fund. Another inference is that the distribution of goods took place within the worship service, because it is mentioned within the context of events recorded in Acts 2:42-47. Several observations may help to put this practice into perspective.

First, while it is possible that some form of almonry (collecting and distributing goods and or money to the needy) was included in worship, it may have been a separate function of certain leaders, such as the elders (see Acts 11:30) or some of the seven Hellenists (Acts 6:1-6).

Second, the decision to sell and share goods was *voluntary* and arose from the believers' spontaneous sense of *koinōnia* with each other, not from con-

---

[72]For a complete listing of these sources, see Laansma, "Lord's Day," p. 684; Aune, *Revelation 1-5,* pp. 83-84.

[73]Laansma, "Lord's Day," pp. 683-84.

[74]See esp. Martin, *Worship of God,* pp. 73-77; Martin, *Worship in the Early Church,* pp. 77-86.

straint. Basically, it was an outward sign and natural consequence of their joyful communal life in the Lord and the Spirit. Barnabas, for example, voluntarily sold his field for the purpose of meeting a specific need at the time. Ananias and Sapphira were punished for their deceit of misrepresentation, not because they failed to comply with a rule of the church (Acts 5:1-11).

Third, the sharing of possessions was a *temporary* practice, initiated, no doubt, as a means of taking care of certain specific and current needs within the body of believers. The Jerusalem church appears to have been a financially poor church, possibly caused by the famine conditions that necessitated a relief offering for all believers in Judea (Acts 11:30; see Gal 2:10, "remember the poor"). However, other conditions may have contributed as well: (1) some of the Hellenistic Jews who permanently returned to Jerusalem from the Diaspora became believers and probably had few material possessions; (2) some believers came from Galilee, where they left their homes, possessions and vocations; (3) the church grew rapidly and may have attracted an unusually large number of believers from the lower economic strata of society in Judea; (4) early Jewish believers may have been persecuted or at least ostracized by unbelieving Jews and thus unable to survive economically on their own; and (5) some members may have expected the imminent return of the Lord and failed to plan for the needs of the future. If true, they were not unlike some saints in Thessalonica who stopped working as they waited for the parousia (see 2 Thess 3:6-13).

It appears that the believers in the Jerusalem church continued to require material assistance. Paul's "collection" of the offering from the Gentile churches, which he later brought to Jerusalem, indicates such a need. However, there is no report in Acts that the communal possession and sharing of goods was prescribed or that it continued. We do not hear anything about it after Acts 5:11. After all, the community could not continue to exist by indefinitely liquidating its assets.[75]

---

[75]Most major commentaries on Acts are helpful in reconstructing various aspects of this section, including similar practices among the Essenes and almonry among first-century Jews. See further, Ben Witherington III, "The Community of Goods" in *The Acts of the Apostles* (Grand Rapids, Mich.: Eerdmans, 1998), pp. 204-10. James Dunn summarizes the issue nicely when he writes: "A community of goods would not be an unexpected feature of a group wholly committed to one another and to what the group represented. The most obvious and immediate parallel is the community of goods practiced not very far away at Qumran. . . . The most obvious difference is that the first Christian sharing of goods was not obligatory (as at Qumran), but wholly spontaneous, an expression of eschatological enthusiasm (note that they did not merely contribute income but sold off property). The procedure is indicated by the Greek: not that everything was sold off at once and put in a common fund, but that possessions were sold off over a period as need arose. The impression is strong of a group whose economic basis (regular jobs and income) was far from secure, but whose imminent expectation (Jesus Messiah returning soon?) allowed them to cope by short-term measures" (*The Acts of the Apostles* [Valley Forge, Penn.: Trinity Press International, 1996], p. 36).

5.7.2. The Collection for the Saints. In a helpful article on this topic, Scot McKnight summarizes the different terminology Paul employs to describe this segment of his mission:

> Paul calls the collection a "fellowship" (*koinōnia,* Rom 15:26), . . . "service" (*diakonia,* Rom 15:25, 31; 2 Cor 8:20; 9:1, 12, 13), "gift" (*charis,* 1 Cor 16:3; 2 Cor 8:6, 7, 19), "generous gift" (*eulogia,* 2 Cor 9:5), "collection" (*logeia,* 1 Cor 16:1), "liberal gift" (*adrotēs,* [sic] 2 Cor 8:20) and "service that you perform" (*hē diakonia tēs leitourgias,* 2 Cor 9:12). 2 Corinthians 8:4 uses three terms at once: "they urgently pleaded with us for the privilege (*charis*) of *sharing* in this *service* to the saints."[76]

While the stated and probably main purpose of this gift was to provide financial relief for the poor "saints" in Jerusalem, a number of scholars have proposed that it had broader applications as well. Some scholars suggest that it symbolized the unity and equality of a church that was now composed of Jewish and Gentile believers (2 Cor 8:13-14). By accepting the offering, the Jerusalem church would, in effect, endorse Paul's mission to the Gentiles and their acceptance into the church. This may lie behind Paul's fear that the offering would be rejected (Rom 15:31) when he made his final trip and delivery to the saints in Jerusalem (Acts 24:17). Unfortunately, neither Luke nor Paul informs us of the results. They may have taken the money but had Paul arrested anyway (Acts 21:17-36).

Other scholars suggest that the Gentiles may have felt some kind of obligation to the Jews for their spiritual heritage and that the offering was a way of expressing their gratitude. Paul implies some kind of "debt" when he writes, "For Macedonia and Achaia have been pleased to share their resources with the poor among the saints at Jerusalem. They were pleased to do this, and indeed they owe it to them; *for if the Gentiles have come to share in their spiritual blessings, they ought also to be a service to them in material things*" (Rom 15:26-27, italics added). Yet this suggestion seems out of character with Paul, who elsewhere declares that there are higher motives to Christian stewardship.[77]

Another possible effect of the offering is what McKnight calls "spiritual provocation," which he explains as follows: "the presentation by Paul and his retinue of Gentile sponsors of the funds to the Jerusalem churches would provoke the nation of Israel to believe in the Messiah, for they would see in that act the

---

[76]Scot McKnight, "Collection for the Saints," *DPL,* p. 143. This article also nicely summarizes the complexity of issues surrounding the significance of the offering.

[77]See Martin, *Worship in the Early Church,* pp. 84-86.

fulfillment of the promise that the Gentiles would bring gifts to Zion (Is 2:2-4; 60:6-7, 11; Mic 4.13)."[78] Unfortunately, this neither led to the conversion of Israel nor did it ameliorate the tensions between Jews and Christians in the first century.

The only New Testament allusion to a *pattern* of giving is in 1 Corinthians 16:1-2: "Now concerning the collection for the saints: you should follow the directions I gave to the churches of Galatia. On the first day of every week, each of you is to put aside and save whatever extra you earn, so that collections need not be taken when I come." We do not know whether this money for Jerusalem was set aside privately or in public worship, nor do we know if it was given above and beyond offerings needed for local expenses. Again, we have no information about how and when the early church took care of its financial needs, including financial support for the apostles.[79] Monetary gifts may be implied in the "sacrifice" mentioned in the *Didache* (*Did.* 14.1-3) and in Justin Martyr, where deacons appear to receive monetary gifts that are distributed to the needy (*Apol. 1* 67).

5.8. The Lord's Supper

It is important to place the Lord's Supper within the context of meals in the ancient world.[80] "To the oriental," notes Joachim Jeremias, "every table fellowship is a guarantee of peace, of trust, of brotherhood. Table fellowship is a fel-

---

[78]McKnight, "Collection for the Saints," p. 146.

[79]For Paul's struggle on this matter, see 1 Cor 9; 2 Cor 11—12. For discussion, see Janet M. Everts, "Financial Support," *DPL*, pp. 295-300. It is also helpful to think of financial support within the context of ancient patronage. See deSilva, "Patronage," pp. 766-71; deSilva, *Honor, Patronage, Kingship and Purity.*

[80]I will use this term (taken from the Greek *kyriakon deipnon* in 1 Cor 11:20) in the discussion unless the context warrants a different one. Other terms used in biblical and theological studies include Eucharist (the noun, taken from the Greek verb *eucharisteō,* "to give thanks," hence "thanksgiving, Mk 14:23; Lk 22:17, 19; 1 Cor 11:24); Holy Communion (1 Cor 10:16: "Is not the cup of thanksgiving for which we give thanks *[to potērion tēs eulogias ho eulogou men]* a participation *[koinōnia]* in the blood of Christ?" [NIV]); breaking of bread (*tē klasei tou artou,* see Lk 24:35; Acts 2:42, 46; 20:7, 11; 27:35; 1 Cor 10:16; 11:24). *Sacrament,* from the Latin *sacramentum* (a translation of the Greek *mystērion*), was originally used by Romans to declare an oath, obligation or loyalty to the emperor but was applied to baptism and the Lord's Supper by the fourth century A.D. (see Günther Bornkamm, "μυστήριον, μυέω," *TDNT* 4:822-28; Arthur G. Patzia, "Mystery," *DLNTD,* pp. 782-84). By participating in the Lord's Supper, believers take the elements of bread and wine as a pledge of loyalty to Jesus. In later theology, *sacramentum* was connected with "sign" (Latin *signum,* Greek *sēmeion*), that is, pointing to some truth beyond itself. The noun *Eucharist* became prominent after the turn of the first century as an attempt to avoid confusion or identification with pagan cultic and religious meals. The Catholic use of the "Mass" is not derived from biblical language but from the Latin, *missio,* meaning "dismissal" of those who were released from a worship service before the Eucharist or Lord's Supper was celebrated.

lowship of life."[81] Thus, eating or sharing a meal was much more significant than just getting together to satisfy one's appetite. Even today, the invitation "come over for dinner" or "let's go out to eat" includes a desire by the participants to enjoy food as well as each other's company and friendship.

Judaism observed a significant number of daily cultic and festal meals. A typical Jewish meal would have included the breaking of bread, the blessing of a cup, words of thanksgiving and prayers. In religious and cultic contexts, table fellowship bound the participants to God (Ex 18:12; 24:11) and became a sacred act that ratified or sealed a covenant between individuals. This appears to have been the case, for example, between Isaac and Abimelech (Gen 26:26-30), Jacob and Laban (Gen 31:54) and David and Abner (2 Sam 3:20).[82] The breaking of table fellowship was considered a heinous crime (Ps 41:9), because by eating and drinking one shared in the blessing of the host.

A common meal was the center of community life for the inhabitants of Qumran as well. One text, now known as *Rule of the Community* or *Manual of Discipline,* states:

> And when they prepare the table to dine or the new wine for drinking, the priest shall stretch out his hand as the first to bless the first fruits of the bread [or the new wine for drinking, the priest shall stretch out his hand as the first to bless the first fruits of the bread] and of the new wine. (1QS 6:4-5)[83]

The Essenes, who did not isolate themselves in the Qumran community (see 1.2.1.6), observed a noon meal that apparently had sacramental overtones. According to Josephus,

> they go into the dining-room, as into a certain holy temple, and quietly set themselves down; upon which the baker lays them loaves in order; the cook also brings a single plate of one sort of food, and sets it before every one of them; but a priest says grace before meat and it is unlawful for anyone to taste of the food before grace be said. The same priest, when he hath dined, says grace again after meat; and when they begin, and when they end, they praise God, as he that bestows

---

[81]Joachim Jeremias, *The Eucharistic Words of Jesus* (Philadelphia: Fortress, 1977), p. 204. The significance of food and table fellowship in the ancient world is discussed by Stephen C. Barton, "Social Scientific Approaches to Paul," *DPL,* pp. 897-98. Here Barton writes, "From a social-scientific point of view, food and meals are a fundamental symbolic means by which a group or society expresses its values and identity. What is *natural* (food and the bodily ingestion of food) is transformed into something *cultural* by being made to carry and express social meanings" (p. 898). See also Barton's "Hospitality," *DLNTD,* pp. 501-7, and "Social Setting of Early Non-Pauline Literature," *DLNTD,* esp. pp. 1104-5.

[82]For other examples, see Bertold Klappert, "Lord's Supper," *NIDNTT* 2:521; Jeremias, *Eucharistic Words of Jesus,* pp. 204-7.

[83]Florentino García Martínez, *The Dead Sea Scrolls Translated* (Leiden: E. J. Brill, 1994), p. 9.

their food upon them; after which they lay aside their [white] garments. (*J.W.* 2.8.5 §§130-31)[84]

Eating and fellowship around meals was an important part of Jesus' public ministry. The Gospels record several occasions where he shared food with such individuals as Matthew (Mt 9:9-10), Zacchaeus (Lk 19:5), Mary and Martha (Lk 10:38-42) and many "sinners," an act that enraged certain religious authorities because such people were considered ritually unclean (Mt 9:11; Mk 2:16; Lk 5:30; 15:1-2). He also ate with his disciples and, on a number of occasions, fed the huge crowds that followed him (Mt 15:32-39; Mk 2:13-17; 6:30-44; 8:6-8; Lk 9:12-17; Jn 6:1-59; 13:2). Some of his teachings and parables predicted a great eschatological messianic banquet to which all peoples and nations would be invited to eat (Mt 22:1-10; 25:1-10; Lk 12:35-39; 13:29; 14:15-24). But there is no doubt that the most significant event in the life of Jesus for our discussion of the Lord's Supper is the Passover meal that he shared with his disciples before the crucifixion (Mt 26:17-29; Mk 14:12-25; Lk 22:7-20).[85]

Scholars face three types of problems (historical, textual and theological) when discussing the Lord's Supper. In the following pages I will outline these problems in the form of questions and observations and then attempt to reconstruct the development of the Lord's Supper in the early church.[86]

5.8.1. Historical. First, although no one seriously denies that Jesus met with his disciples for a meal before his death, the big question centers on the nature, sequence of events, original wording and meaning of the meal. What really happened? Was it a Passover meal? The writers of the Synoptic Gospels indicate that the disciples prepared for a Passover meal (Mt 26:17; Mk 14:12; Lk

---

[84]For further discussion, see Harold G. Kuhn, "The Lord's Supper and the Common Meals at Qumran," in *The Scrolls and the New Testament,* ed. Krister Stendahl (New York: Harper & Row, 1957), pp. 65-93; 259-65. For a brief discussion of pagan meals, see Hans-Joseph Klauck, "Lord's Supper," *ABD* 4:370.

[85]On suggestions, both pro and con, that Jesus and his disciples formed a religious association known as a *ḥᵃbûrâ,* see Jeremias, *Eucharistic Words of Jesus,* pp. 29-31; Neville Clark, *An Approach to the Theology of the Sacraments* (London: SCM Press, 1958), pp. 44-48.

[86]All these issues are addressed in the secondary literature. For additional reading, see William Barclay, *The Lord's Supper* (Nashville: Abingdon, 1967); Johannes Behm "δεῖπνον, δειπνέω," *TDNT* 2:34-35; Brad B. Blue, "Love Feast," *DPL,* pp. 578-79; Eugene LaVerdiere, *The Eucharist in the New Testament and the Early Church* (Collegeville, Minn.: Liturgical Press, 1996); I. Howard Marshall, *Last Supper and Lord's Supper* (Grand Rapids, Mich.: Eerdmans, 1980); Marshall, "Lord's Supper," *DPL,* pp. 569-75; Martin, *Worship in the Early Church,* pp. 110-29; Robert F. O'Toole, "Last Supper," *ABD* 4:234-41; John M. Perry, *Exploring the Evolution of the Lord's Supper in the New Testament* (Kansas City: Sheed & Ward, 1994); John Reumann, *The Supper of the Lord* (Philadelphia: Fortress, 1985); Eduard Schweizer, *The Lord's Supper According to the New Testament* (Philadelphia: Fortress, 1967); Robert H. Stein, "Last Supper," *DJG,* pp. 444-50.

22:8), but they do not record the order of the celebration nor include any of the essential elements.[87]

Second, when was it celebrated? All four Gospels indicate that the crucifixion occurred on Friday (Mt 27:62; Mk 15:42; Lk 23:54; Jn 19:31, 42), but only the Synoptics imply that the Last Supper was a Passover meal. John gives the impression that the Last Supper took place twenty-four hours earlier, on or before the usual time for the meal (Jn 13:1, 29; 18:28; 19:31). Is John correct and the Synoptics wrong? Or are the Synoptics correct and John mistaken? From all the endless debates on this chronology, it seems best to conclude with scholars who believe that there were some calendar differences among the Jews.[88]

Third, is there any relationship between the feeding miracles in the Gospels, especially the multitudes of four and five thousand (Mt 14:13-21; 15:32-39; Mk 6:30-44; 8:1-10; Lk 9:12-17; Jn 6:1-14), and the Lord's Supper? One is struck by the terminology of "blessing," "breaking," "thanking" and "distributing" in the miracle stories, which leads one to ask whether the Evangelists intended their audiences to recall the Lord's Supper when they heard/read these words.[89]

Fourth, is John 6:1-71 the Fourth Evangelist's version of the Lord's Supper? If so, why is it so different from the Synoptics and Paul? Also, what is the purpose of the discourses Jesus gives during the "supper" when he washes the disciples' feet (Jn 13:12-20, 31-35)?[90]

Fifth, how are we to understand the postresurrection appearances and meals that Jesus shared with his followers before his ascension? John 21:1-14 records Jesus appearing to his disciples at the Sea of Galilee, where he prepared breakfast and "broke bread" with them. A similar epiphany took place on the Emmaus road (Lk 24:13-43), where Jesus manifested himself as the resurrected

---

[87]For useful descriptions and analysis, see Barclay, *Lord's Supper,* pp. 20-34; Dunn, *Unity and Diversity,* pp. 161-73; A. J. B. Higgins, *The Lord's Supper in the New Testament* (London: SCM Press, 1952), pp. 9-23; Jeremias, *Eucharistic Words of Jesus,* pp. 41-88; Marshall, *Last Supper and Lord's Supper,* pp. 56-66; Willi Marxsen, *The Lord's Supper as a Christological Problem* (Philadelphia: Fortress, 1970); O'Toole, "Last Supper," 4:236-37; Stein, "Last Supper," pp. 445-47.

[88]Lengthy attempts to explain and harmonize the data are found in Barclay, *Lord's Supper,* pp. 16-20; Harold Hoehner, *Chronological Aspects of the Life of Christ* (Grand Rapids, Mich.: Zondervan, 1975), pp. 65-114; Jeremias, *Eucharistic Words of Jesus,* pp. 11-105; Marshall, *Last Supper and Lord's Supper,* pp. 66-75; Stein, "Last Supper," p. 446. Willi Marxsen solves the riddle (at least for himself) by asserting that in John "theological statements have been historicized" (*Lord's Supper as a Christological Problem,* pp. 19-20).

[89]See Klauck, "Lord's Supper," 4:365.

[90]For discussion of the Fourth Gospel, see Cullmann, *Early Christian Worship;* Higgins, *Lord's Supper in the New Testament,* pp. 74-88; LaVerdiere, *Eucharist in the New Testament,* pp. 112-27; Perry, *Exploring the Evolution of the Lord's Supper,* pp. 83-100.

Lord. His actions and spoken words in Luke 24:30 are similar to the words of institution at the Lord's Supper: "he took bread *[labōn ton arton]* blessed *[eulogēsen]* and broke *[klasas]* it (see below, "the breaking of bread" *[klasei tou artou]* in Acts 2:42). Acts 10:41 also mentions those "who ate and drank with him after he rose from the dead."[91]

Sixth, the "breaking of bread" is mentioned several times as a component of early Christian house gatherings:

☐ Acts 2:42: "They devoted themselves to the apostles' teaching and fellowship, to the breaking of bread *[klasei tou artou]* and the prayers."

☐ Acts 2:46: "Day by day, as they spent much time together in the temple, they broke bread *[klōntes te kat' oikon arton]* at home [NRSV, "from house to house"] and ate their food with glad and generous hearts."

☐ Acts 20:7: "On the first day of the week, when we met to break bread *[klasai arton]*, Paul was holding a discussion with them."

What significance did these meals have for the believers? Were they simply a continuation of the ordinary table fellowship meals that Jesus had had with his disciples during his earthly ministry, or is the expression "the breaking of bread" an equivalent term for the Lord's Supper?[92]

Luke's failure to mention wine (hence the phrase, *sub una,* meaning bread only) or to include any type of liturgy has led to some interesting proposals. Oscar Cullmann, for example, interprets the "breaking of bread" as a continuation of Jesus' postresurrection meals, with their emphasis on the joyful presence of the resurrected Lord.[93] Hans Leitzmann proposed a "Jerusalem" type of meal analogous to the type of fellowship meals Jesus had with his disciples (*ḥabûrâ*) before the resurrection. He suggested that Paul's understanding of the Lord's Supper as a "memorial" or "remembrance" came from a different tradition.[94] Both Marshall and Higgins criticize these theories for setting up a false division or antithesis between Luke and Paul.[95]

---

[91]The word *synalizomenos* in Acts 1:4 could be translated as "eating" or perhaps "sharing a common meal."

[92]If so, this could hardly be the case in Acts 27:35, where Paul presides at a meal with the shipwrecked crew (presumably unbelievers) attempting to make its way to Rome. Here, Paul "took bread *[labōn arton]*; and giving thanks *[eucharistēsen]* to God in the presence of all, he broke it *[klasas]* and began to eat."

[93]Cullmann, *Early Christian Worship,* pp. 14-16.

[94]Hans Leitzmann, *Mass and Lord's Supper* (Leiden: E. J. Brill, 1979). Ernst Lohmeyer recognizes two types of meals—a Galilean and Jerusalem form—but he maintains that both types come from a common tradition in the early church (*Galiläa und Jerusalem* (Göttingen: Vandenhoeck & Ruprecht, 1936).

[95]Marshall, *Last Supper and Lord's Supper,* pp. 130-33; Higgins, *Lord's Supper in the New Testament,* pp. 57-60.

Seventh, what about the so-called agape or love feasts mentioned in the New Testament and early Christian literature? Do these expressions come from the fact that the believers enjoyed eating and fellowshiping *(koinōnia)* together (Acts 2:42) "with glad and generous hearts" (Acts 2:46)? And is it, then, another term for the "breaking of bread" or the Lord's Supper? Jude 12 is the only specific reference in the New Testament where the term is used: "These [false teachers] are blemishes on your love-feasts *[agapais]*, while they feast with you without fear, feeding themselves." The variant reading in 2 Peter 2:13 that substitutes "love feasts" *(agapais)* with "dissipations" *(apatais)* may indicate that the "dissipations" were a mockery of the love feast itself.[96]

Eighth, where does the earliest written account of the Lord's Supper from Paul (1 Cor 11:23-34) fit into the discussion? Paul may have "received" this tradition or a similar version of the Lord's Supper from his association with the early church in Antioch (between A.D. 40-49). He shared that tradition when he founded the church, but now in his letter he clarifies certain features of the rite.[97] Unfortunately, the account is selective because it was written to correct certain abuses and misunderstandings of the Lord's Supper in the Corinthian church. Nevertheless, it is the most complete account of the Lord's Supper in the epistolary literature of the New Testament. What we do not know is whether this early version of the Lord's Supper was normative for all the churches and how this tradition may have influenced the accounts in the Synoptic Gospels.

Historically, then, we are left with a number of questions about Jesus' Last Supper with the Twelve, the postresurrection meals with certain disciples before Pentecost, other meals with believers in the early church, the agape meal and Paul's account of the Lord's Supper. Is there a solution to the historical questions we have raised? How do we understand these components separately, and how do they illuminate our understanding of the development of the Lord's Supper in the early church? Before we attempt to complete the puzzle, however, we must look at some of the textual problems.

5.8.2. Textual. Although many scholars have examined the Synoptic texts (Mt 26:17-29; Mk 14:12-25; Lk 22:7-20) and Paul's version of the Lord's Supper (1 Cor 11:23-34), a number of difficult questions remain unanswered.[98] For example,

---

[96]Brad Blue, "Love Feast," *DPL,* p. 578; Metzger, *Textual Commentary,* p. 634; Richard J. Bauckham, *Jude and 2 Peter,* WBC 50 (Waco, Tex.: Word, 1983), pp. 258-59.

[97]Perry writes, "Paul's account of the 'Last Supper' probably derives from the Passover observance of the Jewish Christians at Antioch" (*Exploring the Evolution of the Lord's Supper,* p. 61).

[98]Some of the most helpful works include Barclay, *Lord's Supper,* pp. 35-55; Higgins, *Lord's Supper in the New Testament,* pp. 24-55; Jeremias, *Eucharistic Words of Jesus,* pp. 138-262;

which account is the earliest? Since Mark is the first written Gospel, is his version (with its strong "Semitic speech") the most original?[99] Why does Matthew add "for the forgiveness of sins" after the phrase, "the blood of the covenant, which is poured out for many" (Mt 26:28)?[100] What about Luke's version, with its two cups (Lk 22:17, 20), and a long and short version in some manuscripts?[101] Luke's and Paul's cup "after supper" (Lk 22:20; 1 Cor 11:25) implies that a meal came between the bread and the cup, but in Matthew and Mark the bread and cup are together. Where does Paul's text fit into the picture? Did the tradition that he "received" and now "passes on" to the Corinthians come from his contact with churches during the early part of his ministry, especially in Antioch?

It is not easy to determine the origin of all these accounts. Do they come from some unknown original versions? Or are the New Testament texts just slightly different renditions that were preserved and adapted to different audiences, Mark and Matthew in Palestine, Luke and Paul with Antioch? On the basis of literary criticism, Jeremias suggests that "all accounts can be seen to represent the result of a living process of growth in the tradition."[102]

There is another major question in the development of the Lord's Supper: In the history of tradition, did the liturgy move from the Last Supper to the Lord's Supper or from the Lord's Supper to the Last Supper? Historically, we know that the Last Supper preceded the Lord's Supper and that this event was foundational for what followed. In other words, without a Last Supper there would be no Lord's Supper. History comes before liturgy![103] However, this does not preclude the possibility that some of the liturgical expressions in the Synoptics came from other traditions of the Lord's Supper in Christian communities and were incorporated into these texts. Could this be why the Last Supper looks more like a celebration of the Lord's Sup-

---

Bertold Klappert, "Lord's Supper," 2:524-30; LaVerdiere, *Eucharist in the New Testament,* pp. 46-95; and Perry, *Exploring the Evolution of the Lord's Supper,* pp. 74-82. Marshall's table 3, "The Development of the Bread-Saying and Cup-Saying" is a helpful visual reconstruction (*Last Supper and Lord's Supper,* pp. 181-83).

[99]On Semitisms in the Synoptic accounts, see Jeremias, *Eucharistic Words of Jesus,* pp. 173-86.

[100]According to Marshall, the idea comes from Jeremiah 31:31-34, God's promise to Israel that he "will forgive their iniquity and remember their sins no more" (*Last Supper and Lord's Supper,* p. 100).

[101]For this textual problem, see Metzger, *Textual Commentary,* pp. 148-50.

[102]Jeremias, *Eucharistic Words of Jesus,* p. 105. Marshall attempts to mitigate the tension of different versions by proposing that each one preserves different features of the "hypothetical" original account (*Last Supper and Lord's Supper,* pp. 39-40).

[103]Thus Jeremias writes, "*at the beginning there stands not liturgy, but historical account*" (*Eucharistic Words of Jesus,* p. 192). This is quite different from calling the accounts "etiological cult legends," that is, stories developed in the Christian communities as attempts to locate the origin of the rite in some historical event (so Marxsen, *Lord's Supper as a Christological Problem,* p. xiii).

per than a Passover meal? This comment requires an understanding of the nature of the Gospels as both historical and theological documents (as literary and redaction criticism have shown). Here, in the context of attempting to reconstruct the Lord's Supper, A. J. B. Higgins provides a helpful reminder:

> What is given [in the Synoptics] is not a description in detail of the last earthly meal of Jesus with his disciples, but an account of the first Eucharist, the institution of the Church's Eucharist as it first began to be celebrated after the resurrection. Because of the special words of explanation uniquely attached by Jesus to the bread and wine, these elements of the meal replaced the lamb as the central feature, and so gave rise to a rite quite different from the annual Passover, to a daily or weekly gathering for the "breaking of bread."[104]

5.8.3. Theological. Theologically, the main questions relate to the meaning and interpretation given to the words of institution attributed to Jesus. All the accounts include elements of Christ's passion: his broken body symbolized by the bread and the shedding of blood symbolized by the wine. This concurs with the tendency in the early church to understand Jesus as the Passover lamb (Jn 1:29, 36) and to interpret his passion from the Old Testament. Paul's credo "that Christ died for our sins in accordance with the scriptures" (1 Cor 15:4) connects Jesus with the "Suffering Servant" of Isaiah 52:13—53:12 (see also Paul's commentary in 1 Cor 5:7-8; 10:14-22, where he sees prototypes of the Lord's Supper in the Old Testament).

All the accounts also have an *eschatological* perspective. Matthew and Mark connect the cup to the coming "kingdom of God" (Mt 26:29; Mk 14:25), while Luke links the Passover meal to the kingdom (Lk 22:15-16). Paul reminds the Corinthians that in their celebration of the Lord's Supper they "proclaim the Lord's death until he comes" (1 Cor 11:26; note *marana tha* ["Our Lord, come"] in 1 Cor 16:22, a prayer for the speedy return of the Lord).

Only Luke and Paul mention the dimension of remembrance (Lk 22:19; 1 Cor 11:25, *anamnēsin*), a concept that conveys not merely the idea of looking back but remembering with the idea of making the event present.[105] Both writers also state that Jesus gave "thanks" (Greek *eucharisteō*) instead of "blessed" *(eulogeō)*, as in Matthew and Mark. This, at least in Paul's context, may account for the designation of the Lord's Supper as the Eucharist. Paul's phrase, "on the night when he was betrayed" (1 Cor 11:23), shows that the tradition of the

---

[104]Higgins, *Lord's Supper in the New Testament*, p. 23.

[105]"To recall, in Biblical thought," writes Martin, "means to transport an action which is buried in the past in such a way that its original potency and vitality are not lost, but are carried over into the present. 'In remembrance of me,' then, is no bare historical reflection upon the Cross, but a recalling of the crucified and living Christ in such a way that He is personally present in all the fullness and reality of His saving power, and is appropriated by the believers' faith" (*Worship in the Early Church*, p. 126).

Lord's Supper never lost its association with the Last Supper.

At the end of his examination of all the texts, William Barclay (as one of many) wonders whether we finally can come to some conclusion about the words that Jesus actually used. His concluding remarks seem like a fitting way to summarize this section of theological observations:

> Without trying to be certain about every word, we may say that there are four elements in the words of the institution. (i) A statement that the bread is the body of Jesus, and that it was for them. (ii) A statement that the cup represents the covenant blood of the new covenant, that is, the new relationship between man and God, made possible at the cost of the life and death of Jesus. (iii) An instruction to repeat this meal in the days to come, so that the memory of Jesus and what he had done and can do is always fresh. (iv) An eschatological saying in which Jesus affirms his confidence in the full coming of the Kingdom.[106]

5.8.4. From Last Supper to Lord's Supper. On the basis of the preceding discussion I will attempt to draw some conclusions about the development of the Lord's Supper in the first century and suggest how it was understood and practiced in the early church.

First, the Last Supper is not a true Passover meal but a supper set within the context of the Passover celebration (see figure 15). There is no way to recover the original words and intent of Jesus through literary and textual analysis. We assume that when the early believers celebrated the Lord's Supper they recalled the traditions about his last meal with the Twelve in the upper room, but it also seems likely that the Evangelists incorporated liturgical sayings into their accounts from later traditions circulating in the early churches. Development, therefore, went in both directions: from the Last Supper to the Lord's Supper and the Lord's Supper to the Last Supper.

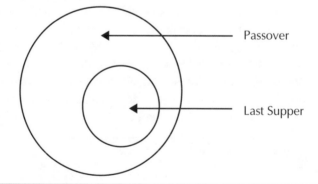

Figure 15. Passover and the Last Supper

[106]Barclay, *Lord's Supper,* p. 55.

The apostle John and the communities to which he wrote certainly celebrated some form of the Lord's Supper. However, no trace of a liturgy exists in
John's Gospel comparable to the Synoptics and Paul that helps us to understand
the meaning and development of the rite for John. Johannine scholars have
closely examined such passages as John 6 (a commentary on the feeding of the
five thousand) and John 13 (footwashing) for their sacramental overtones.
Words about "flesh" and "blood" in John 6:50-58 are clearly reminiscent of the
other accounts, and it appears that John assimilates these (and perhaps other)
traditions and develops them in his discourses.[107] Marshall represents the opinions of a number of scholars on John's presentation and understanding of the
Lord's Supper in the following comment:

> John has presented the equivalent to the words of institution in the context of a dis-
> course which is concerned with the life-giving power of Jesus himself as the true
> bread and with the need to come to him and to believe in him. This has enabled
> John to omit the words of institution in the account of the Last Supper and to
> develop the teaching of Jesus on that occasion, so that again it is the words which
> he speaks, which are spirit and life, which occupy the centre of the stage.[108]

Second, the postresurrection meals likely were a continuation of the meals
and fellowship that Jesus enjoyed with his disciples before his death. The new
element was that Jesus was now in their midst as the exalted Lord. The main
point seems to be that fellowship with Jesus can continue even though his
earthly ministry is over. These are temporary or occasional events that serve as
a transition to the fellowship meals that believers share with each other after the
ascension, when Jesus is present in the Spirit.

Third, the "breaking of bread" *is Luke's way* of identifying the Lord's Supper
in the early church, and thus it becomes the earliest name for the Lord's Supper
as a successor to the Last Supper. Luke may not have included the liturgical elements in Acts because he covered that in his Gospel. In Acts he simply wants to
show that when the newly baptized believers came together to share their common faith and joy, the Lord's Supper was a significant part of their worship.[109]

Acts 2:42 is the earliest account of such a gathering. Here, as we noted earlier, we have to imagine that Luke condenses time and abbreviates events so
that many months likely separate Acts 2:38-41 and 42. It took some time for the

---

[107]In addition to many helpful commentaries on the passages mentioned, there are lengthy discussions in Perry, *Exploring the Evolution of the Lord's Supper,* pp. 83-100; LaVerdiere,
Eucharist in the New Testament, pp. 112-27; Higgins, *Lord's Supper in the New Testament,*
pp. 74-88; Marshall, *Last Supper and Lord's Supper,* pp. 133-39; Cullmann, *Early Christian
Worship.*

[108]Marshall, *Last Supper and the Lord's Supper,* p. 138.

[109]So ibid., pp. 132-33.

apostles to reflect upon all that was happening, to think through the implications of what it meant to be the "true" Israel, to confess Jesus as the Messiah and to be baptized in his name.

Scholars differ in their interpretation of Acts 2:42. Some see four elements in this description of early Christian worship:

☐ the apostles' teaching
☐ a common meal *(koinōnia)*
☐ the "breaking of bread" (the Lord's Supper)
☐ prayers *(proseuchai)*

Others isolate three elements:

☐ the apostles' teaching
☐ a common meal *(koinōnia)* that included the "breaking of bread" (the Lord's Supper)
☐ prayers[110]

After taking all views into consideration, it seems more likely that Luke lists four components of worship, although he really has three in mind because the common meal *(koinōnia)* is followed by the celebration of the Lord's Supper ("the breaking of bread"). Although both *elements* need to be distinguished from each other, *they are viewed as one event.* The early church knew that "breaking bread" was an occasion to eat a meal and then celebrate the Lord's Supper in conjunction with it.

Fourth, it is not easy to know where the agape or love feast terminology fits into this scheme. There appear to be several possibilities: (1) it only describes the fellowship meal; (2) it describes "the breaking of bread" and thus is synonymous with the Lord's Supper; and (3) it describes one *event* (meal *plus* Lord's Supper).[111] The third suggestion seems the most likely from the available evidence:

agape = fellowship meal = breaking of bread = Lord's Supper!

Whereas the common meal and the Lord's Supper were two components of a single event in the New Testament, later history shows that, by the second century, the two were separated. This may have occurred because of the type of excesses noted in the Corinthian church and alluded to in Jude 12 and 2 Peter 2:13. Justin Martyr, for example, describes a celebration of the Lord's Supper (Eucharist) that includes the bread and wine but does not mention the agape (common) meal (*Apol. 1* 65-66).[112]

---

[110]For further elaboration, see ibid., pp. 126-33; Klauck, "Lord's Supper," 4:366.
[111]See Marshall, *Last Supper and Lord's Supper,* pp. 110-11.
[112]For further references to the agape in the church fathers, see Barclay, *Lord's Supper,* pp. 57-61. He shows that the love feast continued separately from the Lord's Supper for several centuries. See also Moule, *Worship in the New Testament,* pp. 28-29.

Fifth, it is unclear how often the early church celebrated the Lord's Supper and who presided. If the phrase "they broke bread" at home (Acts 2:46) is given the same meaning as "*the* breaking of bread" in Acts 2:42 (italics added), one could conclude that the Lord's Supper was a daily celebration.[113] But it is possible to leave the frequency of breaking bread in Acts 2:42 indefinite and take Acts 2:46 as differentiating the meals "from house to house" from the Lord's Supper.

Acts 20:7 is the first reference to the celebration on "the first day of the week," that is, Sunday. This also is the case in the *Didache,* which states: "On every Lord's Day—his special day—come together and break bread and give thanks" (*Did.* 14:1). One concludes that the Lord's Supper had become a weekly celebration and was part of worship on the Lord's Day in most churches. Pliny's letter to Trajan mentions that Christians gather on a "fixed day before sunrise," but he does not identify the day of the week (*Ep.* 10.96).

Nothing is said about the "officiants" of the Lord's Supper in the New Testament. One suspects that Paul presided when he was present, but on different occasions other apostles, teachers, elders, deacons or the head of the household presided. As far as we know, officiating at the Lord's Supper was not an ordained or a "priestly" function during the first century. Bishops and deacons appear to have been responsible for this in the community addressed by the *Didache* (see *Did.* 15:1-2). Ignatius limited this responsibility to the ecclesiastical office of bishop or his delegated leader: "without the bishop's supervision, no baptisms or love feasts are permitted" (Ign. *Smyrn.* 8.1-2). According to Justin Martyr, the Lord's Supper was conducted by a leader, "the president of the brethren," who gave thanks for the elements and then offered them to the "deacons" for distribution to the entire congregation (*Apol.* 1.65).[114]

Sixth, no other texts in the New Testament reflect the celebration of the Lord's Supper. Hebrews contains some linguistic parallels, such as "flesh and blood" (Heb 2:14), "tasted the heavenly gift" (Heb 6:4), the "new covenant" and "the blood of the covenant" (Heb 9:15, 20; 10:29), but the author appears to be developing themes from the Old Testament rather than from the Lord's Supper. Throughout the epistle the readers are exhorted to continue growing in their Christian faith. The author also reminds them not to

---

[113]So Leonard Goppelt on the analogy of the daily Essene meals (*Apostolic and Post-Apostolic Times,* trans. Robert A. Guelich [Grand Rapids, Mich.: Baker, 1970], p. 212).

[114]See Barclay, *Lord's Supper,* pp. 95-104 for discussion and references on changes in the post-apostolic period. He writes, "Whether the movement was in the right direction or not is something which we cannot at the moment lay down, but movement there was from the house to the Church, from real meal to symbolic meal, from simplicity to elaboration, from devotion to theology, from the concrete to the abstract, from the layman to the priest" (p. 104).

neglect meeting together (Heb 10:25), an obvious reference to worship services. It would be surprising if the Lord's Supper had not been a part of their liturgy.

Revelation contains considerable liturgical language in the form of prayers, benedictions and hymns, but this language does not reflect any direct resemblance to the liturgy of the Lord's Supper. Hans-Joseph Klauck, for example, concludes that the liturgical elements in Revelation "take on a different function in a different literary context and cannot (nor do they wish to) reflect the complete sequence of events in an early Christian celebration of the Lord's Supper."[115]

Just as we have no way to reconstruct a worship service from the New Testament, we have no way to outline the proceedings of the Lord's Supper. Scholars who do, such as Leonard Goppelt, read too much back into the early church from later liturgies, such as the *Didache*, Justin's *First Apology* and Hippolytus's *Apostolic Tradition*.[116] While there may be a trajectory or natural development from the first to the second and third centuries, we must let the New Testament texts speak for themselves or at least be more judicious in our use of postapostolic sources.

In terms of the *sequence of events* in the celebration of the Lord's Supper in the early church, this much seems plausible:

Paul: bread—meal—cup

Mark: meal—bread—cup

Justin: meal and Lord's Supper are separate events

In Acts 2:42 the typical gathering of believers includes teaching, "breaking bread" (meal + Lord's Supper) and prayer. As mentioned earlier, emphasis is on the joyful presence of the Lord in their midst. Perhaps the sharing of goods (Acts 2:44-45; 4:32-37) took place during this time as well.

We do not know for certain whether the worship service that Paul describes in 1 Corinthians 11:23-34 (singing, prophesying, teaching, interpreting and exercising spiritual gifts) was a separate event from the celebration of the Lord's Supper. The presence of unbelievers in the worship service (1 Cor 14:22-25) suggests a separation, because one would not expect them to participate in the Lord's Supper (1 Cor 11:27).

Although no order of service for the Lord's Supper can be reconstructed, it seems natural to conclude that the liturgy included prayers, songs, Scripture reading and a benediction. Scholars who propose that 1 Corinthians 16:20-24 belongs to the liturgy of the Lord's Supper include the following elements:

---

[115]Klauck, "Lord's Supper," 4:368.
[116]Goppelt, *Apostolic and Post-Apostolic Times*, pp. 202-21.

the holy kiss, the curse and the *maranatha.*[117]

In some biblical contexts the holy kiss is simply a gesture of friendship and love (Acts 20:37; 2 Cor 13:12; 1 Thess 5:26), but in others it could be connected with the beginning of the Lord's Supper (Rom 16:16, 1 Cor 16:20; 1 Pet 5:14; see also *Did.* 4.2; Justin Martyr *Apol. 1* 65).[118] Similarly, Paul uses the curse *(anathema)* to condemn anyone preaching a false gospel (Gal 1:9), but the *anathema* in 1 Corinthians 16:22 could be a reprimand against those who participate in the Lord's Supper in an unworthy manner, fail to discern the body (church) and stand to be judged (see 1 Cor 11:27-34; note also *Did.* 10.6: "If anyone is holy, let him come. If not, let him repent"). Finally, while *marana tha* (1 Cor 16:20) is certainly intended for the Lord's final coming (parousia), it could be a plea for his presence in the Lord's Supper as well (so *Did.* 10.6).

Throughout this brief examination of the Lord's Supper we have discussed the significance of the rite in the early church and the meaning attributed to certain phrases in the liturgy. In conclusion, I wish to draw attention to several "dimensions" or "perspectives" of the Lord's Supper in the life of the Corinthian church, suggesting that such thoughts were present when the Eucharist was celebrated in other churches as well. The concluding discussion will center around four "looks": the inward look, the backward look, the forward look and the outward look.

First, Paul exhorts the participants to "examine yourselves" (1 Cor 11:28; the *inward* look). In this context the personal examination is necessary because of the abuses that were mentioned in 1 Corinthians 11:17-22. Participation in the Lord's Supper requires a correct understanding of and attitude toward the Lord's death; otherwise, one participates in an "unworthy manner" (1 Cor 11:27). The inward look, however, is meant to bring persons *to the table,* not to drive them away (1 Cor 11:28: "Examine yourselves, and only then eat of the bread and drink of the cup").

By participating "in remembrance of me" the believer looks *back* to the cross and reflects on the broken body and shed blood of the Lord. This dimension is meant to "recall" the passion of the Lord in such a way that he becomes present to the believer. It is a sacred moment to thank God for the redemptive work of Christ.

---

[117]See Klauck, "Lord's Supper," 4:530; Marshall, *Last Supper and Lord's Supper,* pp.144-46; Cullmann, *Early Christian Worship,* pp. 12-36.

[118]So Jeremias, *The Eucharistic Words of Jesus,* p. 119. See William Klassen, "The Sacred Kiss in the New Testament: An Example of Social Boundary Lines," *NTS* 39 (1993): 122-35; Alan Kreider, *Worship and Evangelism in Pre-Christendom* (Cambridge: Grove Books, 1995), pp. 28-30. On the kiss as an act of solidarity and intimacy, see Hurtado, *At the Origins,* pp. 42-43.

The *forward* look is captured in the words "For as often as you eat this bread and drink the cup, you proclaim [*katangellō*] the Lord's death until he comes" (1 Cor 11:26). The enactment of the Lord's Supper is a kerygmatic event because it embodies the essence of the gospel, affirming both the past event of redemption and the future assurance of his return. From this perspective, *marana tha* (1 Cor 16:22) would be a fitting way either to begin or to end the celebration.

Finally, participants are to look *outward*. This dimension captures the social reality of the Lord's Supper expressed elsewhere in the early church by such terms as "fellowship," "love," unity" and "sharing one's possessions." Unfortunately, all this was lacking in Corinth because the members totally rejected these virtues by their gastronomic excesses and selfishness (1 Cor 11:20-22). Thus Paul issues a stern reminder: "So then, my brothers and sisters, when you come together to eat, wait for one another" (1 Cor 11:33). This, too, is the implication of the phrase "discerning the body," where "body" refers to the church, not the physical body of Christ (1 Cor 11:29).[119] Participation at the Lord's table asks believers to look beyond themselves and acknowledge the presence and need of their brothers and sisters in their midst.

In spite of attempts to deal fairly with the available texts and reconstruct the practice and meaning of the Lord's Supper for the early church, many of our questions remain unanswered and our conclusions tentative. Thus it seems fitting to end with a quotation from C. F. D. Moule, who concluded his study on the Lord's Supper with this observation: "What actually took place at a Eucharist? No doubt the answer to that question would vary at different periods and in different areas."[120]

5.9. Baptism

5.9.1. General Observations. It should be understood that baptismal rituals are not unique to Christianity, although Christian baptism is certainly different from other baptisms.[121] Long before the first century and the emergence of the

---

[119]See the discussion in Fee, *First Corinthians,* pp. 562-63.

[120]Moule, *Worship in the New Testament,* p. 25.

[121]For additional reading, see Kurt Aland, *Did the Early Church Baptize Infants?* (London: SCM Press, 1963); John Baillie, *Baptism and Conversion* (London: Oxford University Press, 1964); C. K. Barrett, *Church, Ministry, and Sacraments in the New Testament* (Grand Rapids, Mich.: Eerdmans, 1985); Karl Barth, *The Teaching of the Church Regarding Baptism* (London: SCM Press, 1948); Barth, *Baptism as the Foundation of the Christian Life,* vol. 4, pt. 4 of *Church Dogmatics,* ed. G. W. Bromiley and T. F. Torrance, trans. G. W. Bromiley (Edinburgh: T & T Clark, 1969); George R. Beasley-Murray, *Baptism in the New Testament* (London: Macmillan, 1962); Beasley-Murray, "Baptism," *DPL,* pp. 60-66; Geoffrey Bromiley, *Children of Promise: The Case for Baptizing Infants* (Grand Rapids, Mich.: Eerdmans, 1979); Carrington, *Primitive Christian Catechism;* Oscar Cullmann, *Baptism in the New Testament* (London: SCM Press, 1950); James D. G. Dunn, *Baptism in the Holy Spirit* (London: SCM Press,

church, people practiced various kinds of baptisms and other water rites. Primitive tribes, the civilizations of the ancient Near East, the Greeks and other pagan societies put considerable stress on the cleansing and purifying qualities of water. Water has been widely used to symbolize the ideas of ritual cleansing and initiating people into certain religious societies or organizations.

This reality was true for the Jewish people as well. The Old Testament makes many references to Jewish rites of purification by water. When individual Israelites became unclean in some way, they were instructed to "bathe" in water (Lev 15:5-33) or be sprinkled with water to remove their impurity (Num 19:14-22). This was a ceremonial purification and should not simply be equated with washing some dirt or grease off of one's physical body.

Such washings, sprinklings and purifications were considered to have a profound moral effect on individuals as well. This is especially clear in the prophetic writings that present God acting through these rituals to cleanse the hearts of his people. Ezekiel, for example, says, "I will sprinkle clean water upon you, and you shall be clean from all your uncleannesses, and from all your idols I will cleanse you" (Ezek 36:25). Isaiah connects the outward act of washing with its inner moral nature when he summons God's people: "Wash yourselves; make yourselves clean; remove the evil of your doings from before my eyes; cease to do evil, learn to do good" (Is 1:16). And Zechariah predicts, "On that day a fountain shall be opened for the house of David and the inhabit-

---

1970); W. F. Flemington, *The New Testament Doctrine of Baptism* (London: SPCK, 1948); Lars Hartman, *'Into the Name of the Lord Jesus': Baptism in the Early Church* (Edinburgh: T & T Clark, 1997); Hartman, "Baptism," *ABD* 1:583-94; Joachim Jeremias, *Infant Baptist in the First Four Centuries* (London: SCM Press, 1960); Jeremias, *The Origins of Infant Baptism: A Further Study in Reply to Kurt Aland* (London: SCM Press, 1963); Paul K. Jewett, *Infant Baptism: The Covenant of Grace* (Grand Rapids, Mich.: Eerdmans, 1978); Geoffrey W. H. Lampe, *The Seal of the Spirit: A Study in the Doctrine of Baptism and Confirmation in the New Testament and the Fathers*, 2d ed. (London: SPCK, 1967); Herbert G. Marsh, *The Origin and Significance of the New Testament Baptism* (Manchester: Manchester University Press, 1941); Kilian McDonnell and George T. Montague, *Christian Initiation and Baptism in the Holy Spirit* (Collegeville, Minn.: Liturgical Press, 1991); Albrecht Oepke, "βάπτω κτλ," *TDNT* 1:529-46; Stanley E. Porter and Anthony R. Cross, eds., *Baptism, the New Testament and the Church: Historical and Contemporary Studies in Honor of Reginald E. O. White* (Sheffield: Sheffield Academic Press, 1999); Rudolf Schnackenburg, *Baptism in the Thought of St. Paul* (Oxford: Blackwell, 1964); Max B. Turner, *The Holy Spirit and Spiritual Gifts Then and Now* (Carlisle: Paternoster, 1996); Günther Wagner, *Pauline Baptism and the Pagan Mysteries: The Problem of the Pauline Doctrine of Baptism in Romans 6:1-11 in the Light of Its Religious-Historical Parallels* (Edinburgh: Oliver & Boyd, 1967); Geoffrey Wainwright, "Baptism, Baptismal Rites," *DLNTD*, pp. 112-25; Alexander J. M. Wedderburn, *Baptism and Resurrection: Studies in Pauline Theology Against Its Greco-Roman Background* (Tübingen: J. C. B. Mohr, 1987); Reginald E. O. White, *The Biblical Doctrine of Initiation* (Grand Rapids, Mich.: Eerdmans, 1960).

ants of Jerusalem, to cleanse them from sin and impurity" (Zech 13:1). These rituals of purification may have influenced the development of some Jewish rites of baptism that preceded Christian baptism.[122]

5.9.2. Jewish Proselyte Baptism. One of these rites was proselyte baptism. When Gentiles wished to become Jews, they had to go through several steps of initiation, which included an examination of their intentions, instructions in the ways of Israel, circumcision and a self-administered baptism by immersion. It was more than just another ritual of initiation, for the texts suggest that it effected spiritual cleansing as well. However, our main interest lies in the fact that it served as a *rite of admission* to the Jewish community. It differs from Christian baptism because it did not require repentance or offer the forgiveness of sins.

5.9.3. Baptism in the Qumran Community. Baptism was also practiced by Jews living in the Qumran community, a settlement located near the shore of the Dead Sea in Palestine from about 140 B.C. to A.D. 68. As mentioned earlier (see 1.2.1.6), this community is sometimes identified with the Essenes. Their literature (the Dead Sea Scrolls) teaches that anyone wishing to enter the community had to go through an elaborate period of probation and instruction that climaxed in baptism. While the community practiced a number of ritual purifications, there is evidence that they performed a unique baptism that carried special significance as a rite of *purification and initiation.*

5.9.4. John the Baptist. Readers of the New Testament are well acquainted with John the Baptist. In fact, one is rather struck with his unexpected entrance upon the scene from the wilderness, his strange nomadic dress and his claim to be a forerunner of the Messiah preparing the nation for the coming of the kingdom of heaven (Mt 3:1-12; Mk 1:1-8; Lk 3:1-17). John came "proclaiming a baptism of repentance for the forgiveness of sins" (Mk 1:4).

It appears that John was an immediate success (Mt 3:5; Mk 1:5; Lk 3:10). Many Jews, whose hopes were high with messianic expectations, readily accepted his teaching and baptism. For them, the long-awaited prophecy of Isaiah was being fulfilled as they heard "the voice preparing the way of the Lord." John's message of repentance *and baptism* was also significant. The call to repent (*metanoeō*, which means a turning to God) was a plea that the Jewish people had heard again and again from their prophets. But what is this "baptism of repentance," and why is there no account of what John meant by it?

The most likely explanation is that John's baptism was understood in terms of the washings and baptisms that the Jewish public already knew, even though John

---

[122]On the antecedents to Christian baptism, see Beasley-Murray, *Baptism in the New Testament,* pp. 1-44; Hartman, *'Into the Name of the Lord Jesus,'* pp. 3-8. The issues are complex and controversial and go beyond the scope of this study.

may not have adopted or adapted any one of them. Some scholars believe that John had been a member of the Essene (Qumran) community but broke away from them in order to publicly call the people to turn to God. At any rate, he was another of the great prophets preparing Israel for the coming messianic age.

John's baptism stands closer to Christian baptism than any other rite. Both were initiated by a call to repentance, resulted in conversion with the remission of sins and admitted people into an eschatological community.[123] Yet, his baptism was not Christian baptism and should not be identified with it, in spite of some similarities. The Gospels tell us that John practiced a baptism of water (Mt 3:11; Mk 1:8; Lk 3:16a) and identified this as a "baptism of repentance for the forgiveness of sins" (Mk 1:4-5; Lk 3:3; cf. Mt 3:6, 11; see Josephus *Ant.* 18.2 §§116-19). In this respect it marked the individual's turning from sin to God. But John's baptism was definitely initiatory in that it prepared the baptized for the coming Messiah. In other words, it *initiated* recipients into a new community in which they enjoyed forgiveness and received a new status.

5.9.5. The Baptism of Jesus. The Synoptic Gospels mention that Jesus was baptized by John (Mt 3:13-17; Mk 1:9-11; Lk 3:21-22; see John 1:29-34) and affirm that the baptism was accompanied by the opening of the heavens, the descent of the Spirit as a dove and the approval of the divine voice saying, "You are my Son, the Beloved; with you I am well pleased" (Mk 1:11).[124] There can be no doubt that the Evangelists believed that Jesus' baptism was a very significant event.

However, it is necessary to distinguish between Jesus' baptism and the baptism of the Jewish people. Their baptism was for the remission of sins, and Jesus "was without sin" (Heb 4:15; cf. Mt 3:14). It was also an initiatory baptism into the messianic age, and Jesus was the Messiah. Why, then, was he baptized? Matthew 3:14-15 shows that the early church wrestled with this question. John the Baptist, it states, was hesitant to baptize Jesus, but Jesus replied: "Let it be so now; for it is proper for us in this way to fulfill all righteousness."

This response implies that it was necessary for Jesus to be baptized in order to accomplish his messianic work. It was a deliberate act on his part to identify

---

[123]Hartman's section on John the Baptist is important because he argues repeatedly that Christian baptism is "christianised Johannine baptism" (*'Into the Name of the Lord Jesus,'* pp. 9-21; 31-35). Thus he concludes: "Christian baptism was characterized above as a christianised Johannine baptism. We have also encountered some features which are common to both of these baptisms, particularly the eschatological perspective in which both of them should be understood. Between the two baptisms lay the life and work of Jesus and the events, which led to the conviction that he had risen from the dead. This was also understood in the same eschatological perspective, but had the result that Christian baptism became something more than a renewed Johannine baptism" (p. 35). See also Dunn, *Unity and Diversity,* p. 155.

[124]Note the variants in the NRSV for the phrases "Beloved Son" and "my Son, the Beloved."

himself further with the people, even as he had done during his birth, circumcision and dedication in the temple. Here, in baptism, he wished to leave nothing undone that was part of God's will. His baptism inaugurated his public ministry that eventually would lead to his death by crucifixion in Jerusalem.

While it is true that in his baptism Jesus demonstrates identification, obedience, submission to God's will and commitment to his public mission, his was a unique baptism, quite unlike anything that ever preceded or followed. The early church must have recognized this, because they never appealed to his baptism as a reason for their baptism. Christian baptism finds its source and meaning in the significant redemptive events of Christ's death and resurrection and not in his baptism. Nevertheless, Lars Hartman is correct in suggesting that the "interpretations of his [John's] baptism and of the tradition of Jesus' baptism teach us, on the one hand, how important John and his baptism were in these early Christian circles, and on the other, that the account of Jesus' baptism could also have a bearing on the baptism which the Christian readers had undergone."[125]

5.9.6. The Practice of Jesus. The practice of baptism during the earthly ministry of Jesus is very difficult to reconstruct because so very little is said about it. The Gospel of John indicates that John the Baptist continued to baptize around the Jordan river because of the availability of water (Jn 3:22-23). His movement attracted a number of followers, and those associated with him were identified as the "disciples of John" (Lk 7:18-19; 11:1; Acts 19:1-7). Others, however, followed Jesus. The Fourth Gospel records that Jesus and his disciples also baptized (Jn 3:22; 4:1), but the author is quick to add that *Jesus himself did not baptize* (Jn 4:2).[126]

It is impossible to say with any degree of certainty whether the baptism attributed to Jesus and his disciples was similar to or different from that of John and his followers. At this stage, however, the baptism of the Jesus movement was not a baptism associated with his death and resurrection and thus cannot be regarded as Christian baptism in the way the rite was understood and practiced later. After Jesus' death and resurrection, baptism was performed "in his name" (Acts 2:38; 8:16; 10:48; 19:5) or, as Paul writes, it was a baptism into Christ (Rom 6:1-11; Gal 3:26-27; Col 2:11-12). This became the essence of the early church's concept of *Christian baptism.*

5.9.7. The Baptism of the Spirit. John the Baptist spoke of a messianic baptism with the Holy Spirit in distinction from his own baptism in water (Mt 3:11;

---

[125]Hartman, *'Into the Name of the Lord Jesus,'* p. 27.

[126]See the standard secondary literature for comments, plus John E. Morgan-Wynne, "References to Baptism in the Fourth Gospel," in Porter and Cross, eds., *Baptism, the New Testament and the Church,* pp. 116-35; J. Ramsay Michaels, "Baptism and Conversion in John: A Particular Baptism Reading," in Porter and Cross, eds., *Baptism, the New Testament and the Church,* pp. 136-39.

Mk 1:8; Lk. 3:16). Water baptism, therefore, was not the distinguishing feature of Jesus' ministry. The world was to await another baptism, namely, a baptism with the Holy Spirit. This prophecy of John found its fulfillment on the day of Pentecost, as recorded in Acts 2:1-13. On this occasion, the Holy Spirit was poured out upon all nations, and a new age—the age of the Spirit—was inaugurated. According to Peter, this was a fulfillment of Old Testament prophecy (Acts 2:16-21). Jesus, the exalted Lord, baptized his disciples with the Holy Spirit (Acts 2:33). The prediction of John the Baptist about one coming to baptize with the Holy Spirit had indeed come true (see 2.5.2).

It does not appear that Christian baptism was administered to those who had been baptized by John. There is no record that Peter, John, the other disciples and the 120 (Acts 1:15) were required to be rebaptized "into the name of Jesus." The baptism of the Spirit somehow covered those who were in present in Jerusalem on the day of Pentecost. In Acts 19:1-7, however, one notes the unusual case of some disciples of John who must have left Jerusalem before Pentecost to reside in Ephesus. Consequently, they had been baptized by John and knew nothing about the Holy Spirit. After Paul baptized them in the "name of the Lord Jesus" (Acts 19:5), they had experiences similar to believers in Jerusalem on the day of Pentecost. This is the only recorded incident of a rebaptism in the New Testament.

In Acts 2:38, Peter concludes his sermon with this appeal: "Repent, and be baptized every one of you in the name of Jesus Christ so that your sins may be forgiven; and you will receive the gift of the Holy Spirit." Here, repentance, water baptism and the reception of the Holy Spirit are all part of becoming a Christian. In other words, one receives the Holy Spirit when one becomes a Christian, that is, when one believes and is baptized. The apostle John also refers to the new birth as effected through baptism (born of water) and the Spirit (Jn 3:5). Paul likewise links baptism with the gift of the Spirit in some of his letters (1 Cor 6:11; 12:13; Tit 3:5). One who is "in Christ" is also "in the Spirit" (Rom 8:1, 9-17). There is, therefore, no need for any "Spirit baptism" apart from the reception of the Holy Spirit at the time of one's water baptism.[127]

5.9.8. The Practice of Baptism in the Early Church. Although the New Testament offers no specific instructions on the administration of baptism, it is possible to identify certain important principles about the practice and meaning of this rite in the early church.

First, it was a believers' baptism. This is to say that only believers—people

---

[127]These rather broad statements do not imply unanimity among scholars. For example, Gordon Fee (*First Corinthians*) and James Dunn (*Baptism in the Holy Spirit*) believe that 1 Cor 12:13 (and many other passages where baptism is mentioned) refers to Spirit rather than to water baptism. See Dunn, "'Baptized' as Metaphor," in Porter and Cross, eds., *Baptism, the New Testament and the Church*, pp. 294-310.

who confessed Jesus as Messiah—came to baptism.[128] The frequent references to repentance (Acts 2:38) or having faith in the Lord Jesus Christ were directed toward people who had the intellectual capacity to believe and respond to the kerygma. After people expressed their faith in Jesus the Messiah, they were baptized almost immediately (Acts 2:38, 41; 8:12, 35-38; 9:18; 10:47-48; 18:8; 19:5). Baptism was understood as a unitary event rather than a sequence of three separate experiences. Conceptually, we can visualize Christian initiation as the top portion of figure 16, not the bottom portion.

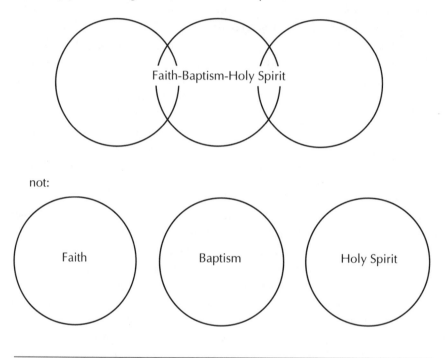

Figure 16. Christian initiation

---

[128]The concept of infant baptism was a later development and cannot be found in the first century. Most scholars today who support infant baptism in the church admit that this practice cannot be defended from the teaching of the New Testament. So, for example, Dunn: "For it has to be recognized that _infant baptism can find no real support in the theology of baptism which any NT writer can be shown to espouse_" (_Unity and Diversity,_ p. 161). Everything that the New Testament says about faith, repentance and belief precludes the idea that infants could be or were baptized in the early church. The same is true in the writings of Tertullian, Clement of Alexandria and Hippolytus, where candidates for baptism (the catechumens) were individuals who could comprehend Christian instruction. On the relevance and authenticity of Hippolytus's statement, "they shall baptize _[baptizein]_ the little children first" (_Apos. Trad._ 21.4), see comments by Paul K. Jewett, _Infant Baptism,_ pp. 22-25.

During the early stage of initiation, the only separation in time between faith and baptism was for logistical reasons. The concept of prebaptismal instruction was a later development in the church. For the early church at least, baptism belonged to the beginning of the Christian life, when one initially expressed faith in Christ, and not to the maturity of the believer.

There is no way of knowing when catechetical instruction began in the church. The earliest believers in Jerusalem may have confessed "Jesus as Messiah" personally at the time of their baptism (see the use of "confession" [homologeō or homologia] in Rom 10:9; 1 Tim 6:12; Heb 3:1; 4:14; 10:23) or had a formula pronounced over them by the officiant. James 2:7 refers to "the excellent name that was invoked over you" (Greek aorist passive of epikaleō, "call upon," "appeal to"), and Ephesians 5:26 seems to imply that baptism ("the washing of water") was accompanied by some spoken "word" (rhēma).[129]

If there was any kind of instruction at this early stage, it was minimal at best. New Testament references to instruction (katēcheō, Lk 1:4; Acts 18:25) or to teaching, traditions, doctrine, and the like in the church come after, not before, baptism. However, as the church expanded, simple confessions may have become more elaborate and additional instructions given to the candidate. This was necessary partially because of the rise of false teaching in the church and partially because of the need to guarantee that those entering the church were genuine in their faith and intentions. The textual variant at Acts 8:37 is an indication that some type of instruction, interrogation and confession was emerging in certain areas and was thus added to this text at a later time. Here the Ethiopian eunuch is instructed by Philip, and when he requests baptism, Philip replies, "If you believe with all your heart, you may." The eunuch replies, "I believe that Jesus Christ is the Son of God."[130]

It is doubtful that the elaborate early baptismal catechisms reconstructed by Philip Carrington and E. G. Selwyn applied to prebaptismal instruction or that Ephesians and 1 Peter are baptismal homilies.[131] The earliest extant nonbiblical literature that comments on baptism is the Didache: "This is how to

---

[129]For suggestions, see Patzia, Ephesians, Colossians, Philemon, p. 271.

[130]Metzger, Textual Commentary, pp. 315-16; see also Cullmann's appendix, "Traces of an Ancient Baptismal Formula in the New Testament," in Baptism in the New Testament, pp. 71-80, where he analyzes the word kōlyō, "hinder," "prevent" or "forbid" in Acts 8:36; 10:47; 11:17.

[131]See Carrington, Primitive Christian Catechism; Selwyn, First Epistle of Peter. For a brief discussion and bibliography on Ephesians as a baptismal homily, see Patzia, Ephesians, Colossians, Philemon, pp. 131-33. The claim that 1 Peter is a baptismal homily is mentioned in most major commentaries on this epistle but is well summarized by Ernst Best, 1 Peter (London: Marshall, Morgan & Scott, 1971), pp. 21-27.

baptize. Give public instruction on all these points, and then baptize" (_Did._ 7:1). Unfortunately, we do not know anything about the content or duration of such instruction. In the postapostolic period there is more evidence of instruction in Justin Martyr (_Apol._ 1.61), Tertullian (_Bapt._ 1.3), Origen (_Cels._ 3.51 and various homilies) and Hippolytus (_Apos. Trad._). Thus Alan Kreider notes that "by the end of the second century a catechetical procedure had come into existence—present with variations in both East and West—in which baptism took place only after a catechesis that was both extensive and intensive."[132]

As one reads through Acts it becomes obvious that there is no consistent pattern or sequence of events to what we have called "Christian initiation," "conversion," "being saved" or "becoming a believer." In Acts we have the following order:

Acts 2:38:	belief—baptism—Holy Spirit
Acts 8:14-24:	belief—baptism—hands—Holy Spirit
Acts 10:44-49:	belief—Holy Spirit—tongues—baptism
Acts 19:1-7:	belief—baptism—hands—Holy Spirit—tongues

Faith, water baptism and reception of the Holy Spirit always appear in these four examples. The two variants are "laying on of hands" and "speaking in tongues." We may track this out even further in Acts by listing all the occasions where Luke refers to people becoming believers (see figure 17).

From this pattern we are able to draw the following conclusions: (1) faith or belief in Jesus, as proclaimed in the kerygma, is the first step in becoming a believer; (2) water baptism and the reception of the Holy Spirit are either mentioned or implied; (3) "hands" and "tongues" apply to specific situations only and not to any normative pattern of Christian initiation.[133] These observations are consistent with the rest of the New Testament literature, where the baptism of believers is taken for granted and tongues, at least for Paul, is a "gift of the Spirit" bestowed only on certain individuals.

Since Luke is not a systematic theologian, nor does he intend to provide his readers with a church manual, we look in vain—and perhaps disappointment—for a uniform pattern of Christian initiation. His exceptions may come from various reports and traditions, or they may simply testify to the sovereignty and

---

[132]Alan Kreider, "Baptism, Catechism, and the Eclipse of Jesus' Teaching in Early Christianity," _TynBul_ 47 (1996): 318. On the _Didache_ and the _Shepherd of Hermas_, see Hartman, '_Into the Name of the Lord Jesus,_' pp. 177-86.

[133]Most commentators take Acts 2:38 as the most normative statement of Christian initiation in the New Testament. See also Joel B. Green, "From 'John's Baptism' to 'Baptism in the Name of the Lord Jesus': The Significance of Baptism in Luke-Acts," in Porter and Cross, eds., _Baptism, the New Testament and the Church,_ esp. p. 157 n. 2.

autonomous character of the Holy Spirit. James Dunn expresses this clearly when he writes:

> We may conclude with some confidence that the primary concern, whether of the first Christians or of Luke, was *not* to establish a particular ritual procedure, far less to determine the action of God in accordance with a cultic action. . . . On the contrary, the evidence of Acts serves to underline the freedom of God to meet faith when and as he pleases, and *what we see in Acts is the early churches adapting themselves and their embryonic ritual in accordance with God's manifest action through the Spirit.*[134]

Scripture	Belief	Baptism	Spirit	Hands	Tongues
Acts 2:1-13	*	—	*	—	*
Acts 2:38	*	*	*	—	—
Acts 2:40-43	*	*	—	—	—
Acts 2:47	*	—	—	—	—
Acts 4:4	*	—	—	—	—
Acts 4:31	—	—	*	—	—
Acts 6:7	*	—	—	—	—
Acts 8:12-17	*	*	*	*	—
Acts 8:36-39	*	*	—	—	—
Acts 9:17-19	*	*	*	*	—
Acts 9:42	*	—	—	—	—
Acts 10:44-48	*	*	*	—	*
Acts 11:21-26	*	—	—	—	—
Acts 13:48-52	*	—	*	—	—
Acts 14:1	*	—	—	—	—
Acts 14:21	*	—	—	—	—
Acts 16:5	*	—	—	—	—
Acts 16:15	*	*	—	—	—
Acts 16:31-33	*	*	—	—	*
Acts 17:34	*	—	—	—	—
Acts 18:8	*	*	—	—	—
Acts 19:4-7	*	*	*	*	*
Acts 22:16	*	*	—	—	—

Figure 17. Christian initiation in Acts

---

[134]Dunn, *Unity and Diversity,* p. 157.

These slight variations do not destroy the basic uniformity and coherence of baptismal practice and theology in the New Testament. Anthony R. Cross expresses the opinion of a majority of scholars when he states that "there is as much justification to argue that there exists within the New Testament a single, coherent and discernible theology and practice of baptism than there is to argue the opposite view."[135]

Second, it was a baptism by immersion. The Greek term for baptism (_baptizō_) means "to dip or to immerse," and there is no doubt among scholars that immersion was the uniform practice of the early church. Both the prepositions "in" (_en_) or "into" (_eis_), when used of baptism, as well as the symbolism of death and resurrection (Rom 6) support this. Other forms or modes developed later in postapostolic times. The first specific example is in the _Didache_, which supports affusion (pouring) probably for reasons of necessity or convenience:

> Now about baptism: This is how to baptize. Give public instruction on all these points, and then "baptize" in running water, "in the name of the Father and of the Son and of the Holy Spirit." If you do not have running water, baptize in some other. If you cannot in cold, then in warm. If you have neither, then pour water on the head three times "in the name of the Father and of the Son and of the Holy Spirit." Before the baptism, moreover, the one who baptizes and the one being baptized must fast, and any others who can. And you must tell the one being baptized to fast for one or two days beforehand. (_Did._ 7.1-6)

Immersion remained the norm for many centuries and still is retained by the Eastern Orthodox Church for the baptism of infants as well as adults.

Third, it was a baptism into the name of Jesus Christ (Acts 2:38; 8:12, 16; 10:48; 19:5; 22:16), the name standing for the person. By being baptized into the name "of Jesus," one actually was baptized into the person of the Lord Jesus Christ (Rom 6:3; 10:8-9; Gal 3:26-27). This signified not only that the one baptized came under new ownership but also that the Lord appropriated the believer for his own.

Scholars are divided on the origin of the phrase "in the name of." Some prefer the Greek secular idea of banking terminology ("to the account of"), others a translation of a Hebrew/Aramaic phrase ("into somebody's name"). Lars Hartman sums up the conclusion of most scholars when he writes: "The formula,

---

[135]Anthony R. Cross, "'One Baptism' (Ephesians 4.5): A Challenge to the Church," in Porter and Cross, eds., _Baptism, the New Testament and the Church_, p. 181. See also Joel B. Green's "discourse-oriented" or "narrative" examination of Luke in "From 'John's Baptism'," pp. 157-72.

linguistically peculiar though it may be, is a literal translation of a Hebrew-Aramaic idiom, which the Aramaic-speaking early church used when speaking of Christian baptism. Accordingly we are brought down to a very early period of the church. In its Greek version the formula became a Christian technical term."[136]

If baptism "into the name" is the earliest formula, what, then, should we do with Matthew 28:19, where the risen Lord instructs his disciples to go to all "nations, baptizing them in the name of the Father and of the Son and of the Holy Spirit"? There is no textual evidence to indicate that this is a later addition to Matthew's Gospel.[137] The most one can say with certainty is that this was a baptismal formula attributed to the risen Lord, known and practiced in Matthew's church, and that it was adopted by other communities as well (see *Did.* 7.1-6).

Finally, baptism incorporated believers into the body of believers, the church. Acts records that those who received the Lord were baptized and "added" to the number of believers (Acts 2:41, 47). In this way new believers identified with others and committed themselves to that local house church in worship and service, whether it was in Jerusalem, Corinth, Colossae, Rome, or elsewhere. Baptism was the rite of entry into the church. For the early believers this was a serious and monumental decision, because it separated them from unbelievers and identified them with the Christian community.

In Paul's letters we discover a further development of the relationship between baptism and church membership. Baptism is "in" or "into" Christ (Rom 6:1-11; Gal 3:26-28; Col 2:11-12). Elsewhere the church is identified as the body of Christ (e.g., 1 Cor 12:27; Eph 4:12; Col 1:24), and believers are baptized into the body (1 Cor 12:12-13). In Christian baptism, then, one is received into the community of Jesus, the body of Christ.

Although we cannot consider all the details of Paul's teaching on the church here, the apostle's argument runs something like this:

the church = Christ's body

baptism = into Christ, into his body

therefore, baptism = into the church

One cannot separate baptism into Christ from baptism into his body, the church. Baptism in the New Testament was never regarded as an "individual"

---

[136]Hartman, *'Into the Name of the Lord Jesus,'* p. 43.

[137]See discussions in major commentaries and monographs on baptism. John Nolland's "Baptism in Matthew" (in Porter and Cross, eds., *Baptism, the New Testament and the Church*, p. 77 n. 28) provides a good current bibliography.

or "private" act, because being united with Christ meant to be united with his body, the church, and thus with every true believer.

5.9.9. The Theology of Early Christian Baptism. Although this brief historical survey is necessary for understanding the rise and practice of baptism in the early church, it does not deal with the theology of baptism, that is, how the early church understood the rite. Several observations can illuminate our understanding and the significance of baptism for believers in the early church.[138]

5.9.9.1. The Relationship Between Faith and Baptism. The previous discussion concluded that a believer's faith and baptism were closely linked. In this concept of "faith-baptism," there was no separation of faith from baptism or baptism from faith; both elements were considered one act. Faith was necessary for baptism; baptism was necessary for faith. One writer has commented on this relationship by stating that "baptism and faith are but the outside and the inside of the same thing."[139]

This combination is illustrated throughout the New Testament. Peter, for example, instructed his hearers to repent—that is, to have faith, to believe—and to be baptized (Acts 2:38). At the time of Paul's conversion, he was told to be baptized, calling upon the name of the Lord (Acts 22:16). Below we shall note many other passages in the New Testament that either state explicitly or imply this essential relationship. In other words, one was not baptized unless one believed, nor did one believe without being baptized. On the basis of this relationship, it is safe to assert that there were no unbaptized believers in the early church.

At this point it is important to consider what the New Testament teaches about becoming a believer and a member of the early church and how the New Testament uses a number of different words and concepts to describe this process. When, for example, one wants to know how to receive salvation (to be saved), we discover several variations: (1) salvation is through *faith* (Mk 16:16;

---

[138]Since the New Testament authors take baptism for granted—that is, as a normal part of becoming a believer—they often do not refer to it specifically. Hartman's observations on this point is helpful: "over and over again it has also become evident that baptism and its meaning cannot be isolated from the combination of events, actions, attitudes, experiences and phenomena which together make up the transition from the past and its conditions to the new, Christian life. Baptism is the ritual focus of this cluster of events, and the close connection between baptism and the other elements may explain why our authors do not always clearly link baptism with repentance/conversion, forgiveness of sins, faith, justification, or the gift of the Spirit. To disregard the circumstance that baptism belongs to such a larger whole may have the result that it is unjustly focused upon, but also, paradoxically enough, that its importance is underestimated" (*'Into the Name of the Lord Jesus,'* pp. 168-69).

[139]Beasley-Murray, *Baptism in the New Testament,* p. 272.

Acts 16:30-31; Rom 5:1; Gal 3:26; Eph 2:8-9); (2) salvation is through *repentance* (2 Cor 7:10; 2 Pet 3:9); (3) salvation is through *confession* (Acts 22:16; Rom 10:9); (4) salvation is through *regeneration* (Tit 3:5); and (5) salvation is through *baptism* (1 Cor 6:11; Gal 3:27; 1 Pet 3:21).

Along with these references are a number of other examples that express this reality as well: salvation is received through (1) faith and baptism (Mk 16:16; Acts 16:31-33; 18:8; Gal 3:25-27; Col 2:11-12); (2) faith and regeneration (Gal 3:2, 14; Eph 1:13); (3) baptism and regeneration (Acts 9:17-18; 10:44-48; Rom 6:4; Tit 3:5); (4) repentance, faith and regeneration (Acts 2:38, 11:18); (5) faith, baptism and regeneration (Acts 19:4-6); (6) baptism, sanctification, justification and the work of the Holy Spirit (1 Cor 6:11).

By studying these various Scripture passages it becomes even more obvious that repentance (faith/belief/confession), water baptism and the gift of the Holy Sprit are all included in the process of becoming a believer. Isolating one or two of these elements, separating them by a period of time or even omitting one confuses the teaching and practice of baptism in the New Testament. All of these components can be assumed to be present even when they are not all explicitly mentioned. Surely Peter, for example, does not mean to exclude "faith" when he called the Jews to repent and be baptized (Acts 2:38), nor would Paul imply that an act of confession and faith that does not involve regeneration, baptism or repentance saves (Rom 10:9).

Some theologians have avoided or misinterpreted certain New Testament texts (e.g., Jn 3:5; Acts 2:38; 22:16; 1 Cor 6:11; Tit 3:5; 1 Pet 3:18-21) because these references link baptism with the forgiveness of sins. However, when these texts are understood within the larger context of what the New Testament teaches about becoming a believer, they become clearer. The New Testament does not teach a doctrine of baptismal regeneration; rather, it teaches a "faith-baptism." All of this means that the early church considered baptism a very normal and important part of becoming a member of the church. The New Testament places baptism squarely within the context of salvation; it was an essential element of early Christian initiation and worship.

5.9.9.2. Baptism as Participation in Christ's Death and Resurrection. The understanding of baptism as participation in Christ's death and resurrection comes largely from the apostle Paul and is found in such passages as Romans 6:1-11; Galatians 3:25-26; and Colossians 2:11-12. Some of this is already implied by baptism "into the name of Jesus" (see Acts), because the name stands for the person. But Paul speaks about a Christian actually participating in Christ's death and resurrection and being united with him in baptism.

From the way Paul develops his theology of baptism in these and other passages, it becomes obvious that baptism is more than just a symbol. The apostle looks back to baptism as the time or place when the believer did, in fact, die to sin and was raised and united with the Lord (see also Col 2:20; 3:1). Baptism, in other words, is the temporal reference point in becoming a believer. It is the occasion when one "strips off" (Col 3:9) the old self and "clothes oneself" as a new person in Christ (Col 3:10). These definitions do not make baptism magical or mechanical (*ex opere operato*) in any sense because Paul continually stresses the response of faith that accompanies baptism.

5.9.9.3. Baptism and the New Life. The idea that baptism has moral or ethical efficacy was implied earlier by John the Baptist, who called people to "a baptism of repentance" and to "bear fruits worthy of repentance" (Lk 3:3, 8). Paul develops this idea in his epistles by showing how baptism relates to new life in Christ. Romans 6 is particularly helpful for understanding this truth. Here Paul is correcting a false understanding of sin and righteousness. Apparently, some believers felt that God's grace and their "freedom in Christ" permitted them to continue in sin even after they became Christians, because God's moral law was no longer binding on them (Rom 5:12-21). This leads Paul to exclaim in Romans 6:1-2: "Should we continue in sin in order that grace may abound? By no means! How can we who died to sin go on living in it?" Then Paul goes on to explain what happened in their baptism. By being baptized into Christ they died to sin (Rom 6:4, 6) and were raised to newness of life (Rom 6:4, 10-11). And since they have died to sin, they can no longer live to sin, for they have been "raised with Christ." From this we can understand the meaning of Romans 6:12-14:

> Therefore, do not let sin exercise dominion in your mortal bodies, to make you obey their passions. No longer present your members to sin as instruments of wickedness, but present yourselves to God as those who have been brought from death to life, and present your members to God as instruments of righteousness. For sin will have no dominion over you, since you are not under law but under grace.

This ethical teaching is brought out in other passages that talk about old and new life, including, for example, Colossians 3:1-17, which can be understood within the context of baptism. When Paul gives ethical instructions to the church, he reminds his readers what took place in their baptism and how their ethical life is to manifest that. There is a similar emphasis in Ephesians 4:17—5:20, where the imagery of "putting away" and "clothing" oneself is related to the ethical teaching of baptism.

All this language and symbolism serves to demonstrate the close relationship between baptism and ethical behavior. Looking at it another way, Paul says: you *are* a believer by virtue of your participation in Christ (the indicative); now *become* what you are (the imperative). As Ephesians 5:8 says: "But now in the Lord you are light. Live as children of light." Baptism, therefore, serves as a wonderful reminder for believers to live out the new life they have received in Christ.

5.10. Summary

It is difficult to speak definitively about some aspects of early Christian worship because the New Testament letters were not written as liturgical documents and thus do not contain a lot of necessary information. However, there are enough "clues" within the New Testament in the form of creeds, confessions, hymns, liturgical expressions, sacramental acts, and the like that we can reconstruct a reasonably good picture of the practice and meaning of worship in early Christianity. At the very least, we can conclude with the following seven points.

First, Christianity emerged within the context of Judaism with the conviction that it was the true Israel of God. However, there are two realities that we must face. One is our lack of knowledge of certain beliefs and practices of first-century Judaism. The second relates to Luke's descriptions of the early church in Acts. It is not always easy to distinguish between Luke's historical objectivity and his theological or apologetic agenda.

Second, the early church developed its internal life and worship within the structural organization of households common in that day. Believers met as a church in private homes until the third century A.D., when specific buildings for meetings were erected.

Third, since Christianity began as a reform movement within Israel, it initially had no intention of separating from Judaism. A "Parting of the Ways," however, became inevitable as the early church developed its theology and worship around the central principle of the gospel that God acted in the person of Jesus Christ to reconcile the world and that through his resurrection Jesus was proclaimed the exalted Lord and Messiah (Acts 2:36).

Fourth, since early Christian worship was characterized by considerable diversity, we must avoid the temptation to harmonize its practices and beliefs according to some assumed preordained model. Worship patterns varied among the churches, ranging between the order of a synagogal model and the rather free expressions of worship evident in Corinth (1 Cor 11—14).

Fifth, some early (late first and early second century) nonbiblical literature can be helpful in reconstructing early Christian worship as long as we remember that worship did not develop in a linear way in all the churches throughout the empire. In short, we must avoid projecting too much later material back into the first century.

Sixth, the New Testament writers did not provide a complete and clear picture of all the churches mentioned in their texts. But they leave no doubt

that the church and its worship are profoundly significant theological concepts. At its very core, the church is the "body of Christ" (1 Cor 10:16;
12:27; Eph 4:12), God's "field" (geōrgion), "building" (oikodomē) and "temple" (naos) in which the Spirit of God dwells (see 1 Cor 3:9-17 and similar
themes in Eph 2:14-22; 1 Pet 2:4-5).

Seventh, liturgical historians walk a fine line between certainty and ambiguity when it comes to reconstructing early Christian worship. Our study has confirmed this delicate balance by looking carefully at the material and
reconstructing possibilities without becoming unduly pessimistic.

CONCLUDING
REMARKS

I t is difficult to end this book because there is so much more that could be said about the emergence of the early church. Many new thoughts and new materials in the form of books and articles keep appearing and should be consulted. One could easily add another chapter or write an entire book on ecclesiology, focusing on such topics as the theology of the church or the images and metaphors used to characterize the church throughout the New Testament. One could even offer critiques of the modern church vis-à-vis the early church. However, much of this has been done by very capable scholars and is available in many of the sources mentioned in the footnotes and bibliography.

Although it was necessary to discuss the emergence of the early church in geographical, historical, sociological, religious and theological categories, I hope that readers caught a glimpse of the church's expansion and what it meant to be a Christian—to be *the church*—in the first century. In many ways, the *nature* of the church was reflected in the various sections that divide the book, even though I did not draw a great deal of attention to this at the time.

Members of the early church came from a Semitic or Greco-Roman background. Just as Jesus' radical call to discipleship meant separation of familial ties (Lk 14:26), conversion to Christianity involved replacing one religion with another by abandoning certain beliefs and practices that were incompatible with a new faith. In many cases, becoming a Christian invited ostracism, hostility and persecutions from family, friends, and religious and secular authorities. We discussed this reality throughout the book and drew attention to the struggles new believers had in making the transition from

Judaism or paganism into the Christian church. Much of the New Testament paraenetic material is directed toward encouraging believers, clarifying who they are as the people of God and reminding them to remain focused on the revelation of God through Christ and the apostolic teaching that was passed on to them.

The early church saw itself as the true Israel of God with a mission not only to reform Judaism but to take the good news of the gospel to the ends of the earth. Part two discussed this conviction, focusing on Jesus' aims and mission and what he envisioned from his disciples. The hopes and dreams that Jesus instilled in his disciples during his earthly ministry were momentarily shattered with his crucifixion but then revived with his resurrection and the promise of the Holy Spirit (Lk 24:13-53).

The resurrection and the subsequent experience of the Holy Spirit at Pentecost revolutionized the followers of Jesus. They realized that God was at work in the risen Lord and readily confessed him as their Messiah. The coming of the Spirit was the fulfillment of a long-awaited prophecy (Acts 2:17-21) that established the believers as an eschatological community and empowered them to take the gospel to the ends of the earth as well.

Part three traced the spread of the church from Jerusalem to Rome, mainly by incorporating material from the book of Acts and the letters of Paul. Since the early believers saw themselves as a missionary community, they established churches in regions and cities throughout the Greco-Roman world. Luke's plan for the expansion of the church (Acts 1:8) was largely fulfilled by the apostle Paul, who was called by God to take the gospel to the Gentiles (Rom 11:13; 15:16; Gal 2:8; cf. Eph 3:8).

The Holy Spirit also manifested itself within the leadership and worship of the early church. Believers were endowed with certain spiritual gifts (*charismata*), which enabled them to serve God and one another in different ways. Part four discussed these ministries and offices and noted how the church ordered itself around the gifts and gifted individuals as it established itself as a credible institution in the Roman Empire.

Above all else, the church was a worshiping community of believers, operating from the conviction that worship was their way to relate to God and each other. Initially, their worship had some affinity with Judaism, but as the church established its own identity, it gradually developed its own patterns of initiation and liturgy. Thus part five attempted to identify the components of worship from the New Testament texts in order to discover the meaning, significance and practice of worship in the early churches.

Apart from these rather broad brush strokes it is instructive to look at the early church from the perspective of personal questions that individual members had about their new identity and how these questions are addressed in the New Testament.

Who Are We?

Initially, Jewish Christians had no problem seeing themselves as the true Israel who confessed Jesus as their Messiah. In Acts, Luke primarily refers to individuals as "disciples" (of Jesus) and "believers" and even defines their identity more specifically as "Christians" (Acts 11:26). Other New Testament writers use a number of different terms, such as "children of God," "saints" and "brothers and sisters." Collectively, believers constitute the church *(ekklēsia)* of God and are his "elect," "flock," "family," "field," "building" and "household." The apostle Paul goes further and develops the nature of the church around the concept of God's "temple" (1 Cor 3:9-17; 2 Cor 6:16-18) and the "body of Christ" (1 Cor 12:27). Peter writes to believers in the Diaspora as those who are "a chosen race, a royal priesthood, a holy nation, God's own people" (1 Pet 2:9; see also Eph 2:19-22).[1]

What Are We to Believe?

If one looks at the four Gospels, it becomes apparent that belief is centered in the person of Jesus as God's Messiah and Savior of the world. The Evangelists use a number of different theological terms to describe Jesus (Son of God, Son of Man, Lord, Messiah, Lamb, Savior, Prophet, etc.) but clearly affirm that people must believe in Jesus. John probably sums this up best when he writes: "But these [the words in his Gospel] are written so that you may come to believe that Jesus is the Messiah, the Son of God, and that through believing you may have life in his name (Jn 20:31).

The earliest recorded response to the proclamation of the gospel in Acts comes after Peter's sermon on the day of Pentecost. Here the hearers ask, "Brothers, what should we do" (Acts 2:37)? Peter's reply that they repent and be baptized in the name of Jesus (Acts 2:38) follows his earlier affirmation that Jesus is "both Lord and Messiah" (Acts 2:36).

All the creeds and confessions of the early church (see 5.4.2) leave no doubt

---

[1]This is not a complete list of the analogies, images and metaphors used throughout the New Testament for the church. Paul Minear, in his classic book, *Images of the Church in the New Testament* (Philadelphia: Westminster Press, 1960), lists ninety-six different terms that describe the church. See also William S. Campbell, "Church as Israel, People of God," *DLNTD*, pp. 204-219; Ronald Y. Fung, "Body of Christ," *DPL*, pp. 76-82; Kevin Giles, "Church," *DLNTD*, pp. 194-204; Dan G. McCartney, "House, Spiritual House," *DLNTD*, pp. 507-11; Peter T. O'Brien, "Church," *DPL*, pp. 123-31; and Rudolf Schnackenburg, *The Church in the New Testament* (Freiburg: Herder, 1965).

that belief is centered in the person of Jesus Christ: his incarnation, death and resurrection. These events form the essence of "the gospel," a widely used term to signify the good news of salvation through faith in Jesus Christ. Throughout the New Testament, believers are constantly reminded to remain true to the gospel that was proclaimed and passed on to them.

What Is Our Mission?

If the earliest disciples in Jerusalem remembered anything about Jesus, it would be his call to follow him and proclaim the good news of the gospel. All the Evangelists except Luke end their Gospel with some kind of commissioning of the disciples (see Mt 28:19-20; the variant reading at Mark 16:15; Jn 20:21). Luke's record of Jesus' charge to his disciples appears in Acts 1:8 ("you will be my witnesses in Jerusalem, in all Judea and Samaria, and to the ends of the earth"), and his history of the early church illustrates that its mission includes the evangelization of the world (part three).

As mentioned earlier, the person and activity of Paul, the apostle to the Gentiles, best exemplify the mission of the church. However, *all believers* are called to be witnesses and testify about the redemptive grace of God in Christ. The very essence of the church is missiological because the church is the people of God in the world. The apostle Peter underscores this when he writes to a community of believers that their mission is to "proclaim the mighty acts of him who called you out of darkness into his marvelous light" (1 Pet 2:9).

How Are We to Live?

This question is partially answered by the preceding ones in the sense that the nature, belief system and mission of the church determine how its members are to conduct themselves in the world. Since they are saints, holy, light in the Lord, a new creation, brothers and sisters, and the like (the indicative), they are to live like saints, be holy, godly, and so forth (the imperative).

Most of the answers to this question of Christian living are brought out in the paraenetical sections of the New Testament, where believers are exhorted to embrace a new way of life. Individually, they are reminded to "put off" certain vices that characterize living in the flesh (Gal 5:16-21; Eph 4:22, 25-31; Col 3:5-11) and to "put on" virtues that characterize living in the Spirit (Gal 5:22-26; Eph 4:24; Col 3:12-17). In addition, as members of a community, they are to live together in fellowship, unity, humility, submission and love.

Although many passages profoundly exemplify the call to Christian living (e.g., Eph 4:1-3; Phil 4:8-9; 2 Pet 1:5-7), I conclude with the words of Ephesians 4:7-16 because they sum up God's vision for the church and its members so wonderfully:

But each of us was given grace according to the measure of Christ's gift. . . . The gifts he gave were that some would be apostles, some prophets, some evangelists, some pastors and teachers, to equip the saints for the work of ministry, for building up the body of Christ, until all of us come to the unity of the faith and of the knowledge of the Son of God, to maturity, to the measure of the full stature of Christ. We must no longer be children, tossed to and fro and blown about by every wind of doctrine, by people's trickery, by their craftiness in deceitful scheming. But speaking the truth in love, we must grow up in every way into him who is the head, into Christ, from whom the whole body, joined and knit together by every ligament with which it is equipped, as each part is working properly, promotes the body's growth in building itself up in love.

Amen. Come, Lord Jesus! (Rev 22:20)

Selected Bibliography

Aune, David E. *Prophecy in Early Christianity and the Ancient Mediterranean World.* Grand Rapids, Mich.: Eerdmans, 1983.

———. "Worship, Early Christian." *ABD* 6:976-82.

Avis, P. *Christians in Communion.* London: Geoffrey Chapman, 1990.

Balch, David L. "Household Codes." *ABD* 3:318-20.

———. *Let Wives Be Submissive: The Domestic Code in 1 Peter.* SBLMS 26. Chico, Calif.: Scholars Press, 1981.

Bammel, Ernst. "Jewish Activity Against Christians in Palestine According to Acts." In *The Book of Acts in Its Palestinian Setting,* pp. 357-64. Edited by Richard Bauckham. BAFCS 4. Grand Rapids, Mich.: Eerdmans, 1995.

Banks, Robert. *Paul's Idea of Community.* Rev. ed. Peabody, Mass.: Hendrickson, 1994.

Barclay, William. *The Lord's Supper.* Nashville: Abingdon, 1967.

Barnett, Paul W. "Apostle." *DPL,* pp. 45-51.

———. *Jesus and the Rise of Early Christianity.* Downers Grove, Ill.: InterVarsity Press, 1999.

Barrett, C. K. *Acts.* 2 vols. Edinburgh: T & T Clark, 1994.

———. *Church, Ministry and Sacraments in the New Testament.* Grand Rapids, Mich.: Eerdmans, 1985.

———. *The Signs of an Apostle.* London: Epworth, 1970.

Barth, Karl. *The Teaching of the Church Regarding Baptism.* London: SCM Press, 1948.

Barth, Markus. *The People of God.* Sheffield: JSOT Press, 1983.

Bartlett, David L. *Ministry in the New Testament.* Minneapolis: Fortress, 1993.

Barton, Stephen C. "The Communal Dimension of Earliest Christianity: A Critical Survey of the Field." *JTS* 43 (1992): 399-427.

Bauckham, Richard. "James and the Jerusalem Church." In *The Book of Acts in Its Palestinian Setting,* pp. 428-34. Edited by Richard Bauckham. BAFCS 4. Grand Rapids, Mich.: Eerdmans, 1995.

———, ed. *The Book of Acts in Its Palestinian Setting.* BAFCS 4. Grand Rapids, Mich.: Eerdmans, 1995.

Beasley-Murray, George R. "Baptism." *DPL,* pp. 60-66.

———. *Baptism in the New Testament.* London: Macmillan, 1962.

Becker, Jürgen. *Paul: Apostle to the Gentiles.* Louisville: Westminster John Knox, 1993.

Behm, Johannes. "δεῖπνον, δειπνέω." *TDNT* 2:34-35.

Belezikian, Gilbert. *Beyond Sex Roles: What the Bible Says About a Woman's Place in the Church and Family.* Grand Rapids, Mich.: Baker, 1986.

Belleville, Linda. *Women Leaders in the Church.* Grand Rapids, Mich.: Baker, 2000.

Betz, Hans-Dieter. "Apostle." *ABD* 1:309-11.

Beyer, Hermann W. "διακονέω, διακονία, διάκονος." *TDNT* 2:82-93.

Bichsel, N. A. "Hymns, Early Christian," *ABD* 3:350-51.

Blue, Bradley B. "Acts and the House Church." In *The Book of Acts in Its Graeco-Roman Setting,* pp. 119-222. Edited by David W. J. Gill and Conrad Gempf. BAFCS 2. Grand Rapids, Mich.: Eerdmans, 1994.

———. "The Influence of Jewish Worship on Luke's Presentation of the Early Church." In *Witness to the Gospel: The Theology of Acts,* pp. 473-97. Edited by I. Howard Marshall and David Peterson. Grand Rapids, Mich.: Eerdmans, 1998.

———. "Love Feast." *DPL,* pp. 578-79.

Bockmuehl, Markus, and Michael B. Thompson, eds. *A Vision for the Church: Studies in Early Christian Ecclesiology.* Edinburgh: T & T Clark, 1977.

Bornkamm, Günther. *Early Christian Experience.* London: SCM Press, 1969.

————. "πρέσβυς κτλ." *TDNT* 6:651-83.

Bourke, Myles M. "Reflections on Church Order in the New Testament." *CBQ* 30 (1968):493-511.

Bradshaw, Paul F. *The Search for the Origins of Christian Worship.* New York: Oxford University Press, 1992.

Branick, Vincent P. *The House Church in the Writings of Paul.* Wilmington, Del.: Michael Glazier, 1989.

Bromiley, Geoffrey W. *Christian Ministry.* Grand Rapids, Mich.: Eerdmans, 1959.

Brown, Raymond E. *The Churches the Apostles Left Behind.* New York: Paulist, 1984.

————. *An Introduction to the New Testament.* New York: Doubleday, 1997.

Brown, Raymond E., and John P. Meier. *Antioch and Rome.* New York: Paulist, 1982.

Bruce, F. F. *The Book of the Acts.* Rev. ed. NICNT. Grand Rapids, Mich.: Eerdmans, 1992.

Burkitt, F. C. *Christian Beginning.* London: University of London Press, 1924.

Burtchaell, James T. *From Synagogue to Church.* Cambridge: Cambridge University Press, 1992.

Cadoux, C. John. *The Early Church and the World: A History of the Christian Attitudes to Pagan Society and the State Down to the Time of Constantine.* Edinburgh: T & T Clark, 1925.

Caird, G. B. *The Apostolic Age.* London: Gerald Duckworth, 1955.

Campbell, R. Alastair. *The Elders: Seniority Within Earliest Christianity.* Edinburgh: T & T Clark, 1994.

Campbell, William S. "Church As Israel, People of God." *DLNTD,* pp. 204-19.

Campenhausen, Hans von. *Ecclesiastical Authority and Spiritual Power in the Church of the First Three Centuries.* London: A. & C. Black, 1969.

————. *Tradition and Life in the Church: Essays and Lectures in Church History.* London: Collins, 1968.

Carrington, Philip. *The Early Christian Church.* Vol. 1, *The First Christian Century.* Cambridge: Cambridge University Press, 1957.

Carson, Donald A. *The Church in the Bible and the World.* Exeter: Paternoster, 1987.

————, ed. *From Sabbath to Lord's Day.* Grand Rapids, Mich.: Zondervan, 1982.

Clapp, Rodney. *A Peculiar People: The Church as Culture in a Post-Christian Society.* Downers Grove, Ill.: InterVarsity Press, 1996.

Clark, Neville. *An Approach to the Theology of the Sacraments.* London: SCM Press, 1958.

Clogg, F. Bertram. *The Christian Character in the Early Church.* London: Epworth, 1944.

Clowney, Edmund P. "Interpreting the Biblical Models of the Church: A Hermeneutical Deepening of Ecclesiology." In *Biblical Interpretation and the Church: Text and Context,* pp. 64-109. Edited by Donald A. Carson. Exeter: Paternoster, 1984.

Collins, John N. *Diakonia: Re-interpreting the Ancient Sources.* New York: Oxford University Press, 1990.

Conniry, Charles J. "Identifying Apostolic Christianity." *JETS* 37 (1994): 247-61.

Conzelmann, Hans. *Acts of the Apostles.* Philadelphia: Fortress, 1987.

Cooke, Bernard. *Ministry to Word and Sacrament.* Philadelphia, Fortress, 1980.

Cullmann, Oscar. *Baptism in the New Testament.* London: SCM Press, 1950.

————. "Dissensions Within the Early Church." In *New Testament Issues,* pp. 119-29. Edited by Richard Batey. London: SCM Press, 1970.

————. *The Earliest Christian Confessions.* London: SCM Press, 1949.

————. *Early Christian Worship.* Translated by A. Stewart Todd and James B. Torrance. London: SCM Press, 1953.

———. *The Early Church.* London: SCM Press, 1966.

Davies, W. D. *Christian Origins and Judaism.* London: Darton, Longman & Todd, 1962.

Delling, Gerhard. *Worship in the New Testament.* Translated by Percy Scott. London: Darton, Longman & Todd, 1962.

deSilva, David A. *Honor, Patronage, Kinship and Purity: Unlocking New Testament Culture.* Downers Grove, Ill.: InterVarsity Press, 2000.

Dodd, C. H. *The Apostolic Preaching and Its Developments.* New York: Harper & Row, 1964.

Dulles, Avery R. *A Church to Believe In: Discipleship and the Dynamics of Freedom.* New York: Crossroad, 1982.

———. "A Half Century of Ecclesiology." *TS* 50 (1989): 419-42.

———. *Models of the Church.* 2d ed. Dublin: Gill & Macmillan, 1988.

Dunn, James D. G. *The Acts of the Apostles.* Valley Forge, Penn.: Trinity Press International, 1996.

———. *Baptism in the Holy Spirit: A Re-examination of the New Testament Teaching on the Gifts of the Spirit in Relation to Pentecostalism Today.* London: SCM Press, 1970.

———. "The Body of Christ in Paul." In *Worship, Theology and Ministry in the Early Church: Essays in Honour of Ralph P. Martin,* pp. 146-62. Edited by M. J. Wilkins and T. Paige. JSNTSup 87. Sheffield: Sheffield Academic Press, 1992.

———. *The Partings of the Ways.* Philadelphia: Trinity Press International, 1991.

———. *Unity and Diversity in the New Testament.* 2d ed. Philadelphia: Trinity Press International, 1990.

———, ed. *Jews and Christians: The Partings of the Ways A.D. 70-135.* Grand Rapids, Mich.: Eerdmans, 1992.

Ellis, E. Earle. "Paul and His Co-Workers." *NTS* 17 (1971): 437-52.

———. *Pauline Theology: Ministry and Society.* Washington, D.C.: University of America Press, 1997.

Esler, Philip E. *Community and Gospel in Luke-Acts.* Cambridge: Cambridge University Press, 1987.

Evans, Craig A. "Christianity and Judaism: Partings of the Ways." *DLNTD,* pp. 159-70.

———. "Prophet, Paul As." *DPL,* pp. 762-65.

Ferguson, Everett. *The Church of Christ: A Biblical Ecclesiology for Today.* Grand Rapids, Mich.: Eerdmans, 1996.

Field, B. "The Discourses Behind the Metaphor 'The Church As the Body of Christ' As Used by St. Paul and the 'Post Paulines.'" *AJT* 6 (1992): 88-107.

Fiensy, David A. "The Composition of the Jerusalem Church." In *The Book of Acts in Its Palestinian Setting,* pp. 237-65. Edited by Richard Bauckham. BAFCS 4. Grand Rapids, Mich.: Eerdmans, 1995.

Filson, Floyd. "The Significance of the Early House Churches." *JBL* 58 (1939): 105-12.

———. *Three Crucial Decades: Studies in the Book of Acts.* Richmond, Va.: John Knox Press, 1963.

Fitzmyer, Joseph A. *The Acts of the Apostles.* New York: Doubleday, 1997.

Flew, R. Newton. *Jesus and His Church: A Study of the Idea of the Ecclesia in the New Testament.* London: Epworth, 1938.

Floor, L. "Church Order in the Pastoral Epistles." *Neot* 10 (1976): 81-91.

Foakes-Jackson, Fredrick J. *The Rise of Gentile Christianity.* New York: George H. Doran, 1927.

———. *Studies in the Life of the Early Church.* New York: George A. Doran, 1927.

Foakes-Jackson, Fredrick J., and Kirsopp Lake. *The Acts of the Apostles.* 5 vols. London: Macmillan, 1920-1933.

Freyne, Sean. *Galilee from Alexander the Great to Hadrian 323 B.C.E. to 135 C.E.: A Study of Second Temple Judaism.* Edinburgh: T & T Clark, 1998.

Friedrich, Gerhard. "εὐαγγελίζομαι, κτλ. " *TDNT* 2:707-37.

———. "κῆρυξ, κτλ." *TDNT* 3:683-718.

Fung, Ronald. "Charismatic Versus Organized Ministry? An Examination of an Alleged Antithesis." *EvQ* 52 (1980): 195-214.

Gardner-Smith, P., and F. J. Foakes-Jackson. *The Expansion of the Christian Church.* Cambridge: Cambridge University Press, 1939.

Gibson, A. F. *The Church and Its Unity.* Leicester: Inter-Varsity Press, 1992.

Giles, Kevin N. "The Church in the Gospel of Luke." *SJT* 34 (1981): 121-46.

———. "Church Order, Government." *DLNTD,* pp. 219-226.

———. "Is Luke an Exponent of 'Early Protestantism'? Church Order in the Lukan Writings." *EvQ* 54 (1982): 193-205; 55 (1983): 3-20.

———. *The Making of Community: Acts 1-12.* Albatross: Sutherland, 1992.

———. *Patterns of Ministry Among the First Christians.* Melbourne: Collins-Dove, 1989.

———. "Prophecy, Prophets, False Prophets." *DLNTD,* pp. 970-77.

———. *What on Earth Is the Church?* Downers Grove, Ill.: InterVarsity Press, 1995.

Gill, David W. J., and Conrad Gempf, eds. *The Book of Acts in Its Graeco-Roman Setting.* BAFCS 2. Grand Rapids, Mich.: Eerdmans, 1994.

Glen, John Stanley. *Pastoral Problems in First Corinthians.* Philadelphia: Westminster Press, 1964.

Goguel, Maurice. *The Birth of Christianity.* London: Allen & Unwin, 1953.

———. *The Primitive Church.* London: Allen & Unwin, 1947.

Goppelt, Leonhard. *Apostolic and Post-Apostolic Times.* Translated by Robert A. Guelich. Grand Rapids, Mich.: Baker, 1970.

Gore, Charles. *The Church and the Ministry.* London: SPCK, 1936.

Grant, Robert M. *Early Christianity and Society: Seven Studies.* San Francisco: Harper & Row, 1977.

Green, Michael. *Evangelism in the Early Church.* London: Hodder & Stoughton, 1970.

Green, Joel B. "From 'John's Baptism' to 'Baptism in the Name of the Lord Jesus': The Significance of Baptism in Luke-Acts." In *Baptism, the New Testament and the Church,* pp. 157-172. Edited by Stanley E. Porter and Anthony E. Cross. Sheffield: Sheffield University Press, 1999.

Gundry, Robert H. *Soma in Biblical Theology.* Cambridge: Cambridge University Press, 1976.

Gunton, Colin and Daniel Hardy, eds. *On Being the Church.* Edinburgh: T & T Clark, 1989.

Haenchen, Ernst. *The Acts of the Apostles.* Philadelphia: Westminster Press, 1971.

Hahn, Ferdinand. *The Worship of the Early Church.* Philadelphia: Fortress, 1973.

Hammer, Jennifer. *The Church Is a Communion.* London: Geoffrey Chapman, 1964.

Hanson, K. C., and Douglas E. Oakman. *Palestine in the Time of Jesus.* Minneapolis: Augsburg Fortress, 1998.

Harnack, Adolf von. *The Expansion of Christianity in the First Three Decades.* London: Williams & Norgate, 1904-1905.

———. *The Mission and Expansion of the Christian Church.* London: Williams & Norgate, 1908.

Harrison, Everett F. *The Apostolic Church.* Grand Rapids, Mich.: Eerdmans, 1985.

Hartman, Lars. *'Into the Name of the Lord Jesus': Baptism in the Early Church.* Edinburgh: T & T Clark, 1997.

Hemer, Colin. *The Book of Acts in the Setting of Hellenistic History.* Tübingen: J. C. B. Mohr, 1989.

———. *The Letters to the Seven Churches of Asia in Their Local Setting.* Sheffield: JSOT, 1986.

Hengel, Martin. *Acts and the History of Earliest Christianity.* Translated by John Bowden. Philadelphia: Fortress, 1980.

———. *Between Jesus and Paul.* Philadelphia: Fortress, 1983.

Hengel, Martin, and Anna Maria Schwemer. *Paul Between Damascus and Antioch: The Unknown Years*. Louisville: Westminster John Knox, 1997.

Hess, Klaus. "Deacon." *NIDNTT* 3:544-49.

Higgins, A. J. B. *The Lord's Supper in the New Testament*. London: SCM Press, 1952.

Hill, Craig C. "Hellenists, Hellenistic and Hellenistic-Jewish Christianity." *DLNTD*, pp. 463-67.

Holmberg, Bengt. *Paul and Power: Authority in the Primitive Church As Reflected in the Pauline Epistles*. Philadelphia: Fortress, 1980.

Hopwood, Percy G. S. *The Religious Experience of the Primitive Church: The Period Prior to the Influence of Paul*. New York: Scribner's, 1937.

Hort, Fenton John Anthony. *Christian Ecclesia*. London: Macmillan, 1908.

Hultgren, Arland. "The Church in the NT: Three Polarities in Discerning Its Identity." *Dialog* 33 (1994): 111-17.

Hunter, Archibald M. *Paul and His Predecessors*. Rev. ed. London: SCM Press, 1961.

Hurtado, Larry W. *At the Origins of Christian Worship*. Grand Rapids, Mich.: Eerdmans, 2000.

Jeffers, James S. *The Greco-Roman World of the New Testament Era*. Downers Grove, Ill.: InterVarsity Press, 1999.

Jeremias, Joachim. *The Eucharistic Words of Jesus*. London: SCM Press, 1966.

———. *Jerusalem in the Time of Jesus: An Investigation into Economic and Social Conditions During the New Testament Period*. Philadelphia: Fortress, 1969.

———. *The Prayers of Jesus*. London: SCM Press, 1967.

Jervell, Jacob. *Luke and the People of God*. Minneapolis: Augsburg, 1972.

Jewett, Paul K. *Man as Male and Female: A Study in Sexual Relationships from a Theological Point of View*. Grand Rapids, Mich.: Eerdmans, 1975.

Johnston, George. *The Doctrine of the Church in the New Testament*. Cambridge: Cambridge University Press, 1943.

Judge, E. A. *The Social Pattern of the Christian Groups in the First Century: Some Prolegomena to the Study of New Testament Ideas of Social Obligation*. London: Tyndale Press, 1960.

Kee, Howard C. *Community of the New Age*. Philadelphia: Westminster Press, 1977.

Keener, Craig S. Paul, "Man and Woman." *DPL*, pp. 583-92.

———. "Woman and Man." *DLNTD*, pp. 1205-15.

———. *Women and Wives: Marriage and Women's Ministry in the Letters of Paul*. Peabody, Mass.: Hendrickson, 1992.

Kelly, J. N. D. *Early Christian Creeds*. London: Longmans, Green, 1950.

Kingsbury, Jack D. "The Verb ἀκολουθεῖν ('To Follow') as an Index of Matthew's View of His Community." *JBL* 97 (1978): 56-73.

Kittel, G. "ἀββᾶ." *TDNT* 1:5-6.

Klappert, Bertold. "Lord's Supper." *NIDNTT* 2:520-37.

Klauck, Hans-Josef. *Hausgemeinde und Hauskirche im frühen Christentum*. Stuttgart: Verlag Katholisches Bibelwerk, 1981.

———. "Lord's Supper." *ABD* 4:362-72.

Knight, George W., III. *The New Testament Teaching on the Role Relationship of Men and Women*. Grand Rapids, Mich.: Baker, 1977.

Knight, Jonathan M. "Alexandria, Alexandrian Christianity." *DLNTD*, pp. 34-37.

Knox, Wilfred L. *St. Paul and the Church of Jerusalem*. Cambridge: Cambridge University Press, 1925.

Kress, Robert. *The Church, Communion, Sacrament, Communication*. New York: Paulist, 1985.

Kroeger, Catherine. "Women in the Early Church." *DLNTD*, pp. 1215-22.

Kroeger, Richard C., and Catherine C. Kroeger. *I Suffer Not a Woman: Rethinking 1 Timothy 2:11-15 in Light of Ancient Evidence*. Grand Rapids, Mich.: Baker, 1992.

Kruse, Colin G. "Apostle." *DPL,* pp. 27-33.

————. "Apostle, Apostleship." *DLNTD,* pp. 76-82.

————. "Ministry." *DPL,* pp. 603-08.

————. *New Testament Models for Ministry: Jesus and Paul.* Nashville: Nelson, 1984.

Laansma, Jon C. "Lord's Day." *DLNTD,* pp. 679-86.

Lampe, G. W. H. *The Seal of the Spirit: A Study in the Doctrine of Baptism and Confession in the New Testament and the Fathers.* London: Longmans, Green, 1951.

Latourette, Kenneth Scott. *A History of Christianity.* New York: Harper, 1953.

LaVerdiere, Eugene. *The Eucharist in the New Testament and the Early Church.* Collegeville, Minn.: Liturgical Press, 1996.

Lietzmann, Hans. *The Beginnings of the Christian Church.* Translated by Bertram Lee Woolf. New York: Scribner's, 1949.

Lightfoot, J. B. "The Christian Ministry." In *St. Paul's Epistle to the Philippians,* pp. 181-269. London: Macmillan, 1879.

Lim, David S. "Evangelism in the Early Church." *DLNTD,* pp. 353-59.

Lohfink, Gerhard. *Jesus and Community.* Philadelphia. Fortress, 1984

Loisy, Alfred. *The Gospel and the Church.* New York: Prometheus, 1988.

Longenecker, Richard N. *The Christology of Early Jewish Christianity.* London: SCM Press, 1970.

————. *New Wine into Fresh Wineskins: Contextualizing the Early Christian Confessions.* Peabody, Mass.: Hendrickson, 1999.

Luz, Ulrich. "The Disciples in the Gospel of Matthew." In *The Interpretation of Matthew,* pp. 115-48. Edited by Graham Stanton. Edinburgh: T & T Clark, 1995.

Manson, T. W. *The Church's Ministry.* London: Hodder & Stoughton, 1948.

Manson, William. *Jesus and the Christian.* Grand Rapids, Mich.: Eerdmans, 1967.

Marshall, I. Howard. "Church." *DJG,* pp. 122-25.

————. "Early Catholicism in the New Testament." In *New Dimensions in New Testament Study,* pp. 217-31. Edited by Richard N. Longenecker and Merrill C. Tenney. Grand Rapids, Mich.: Zondervan, 1974.

————. *Last Supper and Lord's Supper.* Grand Rapids, Mich.: Eerdmans, 1980.

————. *Luke: Historian and Theologian.* Downers Grove, Ill.: InterVarsity Press, 1998.

————. "New Wine in Old Wineskins. The Biblical Use of the Word 'Ekklesia.'" *ExpT* 84 (1972-1973): 359-64.

Martin, Ralph P. *The Family and the Fellowship.* Grand Rapids, Mich.: Eerdmans, 1979.

————. *A Hymn of Christ: Philippians 2:5-11 in Recent Interpretation and in the Setting of Early Christian Worship.* Downers Grove, Ill.: InterVarsity Press, 1997.

————. "Hymns, Hymn Fragments, Songs, Spiritual Songs." *DPL,* pp. 419-23.

————. "Worship and Liturgy." *DLNTD,* pp. 1224-38.

————. *Worship in the Early Church.* Grand Rapids, Mich.: Eerdmans, 1983.

————. *The Worship of God.* Grand Rapids, Mich.: Eerdmans, 1994.

Marxsen, Willi. *The Lord's Supper As a Christological Problem.* Philadelphia: Fortress, 1970.

McCartney, Dan G. "Household, Family." *DLNTD,* pp. 511-13.

McDonald, Margaret Y. *The Pauline Churches: A Socio-historical Study of Institutionalization in the Pauline and Deutero-Pauline Writings.* Cambridge: Cambridge University Press, 1988.

McKnight, Scott. "Collection for the Saints." *DPL,* pp. 143-47.

————. *A Light Among the Gentiles: Jewish Missionary Activity in the Second Temple Period.* Minneapolis: Fortress, 1991.

Meeks, Wayne A. *The First Urban Christians: The Social World of the Apostle Paul.* New Haven, Conn.: Yale University Press, 1983.

Meeks, Wayne A., and Robert A. Wilken. *Jews and Christians in Antioch in the First Four Cen-*

turies of the Common Era. Missoula, Mont.: Scholars Press, 1978.

Menzies, Robert P. *The Development of Early Christian Pneumatology.* Sheffield: JSOT, 1991.

Metzger, Bruce M. *A Textual Commentary on the Greek New Testament.* 2nd ed. New York: American Bible Society, 1994.

Meyer, Ben. *The Aims of Jesus.* London: SCM Press, 1979.

Mickelsen, Alvera, ed. *Women, Authority and the Bible.* Downers Grove, Ill.: InterVarsity Press, 1986.

Minear, Paul S. *Images of the Church in the New Testament.* Philadelphia: Westminster Press, 1960. Repr., Eugene, Ore.: Wipf & Stock, 1998.

Moule, C. F. D. *Worship in the New Testament.* Richmond, Va.: John Knox Press, 1961.

Neufeld, Vernon H. *The Earliest Christian Confessions.* Grand Rapids, Mich.: Eerdmans, 1963.

Newbigin, Leslie. *The Household of God.* London: SCM Press, 1953.

Newman, Carey C., ed. *Jesus and the Restoration of Israel.* Downers Grove, Ill.: InterVarsity Press, 1999.

O'Brien, Peter T. "Church." *DPL,* pp. 123-31.

Osborne, Grant. "Elder." *DJG,* pp. 201-3.

Osiek, Carolyn, and David L. Balch. *Families in the New Testament World: Households and House Churches.* Louisville: Westminster John Knox, 1997.

O'Toole, Robert F. "Last Supper." *ABD* 4:234-41.

Pannenberg, Wolfhart. *The Church.* Translated by Keith Crim. Philadelphia: Westminster Press, 1983.

Patzia, Arthur G. *The Making of the New Testament.* Downers Grove, Ill.: InterVarsity Press, 1995.

Pearson, Birger, A. "Christianity in Egypt." *ABD* 1:954-60.

———. "Christians and Jews in First-Century Alexandria." *HTR* 79 (1986): 206-16.

Perkins, Pheme. *Ministering in the Pauline Churches.* New York: Paulist, 1982.

Perry, John M. *Exploring the Evolution of the Lord's Supper in the New Testament.* Kansas City: Sheed & Ward, 1994.

Peterson, David. "The Worship of the New Community." In *Witness to the Gospel: The Theology of Acts,* pp. 373-95. Edited by I. Howard Marshall and David Peterson. Grand Rapids, Mich.: Eerdmans, 1998.

Peterson, J. M. "House-Churches in Rome." *VC* 23 (1969): 264-72.

Porter, Stanley E., and Anthony R. Cross, eds. *Baptism, the New Testament and the Church: Historical and Contemporary Studies in Honor of Reginald E. O. White.* Sheffield: Sheffield Academic Press, 1999.

Ramsay, William. M. *The Church in the Roman Empire.* Grand Rapids, Mich.: Baker, 1954.

Rapske, Brian M. "Roman Empire, Christianity and The." *DLNTD,* pp. 1059-63.

Reasoner, Mark. "Rome and Roman Christianity." *DPL,* pp. 850-55.

Reinhardt, Wolfgang. "The Population Size of Jerusalem and Numerical Growth of the Jerusalem Church." In *The Book of Acts in Its Palestinian Setting,* pp. 237-65. Edited by Richard Bauckham. BAFCS 4. Grand Rapids, Mich.: Eerdmans, 1995.

Rengstorf, Karl H. "διδάσκω, διδάσκαλος, κτλ." *TDNT* 2:135-65.

———. "ἀποστέλλω, κτλ." *TDNT* 1:398-447.

Reumann, John. *The Supper of the Lord.* Philadelphia: Fortress, 1985.

Riesner, Rainer. *Paul's Early Period: Chronology, Mission Strategy, Theology.* Translated by Doug Stott. Grand Rapids, Mich.: Eerdmans, 1998.

———. "Synagogues in Jerusalem." In *The Book of Acts in Its Palestinian Setting,* pp. 179-212. Edited by Richard Bauckham. BAFCS 4. Grand Rapids, Mich.: Eerdmans, 1995.

Roetzel, Calvin. *The Letters of Paul.* 4th ed. Louisville: Westminster John Knox, 1998.

Ropes, James Hardy. *The Apostolic Age in the Light of Modern Criticism.* New York: Scribner's, 1906.

Sanders, E. P. *Jesus and Judaism.* Philadelphia: Fortress, 1985.

————. *Judaism: Practice and Belief 63 B.C.E.-66 C.E.* Philadelphia: Trinity Press International, 1992.

Schillebeeckx, Edward. *The Church with a Human Face.* London: SCM Press, 1985.

————. *Ministry: A Case for Change.* London: SCM Press, 1981.

Schlatter, Adolf. *The Church in the New Testament Period.* London: SPCK, 1955.

Schnabel, Eckhard J. "Mission, Early Non-Pauline." *DLNTD,* pp. 752-75.

Schnackenburg, Rudolf. *The Church in the New Testament.* Freiburg: Herder, 1965.

Schrage, Wolfgang. "'Ekklesia' und 'Synagoge' Zum Ursprung des Urchristlichen Kirchenbegriffs." *ZTK* 60 (1963): 178-202.

Schweizer, Eduard. *Church Order in the New Testament.* SBT 32. Naperville, Ill.: A. R. Allenson, 1961.

————. "The Concept of the Church in St. John." In *New Testament Essays in Honour of T. W. Manson,* pp. 230-45. Edited by A. J. B. Higgins. Manchester: Manchester University Press, 1959.

————. *The Lord's Supper According to the New Testament.* Philadelphia: Fortress, 1967.

————. "Matthew's Church." In *The Interpretation of Matthew,* pp. 129-55. Edited by Graham Stanton. Philadelphia: Fortress, 1983.

Scott, Ernest F. *The Beginnings of the Church.* New York: Scribner's, 1925.

Seccombe, David. "The New People of God." In *Witness to the Gospel: The Theology of Acts,* pp. 349-72. Edited by I. Howard Marshall and David Peterson. Grand Rapids, Mich.: Eerdmans, 1998.

Snodgrass, Klyne, ed. *The Church: Symposium on Theological Interpretation of Scripture. Ex Auditu.* Chicago: North Park Theological Seminary, 1994.

Stark, Rodney. *The Rise of Christianity.* Princeton, N.J.: Princeton University Press, 1996.

Stein, Robert H. "Last Supper." *DJG,* pp. 444-50.

Stemberger, Günter. *Jewish Contemporaries of Jesus: Pharisees, Sadducees, Essenes.* Minneapolis: Augsburg Fortress, 1995.

Streeter, Burnett Hillman. *The Primitive Church, Studied with Special Reference to the Origins of the Christian Ministry.* New York: Macmillan, 1929.

Sunquist, Scott. "Syria, Syrian Christianity." *DLNTD,* pp. 1150-53.

Taylor, Vincent. "The New Testament Origins of Holy Communion." In *New Testament Essays,* pp. 48-59. London: Epworth, 1970.

Thompson, Michael B. "Teaching/Paraenesis." *DPL,* pp. 922-23.

Thornton, L. S. *The Common Life in the Body of Christ.* 3rd ed. London: Dacre, 1950.

Towner, Philip H. "Household Codes." *DLNTD,* pp. 513-20.

————. "Households and Household Codes." *DPL,* pp. 417-19.

Turner, Max. *The Holy Spirit and Spiritual Gifts: Then and Now.* Carlisle: Paternoster, 1996.

————. *Power from on High.* Sheffield: Sheffield Academic Press, 1996.

Tyson, Joseph B. "The Emerging Church and the Problem of Authority in Acts." *Int* 42 (1988): 132-45.

Wainwright, Geoffrey. "Baptism, Baptismal Rites." *DLNTD,* pp. 112-25.

White, Reginald E. O. *The Biblical Doctrine of Initiation.* Grand Rapids, Mich.: Eerdmans, 1960.

Wilkins, Michael J. "Teaching, Paraenesis." *DLNTD,* pp. 1156-59.

Wilkins, Michael J., and Terence Paige, eds. *Worship, Theology and Ministry in the Early Church: Essays in Honor of Ralph P. Martin.* JSNTSup 87. Sheffield: Sheffield Academic Press, 1992.

Williams, David J. *Acts.* NIBCNT 5. Peabody, Mass.: Hendrickson, 1990.

Wilson, Stephen G. *The Gentiles and the Gentile Mission in Luke-Acts.* Cambridge: Cambridge University Press, 1973.

Winter, Bruce W., and Andrew D. Clark, eds. *The Book of Acts in Its Ancient Literary Setting.* BAFCS 1. Grand Rapids, Mich.: Eerdmans, 1993.

Witherington, Ben, III. *The Acts of the Apostles.* Grand Rapids, Mich.: Eerdmans, 1998.

———. *The Jesus Quest.* Downers Grove, Ill.: InterVarsity Press, 1994.

———. *Women in the Earliest Churches.* SNTSMS 59. Cambridge: Cambridge University Press, 1988.

Wright, David F. "Creeds, Confessional Forms." *DLNTD,* pp. 255-60.

Wright, N. T. *Jesus and the Victory of God.* Minneapolis: Fortress, 1996.

———. *The New Testament and the People of God.* Minneapolis: Fortress, 1992.

Wu, Julie L. "Liturgical Elements." *DLNTD,* pp. 659-65.

———. "Liturgical Elements." *DPL,* pp. 557-60.

———., and Sharon C. Pearson. "Hymns, Songs." *DLNTD,* pp. 520-27.

Scripture Index